DREAM NO LITTLE DREAMS:
A BIOGRAPHY OF THE DOUGLAS GOVERNMENT
OF SASKATCHEWAN, 1944–1961

In 1944, the people of Saskatchewan elected the first socialist government in North America. *Dream No Little Dreams* is the biography of that government, led by the great Tommy Douglas of the Co-operative Commonwealth Federation (CCF, later the New Democratic Party). Providing a case study in the art and practice of governing, A.W. Johnson analyses the policy decisions of the CCF with the added benefit at times of having an insider's viewpoint. Johnson, a senior public servant in Saskatchewan during most of the Douglas years, begins by introducing the government's central mission – the transformation of the role of the state – and describes how it achieved this goal over some seventeen years.

Johnson analyses the roots of the CCF in Saskatchewan history and Prairie politics, and its philosophy as it prepared to govern. He describes the policies and programs introduced by the Douglas government, the changes to the machinery of government and the processes of governing, and the creation of a professional public service.

Medicare is viewed by many as the greatest achievement of the Douglas government. *Dream No Little Dreams* offers rich insight into the initial planning stages of medicare and details the protracted struggle with the medical profession that followed as Douglas fought to implement it. Johnson also addresses the question of how socialists were going to pay for all their ambitions, and situates the answer in the context of developments in national policy and in federal-provincial fiscal arrangements from the war years through to the 1960s.

A.W. JOHNSON has served as Deputy Minister of Finance for the Government of Saskatchewan, Assistant Deputy Minister of Finance for the Government of Canada, Deputy Minister of the Treasury Board and of Welfare, and as a constitutional adviser to Prime Minister Trudeau. He was President of the CBC from 1975 to 1982 and a professor in the Department of Political Science at the University of Toronto from 1983 to 1989.

IPAC
The Institute of
Public Administration of Canada

IAPC
L'Institut d'administration
publique du Canada

The Institute of Public Administration of Canada
Series in Public Management and Governance

Editor: Donald Savoie

This series is sponsored by the Institute of Public Administration of Canada as part of its commitment to encourage research on issues in Canadian public administration, public sector management, and public policy. It also seeks to foster wider knowledge and understanding among practitioners, academics, and the general public.

Networks of Knowledge: Collaborative Innovation in International Learning, Janice Stein, Richard Stren, Joy Fitzgibbon, and Melissa Maclean

The National Research Council in the Innovative Policy Era: Changing Hierarchies, Networks, and Markets, G. Bruce Doern and Richard Levesque

Beyond Service: State Workers, Public Policy, and the Prospects for Democratic Administration, Greg McElligott

A Law unto Itself: How the Ontario Municipal Board Has Developed and Applied Land Use Planning Policy, John G. Chipman

Health Care, Entitlement, and Citizenship, Candace Redden

Between Colliding Worlds: The Ambiguous Existence of Government Agencies for Aboriginal and Women's Policy, Jonathan Malloy

The Politics of Public Management: The HRDC Audit of Grants and Contributions, David A. Good

Dream No Little Dreams: A Biography of the Douglas Government of Saskatchewan, 1944–1961, Albert W. Johnson

A.W. JOHNSON

With the assistance of Rosemary Proctor

Dream No Little Dreams

A Biography of the Douglas Government
of Saskatchewan, 1944–1961

IPAC IAPC
The Institute of
Public Administration of Canada
L'Institut d'administration
publique du Canada

UNIVERSITY OF TORONTO PRESS
Toronto Buffalo London

© University of Toronto Press Incorporated 2004
Toronto Buffalo London
Printed in Canada

ISBN 0-8020-8954-2 (cloth)
ISBN 0-8020-8633-0 (paper)

Printed on acid-free paper

National Library of Canada Cataloguing in Publication

Johnson, A.W. (Albert Wesley), 1923–
  Dream no little dreams : a biography of the Douglas Government of
  Saskatchewan, 1944–1961 / A.W. Johnson ; with the assistance of
  Rosemary Proctor.

  (The Institute of Public Administration of Canada series in public
  management and governance)
  Includes bibliographical references and index.
  ISBN 0-8020-8954-2 (bound)   ISBN 0-8020-8633-0 (pbk.)

  1. Saskatchewan – Politics and government – 1944–1964.
  2. Saskatchewan – Social policy.   3. Co-operative Commonwealth
  Federation.   I. Proctor, Rosemary   II. Title.

  FC3525.2.J64 2004   320.97124'09'045   C2003-905132-3

University of Toronto Press acknowledges the financial assistance to its
publishing program of the Canada Council for the Arts and the Ontario
Arts Council.

University of Toronto Press acknowledges the financial support for its
publishing activities of the Government of Canada through the Book
Publishing Industry Development Program (BPIDP).

To Ruth
and our four:
Andy, Fran, Jane, and Geoff

We should never, never be afraid or ashamed about dreams. The dreams won't all come true, we won't always make it, but where there is no vision a people perish. Where people have no dreams and no hopes and no aspirations, life becomes a dull and meaningless wilderness.

– Tommy Douglas

Contents

Foreword

Gregory P. Marchildon

Much has been said about Tommy Douglas's vision of a New Jerusalem and his provincial government's ability to turn a relatively isolated and poverty-stricken province into Canada's most important social policy laboratory from 1944 until the early 1960s. At the same time, virtually nothing has been written on how this was actually accomplished. The one exception was a Harvard Ph.D. dissertation completed in 1963.[1] Its author was A.W. Johnson, a Saskatchewan civil servant on educational leave from the provincial government.[2] While difficult to obtain, Johnson's thesis filled such an important gap in the literature that it was actively sought out and cited in subsequent articles and monographs dealing with the Saskatchewan government during the CCF years. And although much has been published on Tommy Douglas and the political dimension of his government, very little touches on Douglas's actual administration, including policy implementation and program management. This would have been reason enough to publish the dissertation four decades after it was written.

What follows, however, is much more. Rather than simply allowing his dissertation to be published in its existing form, Johnson spent more than three years rewriting. Instead of spending time with family and friends that should have been the reward for a lifetime devoted to the public interest, he closeted himself in his home office reviewing and summarizing all the secondary literature so that he could evaluate and rewrite what he had written before. He phoned up old colleagues with whom he had worked and asked for their recollection of this or that policy, program, department, agency, or commission as a check against the secondary sources, his own memory, and what he himself had recorded. He then summarized what he discovered in new passages throughout the manuscript. The end result of all this hard labour is, at long last, the published biography of what is now regarded as Canada's most socially innovative government of the twentieth century. Johnson's major contribution is to explain, in detail, just how the Douglas government achieved most of its ambitious objectives. In particular, he describes the evolution of what Christopher Dunn calls the institutionalized cabinet, a move that predated all other provincial governments and went further in some respects than parallel developments in Ottawa.[3] A desire for effective planning was at the heart of this development, and Johnson was one of those lucky young individuals who joined the government just as it was beginning to experiment with these new structures.

Planning and the Institutionalized Cabinet

Before the end of its first term, the Douglas government had established the central agencies that would spearhead its planning efforts. Two remarkable advisors were behind these early developments – George Cadbury and T.H. McLeod. Though heir to the wealthy English chocolate family, Cadbury was a Fabian socialist who understood modern planning techniques and organizations. Brought into the government by Tommy Douglas shortly after the end of the war, Cadbury established the Economic Advisory and Planning Board (EAPB) as well as the secretariat that would support it. Despite the fact that the EAPB was a cabinet committee, Cadbury acted as its first Chair. Its mandate was long-term planning generally, but it concentrated on the economic development policies that would put the province on a more prosperous trajectory after the devastation of the Great Depression.[4]

T.H. McLeod had been Tommy Douglas's urban organizer before and during the successful political campaign of 1944. After the election, he turned his hand to government organization, eventually working with Cadbury on the new planning structures. McLeod became the secretary of the EAPB and managed the new planning secretariat. This body would soon spin off two new central agencies – the Budget Bureau and the Government Finance Office. After examining the U.S. Bureau of the Budget, McLeod adapted the basic structure to a small Westminster-style cabinet government, allowing for a more dynamic and systematic approach to expenditure budgeting and planning. The Budget Bureau would soon become the secretariat for a revitalized Treasury Board, a cabinet committee made up of the provincial treasurer as Chair and two additional cabinet ministers with the deputy provincial treasurer acting as secretary, the position soon taken up by McLeod.[5]

In contrast, the Government Finance Office (GFO) was responsible for overseeing the operations of the province's public enterprises through the GFO Board, a third cabinet committee that acted as the Treasury Board for the province's Crown corporations. Cadbury oversaw the GFO in this initial stage, but it was a Rhodes scholar and lawyer by the name of Allan Blakeney, who came from Nova Scotia via Oxford University, who would put his stamp on the central agency as the GFO's secretary and legal advisor from 1950 until 1955.[6]

Al Johnson was both a witness to, and a direct participant in, these developments. Born and raised in small-town Saskatchewan, Johnson did his first degree at the University of Saskatchewan and then moved on to graduate work in public administration at the University of Toronto. The election of a new and exciting government at home emitted its siren call. In July 1945, immediately after completing his degree, he came home to work in the highly controversial Adult Education Division.[7] Then in the fall of 1946, he was plucked out of his job to join what would soon become the new Budget Bureau under T.H. McLeod. Beyond the tasks of expenditure planning and control, both Cadbury and McLeod wanted the Budget Bureau to provide an ongoing stream of advice on the machinery of government generally in order to improve performance on a systematic basis. Who better to bring in than a young and energetic analyst who had been formally tutored in government administration and who was already showing some aptitude for fusing policy objectives with the organizational structures and processes required to achieve them?[8]

By 1949 the Budget Bureau had become a real organization with a small but expert staff. Johnson was officially named the director of administrative management, the arm of the Budget Bureau responsible for providing ongoing advice to the Douglas cabinet on the machinery of government. Johnson had a staff of five analysts, a number that would double over the next three years. Informally known as the Organization and Methods (O & M) unit, it completed roughly two major departmental organization surveys plus five to six smaller studies per year. He would describe the work of the new unit, as well as its potential for governments beyond Saskatchewan, in his first major presentation to the Institute of Public Administration of Canada (IPAC), an organization that was created by civil servants like him in large part to facilitate the exchange of ideas among the new breed of public sector managers in the country.[9]

The dissemination of what he considered to be major advances in public policy and administration would be a recurring theme in Johnson's life. As a regular contributor to the IPAC journal as well as other scholarly publications, Johnson used his practical and theoretical knowledge to challenge existing policies and practices as well as to explore new policies and organizational forms. He became part of a coterie of modernizers who saw government as a positive catalyst of change in post-war Canada. In his words, IPAC was the meeting ground to discuss 'the methods and problems of government administration in Canada.' Since these gatherings facilitated the 'open examination' of what had 'formerly been guarded from public scrutiny,' IPAC quickly attracted an academic membership eager to explore the secrets of cabinet government. In Johnson's view, IPAC's ultimate objective was to ensure that government decision-making be done 'within a framework' that provided 'as far as possible for an objective consideration of the facts and implications involved in any policy question under consideration.'[10] He contributed to this through writing dozens of articles that appeared in both journals and edited book-length collections, becoming quite possibly the most published civil servant in Canada during the past half century, a major accomplishment given the hectic life of a senior official. This work would be recognized when Johnson received the Gold Medal from the Professional Institute of the Public Services of Canada in 1975, the Vanier Medal from IPAC a year later, and the Public Policy Forum's award for public service in 1996. This pronounced ability to mix practice with scholarly detachment was noted when Johnson was showered with honorary doctorates from universities across the country as well as being made a Companion of the Order of Canada.

In 1952, Johnson was promoted to the position of deputy provincial treasurer and secretary to the Treasury Board, positions he would hold for the next twelve years. During all these years, he was also a sitting member of the Planning Board as well as the GFO Board. Simply put, his job was to raise revenues adequate to the government's program requirements and to manage overall expenditures so that they would not exceed revenues. But this was no mere technical exercise in Johnson's view. He would later describe a budget as 'the meeting point of the decision-making process, the point at which all government's diverse priorities and policies and programs must somehow be brought together into an integrated and hopefully harmonious whole.'[11] Compare this to the analogy (often used by senior treasury officials) of the budget-making process as sausage making!

During this time, Johnson became steeped in intergovernmental relations. He was a key member of the Continuing Committee on Fiscal and Economic Matters, first established in 1955. Over its long life, the committee would focus on three issues: (1) designing and fine-tuning equalization; (2) financing of shared-cost programs; and (3) managing taxation in fields occupied by both governments. Johnson used his intergovernmental experiences in these early years to formulate some definitive views concerning the federation; in particular, the leadership role of the federal government in furthering the national dimensions of key social policies and programs such as medicare and post-secondary education, and in ensuring that these services were made available to all Canadians.[12]

Johnson's minister throughout this extraordinary period was Clarence M. Fines, an enigmatic character whose legacy was to act as the fiscal balance wheel in the Douglas government. His directing of the Provincial Treasury as well as the Treasury Board would produce balanced budgets for the sixteen years of his tenure, and his department's Budget Bureau provided the organizational advice that would keep the rest of the government's machinery at the cutting edge.[13] Fines was not an easy man to know or understand. He developed the reputation of being the one minister who was always prepared to sacrifice the dreams of the CCF on the altar of fiscal probity, but, in fact, he was one of the original founders of the party, with a deep belief in its philosophical objectives.[14] Johnson had tremendous respect for Fines, and this respect was reciprocated, the product of each understanding his respective role. In the gray area of policy origination, the trick was to provide policy suggestions and options without appropriating the right of the minister to set the general direction of policy. When Johnson wrote his now famous article on the role of the deputy minister in 1961, he must have had Clarence Fines in mind when describing the special relationship between a deputy and his minister: 'Each of them comes to know each other: his strengths and weaknesses, his interests and his blind spots, his insights and his obtuseness. So in the process of formulating policy each comes to look to the other to contribute those particular capacities and talents which he knows him to possess.'[15]

In the same way that Johnson and Fines complemented each other with their very different skills and compensated for each other's weaknesses, Fines and Tommy Douglas complemented (and compensated for) each other as the senior political leaders of the CCF government. While Fines led the government from an administrative and financial perspective, Douglas provided the vision and long-term political direction. History has largely ignored Fines, but you cannot walk away from this book without the impression that he was an essential ingredient in the success of the Douglas government.

Clarence Fines was effective, in part, because he left the management of his department to his most senior official while he provided the political direction. Al Johnson, in turn, was committed to bringing in the most talented young individuals he could find anywhere in the country. Like all central agency staff, Budget Bureau analysts were hired through Orders in Council rather than through the Public Service Commission. This allowed a large number to be hired directly from universities throughout Canada without having had previous government experience. Through his personal contacts with prominent professors in numerous universities, Johnson received inside information on 'up and coming' students. He also welcomed opportunities to give seminars on public administration and policy at universities to interest bright young minds in a career in government.[16] He publicly stated that one of the most important jobs of any senior public executive is to attract and develop 'precious' individuals, those that stand out among the rest because of their talent, devotion, and hard work. Many will agree in principle, but few in practice. To make his point, he asked a series of rhetorical questions:

> What percentage of the time of senior executives in departments is devoted to finding top flight people for the public service? What percentage of their time is devoted to giving seminars in universities to make known to students and professors alike the nature of the work of particular agencies of government and thus to making attractive to the best of them work in the public service? What emphasis do senior executives give to ensuring that their most promising people get the right mixture of training and at the optimum pace – experience in jobs of different kinds, educational leave, a posting to another government, language training, even a permanent appointment to another department?[17]

Johnson's emphasis on the quality of individual civil servants was based on his personal philosophy that the most important input to an organization that produced policies and programs was people. In his view, creativity was a personal act, 'the product of creative minds, not of structures or committees or manuals of instruction. So to ask what are the conditions of creativity in government, or anywhere else for that matter, is to ask what are the conditions which unleash, and enlarge, and enhance the creativity of the human mind.'[18]

Budget Bureau trainees who were not recruited directly from the University of Saskatchewan came to the province from other Canadian universities, with a concentration from Queen's University, Carleton University, and the University of Toronto. They would work in the Budget Bureau for a couple of years and then move on to more senior appointments in the line departments, a natural progression that became a distinguishing mark of the Saskatchewan public service until the early 1980s. After the defeat of the CCF government in 1964, a sizeable number of the graduates of the Budget Bureau went to the federal government as senior public servants, where they would influence the direction of the country itself.

A.W. Johnson and the Saskatchewan Diaspora

In 1961, shortly after passing the legislation that gave birth to medicare in the province, Tommy Douglas left the Premier's Office to become the national leader of the newly created New Democratic Party. As Douglas's successor, Woodrow Lloyd implemented the program in the face of a powerful coalition that had mobilized against it. The doctors' strike of 1962, and the polarization and bitterness that accompanied it, affected Al Johnson and his colleagues for life.[19] The aftershock of this policy, combined with the growing public desire for changing a government that had been in power for two successive decades, helped elect the Liberals under Ross Thatcher in 1964.

Many months before the election, having decided that it was time to tackle new challenges, Johnson had accepted the position of assistant deputy minister in the federal Department of Finance. Everyone came to know this, including Thatcher, who asked Lloyd if he could seek advice on the public service from Johnson, given the fact that he was leaving the government anyway. Lloyd agreed and Johnson ended up talking to Thatcher. Emphasizing the competence and ability that had been built up over the years, he convinced Thatcher to keep some of the people in the Budget Bureau and other central agencies, but nothing could stop some from leaving voluntarily and others from being fired, given Thatcher's electoral promise to get rid of all the 'CCF bureaucrats.'[20]

The exodus of these civil servants would hurt Saskatchewan but enrich the rest of the country. While some provincial governments, in

particular the modernizing Robichaud administration in New Brunswick, would profit from this exodus from Saskatchewan, the federal government benefited most. Elected just the year before, Prime Minster
Lester B. Pearson was building a modern welfare state, and a large number of the Saskatchewan diaspora found a more congenial home for
their talents. Aside from Johnson, other important catches included
Tommy Shoyama and Don Tansley.

Tommy Shoyama was one of a small coterie of Japanese Canadians
brought into the Saskatchewan public service at a time when they faced
a high degree of discrimination elsewhere.[21] As secretary to the Economic Advisory and Planning Board from 1950 until 1964, Shoyama was
a key advisor on economic and social policy to Tommy Douglas and
then Woodrow Lloyd. He came into the Pearson government via the
new Economic Council of Canada under John Deutsch and eventually
became the deputy minister of finance in the Trudeau government.[22]

Don Tansley had run the Budget Bureau for many years, and for one
year had been acting deputy treasurer while Johnson was on leave at
Harvard. He had also served as Chair of the Medical Care Insurance
Commission, which had been charged with medicare's implementation
in the early 1960s.[23] After serving as deputy minister of finance and
industry in New Brunswick, Tansley went to Ottawa as senior vice-president of the Canadian International Development Agency, eventually
becoming the first deputy minister of fisheries and oceans.[24]

The other bureaucrats from Saskatchewan were spread out through
the federal public service, although a particularly large number clus-
tered in the Department of Finance. Collectively, they became known –
with both affection and respect – as the 'Saskatchewan Mafia.' From the
beginning, Al Johnson was seen as their leading member. In a *Maclean's*
cover story on 'The Ottawa Establishment' just months after his arrival
in Ottawa as assistant deputy minister of finance, Johnson was identified
by Peter Newman as a member of the country's exclusive power elite.
Classified as one of eleven sub-mandarins, he was placed in the same
company as Simon Reisman (deputy minister of industry) and A.E.
Ritchie (deputy under-secretary of state for external affairs).[25] In charge
of federal-provincial relations and tax policy, he played a pivotal role in
establishing equalization, helping expand post-secondary education
through a workable federal funding formula, and finding an intergovernmental solution to the implementation of national medicare.[26]

Through the support and active sponsorship of Robert Bryce, the
deputy minister of finance, Johnson was thrust into the heart of the

Pearson administration, and his impact on the government's domestic policy direction was arguably second only to Tom Kent, Pearson's chief policy advisor in the Prime Minister's Office. The national medicare story is briefly recounted here as a postscript to the Saskatchewan medicare story, and the evolution of equalization is touched upon in the Annex, but you will find no mention of federal funding of post-secondary education in this book. It is worth a comment.

As a country, we have largely forgotten the intergovernmental statecraft that would allow the federal government to partner with the provinces in the remarkable expansion of post-secondary education – with enrolment of eighteen- to twenty-four-year-olds doubling within a decade, more than responding to the baby boom. Moreover, this expansion was funded on the back of an intergovernmental agreement that did not infringe on provincial jurisdiction over education and included Quebec on the same terms and conditions as all other provinces.[27] Johnson played a central role in forging this 1967 agreement. He learned much about the political and economic dynamics of the Canadian federation from these and similar experiences, which he attempted to summarize in the inaugural issue of the *Canadian Journal of Political Science* early in 1968.

Thinking long and hard about the very nature of the country, Johnson came to the conclusion that federalism was by definition 'a compromise between the conflicting elements of unity and diversity within a single state' and that this compromise is subject to continual change within a federation as dynamic as Canada's. Surprisingly for a civil servant, he bluntly spelled out the country's future options, including associate state status for Quebec.[28] Shortly after, Pierre Trudeau took over from Lester B. Pearson as prime minister. He appointed Johnson as his economic advisor on the constitution, an open-ended position that gave Johnson the latitude to work on federal-provincial issues free of major administrative responsibilities.

In 1970, Johnson was made secretary (the equivalent of deputy minister) to the Treasury Board, and he returned to the familiar business of fiscal planning and budgeting, but now on a national scale.[29] His Saskatchewan experience had a direct impact, however, in the manner in which the Treasury Board secretariat conducted its program reviews. In a manner similar to how the major department organization surveys were conducted by the Budget Bureau, he insured that his secretariat personnel worked jointly with the personnel of the department affected by any given program review. In the same way that Tommy Shoyama had sat in on Treasury Board meetings and Johnson on Economic Advisory and Planning Board meetings in the Douglas government, it was arranged that one official from the secretariat supporting the Cabinet Committee on Priorities and Planning would sit in on Treasury Board meetings and vice versa.[30]

Johnson remained secretary of the Treasury Board until early 1973 when Trudeau decided to launch a major review of Canada's social security system. Johnson suggested that it be a joint federal-provincial review, given the primary role of the provinces in providing income security and social services. Trudeau agreed despite his own, more centralist, view of the federation. In the throne speech that year, the government of Canada announced that it would attempt to harmonize, integrate, and rationalize the federal and provincial elements of the current system in order to provide individual Canadians with a far more effective system.[31]

To accomplish this, Trudeau appointed his most trusted cabinet member, Marc Lalonde, as the new minister of national welfare, and Johnson as the new deputy minister. By April, the new minister and his deputy produced a working paper on social security in Canada that set out some basic principles and objectives from the national perspective. Dubbed the orange paper because of the colour of its cover, this document launched the three-year review with the provinces. While rejecting a single guaranteed income system as a replacement for all of the existing federal and provincial income security programs, it did put forward a series of strategies to achieve a more universal system to replace the various means-tested income supplementation systems in the country.[32]

These years in the Trudeau administration marked a period of consolidation for Johnson as he took his past experience and applied it to improving the existing system both in terms of public administration and in terms of updating and improving social policies and programs. It would end with his appointment as president of the CBC and his entry into the world of radio and television broadcasting in 1975.

President of the CBC

Although new to the CBC, Johnson was no stranger to cultural affairs. Always a great patron of the visual arts, Johnson had initiated a policy in Saskatchewan as deputy provincial treasurer that every new building financed by the government be required to set aside 1 per cent of capital costs for the purchase of works of art. Combining his position in government with his membership on the University of Saskatchewan's board of governors, he supported the creation of a Faculty of Fine Arts at the (then) Regina campus of the university. It would soon become famous as the home of a nationally renowned group of painters known as the Regina Five. As secretary of the Treasury Board in Ottawa, he helped steer through the idea of the Art Bank, which was instrumental in getting Canadian works of art into almost all federal government offices and encouraging painters and sculptors throughout the country. In addition, Johnson had been a board member of the National Film Board since 1970.

For Johnson, the CBC was an institution that mirrored the country. Just as Canada was 'economically implausible, painfully diverse, and full of contradictions' but also 'one of the freest, most creative, most humane, most exciting, most successful countries on earth,' so was the CBC. Johnson used a musical metaphor. The breadth of intelligence and talent that resided within its creative body ensured that the CBC understood 'the point-counterpoint character of Canada,' with the 'point being the voice of nationhood and the counterpoint being the linguistic, and cultural and regional voices.'[33] The national dimensions were important to building the country, but the diverse regional, cultural, and linguistic voices also had to be heard, and Johnson was a staunch supporter of regional programming and centres.

He saw the CBC as an 'agent of development for the skills of the Canadian creative community.' Returning to Johnson's musical metaphor, the CBC was the conductor, ensuring the proper 'combination of simultaneous voice parts, each of them independent,' but all producing a coherent and integrated piece of work.[34] To succeed, no one voice should be allowed to overwhelm or drown out the others, and some voices would have to be encouraged.

At the onset, Johnson had two principal objectives. The first was to increase the quantity, quality, and exposure of Canadian programs and programming. The second was to modernize the CBC, so that it would become a catalyst in broadcasting and the evolution of Canadian culture in light of the information and communications technology revolution.[35] He found radio in very healthy shape; in his view (shared by many), CBC Radio was quite simply the best in the world. CBC TV was another story. American television was in danger of overwhelming Canadian broadcasting, and he sought greater resources to invest in new Canadian programming as well as a proposed new channel that would distinguish itself from commercial television. Despite some considerable achievements on other fronts, Johnson would be disappointed both by the government of Canada and its regulatory arm, the Canadian Radio and Television Commission (CRTC), in rejecting his 'Canadianization' strategy. After leaving the CBC in 1982, Johnson wrote of his disappointment with government and CRTC support, and continued to put forward policy prescriptions to improve the state of Canadian broadcasting and, with it, an independent cultural space for the country.[36]

Academic and Consulting Life

Now closing in on sixty years of age, Johnson became an academic, a career for which he had been preparing for decades. After a one-year appointment as Skelton-Clark Fellow at Queen's University, he joined the Department of Political Science at the University of Toronto as a professor of public policy and administration. For seven years, he would commute between Ottawa and Toronto, working on a comprehensive methodological approach to policy-making, while teaching about the real world of government. Many of his students were struck by the way in which he combined a far-sighted and progressive vision with an equally tough-minded emphasis on structure and prudent fiscal administration. For Johnson, idealism was a vital quality in the public service, always providing it could be translated into effective and sustainable action. In this, he simply reflected the prevailing ethos of the Douglas government.

Following a further two-year stint as a senior research fellow at the Canadian Centre for Management Development (CCMD) in Ottawa, Johnson returned to the front lines as an international public administration consultant in 1991.[37] First, he went to Indonesia on behalf of the International Monetary Fund to study and report on national-provincial fiscal arrangements. Then he led a mission to the Republic of South Africa as that country began to undergo its transition to a multiracial democracy. This was succeeded by a more permanent program on governance in South Africa that Johnson would direct until 1999. His experience as a provincial and federal civil servant was directly relevant to the job of helping the South Africans establish provinces within a new federation. From the beginning, his trusting relationship with senior members of the new ANC government and Nelson Mandela's support of the program were the cornerstones of the initiative.

I first met Al Johnson in Johannesburg, South Africa. A participant in his governance project, I was on my way to Bloemfontein to discuss cabinet committee systems with the provincial government of Free State, based upon my experience as cabinet secretary in Saskatchewan. I had just finished reading Al's thesis in the course of trying to understand the evolution of the cabinet system in Saskatchewan, and asked him whether he had ever considered getting it published. 'Not really' was the answer. He had found himself back on the front lines of government work the moment he left Harvard, having to finish his dissertation while assisting the government during the last difficult months of the introduction of medicare. While he spent evenings and weekends working on articles throughout his career, he never had the time to work on a full-length book.

In 1999 Johnson returned to Canada permanently, and I raised the issue again. No longer on the front line, he seemed more receptive. But since he also knew it would involve a considerable investment of time, he insisted that an independent third party read the manuscript to see if it was worth reworking into a book. So the thesis was sent to Peter Aucoin, a highly respected professor of political science and public administration at Dalhousie University for another review. When Aucoin concluded that the investment of time would indeed be worthwhile, Johnson began work on the manuscript.

When visiting Ottawa on other business, I would stop in at the Johnson household and ask about some of the obvious themes emerging from the manuscript. But on one occasion I asked a less obvious, and more intrusive, question. Why had he never become a politician himself? After all, he was hardly the traditionally dispassionate and apolitical civil servant. He shared fully in the ideals and objectives of the Douglas government. He had gone far beyond the call of bureaucratic duty in furthering the progressive social agenda of the Pearson government.[38] And he was as close to politicians as civil servants can get in their careers. In response, Johnson cast his mind back to when he was seventeen years old and a long conversation he had had with J.S. Woodsworth in Vancouver in 1941.

Johnson knew Woodsworth through his father, who was a United Church minister. Reverend Johnson had studied theology in Winnipeg's Wesley College, when Salem Bland was still teaching there, and when J.S. Woodsworth was leading the All Peoples Mission in that city. Then trying to recover from a stroke at home, Woodsworth had asked to see Johnson, who was working in British Columbia for the summer break from the University of Saskatchewan. Woodsworth spent more than three hours recounting the story of his life as a social activist and political leader. As Johnson was preparing to leave, he was told the real reason for the invitation to talk. Woodsworth wanted him to go into politics, the best possible way to realize the ideal of a more just society.

Understandably, Johnson was moved by Woodsworth's vision and his advice. For many years, he continued to believe that he might become a politician. But after spending considerable time in the Saskatchewan public service and watching that great master politician Tommy Douglas, he concluded (not surprisingly, given his point of reference) that he did not possess the required range of qualities and talents. Moreover, he realized that a role behind the scenes was much more congenial to his personality. Behind the scenes these roles may have been, but his work as a public servant had an appreciable impact on the evolution and direction of Canadian government and society. And many of Johnson's most important achievements had their origins in the Douglas government of Saskatchewan.

Notes

1 Albert Wesley Johnson, 'The Biography of a Government: Policy Formulation in Saskatchewan, 1944–61' (Ph.D. diss., Harvard University, 1963).
2 On the Douglas's government's policy of educational leave, see Robert I. McLaren, *The Saskatchewan Practice of Public Administration in Historical Perspective* (Lewiston, NY: Edwin Mellen Press, 1998), 99–100.
3 Christopher Dunn, *The Institutionalized Cabinet: Governing the Western Provinces* (Montreal and Kingston: McGill-Queen's University Press, 1995).
4 Robert I. McLaren, 'George Woodall Cadbury: The Fabian Catalyst in Saskatchewan's "Good Public Administration,"' *Canadian Public Administration* 37.1 (Spring 1994): 51–64; George Cadbury, 'Planning in Saskatchewan,' in *Essays on the Left*, ed. Laurier LaPierre et al. (Toronto: McClelland and Stewart, 1971). Interview with George Cadbury, 15 June 1981 and 21 Jan. 1982, Saskatchewan Archives Board (Regina), R-8343 to R-8345.
5 A.W. Johnson, 'The Treasury Board in Saskatchewan,' *Proceedings of the 7th Annual Conference of the Institute of Public Administration of Canada* (1955); T.H. McLeod, 'Public Enterprise in Saskatchewan: The Development of Public Policy and Administrative Controls' (Ph.D. diss., Harvard University, 1959); T.H. McLeod and Ian McLeod, *Tommy Douglas: The Road to Jerusalem* (Edmonton: Hurtig, 1987). Interview with T.H. McLeod, 25 and 28 Nov. 1981, Saskatchewan Archives Board (Regina), R-8444 to R-8448.

6 On the GFO, see Dennis Gruending, *Promises to Keep: A Political Biography of Allan Blakeney* (Saskatoon: Prairie Books, 1990); Allan Blakeney and Sandford Borins, *Political Management in Canada* (Toronto: University of Toronto Press, 1998), 133–7; and McLaren, *The Saskatchewan Practice of Public Administration*, 115–18.

7 Michael Welton, 'Conflicting Visions, Divergent Strategies: Watson Thomson and the Cold War Politics of Adult Education in Saskatchewan, 1944–46,' *Labour / Le Travail* 18 (Fall 1986): 111–38.

8 Interview with A.W. Johnson, 9 Feb. 1982, Saskatchewan Archives Board (Regina), R-8426 to R-8427.

9 Walter Gordon and A.W. Johnson, 'Government, Organization and Method Units versus External Management Units,' *Proceedings of the 4th Annual Conference of the Institute of Public Administration of Canada* (1952), 27–47.

10 Johnson, 'The Treasury Board in Saskatchewan,' 112.

11 A.W. Johnson, 'The Treasury Board of Canada and the Machinery of Government of the 1970s,' *Canadian Journal of Political Science* 4.3 (Sept. 1971): 347.

12 This was most clearly expressed in A.W. Johnson, 'Federal-Provincial Fiscal Relations: An Historical Perspective,' in *Ottawa and the Provinces: The Distribution of Money and Power*, ed. David W. Conklin (Toronto: Ontario Economic Council, 1985), 107–43.

13 See Gruending, *Promises to Keep*, 31. Fines resigned just before the general election of 1960, perhaps because of the controversy surrounding his marital situation (Fines had left his wife) and the 'constant gossip about the wealth he had accumulated from shrewd personal investments while he was Treasurer.'

14 At least this is Johnson's assessment, and he got to know Fines better than anyone else in the government, with the possible exception of Tommy Douglas.

15 A.W. Johnson, 'The Role of the Deputy Minister: III,' *Canadian Public Administration* 4.4 (Fall 1961): 369. This article was reprinted in Kenneth Kernaghan, ed., *Public Administration in Canada* (Toronto: Methuen, 1985).

16 A.W. Johnson, 'Education and the Development of Senior Executives,' *Canadian Public Administration* 15.4 (Fall 1972).

17 A.W. Johnson, 'Productivity, People and the Public Service,' *Optimum* 2.1 (1971): 17.

18 A.W. Johnson, 'Public Policy: Creativity and Bureaucracy,' *Canadian Public Administration* 21.1 (Spring 1978): 3.

19 Robin F. Badgely and Samuel Wolfe, *Doctors' Strike: Medical Care and Conflict in Saskatchewan* (Toronto: Macmillan, 1967).

20 For two different views on the transition, see Norman Ward, 'Changing the Guard at Regina,' *Canadian Forum* 44 (Sept. 1964): 127–8; and Meyer Brownstone, 'Another View on the Saskatchewan Government,' *Canadian Forum* 44 (Dec. 1964): 198–200.

21 Others included George Tamaki (first secretary of the GFO under George Cadbury) and Arthur Wakabayashi (Budget Bureau analyst and later deputy provincial treasurer).

22 'Thomas Kunito Shoyama,' in *Canadian Who's Who* (Toronto: University of Toronto Press, 2001), 1181.

23 The commission was established in 1962. According to Dennis Gruending (*Promises to Keep*, 39–40), the government could not find a doctor acceptable to the profession to chair the commission, forcing it to look to the civil service. Tansley apparently took the job after asking if the position 'included danger pay.'

24 'Donald Dougans Tansley,' in *Canadian Who's Who* (Toronto: University of Toronto Press, 2001), 1263; Della M.M. Stanley, *Louis Robichaud: A Decade of Power* (Halifax: Nimbus, 1984), 93–4.

25 Peter Newman, 'The Ottawa Establishment,' *Maclean's*, 22 Aug. 1964, pp. 7–9, 30–8.

26 In *A Public Purpose: An Experience of Liberal Opposition and Canadian Government* (Montreal and Kingston: McGill-Queen's University Press, 1988), 366, Tom Kent generously gave Johnson full credit for finding the solution.

27 A.W. Johnson, 'Stop Neglecting Research,' *Policy Options* 7.4 (May 1986): 12–15. On the history of the post-secondary federal-provincial arrangement, see A.W. Johnson, *Giving Greater Point and Purpose to the Federal Financing of Post-Secondary Education and Research* (Ottawa: Task Force Report for the Secretary of State of Canada, 1985); and Johnson, 'Federal-Provincial Fiscal Relations.'

28 A.W. Johnson, 'The Dynamics of Federalism in Canada,' *Canadian Journal of Political Science* 1.1 (March 1968): 18–39; reprinted in Peter Meekison, ed., *The Dynamics of Federalism in Canada: Myth or Reality* (Toronto: Methuen, 1968).

29 Of course, the nature of budgeting itself had evolved since his Saskatchewan days, as he himself described; see A.W. Johnson, 'Planning, Programming, and Budgeting in Canada,' *Public Administration Review* 63.1 (Jan./Feb. 1973): 23–31.

30 On the administrative and policy objectives behind the Treasury Board secretariat, see A.W. Johnson, 'The Treasury Board of Canada and the Machinery of Government in the 1970s,' *Canadian Journal of Political Science* 4.3 (1971): 346–66.

31 A.W. Johnson, 'Canada's Social Security Review, 1973–75: The Central Issues,' *Canadian Public Policy* 1.4 (1975): 457.

32 Government of Canada, *Working Paper on Social Security in Canada*, 2nd ed. (Ottawa: Minister of National Health and Welfare, 18 April 1973). See also A.W. Johnson, 'Canada's Social Security Review: The Central Issues,' *Canadian Public Policy* 1.4 (1975): 456–72; and 'A Perspective on Social Policy Legislation and Reform,' in *Report on the Policy Forum on Universality and Social Policies in the 1990s*, ed. Alan Green and Nancy Olewiler (Kingston: John Deutsch Institute, 1985), 1–6.

33 A.W. Johnson, 'Fifty-Fifty TV,' *Policy Options* 9.3 (April 1988): 18.

34 Ibid.

35 A.W. Johnson, 'Culture, Broadcasting and the Canadian Identity,' *SMPTE Journal* 91 (April 1982): 346–52.

36 See A.W. Johnson, 'Prescriptions for Broadcasting in Canada: Looking through the Burlap Bag,' *Queen's Quarterly* 90.2 (1983): 457–65; 'Broadcasting in Canada: The Ideal and the Reality,' *Policy Options* 4.2 (1983): 6–12; and 'Fifty-Fifty TV,' *Policy Options* 9.3 (1988): 18–22.

37 During his time at CCMD, Johnson wrote his most important monograph: *What Is Public Management? An Autobiographical View* (Ottawa: CCMD, 1993).

38 A.W. Johnson's own view of Pearson and his legacy can be found in *Pearson: The Unlikely Gladiator*, ed. Norman Hillmer (Montreal and Kingston: McGill-Queen's University Press, 1999), 172–4.

Preface

Saskatchewan is a small province in population, and given its size and its remoteness from Canada's major population centres it seldom receives much attention from the media or the public at large. Yet the Douglas government which was elected in Saskatchewan some sixty years ago continues to be known both to students of government and to a substantial body of Canadians. It is most recognized for its pioneering in public policy, notably for the creation of medicare. It is known too for its contribution to political thought in Canada and for its innovation in the organization of government and in the art of governing.

The story of that government, from its roots in Saskatchewan history and politics through five terms in office, is an ideal candidate for a history of a whole government – and for an exploration of the many aspects and facets of governance.

A biography of the Douglas government is indeed a story of many dimensions. It is first and foremost a chronicle of the voyage of a whole government – proceeding well beyond the more familiar and particular studies of individual areas of public policy or administration – and reflecting, I hope, the drama and the adventure of the life of a government.

My overriding objective in writing the book is to give the reader an insight into the functioning of a government that led the way, after the Second World War, in refashioning the goals and the purposes of government in Canadian society. In its perspective it is partly an insider's view, since I was a senior public servant in the province during most of the Douglas years, and partly an academically inspired study, it being based on my Ph.D. thesis for Harvard University.

When I first told Premier Douglas of my intention to write my thesis on his government, he was enthusiastically supportive, promising to assist me in any way he could, subject to one condition: that I was to 'write it as I saw it,' unaffected by the fact that I was in the employ of the government of Saskatchewan (albeit on leave without pay at that point). Need I say how indebted I felt and still feel?

The challenge was and is to select the policy areas and the other aspects of governance – the facts and the analysis – that reflect with fidelity the substance and the 'feel' of this seventeen years of government. It was a task whose difficulty lay in the necessary but formidable business of deciding what and who must be omitted from this wealth of government activity. I can only hope that my many friends and colleagues of those days – many of whom are still living – will be as tolerant in their reaction to what I have chosen to write about, and how I have done so, as they once were to the positions I took when we were working together.

For me, this biography of the Douglas government is at once a history of this remarkable government and a case study of the art and the practice of governing. And given the many elements of governance, it is a case study, as well, on each of a large number of such elements. These range from the electoral system, the party system, and the reflection of both in the Legislative Assembly; to the parliamentary and cabinet system; to the machinery of government serving the premier and the cabinet, plus the departmental structures created to plan and deliver public services; through to public administration more generally, including such processes as budgeting and staffing.

The study includes, as well, the development of public policy, and the creation of particular policies in both the social and the economic policy fields. I note, particularly, the resolution of the state's role in economic policy, provincially, and its role in public utilities and in economic development. In the social policy field, the state's role came to include, of course, the provision of essential public services in the fields of health and welfare and education, as well as its contribution to the arts and culture.

Then, beyond all these elements of governance, and more in the realm of political theory than of public administration, lie the relationships among the principal participants in politics and government, involving various and varying measures of influence, authority, power, and legitimacy. All these are depicted at one time or another, and in one measure or another, in this book.

Which brings into play the people involved in the Douglas government. Only a few of them – those who figured most prominently in particular programs and particular agencies – are named specifically in the text. But in mentioning them, I have in mind too, as will the readers, I am sure, the legion of others who laboured with equal dedication and equal effectiveness in realizing the Douglas government's goals.

Taken as a whole, the story of the Douglas government reflects, then, on the interaction of all of these elements of governance. You the readers will perceive, I believe, that forty years later this history, beyond its interest to the general public, still provides insights for scholars and students and practitioners of political science and public administration.

Acknowledgments

I want first to acknowledge the contribution of Rosemary Proctor to the production of this book: quite simply, without her it would not have been written. It was she who 'edited down' my Ph.D. thesis – the foundation of this work – from its original seven hundred pages to book length, and then proceeded to serve as an editor throughout the writing of the book. It was she, too, who served as a colleague in discussions concerning the introduction into the manuscript of selected material from relevant post-thesis literature, as well as in helping to formulate the consequential restructuring that would be called for. More, Rosemary read the drafts of all the chapters as I produced them, and proposed revisions and sometimes reformulations. Thanks, R.P., for bringing your rich and varied talents and your impressive governmental experience to this enterprise.

Next, I want to acknowledge the singular contributions of Greg Marchildon. It was he who pressed me, successfully, to transform and publish my Ph.D. thesis, 'Biography of a Government: Policy Formulation in Saskatchewan, 1944-61.' I was about to enter the fifty-fifth year of my career, he knew, and because he is a prolific writer himself he was able compellingly to say that the formidable task he was proposing was indeed 'doable.' To his credit, he never said it would be easy! Equally to his credit, as soon as we had a preliminary manuscript, Greg read the manuscript thoroughly and gave me copious notes on how he thought it could be improved. That done, he went on to prepare a reading list of books and articles that had been published about the Douglas government of Saskatchewan or were relevant to it, over the post-Douglas years. For that, and for your initiation and your authorship of the foreword, as well as for your considerable insights, I thank you Greg.

The third acknowledgment is a collective one: to seven former colleagues and friends who read the manuscript, who sent me their very helpful comments and suggestions, and who gave me insights and recollections on some aspect or other of the Douglas government. They are Allan Blakeney, Grant Botham, Nancy Kenyon, Tommy McLeod, Tommy Shoyama, Don Tansley, and the late Bob McLarty. All are former public servants in the Douglas government in Saskatchewan, and as such they all have an insider's view – if from differing vantage points – of policy formulation and execution during those years. As well, all have held significant posts in the government of Canada or other provinces, and thus brought to their critiques a comparative government perspective. And, as a former premier of Saskatchewan, Allan Blakeney contributed exceptional insights and perspectives, always with disciplined objectivity. What is more, they all shared the ability to make their suggestions sound like compliments. Naturally I appreciated this, but more particularly I am grateful to them for their thoughtful and helpful critiques.

Three people gave me immense help with the research required for this book. The first is Nancy Kenyon, who did the research for the original thesis in 1961–2. Thanks to Tommy Douglas, I had gained access to all his papers as well as to the CCF Party's papers, and Clarence Fines had similarly opened his papers to us. Armed with these, and with the framework and intended orientation of the thesis that I had developed, Nancy did all the research for the original thesis. It was a formidable task, and she accomplished it with all the intelligence and the class for which she is known.

Larissa Lozowchuk did the research for the Annex to this book. In particular, she developed the revenue and the expenditure data of the government of Saskatchewan, presented in four-year periods: a quite original approach that required for its execution an equally original mind – which Larissa demonstrated in her work, along with her executive skills. My thanks to you, Larissa.

And then there was Michele Howland of the Legislative Library of Saskatchewan, to whom I turned for the most arcane facts during the writing and revising of the book. Michele not only answered my questions, but she always did so within a larger context – one that informed me and informs the narrative. Thank you, Michele.

Thanks to the many others who have helped me and influenced me as I wrote this remarkable story, beginning with Professor Stefan

Dupré, who was my Harvard thesis advisor, as I wrote the first version of this biography, and extending to my contemporary friends of the Rideau Club Round Table in Ottawa, who have willingly shared with me their experiences in the writing and the publishing of their first books.

Finally, I want to pay tribute to University of Toronto Press ... to Len Husband, Ken Lewis, and Frances Mundy and all the others involved in this publication. Rosemary Proctor and I appreciated your experience, your insights, and yourselves. Equally I recognize with pleasure the role played by the Institute of Public Administration of Canada in the publication of this work: it marks in a particular way my fifty-year association with IPAC.

DREAM NO LITTLE DREAMS:
A BIOGRAPHY OF THE DOUGLAS GOVERNMENT
OF SASKATCHEWAN, 1944–1961

1

The Roots of the CCF in Saskatchewan and Canada

On 15 June 1944 North America's first socialist government was elected in Saskatchewan. The Co-operative Commonwealth Federation, as it was called, won 53 per cent of the popular votes and forty-seven of the fifty-two seats in the legislature. The opposition Liberal Party was left with only five members. Friends of the Co-operative Commonwealth Federation greeted the victory as the opening of the door to the promised land. The CCF newspaper proclaimed:

> Saskatchewan is now all set to make history. The people in the province have left no doubt in anyone's mind that they are ready for a new kind of government – and a new kind of government is undoubtedly what they are going to get. It is going to be the first real 'people's government' in the history of Canada.[1]

Opponents of the CCF looked forward to socialist rule with anxiety and foreboding. Predictions were freely made that all private property would be socialized, that there would be no more elections, and that pictures of Lenin and Stalin would be hung in every schoolroom. On the day before the election, the *Regina Leader Post* had warned:

> The question to be decided in tomorrow's vote is whether or not Saskatchewan is to become a socialist state ... It is just plain stupid to say it does not matter who wins in this election where the answer to the question will affect vitally the way of living of every individual, will affect the right to own and use property, will enthrone a stultifying dictatorial system; and may start Canada on the road to strife and devastation that has been fol-

lowed by European countries which faced the same issue and failed to settle it decisively on the first vote.[2]

Notwithstanding such extremist views, the victory of the Co-operative Commonwealth Federation in Saskatchewan was in a sense a triumphant denouement. The province had suffered through the worst depression in history, along with the rest of Canada and beyond. Through most of the 1930s it had experienced unimaginable crop failures and desperate declines in farm and family income. A great many had to endure the humiliation of going on 'relief' (welfare) just to survive. Clearly the economic system had failed: the crash of 1929 and the ensuing economic depression were surely evidence of that.

Then came the war and, with it, full employment. Canada's national government mounted a panoply of economic measures to gear up the nation's capacity to produce the weapons of war and to finance the armed forces; to control the incomes of the labour force of Canada and the prices of the goods and services they consumed; and to attempt to distribute with some fairness the costs of the war effort. The economy strained the limits of its capacity, and Canadians came to know and to experience full employment.

As the war neared its end, people looked forward to the brave new world that was being promised. It was a period characterized by discussions of the Beveridge Report,[3] of Roosevelt's four freedoms,[4] of Keynesian relief from unemployment, and of post-war planning. It was a time that produced the Labour government in Britain, the Council of Economic Advisors and the promise of full employment in the United States, and in Canada the White Paper on Employment and Income plus the famous 'Green Book Proposals,' Canada's charter for full employment and social security.

People were ready for change, and the election of the CCF in Saskatchewan became the portent of that change. The role of the state, which had changed immeasurably during the war, would unquestionably have to change once more: to assure full employment after the war; to assure the health and social well-being of the public at large; and to manage the economy in a way that would sustain these new goals.

How all this would be accomplished was of course the critical question. But the CCF had no doubt as to the answer: a Canadian version of democratic socialism.

The social policy goals of the CCF were clear, and the nature of the programs by which they would be realized seemed equally clear. Similarly their economic goals were clear: the government must assume responsibility for the management or some kind of social direction of the economy. The policy instruments by which this might be achieved were not as self-evident in the mid-1930s, when the CCF's Manifesto was written. But in these early years the party was sure that such management or direction of the economy called for social ownership of the key engines of the economy and of those enterprises that served essentially social needs. What this meant for a province or a provincial government – let alone a national government – would have to be worked out.

But the hope inspired by the CCF in Saskatchewan and its willingness to reach out to new frontiers of public policy were unmistakeable. And that was what the majority of Saskatchewanians were looking for.

The provincial Liberal Party and government, in its election platform, offered no alternative inspiration. It put forward a four-point agricultural program and new promises of health and education measures – the latter inspired no doubt by the post-war reconstruction measures being promised by the national Liberal government. But the Saskatchewan Liberals were encumbered by their performance as a government over the preceding ten years, and by the fact, unprecedented in Canadian history (with one exception some twenty-eight years earlier), that the government had extended its own life by one year through legislative rather than electoral action.[5]

During half of its last ten years, the government had, it must be said, been 'occupied with the problems of debt, drought and depression.'[6] But few reforms were forthcoming even after these years, whether in farm security or health or education or welfare – these being the leading planks of the CCF platform. Indeed, the government seemed to be suffering from inertia – inertia in policy, in public administration, and in leadership.

The paralysis in policy, in the fields of health, welfare, and education, to take these examples, was not born of a lack of human sympathy – to suggest otherwise would be churlish. Rather, it flowed from an apparent inability or unwillingness to challenge existing attitudes and institutions in these fields. The Saskatchewan Liberal Party simply seemed satisfied with the status quo.

In the field of health, municipal doctor plans, the earliest version of public medical care, had been developed locally and then sanctioned by the provincial government in 1919. But that sanction depended, municipality by municipality, upon a favourable local ballot before new plans could be launched. By 1943, only one-third of the municipalities together with seventy-one villages and towns had established doctor plans.[7] To introduce universal medicare would require a new province-wide system and institutional structure, and quite different relationships with doctors and patients and local governments alike.

In the field of education, legislation had been passed in 1940 providing for the consolidation of Saskatchewan's miniature school districts into consolidated districts, which might become larger school units if the residents so determined. By 1943 there were forty-one consolidated districts (not yet school units).[8] Even given the evident benefits of consolidating small schools with multiple-grade classrooms, there was no undertaking to initiate a province-wide education reform.

At the time, the province's rural and urban municipalities also administered social assistance, with the provincial government providing a share of the financing, and with the federal government assisting in varying ways during different periods of the Depression. The principles by which social assistance (relief) was administered were based on the belief that 'unemployment – especially endemic unemployment – was unthinkable in the land of economic promise.'[9] So social assistance was not seen as part of a social insurance program or an employment creation plan, but rather as an act of charity – and one that should be offered at the bare minimum and with strict qualifications. This cast of mind was clearly antithetical to the post-war views on social security measures that would emerge in the early 1940s.

Public policy, in short, was in a state of stagnation in Saskatchewan when the election was called in 1944. On the public administration front, the public service was in the same state. It had been re-politicized by the Liberals when they defeated the short-lived Conservative-Progressive (or 'Anderson') government of 1929–34. 'The three man public service commission [that had been established] was abolished ... and a single commissioner appointed. His powers were reduced to leave discretion at the ministerial level. The Liberals made almost a clean sweep of the appointees of the Anderson government, replacing them with "friends."'[10]

These illustrations provide a measure of the state of government in Saskatchewan in 1944. Clearly it was not a government that could fulfil the hopes and dreams of the post-war period, which would be the central theme of the CCF in the election campaign.

The personalities of the party leaders also played a prominent role in the campaign. The Liberal premier, Billy Patterson, 'did not have a flare for reform nor did he catch the imagination of the people ... He was a businessman who believed in the free enterprise system, individual liberty and sound credit ratings.'[11] Tommy Douglas, on the other hand, was a vibrant and committed believer in 'humanity first': a man who through reason and passion and wit and humour was able to attract widespread support for his cause. He was, in short, a born leader – and, as it turned out, a born premier.

This is a picture of the government that had been displaced in 1944, and an indication of the changes that would have to be made if the CCF was to realize its goal of humanity first, which, as it turned out, the party would have twenty years to accomplish – seventeen years of the Douglas government (1944–61) and three years of the Woodrow Lloyd government (1961–4). This is a biography of the Douglas government, which continues into the Lloyd government in order to complete the story of medicare. It begins, as a biography might be expected to, with the origins and the roots of the biographee: in this case, with the origins of the CCF party and government, and with the beliefs and objectives that they developed in their formative years. These beginnings are to be found in the history of Saskatchewan and its people; in the reform movements of the early years of the twentieth century and in the 1930s, and their impact on the formation of the CCF party; in the actual creation of the party, and the development of its credo, the Regina Manifesto; in the intellectual heritage of the CCF; and in the social and economic ideology of the party itself – most particularly that of the Saskatchewan CCF.

Saskatchewan – Its People and Their History

One of the pre-eminent roots of the CCF party and the government it formed was the people of the province itself and their history. Saskatchewan is a vast land of plains and woods, of harsh climate and rich resources. The plains of the southern half of the province slope gradually to the east and to the north, and merge with the Precambrian rock formation that makes up the provinces northern half. Beneath the plains lies the sedimentary basin, where the rich deposits of potash and oil were waiting to be found, and beneath the Precambrian shield was great mineral wealth that awaited discovery.

Saskatchewan's new settlers came from the United Kingdom, continental Europe, Eastern Canada, and the United States, encouraged by Canada's early immigration policies (beginning effectively around 1897). It was a young province: during the thirty-year period beginning at the turn of the century, the population rose from less than a hundred thousand to nearly a million people. Even then, it was a sparsely settled province; by the 1920s there were little more than four persons per square mile.[12] The people who came to pioneer in the province differed in ethnicity, language, religion, and occupation. Their common traits were a freshness of outlook, a certain energy, and a passion for education and self-improvement. Their common challenge was to populate and develop the vast and empty land.

For these settlers, life was harsh. Farming was a hazardous business, with a short growing season, recurring droughts, and animal and plant pests and diseases. There had not yet developed a 'technology' of agriculture for the plains that could determine the potential of the land, the economic size of a farm, and the appropriate farming methods. The economics of the enterprise and the extent of the natural hazards were unknown. There were also man-made obstacles. The Prairie farmer was completely dependent upon the railroads, both to transport his products to distant markets and to bring in the implements of production and the necessities of life. But the new farmers had no influence over the freight rates charged nor over the allocation of the cars that carried their grain to market. The farmers were equally dependent upon the highly structured marketing organization that bought, stored, and sold their grain – the Winnipeg Grain Exchange and the grain elevator companies.[13] 'By 1900 almost three-quarters of the grain elevators in Western Canada were owned by five companies. Monopoly control of elevator and grain companies was further strengthened by the formation of the Manitoba and North-West Grain Dealers' Association, which included most of the grain dealers and "soon had command of the situation from the buyers' standpoint."'[14] The markets themselves were distant and unknown, far beyond the control of the isolated farmers on the western plains.

Political Developments in the Early Twentieth Century

In this land of scattered farms and small, isolated towns and villages, where a harsh climate was a constant threat to survival and arduous transportation was a challenge to co-operation and community, people had to rely on their own strength and that of their neighbours to survive. If the farmers perceived the markets for their grain as being beyond their control, the national political forces were equally distant from the Saskatchewan grain growers.

Even after Saskatchewan became a province in 1905, its representation in Canada's House of Commons was small; in 1908 the province had 10 members out of 221. The views of Western members seemed lost in the caucuses that forced them to hew to a party line that had been established 'in the East.' The outstanding example was the tariff issue. The National Policy of 1879 had established high tariffs in order to stimulate industrial development, most of which took place in Central Canada, and westerners felt totally unable to achieve the lower tariffs so important to them as primary producers. It seemed obvious to the farmers that 'in times of prosperity and in times of depression alike, the deadweight burden of the tariff bears more heavily upon Saskatchewan than upon any other province of the Dominion,'[15] yet they felt helpless to do anything about it.

So the settler felt alone: alone against the elements, alone in his efforts to develop his farm, alone against the organizations that supplied his needs and bought his products, and alone even against those who governed him from Ottawa. Here was fertile ground for co-operative and community action – to conquer the forces of nature and to combat the external forces with which the agricultural industry contended – in short, to grasp the power which would give the farmers some control over their destiny.

The political history of the province in the first decades of the twentieth century is a story of continuous efforts to work collectively. In these efforts and the challenges the farmers faced may be found the early seeds of more radical political thought and organization. The grievances against the elevators and the railways ultimately served as the focal point around which the farmers successfully organized.

In 1901 a bumper crop, almost twice the size of anything previously known, was harvested, and the railways were unprepared to handle it. Almost half of the crop was lost because of the shortage of boxcars to move it. Out of the ensuing protests and meetings, in 1901 the Territorial Grain Growers' Association (a co-operative) was established. Named the Saskatchewan Grain Growers' Association in that province, after Saskatchewan was established as a province in 1905, it grew rapidly and in fifteen years it had three hundred locals and a membership of 28,000.[16]

The Association pressed for two major reforms: the supply of railway boxcars to farmers as well as to elevator companies, and better grain prices from the companies. It was successful within a year, when the federal government passed legislation requiring the railway companies to assign freight cars on a 'first come – first served' basis. But the railways continued to favour the elevator companies. This time the Grain Growers' Association responded with a lawsuit, which induced the CPR to refrain from trying to buttress the monopoly position of the elevator companies.

But for the farmers further reforms were called for – all related to the development of the land and the distribution of its riches. At its 1907 convention, the Grain Growers' Association expanded its objectives and called for a government-owned telephone system and for government ownership and control of undeveloped oilfields and coal lands. In 1909 the Association advocated government ownership of 'timber, coal or other mines,' in order that 'the profits and benefits be shared by all alike.'

In 1908, another element was added to the promotion of Western radicalism – the establishment of the famous *Grain Growers' Guide*. It 'became the forum of the expression of the organized farmers' aspirations and discontents. Into it as into a fiery melting pot was cast the diverse stock of political ideas, panaceas, and projects of the growing, agitated West.'[17] Equally important, the *Guide* voiced the feeling of impotence that the farmers felt in the arena of political action. The remedy lay, it seemed clear, in displacing the 'control of government by the money power' with 'direct legislation [meaning the initiation of legislative proposals by the public (the initiative) and the referendum] ... or the submission of draft legislation to the electorate for adoption or rejection. To these [instruments of direct democracy] were added the recall, the power of a defined percentage of his constituents to recall, or unseat, a representative. The effect of direct legislation would have been to transfer a large part of the legislative process from representative assemblies to the electorate and [thus] to increase the power of the electorate over its representatives.'[18]

Increasingly, in the second and third decades of the century, the Prairie farmers began to turn to community and political action. One of the intransigent problems, of course, was the national tariff policy that protected industries in Eastern Canada but raised the costs of Prairie farmers. Defeated over the tariff issue in the election of 1911, unable to bring the private elevator companies under their control, and beset by declining wheat prices after 1909, the farmers concluded that provincial or municipal government action was necessary, alongside the co-operative movement, to meet the hazards of farming and the hardships of the frontier.

The most notable of the co-operative initiatives was the establishment in 1911 of the Saskatchewan Co-operative Elevator Company. By July 1914 it owned 192 of the province's elevators and was supported by one-seventh of the farmers. By 1915, government partnership with private or co-operative enterprise had been tried in the building of railway branch lines, in creameries, and in poultry and local marketing.[19] The farm movements were ready for more. In 1916 the Farmers' Platform, drawn up by the Canadian Council of Agriculture (with which the Grain Growers' Association was affiliated), pressed for the 'nationalization of all railways, telegraphy and express companies, the future alienation of natural resources under short-term leases only, and complete provincial control of the liquor trade.'[20]

During 1916 as well, the Non-Partisan League, an American populist movement, migrated from North Dakota to the Canadian prairies and became 'the first significant expression of elements of social democratic populism in Saskatchewan and Alberta.'[21] It argued that the farmers and the workers formed a single class, and that their prime goal was the political supremacy of the common people. Though short-lived in its existence, the League played a noteworthy role in persuading Prairie leaders that political action, though not through existing parties, was required if the goals of farm organizations were to be realized.

More significant on the national political scene, and more dramatic in its direct political action, was the Progressive movement. As a group, the Progressives were suspicious of big business and the 'interests': they believed that the 'interests' discriminated against the farmers and were able to do so effectively because of their economic and political power. The evidence was plain to see – the tariff, the power of the railroads, banks, and elevator companies, and the inability of the West to achieve its goals through traditional party politics. The Progressives supported a 'reform' platform, believing in good government and good citizenship. They advocated women's suffrage, civil service reform, prohibition, child welfare legislation, and improved public health measures. They wanted to reform parliamentary government too, and consistently had proposed direct legislation (the initiative and the referendum) and proportional representation as methods for representing more accurately the people's will. But as their efforts in electoral politics demonstrated, they tended at first to view their role 'as an exercise in modified interest-group pressure on a reformable Liberal Party.'[22]

For most of the 1920s, 'the Progressive movement ... [emerged as] the focus of prairie reform activity and intellectual debate,' and became 'the forerunner of the "protest" parties of the 1930's.'[23] In the

1921 federal election, the National Progressive Party, as it had become, swept the Prairies: not a single government candidate survived in the West, and in Canada as a whole sixty-five Progressives were elected, becoming the second largest group in the House of Commons.[24] West of Quebec, only Saskatchewan retained the Liberal Party in the province's government into the 1920s – it being the government that accommodated itself to the farmers' movement and indeed used that movement to remain in power.[25] In Alberta, Manitoba, and Ontario, United Farmers parties came to power provincially. But in the federal election of 1926, the Progressives virtually disappeared from the national scene, with some of its members joining the Liberal Party and the more radical members, mostly from Alberta, forming the 'Ginger Group' in Parliament.[26]

In Saskatchewan, the farmers' political activity focused on the creation of a co-operative agency for marketing their wheat: a wheat pool that would buy the wheat and sell it on the world market as the short-lived Wheat Board had done in 1919. Despite extensive opposition from the elevator companies and the press, the farmers persisted. For the first time there was a break in the ranks of the Saskatchewan Grain Growers Association. Within the organization, a growing impatience had developed over the close relationship between the Association's leaders and the provincial government, and over 'their attempts to neutralize ... the radical implications of cooperative ideals.'[27]

In 1921 a small group formed the Farmers' Union 'with the object ... of supporting and affiliating with farmers' organizations in all the large producing countries to obtain control of all main farm produce, to regulate and obtain reasonable prices above cost of production, and also to protect the farmers' interests by the support and strength of their own organization.'[28] The newly formed Farmers' Union proceeded as farmers had done in the past: volunteer workers canvassed their neighbours, urging them to enter into a contract to turn over their wheat to the Wheat Pool for a period of five years. Within a year, 45,000 farmers had signed up.

By the end of 1923, the Farmers' Union, along with the Saskatchewan Grain Growers Association, had come to an agreement as to the kind of pool that should be established, and a sufficient number of farmers, holding the aggregate acreage required to make the Wheat Pool a success, had signed up. The Saskatchewan Wheat Pool began its operations in 1924.[29]

This having been accomplished, the Grain Growers Association and the Farmers' Union merged in 1926 to form the United Farmers of Canada (Saskatchewan Section). Like its predecessor organizations, it was clearly committed to the co-operative movement and to economic action of the kind represented by the Wheat Pool. But the UFC continued at first to oppose direct political action. Within the UFC (SS), however, a left-wing faction was pressing not only for political action but also for a radical political program.[30]

This faction was led by George H. Williams. A year earlier, he had founded the Saskatchewan Farmers' Political Association, 'and presented it as an organization for all producers working against capitalist interests.'[31] Williams rapidly assumed prominence within the UFC (SS) and was elected president in 1929, at the age of thirty-five. From that position, he was able to promote his strongly held views that the United Farmers of Canada should form its own (left-wing) political party.

In the late 1920s and early 1930s, M.J. Coldwell, a Regina school principal with Fabian Society views, and Clarence Fines, an assistant school principal, were intensely promoting and building an Independent Labour Party,[32] which had been established in 1925.[33] Aided by the influence and participation of Canada's leading socialist, J.S. Woodsworth, they met in three Prairie cities under the banner of the Western Conference of Labour Political Parties, seeking support from others interested in a new social order. By the time the UFC (SS) was prepared to reverse itself and endorse direct political action, Clarence Fines, the president of the Western Conference, was likewise poised to pursue the question of a jointly sponsored, new party.

The first step in this direction was taken in 1929. The Independent Labour Party, led by Coldwell, and the Farmers' Political Association, led by George Williams,[34] co-operated to nominate candidates in the 1929 provincial election and in the 1930 federal election under the banner of the Farmer Labour Party. The significance of the FPA-ILP participation in the election lay not only in their unexpectedly good showing at the polls, but also in their consistently left-wing platform. They looked to the establishment of a 'co-operative commonwealth' where wealth would be more equitably distributed, where resources would be publicly owned and developed, and where no economic group would be allowed to dominate others in society. The first intimations of a left-wing government came in 1929, before the stock market crash, when the Conservatives and Progressives elected to the Legislative Assembly formed a coalition, led by J.T.M. Anderson, unseating the Liberals after nearly twenty-five years in power.

Political Developments in the 1930s and the Formation of the CCF

While the farmers and the co-operative movement played a fundamental role in the social action that led to the formation of the CCF, it was the decade of the 1930s that finally determined the future course of politics in Saskatchewan. The economy was virtually paralysed by the Depression, which began in 1929, and by the drought that persisted through most of the decade. Wheat yields fell sharply, and the drop in prices was even more catastrophic. Farm income fell from $610 million during 1926–30 to minus $74 million during 1930–5, and to plus $172 million during 1936–40.[35] In Saskatoon, a representative urban area, almost one in five residents was on relief in the mid-1930s. Farm debt rose and the farmers moved on; the population of Saskatchewan declined by some 25 per cent by 1946.[36]

The statistics tell a depressing story, but only those who lived through the 1930s in Saskatchewan can have some feeling for the emotional impact of the Depression. There were the hot dry summer days when clouds of grasshoppers formed a sheen against the sun, and when the crops and the gardens and even the leaves on the few trees were devoured by the insects. There were the dust storms that sometimes so darkened the skies that school children were not released from school until the winds dropped. There was the grit that the storms left in their wake – on the window sills and even in one's teeth. The dryness seemed relentless; the clouds that loomed hopefully on the horizon failed to arrive, or if they did, even those were dry – 'just empties going back,' the farmers said. The sons of these farmers graduated from high school to 'ride the rails' by the thousands, searching elsewhere for work.

In 1931 the United Farmers of Canada (Saskatchewan Section) again debated the question of direct political engagement. This time, it was agreed that the organization should become engaged in political action: George Williams, now president, had won. The UFC (SS) convention also endorsed an openly socialist platform: it blamed the Depression on the inherent contradictions of capitalism and asserted that social ownership and co-operative production were the only satisfactory alternative. The platform went beyond the usual nationalization of the railways and abolition of the Grain Exchange, and proposed 'use leases' as an alternative to the private ownership of land. This was almost foolhardy idealism in a province where two-thirds of the farms were farmer-owned.[37] But the temper of the times, generated by foreclosures, evictions, and seizures of land, meant that the convention was prepared to adopt this alternative to the seeming insecurity of private ownership.

Also in 1931, at a meeting of the Western Conference of Labour Political Parties, Clarence Fines was elected president, and over the next year he devoted himself to promoting a union between the UFC (SS) and the ILP.[38]

In July 1932, the two organizations met in Saskatoon and joined to form the Saskatchewan Farmer-Labour Party. George Williams, a likely candidate for the leadership of the party, did not stand for office – his name having been clouded by an apparently sympathetic visit to the Soviet Union (though clearly he was not a communist). M.J. Coldwell was elected unanimously, and Williams took over the chairmanship of the party council.[39] The name of Tommy Douglas, a twenty-eight-year-old Baptist preacher in Weyburn, appeared as a member of the party's council.[40] The Saskatchewan Farmer-Labour Party having been formed, the delegates went on to the Calgary convention of farmers, labour, social reformers, and socialists, where the CCF was founded.

The story of the creation of the CCF as a national and then a provincial party has been told many times elsewhere: only the essence need be recalled here.[41] The founding group included J.S. Woodsworth, then the Independent Labour Party MP from Winnipeg, Agnes Macphail for the United Farmers of Ontario, M.J. Coldwell for Saskatchewan, and Robert Gardiner for the United Farmers of Alberta. For Manitoba and British Columbia, the Independent Labour Party and the Socialist Party of Canada, respectively, were asked to assume organizational responsibility. Clarence Fines of Saskatchewan, whose name figures prominently in this biography, was the secretary and principal organizer. The co-operating groups met in Calgary in August 1932.

The air was charged with enthusiasm, and with a new hope that some solution might be found to the desperate problems that beset the nation. Certainly, there were few signs of friction as the delegates proceeded earnestly with their task. The conference set itself three tasks: to form 'a national federation of organizations interested in a "co-operative Commonwealth"';[42] to fashion a preliminary program for the new organization, and to find it a name.

The first objective was quickly achieved; J.S. Woodsworth, the passionate spiritual leader of all the antecedents of the CCF, was chosen president by acclamation. A national council of eight, from the five provinces represented, was selected to serve until a platform had been approved. It was chaired by J.S. Woodsworth and included such prominent figures as

Angus MacInnis, MP (British Columbia), William Irvine, MP (Alberta), George H. Williams (Saskatchewan), Louise Lucas (Saskatchewan), and A.R. Mosher (Ottawa).[43] The second task caused more debate, but no serious rifts developed. The provisional eight-point program called for social ownership of utilities, natural resources, banking, and credit, and for broad welfare measures, including the socialization of health services and an extension of social security measures. The basic principle that was to govern in the hoped-for co-operative commonwealth was to be 'the supplying of human needs instead of the making of profits.'[44]

Naming the new party caused the most debate. Many delegates favoured a name which proclaimed the socialist character of the party, or at least by reference linked it with the labour parties which in Britain and elsewhere were known to be socialist. But the majority favoured emphasizing in the name the federative nature of the organization and the notion of a Canadian or a co-operative commonwealth. So the name chosen, the Co-operative Commonwealth Federation, lent emphasis to the fact that it was a Canadian party, and to the pragmatic temper of the delegates, the word *socialist* having been omitted from the party's name. The really fundamental debate would come a year later when the new party's delegates met in Regina to construct the CCF's program, or manifesto.

The Intellectual Heritage of the CCF

Several strands of radical thought were represented in Regina in 1933, and the Manifesto sought to fashion these into a systematic ideology.

The first of these was the political thought of the co-operative and farmers' movements. While they were not represented as such at the Regina meetings, their influence was felt through the participation of the delegates at large and through the role these movements had played in the development of Western political thought – in particular, in the concept of 'socialization' by way of the establishment of co-operatives and credit unions (as well as by governments). This strand of thought was expressed both in terms of principle – 'the key to the political philosophy of the United Farmers is cooperation'[45] – and in terms of practice: the establishment in Saskatchewan of co-operative elevators, the Wheat Pool, the struggle for a 100 per cent compulsory pool (later to become the Wheat Board), and more. By 1933 socialization by way of co-operatives had proven itself.

A second facet of co-operation and socialization came into play when the issues confronting the farmers exceeded their reach by way of direct

co-operative action. Here the farmers co-operated in pressing for socialization through governments – provincial ownership of telephone systems and of all mineral rights and forest resources, and national
ownership of banks and railways. And they pressed, too, for the removal
of 'hostile' government policies – notably tariffs.

Along side this strand of thought was the ideology advocated by
Henry Wise Wood and the United Farmers of Alberta.[46] Wood believed
that industrial society was guilty of the worst feature of competition –
that of selfish aggrandizement. The form of competition envisaged by
the liberal economists of the nineteenth century had given way to con-
centrations of power in monopolies. This 'plutocracy,' as he described
it, had destroyed healthy competition and brought about a new and
unhealthy kind of economy – the object of which, of course, was profit-
making. The consequences of such an economy, unless counteracted,
would be poverty for the great masses of the people. In counteraction,
Wood proposed co-operation: the formation by producers of economic groupings that would co-operate to defeat the competitive social
order and substitute for it a producers' co-operative economy. Wood
was not too explicit as to which economic groups he had in mind, save
the farmers, but he was supremely optimistic that they would be
formed, that they would co-operate, and that a new social order would
dawn.

Whether one viewed the co-operative movement through the eyes of
the United Farmers of Saskatchewan or through the eyes of Henry Wise
Wood and the United Farmers of Alberta, the importance of the co-
operative farmers movement on the Prairies was indisputable. To quote
the Reverend Salem Bland, when speaking about the spirit and practice
of co-operation among grain growers: 'I question if any more construc-
tive and distinctively Canadian contribution has been thrown into the
discussion of our national policies.'[47]

The belief in co-operation and co-operatives, then, constituted the
primary intellectual heritage of the farmers' movements. But there was
another element in that heritage that emerged in Saskatchewan when
the UFC (SS) decided to establish its own party (as the United Farmers
of Alberta had done in 1919). The political views of the Saskatchewan
UFC were, or were to become, much more akin to the democratic
socialism of the urban/labour parties.[48] The transition came about
more or less naturally: it was a matter of extending 'social ownership' to
comprehend not only co-operative ownership but also government ownership, provincial and national. And it was a matter of doing so as part
of a political philosophy, not simply as part of a protest movement.

Put another way, the broadening of co-operative beliefs to comprehend wider social or political action, by way of the state, could be looked upon as an emanation from co-operative beliefs – and one that was consistent with social democracy. For many, indeed, to be a Prairie social democrat required a commitment to co-operatives as central institutions in the transition to, and as a feature of, socialism.[49]

The second strand of the CCF's heritage was the socialist theory advanced by the labour parties that assisted in its formation.[50] From Manitoba, the Independent Labour Party brought to the CCF the 'urban socialist' viewpoint. The leaders of the ILP had nearly all come from Great Britain, and in one way or another they had had long experience in the British and Canadian labour movements.[51] They spoke of society divided into classes, the exploiter and the exploited, and advocated placing human welfare before profits and property. They thought in urban and labour terms, and yet they held many views in common with the farmers (such as opposition to the 'interests,' social reform, holding their members of Parliament accountable to them), even if they were inclined to frighten the agrarians with their sometimes-Marxist noises. From the West Coast, the Socialist Party of Canada gathered most of the diverse strands of a politically splintered labour movement.[52]

More than anyone else, it was J.S. Woodsworth who succeeded in bypassing the pure Marxian doctrine, the revolutionary view (though it must be acknowledged that its exponents showed no sign of erupting into any revolutionary action). He argued that Canadian socialism should be indigenous to Canada. His was a doctrine of gradualism, more in the tradition of the British Labour Party, but adapted to Canadian conditions:

> In developing a constructive programme, we face our most difficult task. We are passing though a hitherto untravelled land ... There are those who would frighten us with the horrible example of failure in England or Germany, or captivate us by idealizing the experiments in Russia. The trouble is that we are inclined to think altogether too much in terms of Europe and in terms of the past ... I refuse to follow slavishly the British model or the American model or the Russian model. We in Canada will solve our problems along our own lines.[53]

Woodsworth preached democratic socialism wherever he went, and it was his approach to social and economic problems that Saskatchewan's reformers embraced. The Saskatchewan tradition lent itself more to this approach. The Grain Growers Association, for example, which had advocated government ownership, compulsory marketing, social planning, and a more equitable distribution of income, had been influenced, not by Marxism, but by the socialist idealists and by 'Christian socialism.'[54]

These were two of the strands of radical thought that were represented in Regina in 1933 and that the intellectuals who drafted the Manifesto sought to fashion into a systematic ideology. To be sure, the debate over the Manifesto revealed the differences that existed between the groups. But other forces made possible the achievement of harmony. Among the seemingly diverse elements at the conference there was general agreement that a unified party was necessary. For too long the farmers' organizations and the labour parties had been operating independently. And there was the compelling imperative of a deepening depression, which persuaded the most doctrinaire of the necessity to establish a co-operative commonwealth in Canada. Finally, coming from similar backgrounds, they understood and responded to the use of the Westminster parliamentary tradition. There were no competing traditions of government.

For most of the delegates at the Regina Conference there was as well a third, unspoken, and more pervasive heritage, the 'Christian ethic,' which motivated such a large number of them. Many of the leaders in the radical movements in Canada were ministers, and many of the delegates had been exposed to the 'social gospel' as taught by men like Salem Bland of Wesley College in Winnipeg. Bland's strong views are captured in the following challenge:

A profit-seeking system will always breed profiteers. It cannot be cleansed or sweetened or ennobled. There is only one way to Christianize it, and that is, to abolish it. That is, it may well be believed, the distinctive task of the age that is now beginning, as the abolition of the liquor-traffic was of the age that is closing, and the abolition of slavery of a still earlier age ... This whole present industrial and commercial world, ingenious, mighty, majestic, barbaric, disorderly, brutal, must be lifted from its basis of selfish, competitive profit-seeking and placed squarely on a basis of co-operative production for human needs.[55]

Again, Woodsworth consistently expressed this view:

We dream of a socialistic state and yet sympathize with Mr. Brooks when he says that the 'Mecca of the Cooperative Commonwealth is not to be reached by setting class against class, but by bearing common burdens through toilsome stages along which all who wish well to their fellows can journey together.' If there must be a fight then it is a fight for the rights of the many weak against the privileges of the few strong, and we stand with the many weak.[56]

Scarcely consistent with dialectical materialism, this social gospel was more akin to the nineteenth-century idealism upon which the English Fabians had built and which provided the intellectual foundations of the British Labour Party. The philosophy expounded by Woodsworth was remarkably similar to the writings of the nineteenth-century idealists, such as T.H. Green and Bernard Bosanquet. Their philosophy was 'characterized by the search for a formula to define the moral task of the state, and to set a single standard of value that would guide men in their public and private actions':[57]

> [It] is an ethical creed. It preaches continuous striving by the individual at self-improvement, at translating into action those moral precepts, about which the civilized world has grown so blasé. In the second place it would flow logically from its tone that idealism should advocate a concept of the state which would make it a serviceable instrument of social and economic reform.[58]

The goal, of course, was individual self-realization: 'Man is endowed with a sense of dignity and independence ... and by a clear conception of what he is and what he wants. Society should help him to arrive at that conception, but the act of willing, the striving for self-realization must be his ... The argument [for the concept of moral freedom] ... sees that under suitable social conditions man can realize the ideal ...'[59]

It seems clear from Woodsworth's writings and teachings that this was the philosophy that motivated him and his followers. The important question, of course, is whether the Saskatchewan CCF, when it drew up its 1944 election platform, was motivated by these same theories, and if so how its leaders interpreted them.

The Regina Manifesto

This was the range of beliefs and influences that were embodied, in one measure or another, in the views of the CCF delegates as they met in Regina to construct their program. The Regina Manifesto, as it has come to be known, had been drafted by a committee of the League for Social Reconstruction made up of several of Canada's leading intellectuals (including Frank Underhill, Frank Scott, and Eugene Forsey) and then revised by the National Council of the CCF. It was a strongly worded document, calling for fundamental social and economic reform, and culminating in a declaration that the CCF would not rest content until capitalism had been eradicated and a co-operative commonwealth established. The basic propositions of the Manifesto were found in its second and third paragraphs:

> We aim to replace the present capitalist system, with its inherent injustice and inhumanity, by a social order from which the domination and exploitation of one class by another will be eliminated, in which economic planning will supersede unregulated private enterprise and competition, and in which genuine democratic self-government, based upon economic equality will be possible. The present order is marked by glaring inequalities of wealth and opportunity, by chaotic waste and instability; and in an age of plenty it condemns the great mass of the people to poverty and insecurity. Power has become more and more concentrated into the hands of a small irresponsible minority of financiers and industrialists ...
>
> What we seek is a proper collective organization of our economic resources such as will make possible a much greater degree of leisure and a much richer individual life for every citizen.[60]

The Manifesto went on to outline the economic, social, and international policies of the CCF, including 'the establishment of a planned, socialized economic order, in order to make possible the most efficient development of the national resources and the most equitable distribution of the national income.' It called for government control of finance: 'the socialization of all financial machinery – banking, currency, credit, and insurance, to make possible the effective control of currency, credit and prices, and the supplying of new productive equipment for socially desirable purposes' – along with social ownership of 'all ... industries and services essential to economic planning.' Some of the 'eligible' industries were listed – transportation, communications, electric power, natural resources, mining, pulp and paper, and certain distributive industries. While the Manifesto did not identify clearly the dividing line between the public and private sectors, it did restrict socialization to 'industries and services essential to economic planning,' and admitted the impossibility of deciding 'the policies to be followed in particular cases in an uncertain future.' At the same time, the Manifesto insisted, 'the welfare of the community must take supremacy over the claims of private wealth.'

The Regina Manifesto went on to advocate special policies to address the emergency created by the Depression. These included a program of public expenditures on public works, as well as a long-term program for agriculture aimed at increasing domestic demand for farm produce, enlarging foreign markets, and, through greater demand, increasing the prices of farm commodities. It advocated, as well, a reduction in the costs of production by means of lower tariffs, co-operative or social ownership of the 'monopolistic corporations' which supplied the farmers, and 'a planned system of agricultural development.' Above all, the farmer was to be guaranteed security of tenure 'by individual provinces,' and insured 'against unavoidable crop failure.' Finally, the Manifesto encouraged the development of co-operative enterprises, such as the Saskatchewan Wheat Pool.

The Manifesto's social policies, which ranked equally with its economic policies, ranged from the advocacy of socialized health services to the guarantee of the rights of the individual. A National Labour Code provided for a complete social security plan, including 'insurance covering illness, accident, old age and unemployment.' The Code limited the hours of work, granted undisputed right to freedom of association, and secured for the worker 'maximum income.'

The Manifesto promoted 'freedom of speech and assembly for all ... [and] equal treatment before the law of all residents of Canada irrespective of race, nationality or religious or political beliefs.' Throughout the document ran a strong thread of egalitarianism: income in accordance with family needs, equality before the law, and 'a new taxation policy designed ... to lessen the glaring inequalities of income and to provide funds for social services.'

Essentially the Manifesto performed two difficult tasks. It presented a consensus statement of ethical principles and social and economic theories representing the views of the 131 delegates and their supporters. It also outlined a complex of policies that would both conform to these principles and reflect the points of view that had come to Regina from across the nation.

Political Developments in Saskatchewan from 1934 to 1944

In Saskatchewan, the socialist ideology and the welfare program of the new CCF Party were wholeheartedly adopted by the Farmer-Labour

Party, and formed the foundation of the party's campaign in the 1934 provincial election. The candidates met bitter opposition. Their opponents attacked them as communists and Bolsheviks and pointed to evidence of the party's intention to nationalize everything. The press was against them, and the Catholic Church openly attacked them.[61] M.J. Coldwell, a schoolteacher, was told by his board to get out of politics or risk dismissal: he was dismissed.

The results of the 1934 election were also discouraging: the Farmer-Labour coalition won only 25 per cent of the popular vote. And the results in terms of the party and in terms of harmony within the party's leadership ranks were equally disconcerting. Coldwell, the party president, was defeated, as was Tommy Douglas. George Williams, who was elected and would become leader of the opposition in Saskatchewan's legislature, rejected as 'ridiculous' any suggestion that a seat should be opened up for the party president, M.J. Coldwell, to run (through the resignation of one of the Farmer-Labour members).[62] Relations between the two men, already fragile, were effectively ruptured.

Williams's 'capacity to ruffle feathers,' as one historian put it,[63] was manifested once again in the run-up to the federal election of 1935, when he attacked Tommy Douglas for having 'accepted' Social Credit Party support in his home constituency (thus to avoid splitting the anti-Liberal vote). Williams demanded of Coldwell that Douglas be repudiated: Coldwell refused.[64] Even after the election, which Douglas won, there were demands within the CCF executive that he be removed from the party.[65] The issue, arising out of the interpretation of party policy regarding the Social Credit Party, was settled within the Council of the CCF.

The results of the 1935 federal election were also disappointing. Only two CCF members were elected – M.J. Coldwell, who would become the second national leader of the CCF, and Tommy Douglas. Moreover, the CCF garnered only 19 per cent of the popular vote, while the Social Credit Party received 20 per cent. Given these results, the newly formed CCF turned its attention to two troublesome questions: first, was their platform too doctrinaire, too ideological? And secondly, should the leaders have listened to those in the CCF who had been advocating coalition with the Socreds and other protest groups (the 'unity' wing)? In the event, the national convention of the CCF in 1937 passed a strong resolution opposing such 'unity.' But there seems to have been a conscious decision with respect to the party's program to speak less in doctrinaire and more in pragmatic terms: the new provincial program omitted any reference to 'use lease' of land or to socialism.

In a pamphlet titled 'Social Democracy in Canada' (1936), George Williams asserted: 'This is not a treatise on Socialism according to Marx, Lenin, Stalin, Henderson, Bellamy, or Engels. The writer does not pretend to be outlining a theoretical socialism ... the people of Canada are not interested in ascertaining whether a proposed economic system agrees with Marxism or any other "ism"; they want to be reasonably sure it will work.'

In this mood, the CCF entered the 1938 provincial election. It had not so much changed its outlook as it had decided to be more pragmatic, at the expense if necessary of theoretical consistency. This election was fought at a time when Saskatchewan was in a desperate condition. The crop of 1937 had been a disastrous failure, and some two-thirds of the farm population was on relief. Despite these economic circumstances, the Liberals were re-elected, but their majority was much reduced. Of the fifty-two seats, the CCF elected ten members, the Social Credit two, and the Unity candidates two, while the Liberal majority fell from fifty to thirty-eight. Those in the party who had supported a united CCF-Socred front almost immediately repented and joined with the others in looking forward to a CCF victory in the next election. In firm tones, the CCF reaffirmed its 'faith in the CCF platform, the CCF organization and the ultimate victory of the CCF.'[66]

The federal election of 1940 found further support for the CCF. The party elected five members to Parliament out of twenty-one seats, and captured nearly as many votes in the rural constituencies as did the Liberals. The CCF was thriving. Memberships poured in, and people openly supported the CCF where formerly they had been fearful of doing so. More and more officials of interest groups – the Wheat Pool, the Teachers' Federation, and the trade unions – sided with the CCF. And of great importance for the forthcoming provincial election, money was rolling into the treasury. The breadth of support may be judged by two measures: first, the contributions to the party were nearly all individual subscriptions; and secondly, the CCF candidates in the 1944 election were widely representative, including thirty farmers, six railroaders, seven schoolteachers, three merchants, two housewives, one lawyer, one Wheat Pool field man, and one veterinarian.[67]

The years 1943 and 1944 saw a confluence of events that was bound to favour the CCF. For one thing, the Liberal government in Saskatchewan was held by many to be responsible for a long and sorry period of Saskatchewan history – from 1935 to 1941. And as if to exacerbate this sentiment, the premier, in that serious lapse of judgment I have alluded to, prolonged the life of the legislature by one year in 1943. More than that, however, was the fact that the early 1940s saw the beginning of the post-war idealism, when across Canada the belief spread that governments, by acts of conscious planning, could bring to the nation the same prosperity that had been achieved in wartime. Moreover, the party was well organized, well financed, and self-confidently a part of a growing trend.

There had been as well a series of changes in the leadership cadre of the CCF in Saskatchewan that brought 'new approaches, new leadership, new vigour to the party.'[68] George Williams, an active leader in the farmer movement and in farmer-labour politics for nearly twenty years, enlisted in the armed forces in Canada in 1939 and was posted overseas in 1941. He resigned from the presidency of the party and was succeeded by Tommy Douglas. Clarence Fines became vice-president. Then, at the 1942 convention, Williams reversed himself and offered his candidacy for the party's leadership – in absentia. Douglas, known to be the strongest candidate for the post, was persuaded to leave his name on the ballot, and was elected by acclamation. His talents, both as a leader and a diplomat, became apparent as he quickly assuaged any residual tensions in the party.[69]

Douglas had, indeed, proven himself both in the House of Commons and on the hustings in Saskatchewan (1935–44) to be a brilliant and vibrant politician. And he exerted a powerful influence in the 1944 election campaign. He was an exceptional and a persuasive speaker. And he 'understood' peoples' problems and their needs, a capacity which was to serve him much better than any doctrinaire presentation of the CCF ideology and platform. In fact, Douglas was not enamoured with socialist theory for the sheer sake of theory. He was concerned that governments should seize the opportunity – their responsibility, he said – to meet human needs, both social and economic. If a socialist-oriented program was the most promising method for achieving his humanitarian goals, then he would, and did, embrace socialism. Besides, the fact that he was a Baptist minister made it more difficult to accuse him and the CCF of being 'godless communists.'

The Values and Ideology of the CCF

The values and the goals that would guide the new CCF government were thus determined long before it was elected in 1944. So, too, were the economic and social policies – or policy directions – which were to be seen as a blueprint for future CCF governments. These had been articulated in the Regina Manifesto. But the important question, here, is whether and to what extent the Saskatchewan CCF was motivated, when it drew up its 1944 election platform, by the same positions and theories, and further how its leaders interpreted these positions. A further consideration is whether the ideology and the objectives themselves had changed in the ten years since the Regina Manifesto had been written, in the light of Canada's wartime economic experience or in response to the political reactions evoked by the Manifesto itself. The answer is to be found only by piecing together a great variety of party pronouncements – convention resolutions, provincial council or executive decisions, statements by political leaders, pamphlets distributed by the Saskatchewan CCF, as well as statements by national leaders which seem to have been endorsed by the Saskatchewan section of the CCF.

The CCF ideology thus expressed seems to have been based upon the premise that individual growth and development is the first concern, the 'root value.' Douglas articulated this view in the 1944 election campaign:

> A new economic system is only a means to an end and not an end in itself ... We are desirous of building a more just and secure economy; but we are conscious of the fact that when we have improved the economic lot of mankind, we have only begun the much greater task of building a new society ... After all, 'a man's life consisteth not in the abundance of things which he possesses': life at its best consists of spiritual values such as a regard for truth, a love of beauty and a seeking after righteousness.[70]

Clarence Fines, in his presidential address to the Eighth Annual Convention of the Saskatchewan CCF, put it this way: 'The function of any well-organized society should not be primarily "to provide employment" but should be to develop its resources and industries co-operatively in such a manner as will provide full personal development and expression for all.'[71]

The opportunity to live a 'dignified, and a rich and varied life'[72] was to be achieved through the establishment of a co-operative, as opposed to a competitive, order; this was to be the incarnation of the brotherhood of man in which the CCF believed. It followed that capitalism, as it was then known, was wrong in moral terms, for it rested upon a purely competitive order. Surely humanity should come before finance and use before profit. It was one of the profound weaknesses in capitalism that the opposite was the case. 'Isn't it strange,' said Douglas, 'that during the depression years our per capita expenditure for education should have dropped 40 per cent but our interest payments to the provincial bondholders were carefully maintained ... It is a sad reflection upon us when we have to maintain our credit at the expense of our school children ...'[73]

The advocacy of democratic socialism was not considered in any way to be inconsistent with the CCF's emphasis on individualism and individual development. One prerequisite of individual self-realization is freedom, and freedom, said Saskatchewan party leaders, is not possible where there is poverty and insecurity. 'We are not disparaging the political freedom which we have ... it was bought ... at great cost,' said Tommy Douglas. 'But it is of little use being free if you are only free to go hungry, or free to go without a job.'[74] A minimum of economic well-being was one condition of true freedom, and hence of the full development of the individual. And there were others – a sufficient measure of social security, security of tenure on the farm and in the home, and the opportunity for an adequate education. 'The whole of our democracy is based upon the principle of equal educational opportunity for all. Inequality in educational structure means inequality in the whole structure of society. It means undeserved privilege for some and undeserved neglect for others. It means that some people can buy social and economic advantage.'[75]

Here was one of the important features of the CCF's ideology – the belief in greater equality. The party held that marked inequality meant that some people would find themselves in a condition of near-poverty, and 'borderline living' inevitably involved minimal freedom. On the opposite end of the scale, affluence brought with it power, not only to satisfy one's own wants but also power over others. Both economic freedom and greater equality must accompany the conventionally accepted freedoms.

Accompanying this individualism was the CCF's quest for the brotherhood of man – whose incarnation in Saskatchewan was to be seen, it was held by many, in the province's co-operative movement. 'This is more than a political movement,' said Douglas about the CCF; 'it is a people's movement, a movement of men and women who have dedicated their lives to making the brotherhood of man a living reality.'[76]

The conditions for achieving these fundamental goals – equally a part of the CCF's value system – were freedom and democracy and equality of economic and social opportunity. As one of the founders of the CCF is quoted: 'Because the CCF aimed to create a society of freedom, equality and economic security, a vote for the CCF contributed to "an environment in which each human soul may have a chance to be the best that its potentialities will permit."'[77]

These were widely held values – individualism, the brotherhood of man, freedom and democracy and equality – unlikely to arouse the controversy that the development of democratic socialism did. It was in choosing the instruments or vehicles for achieving these goals and for realizing these values that the real controversy began. And this was where the CCF became vulnerable politically and often divided in its ranks. This was evident in the translation of the party's economic and social theories into a platform for the CCF for the 1944 election.

The CCF's Economic Policies

The CCF's economic theories, as postulated in the Regina Manifesto, were the most contentious in the political arena and among party members. But what exactly did the leaders think? The CCF's economic policies emerged from several different explanations of the failures of capitalism, and from the effort to find or develop practical solutions to the social and human problems caused by the Depression. Clearly, the CCF disapproved of unqualified capitalism on ethical grounds, but its disapproval was more often expressed in economic and social terms. For example:

> Socialism will come into being because of the failure of Capitalism ... The things which have caused Capitalism to fail are concentration of wealth in the hands of a few, unemployment, lack of purchasing power, lack of constructive planning, the creed of 'no profit no sale,' lack of social consciousness, disregarding the rights of humanity in a frantic attempt to maintain profit-taking, the insistence upon the private ownership of public property.[78]

But while the human goal involved in the arguments was clear, the economic reasoning regarding the failure of capitalism and its cure was less self-evident.

True, the CCF's diagnosis of the reasons for the failure of capitalism was plausible enough – particularly so in the 1930s. High ('exploitive') prices had led to declines in demand, or consumption, which led to lower profits and cuts in production, which in turn brought about reductions in employment and consequent reductions in consumption – a vicious circle, or cycle, brought on by two fundamental flaws in the economic system.

The first lay in the very ethos of capitalism – production for profit and not for human need. And there was, it seemed clear in the midst of the Depression, no mechanism by which these two ends of the economic system – human need and profit – could be reconciled, or harmonized. The second, and related, reason for the failure of capitalism, in the view of the CCF, was that in practice private corporations refused to meet public needs unless their returns were unreasonably high. They were able to achieve this, the party believed, because a large proportion of business enterprises were monopolistic and therefore able to fix their prices and control the supply of the products they produced.

The Manifesto's prescription for change in the system was, effectively, a planned economy. And that would be achieved by placing under public ownership, or direction, three categories of industry: the banking and finance corporations which were responsible for managing a large part of the nation's savings and whose credit policies could influence the direction of the national economy; other industries and services that were essential to economic planning; and natural resources industries, the profits of which, where derived from public resources, should go to the people.

In 1931 the Farmer-Labour Group said its objective was 'the social ownership of all resources and the machinery of wealth production to the ends that we may co-operatively produce and distribute for use and service rather than for private gain.'[79] In 1944 Douglas suggested much the same thing: 'Not only would the social ownership of finance and key ... industries enable us to prevent exploitation, but it would then be possible to plan our production in terms of the needs of the people.'[80]

Effectively, the CCF was advocating a 'new economics' involving fundamental changes in the existing economic system. The sheer scale of the transformation was daunting. More, the system to be introduced was by definition untried and untested, and bound therefore to inspire unease and uncertainty. This uncertainty was reinforced by the ambiguities that are almost inherent in broad blueprints for the future – in this case, a lack of clarity as to which industries would come under public ownership and which would not, and what the role of the provinces would be in an economic system that was characterized by national planning and national direction. All this engendered widespread unease, and often downright opposition: among the public generally and within the CCF party itself. It soon became clear that the party would have to clarify and to attenuate its 'nationalization program' if it were to maintain or indeed to extend its public support.

'By the late 1930's, CCF candidates and leaders moderated their pitch for state ownership in response to public opposition to rapid and extensive conversion of the private economy ... A combination of electoral experience and increased confidence in the ameliorative powers of state planning was leading [not only the CCF but] all Anglo American democratic parties on the left from an unqualified faith in massive public ownership.'[81]

In 1944 the Saskatchewan CCF Committee on Socialization of Industry and Natural Resources said that industry should not be socialized for the sake of socialization, but only under certain defined circumstances. Also in 1944, the CCF's national convention had this to say: 'The socialization of large scale enterprises, however, does not mean taking over every private business. Where private business shows no signs of becoming a monopoly, and operates efficiently under decent working conditions, and fulfils its obligations to the community, it will be given every opportunity to function, to provide a fair rate of return and to make its contribution to the nation's wealth.'[82]

During the election campaign that year, Douglas and his colleagues faced the same questions about the CCF's position on socialization. And they came up with their own answer, '[as the Saskatchewan party] had always done, changing the CCF policy to suit what they saw as the Saskatchewan conditions.'[83] Douglas clarified their position in this way:

> The CCF does not want the government to own everything. In fact we recognize that even if it were desirable, it would be physically impossible for any government to own and operate all of our economy ... [It] would break down under the weight of bureaucracy and red tape ... There are [however] certain features of our economic life which by their very nature must be owned and operated by the people through their federal, provincial or municipal government.[84]

Douglas clearly was speaking of socialization in the broadest sense, and in pragmatic terms. 'Every civilized country in the 20th century has had some experience of social ownership,' he said. And he went on to give some examples of the Canadian experience, differentiating between national ownership (CNR, CBC, Bank of Canada), provincial ownership (telephones, electrical utilities), municipal ownership (public transit, water works), and co-operative ownership (wheat pool, co-op refineries, credit unions). If these had worked – as indeed they had – then why not expand upon them where needed? 'When someone owns something that enables him to control the lives of his fellow citizens ... only then do we hold that the community as a whole should own that monopoly through ... government or cooperative ownership ...' Douglas went on to make the case for the public ownership and exploitation of natural resources, pointing out that his policy provided lots of room for private ownership and enterprise: 'This leaves a wide field for private ownership and private enterprise. [Where] there is sufficient competition among [enterprises] to guarantee that they cannot exploit the community ... there is no reason why they ought not to continue as they do now.'[85]

As we shall see, however, this was not enough to resolve the question of socialization, nor to reconcile conflicting views within the party. In the final analysis, going back to the broader national scene, what really set to rest the question in Canada of public ownership as a central economic policy instrument was the nation's experience in directing the war economy and in adopting after the war new economic policies for achieving high levels of employment and income. Canada's record in directing the war economy was exemplary. 'The government helped to determine what would be produced, how and by whom, the terms on which goods would be exchanged, and how income would be divided [all] in association with the markets.'[86] And it worked.

Then, at the end of the war in 1945, the national government published its White Paper on Employment and Income, 'being an adaptation of Keynesianism to Canada's economy and federal constitution.'[87] The Green Book on Reconstruction, published the same year, 'set out the need for high and stable spending on exports, consumption and private investment [and] re-affirmed the Government's determination to pursue high and stable levels of employment and income ...'[88] New or better understood policy instruments would come to be employed to achieve this goal: monetary policy, fiscal policy, debt management policy, trade policy, balance of payments policy, and more targeted policies such as public investment.

It is an interesting irony that J.S. Woodsworth and William Irvine were later said to have been responsible for 'the earliest Canadian attempt to construct a general body of doctrine to explain cyclical fluctuations in employment and income,'[89] and the first to advocate the use by government of fiscal and monetary measures to combat economic depressions.

More, the 'under-consumption theory' which they embraced led them to propose government spending and the expansion of credit as devices for creating employment. 'There is no disputing, then, the radical character of Woodsworth's theoretical speculations on economic matters through-out the inter-war years. He moulded the three parts of his economic doctrine – monopolies, under-consumption, and the quantity theory of money – into a case for statist socialism.'[90] But it was of course some years later that the Keynesian solution was fully established in Canada.

Government would, in short, continue to have a hand in directing and managing the Canadian economy. Thus, nationalization as a major economic policy was overtaken by Keynesian economic policy instruments. But this was becoming clear only after the CCF had been governing Saskatchewan for some time.

The CCF's Social Policies

The social policies of the CCF, while less complex than the economic, were equally sweeping for their time. The core of the CCF's position on social policy was that the services that were essential to the development and well-being of members of the community should be removed from the private, for-profit sector and be provided through the public, non-profit sector. The party was talking, of course, about education, health, and social security and services.

The CCF's expression of its policies was embodied in comprehensive programs of social reform that included education, social security, health, labour, and individual rights. Their social security program advocated, in effect, a 'national employment' budget in order that high and stable levels of employment would be achieved.[91] And 'for those who cannot contribute their labour to ... society,' they advocated food, clothes, and shelter according to modern standards, and an 'opportunity to live a dignified, and a rich and varied life.'[92]

They advocated, as well, detailed social welfare measures, special programs for the relief of the unemployed, a labour policy which would increase the 'dignity and status of employees,'[93] and sweeping changes in education. In all of these positions, the recurring theme was the provision of minimum standards of living for every citizen, social and economic security for everyone, and individual or personal security. These, the CCF held, are the conditions that must obtain before individual self-realization can be achieved.[94] They rejected both the view that the individual would develop best in a competitive situation, and that the welfare state would stifle the individual.

While neither would have recognized it, the ultimate goals of the socialists and the exponents of economic liberalism were the same: the creation of the conditions in which the individual could most fully and richly develop. Where they differed, and differed profoundly, was in the conditions that they believed would foster this self-realization and in the social ethics that should prevail.

There was never any doubt or qualification in the minds of Saskatchewan's CCF leaders about this aspect of the party's ideology. Indeed, its social security policies enjoyed respectable company in the early and mid-40s. This is when the Mackenzie King government in Ottawa announced in the throne speeches of 1943 and 1944 its intention to discuss with the provinces the establishment of a universal social security plan, and published its Green Book on Reconstruction (discussed in the Annex). This is not to say that there was no opposition to the plan – indeed there was. It was not, in fact, until 1958 and 1968 that national hospitalization and medicare plans were established. But this part of the CCF's ideology was secure.

The CCF's Democratic Theories

If the economic and social policies of the CCF were unconventional, so too were its political theories. A large body of CCF opinion held that the electorate should be consulted directly whenever possible: 'The CCF maintains that ... the Government, Municipal, Provincial and Federal, shall be made truly democratic – by means of the initiative, referendum, recall and other measures making for popular government.'[95] The party held that Parliament should be as representative of the electorate's views as possible: in 1936 Williams advocated the introduction of proportional representation. And in the same year, the Directive Board of the CCF (SS) inserted in the draft constitution for the party a provision for recall of CCF members of the legislature.[96]

The same general point of view found expression in elaborate suggestions as to how the cabinet and the legislature might be 'controlled' by the party. In 1943 Douglas expressed the principle:

The policies of the CCF are the outcome of the needs, and the aspirations of the common people as expressed in provincial and national conventions. Those of us who occupy positions of responsibility in the CCF have no power to add ... or subtract one sentence from the programme laid down by the people themselves. We are merely their servants appointed to carry out their wishes as expressed from time to time in convention assembled.

Much more important ... is the fact that if we do form a government in this province or in the Dominion we shall be required to appear before the regular annual and biennial conventions in order to give an accounting of our stewardship.[97]

The CCF held the view, further, that if it formed the government, the party should have some say in the selection of the premier and his cabinet and in the legislation that was presented.[98]

There was, as might be expected, some disagreement over the more extreme 'direct democracy' views, and increasingly, over time, the party inclined to support the conventions of cabinet government. Moreover, party control over an elected CCF government, which would scarcely have been consistent with the government's responsibility to the Legislative Assembly and the electorate, was sometimes questioned, and party influence was advocated instead. For example, it was acknowledged that the premier must accept final responsibility for his cabinet, and that a CCF cabinet would, because it believed in the supremacy of Parliament, submit its five-year economic plans to the House.[99]

What was new about the CCF political theory, as it had emerged in 1944, was the institutionalization of party and public influence in the processes of government. The belief that cabinet ministers should be 'accountable'[100] to the party was new in Canada, as was the view that the party should advise the premier on his cabinet selections and on legislation. Direct democracy was to be achieved by a combination of constituency control, party influence, and the influence of interest groups.[101]

This, then, is the story of the values and the ideology of the CCF as they guided the party in the drafting of its policy platform for the election of 1944 and for the years that followed. It becomes apparent that despite the many differences of opinion within the Saskatchewan CCF there was a relatively consistent thread of philosophy in its policies and programs. It consisted of a passionate belief in the common man: in his ability and his right to govern himself; his right to the dignity and self-assurance to which all men are born; and his right to the kind of economic and social security which the CCF believed to be essential to self-realization.

Underlying this core of belief was the influence of the farmer-labour movements, the co-operatives, and the more directly political movements, notably the Progressives – underpinned by the beliefs of Salem Bland and his followers. But the wellsprings of the CCF's political philosophy and its associated ideology were primarily the nineteenth-century idealists, as reflected in the British Labour Party and the Fabian Society, coupled with tinges of the theories of European socialists and those of American populists like Henry Wise Wood. These were the foundations upon which the CCF election program of 1944 was built, and the base upon which the CCF government would build for the next seventeen years.

2

Planning the Program for a CCF Government

The 1944 election platform of the CCF, entitled *Program for Saskatchewan*, set forth a sweeping set of positions and commitments to the province. Its origins, of course, were to be found in the CCF's philosophy and its economic and social theories: they served quite naturally as the reference point both in diagnosing the problems Saskatchewan had experienced, and in prescribing the remedies to these problems.

In its essence, the *Program* reflected the CCF's conception of a post-Depression, post-war state: one in which government would play an active role in creating the economic and social conditions under which individual freedom and human well-being might flourish. This, as we have seen in chapter 1, was the beacon that was to guide the CCF government through all its years.

The most notable characteristics of the *Program*, however, were its comprehensiveness and its inter-connectedness. It recognized, first, the prime importance of resources and industrial development – of economic growth – both for rebuilding the province and its economy, and for financing the CCF's ambitious social programs. It addressed itself to the full range of mineral and forest resources and how they might be developed, and similarly to industrial development, and the apparently intractable problem of attracting 'Eastern capital' to a province like Saskatchewan. Alternative means for realizing development in all sectors were explored – with the strongly held view that if industrial development were to occur in Saskatchewan at all, it would have to come about through public initiative.

The sections of the *Program* devoted to agriculture addressed in substantial measure the detritus of the 1930s, reflected in the high levels of farm debt and in the accompanying decline in the security of farm tenure. These were the starting point for any policies that might address the future development of the agricultural industry.

The *Program* went on to set out very detailed plans for comprehensive reform and development in health, education, and social services. It laid the foundations for the development of a universal public health care system – referred to as 'socialized' medicine. It proposed increases in economic security for the elderly and single mothers. It enumerated detailed changes to raise the quality of education throughout the province and to make it more accessible.

The *Program* turned in some detail, as well, to the machinery of government that would be required – the reforms to the public service that clearly were needed to effect such an enormous undertaking. And it addressed the evident financial issues that would confront the government – in particular, the source and the scale of the revenues required to finance the *Program*.

In one sense, there is nothing unusual about a political party planning its platform for an election, and laying the basis for its performance should it form the next government. What was unusual about the CCF's planning, however, was its thoroughness and the comprehensiveness of the resulting policies and programs. The planning was done almost as if the participants had already formed the government. Certainly it was obvious that they intended to do so. But how the CCF went about the process of translating its goals into policies and of elaborating its policies into programs is a particular and revealing story in itself. It is also the essential first chapter in the process of policy formulation in the CCF government. For it was the party that planned the program for the first term of office and, in so doing, set the direction for government policies for the next twenty years.

The Structure and Process of Planning the Platform

The organization of the party was well suited to the task of planning a program. It provided strong leadership roles, which the party leaders would need to develop an integrated program, and at the same time it preserved the principle of direct democracy in the annual conventions at which all party policies had to be debated and accepted. The organization of the party was important, too, in its influence in shaping a new relationship between government and party, once the CCF had come to power.

The constitution of the CCF made its annual provincial convention the supreme body of the party: it was 'the governing body of the Association and shall have the power to alter or amend the Constitution and Platform.'[1] The annual conventions adopted the 'suggested changes in the program and platform'[2] and selected the political leader and other officers of the party. In practice, the convention, its delegates, and the constituencies from which they came were extremely active in proposing policies and programs on an *ad hoc* basis. They looked to their leaders for general guidance but jealously guarded their right to initiate individual policies.

The convention comprised ten delegates from each of fifty-two provincial constituencies (electoral districts), all of the CCF members of Parliament (MPs) and members of the Legislative Assembly (MLAs), and the members of the Provincial Council. For the purposes of program deliberation, the convention was organized into 'panels,' each of which was responsible for a broad area of provincial policy. In these panels, the delegates considered the proposals that had been generated by party leaders or come directly from constituency organizations. The delegates in these panels deliberated and then took decisions in the form of recommendations that were sent, along with the resolutions that had been debated, to the convention's plenary session, where the final decisions were made.

Just as the provincial CCF met in convention each year, so did its constituency organizations. Each constituency was empowered 'to review and suggest amendments to the Platform of the CCF,' and they did this at their annual conventions. Constituency conventions comprised three delegates from each poll (electoral subdivision), members of the constituency executive, the MLA and MP (or candidates) for the area, and representatives of the CCF women's and youth organizations. Their main business was to debate policy resolutions and to select delegates for the provincial convention. Their meetings were often long, and sometimes electric, but it was not difficult for an individual party member to get his or her ideas before the constituency convention.

Between conventions, the Provincial Council was 'responsible for the direction of the affairs of the Association,' and was answerable to the provincial convention.[3] Eight of the councillors during the late 1930s and early 1940s became cabinet ministers – Tommy Douglas, Clarence Fines, J.H. Brockelbank, J.T. Douglas, Joe Phelps, Joe Burton, Toby Nollett, and Jim Darling. Fourteen more were, or later became, members of the Legislative Assembly, and five were, or became, CCF members of Parliament. Other leaders in this Provincial Council included Professor

Carlyle A. King, who became president of the Saskatchewan CCF, and two editors of the party newspaper, the *Saskatchewan Commonwealth*. One council member, W. Ross Thatcher, later defected from the CCF, and became the leader of the Saskatchewan Liberal Party and leader of the opposition in 1960.

The real working body was the provincial executive, which met at least every two months. The executive comprised the president, the vice-president, the political leader, and six others elected by and from the council.[4] Beyond the executive was a Board of Strategy made up of the president and two other executive members (chosen by the executive); it acted for the executive when neither it nor the council was in session. One other committee had an important part to play in the story after the 1944 election. It was the Legislative Advisory Committee, with five members – three chosen by the council from among its members, and two CCF MLAs elected from among their number. Its purpose, when the CCF formed the government, was 'to assist the CCF Legislative Group in preparing legislation in conformity with CCF policies,' and to advise the premier on the composition of his cabinet.[5] Here was direct democracy in action.

But it was the Provincial Council and the provincial executive that took the initiative in drafting the 1944 election platform. The work actually started following a Provincial Council motion in September 1941 to the effect that 'the Education and Publicity Committee be a committee for the purpose of writing a manifesto interpreting the Provincial platform, and this committee to have power to add to their number.'[6] In addition the council established two general committees, a Planning Committee and a Budgeting Committee. During 1942 the functioning committees were Planning, Education, Social Services, and Labour. Early in 1943, the committee organization was changed and the Planning Committee was asked to recommend a series of sub-committees to work under its direction. Four were established: Education, Social Services, Housing, and Natural Resources. Later, separate committees were formed for agriculture and health, and a new Industrial Development Committee was established.[7] In January 1944, the Planning Committee added a committee on the machinery of government as well.[8]

The sub-committees developed, in their areas, the policies and programs that seemed most likely to address Saskatchewan's problems and which were consistent with CCF objectives and principles. The Planning Committee received these recommendations and was responsible for reviewing them and integrating them into a single and coherent whole.

In some ways, this highly structured organization resembled the CCF's 'shadow cabinet' in the Legislative Assembly. But the job of the committees differed importantly: they were not to act as critics of the current government but were to restrict themselves to developing a comprehensive election platform. Nevertheless, the two groups were coordinated, with many of the CCF MLAs serving as members of the party committees.

The members of the committees were, again, largely prominent members of the party.[9] The Planning Committee (later merged with the Budgeting Committee) included Tommy Douglas, MP, later the premier; Clarence M. Fines, to become provincial treasurer; J.H. ('Brock') Brockelbank, MLA, later minister of municipal affairs; Oak W. Valleau, MLA, later minister of social welfare; Carlyle A. King, later president of the Saskatchewan CCF; Joe Phelps, later minister of natural resources; and Woodrow S. Lloyd, president of the Saskatchewan Teachers' Federation and later minister of education and then premier. Prominent members formed the other committees too. The Provincial Council and the Provincial Executive, to whom these planning committees reported, were composed of members who were well known, including the future premier and cabinet ministers, MLAs, and other leaders.

More important than the names themselves, at this point, is the fact that a relatively small number of people, many of them capable of becoming distinguished public leaders, were responsible for drafting the program which would have such a lasting influence on government policies in Saskatchewan. Few of them were experts, in the usual sense, though many of them were professionals in their own right. Tommy Douglas, for example, was a theologian and a sociologist; Woodrow Lloyd and Clarence Fines were school principals; and Gertrude Telford was also a trained sociologist as well as being a political activist. The majority, however, did not have professional qualifications, but rather an intangible quality of insight or perception that helped in clarifying the party's goals and fashioning broad public policies based upon those goals. While they held positions of authority and while they enjoyed in their own right a certain prestige, in another sense they were agents of the party. The supreme authority was the provincial convention, and the party leaders were keenly aware, if for no other reason than the direct democracy ideal that pervaded the CCF, that their election program must meet with convention approval. Moreover, the Provincial Council, which tended to mirror convention opinion, kept a firm hand on the formulation of the program.

There is another sense in which the party leaders themselves were influenced, at the same time that they were exerting influence. To the extent that they were the products, the adherents, of CCF ideology and ethics, they were – they had already been – influenced by the pioneer leaders such as J.S. Woodsworth, M.J. Coldwell, and George Williams, and by contemporary national leaders such as David Lewis, Stanley Knowles, and Andrew Brewin. They could be expected to develop a program consistent with the views that they themselves had adopted.

The party executive, indeed, consciously sought out the views of contemporary provincial and national CCF leaders, in examining the party's policy papers as they emerged and supplementary position papers that had been prepared at the executive's request. This culminated in a special three-day conference of seventy-two leading members of the national and provincial sections of the CCF, held during the Christmas season of 1943. Among those attending were members of the CCF provincial executive – Clarence Fines, J.H. Brockelbank, Oak Valleau, Woodrow Lloyd, Joe Phelps, and, of course, Tommy Douglas. From the national CCF office, Frank Scott and David Lewis attended; two other provincial leaders present were Harold Winch (British Columbia) and Elmer Roper (Alberta). 'The meeting subjected the policy papers ... and other ideas (for labour legislation, health care, provincial budgeting, natural resources and public ownership) to searching examination ... when the party entered the 1944 election, its program had already undergone a baptism of fire.'[10]

In the whole of the process of 'policy-making' within the party, there were of course points at which the leaders exerted commanding influence: notably where elements of the party's philosophy were not entirely homogeneous or where inconsistencies were discovered in the process of refining goals into policies. At any of these points, the leaders were compelled to make choices, and when choices had to be made the leadership was inevitably better equipped to persuade the convention to accept the proposals than the members were to resist them.

During 1943 and 1944, the course seemed unequivocally clear. Leaders and followers alike subscribed to the social ethos that motivated the CCF Party in its policy deliberations. They shared a common heritage in the farmers' and co-operative movements, from which most of them sprang. And they were influenced by a common social experience, as pioneers of a frontier community.

The CCF and Relations within a Federal State

Before embarking upon the details of the 1944 election platform, it is important to recall the limits on a province's power in a federal state, and to reflect on the Saskatchewan CCF's attitudes to Canadian federalism. Clearly the Canadian constitution imposes limits on the provinces' powers, in the interest of providing to the national government the transcending powers required to develop and maintain a healthy national economy, and to contribute to the realization for all Canadians of reasonably equal levels of basic public services, notably health, welfare, and (arguably) education, through the exercise of the spending power. The CCF recognized this reality. The party *Program* asserted: '... the CCF has always recognized that it is not constitutionally possible to set up a complete co-operative commonwealth within the boundaries of a single province.'[11] Douglas consistently took the position that no CCF Government would ever be elected in Saskatchewan by promising to do things which were known perfectly well to be beyond the powers of a provincial government.

At the same time, however, the party believed in strong provincial powers. It recognized that the provinces required the financial power as well as the constitutional power to provide the public services called for in their platform and later by provincial legislation. For example, Douglas argued in 1937 that the CCF was likely to come to power in one of the Western provinces and would need wide provincial powers to carry out its program.[12] In 1944 he advocated strengthening the financial base of the provinces, so that they could discharge their responsibilities more effectively: 'A CCF Government in Saskatchewan would urge upon whatever government was in power in Ottawa, the need for a complete overhaul of federal-provincial relations. At the present time, the federal government has all the sources of revenue, and the provincial government has all the responsibility for social services.'[13]

For the CCF this reform of federal-provincial relations meant a redistribution of personal income and corporation tax revenue to help the poorer provinces, effectively a measure of equalization, as it came to be known, plus federal grants to assist all provinces in providing better social services. These arguments were to be consistently part of the CCF government's positions in the federal-provincial conferences and discussions of the 1940s and the 1950s.[14]

At the same time, the CCF was entirely willing to assign to the federal government the responsibility for programs which, if it were left to the provinces, would not be implemented. At one time, the provincial convention advocated a national labour code, and at another time it seemed prepared to accept federal responsibility for a nationwide health scheme. The compromise of conditional grants was accepted in many other fields. This implied federal assistance to the provinces in order to get a program started and to establish minimum national standards of service, and provincial administration of the program to ensure it was adapted to local conditions.

On balance, the CCF seems to have leaned toward strong central or national powers, simply because its main concern was with building a welfare state out of the devastation of the Depression and the upheaval of world war. The federal government would require broad powers in order to discharge its responsibilities for national economic planning and for stimulating the development of national standards of health and welfare. At the same time, the CCF also acknowledged that the provinces must enjoy wide powers if they were to introduce the policies and programs these national standards would imply, and that they must be guaranteed sufficient tax potential to fund the programs. Here, as elsewhere, the Saskatchewan CCF revealed a certain pragmatism in its analysis and approach.

The Program for Natural Resources and Industrial Development

Turning, then, to the deliberations of the CCF's Planning Committee and its policy sub-committees, the most active and controversial of these was the Natural Resources and Industrial Development Committee, led by Joe Phelps. The committee considered extensive proposals for both natural resources and industrial development, and foresaw a significant new provincial role in both areas. Its premise was clearly that the development of resources would, or should, take place under public rather than private auspices.

In Saskatchewan, where the province already owned some 70 per cent of mineral rights, this presumably would mean, as a first step, acquiring the privately owned mineral rights, thus bringing all mineral rights under public ownership.[15] The next question would concern the exploration for oil and minerals and their exploitation upon discovery: would this be done by the public sector or 'contracted out' to the private sector?

In one report, the committee argued that 'the CCF Provincial Government [should] plan for the eventual and complete socialization under provincial administration of all natural resources now controlled by the Province ...'[16] It suggested that, as an immediate objective, the province should 'plan to prevent any further alienation of natural resources,' and should consider whether and which of the already alienated resources should be restored to public ownership. This point of view was consistent with CCF ideology and was accepted by the Provincial Council. The 1944 *Program* asserted, '... we must proceed to the public development and public ownership of our natural resources.'[17]

Resource development was intended to serve two basic objectives, the first being economic growth and development. This was stated most clearly by an advisor, C.A.L. ('Vern') Hogg (subsequently deputy minister of natural resources), who pointed out the need for economic diversification in Saskatchewan. He acknowledged the importance of strengthening the agricultural industry, but argued that Saskatchewan's dependence upon a single and unstable industry was undesirable, and that the most likely avenue of diversification was resource development. This was not a particularly radical position: Saskatchewan's Industrial Development Board had argued it earlier.[18] In the end, the CCF *Program* laid greater stress upon social ownership and social benefits than it did upon the economics of development, but it did state that 'our natural resources [must] be developed to the fullest extent ...'[19]

The second objective, then, was to maximize the benefits to the people of the province from the profits of resource development; this objective was to be achieved largely through social or public ownership. The Committee on Natural Resources and the Planning Committee envisaged the revenues from natural resources being made available to finance social services, though they realized this source of income would take some time to develop.[20] The *Program* spoke of the development of natural resources 'for the public benefit' and said 'a CCF Government can obtain revenue from the development of natural resources under public ownership.'[21]

But the party did not visualize exclusive government ownership. It also spoke of collecting royalties and taxes from privately owned enterprises. The Planning Committee agreed, for example, that a 'severance tax' should be applied to resources that were being developed privately,[22] and the Chair – later the minister of natural resources – announced in the legislature in March 1944 that the CCF would not socialize the Hudson Bay Mining and Smelting Company, but instead would raise their royalties.[23] For that matter, the 1944 *Program* made no mention of the Natural Resource Committee's recommendation that privately owned resources should be restored to the Crown.

Nevertheless, the party had quite a clear idea of how to proceed with resource development. The first steps included 'a survey and a stock-taking by geologists, chemists, engineers and other specialists.'[24] Vern

Hogg had proposed a provincial bureau of mines that would undertake geological mapping, prospector training, and preliminary mining development, but he also advised against socialization of the mining industry.[25] Other resources, such as oil, natural gas, and potash, remained undiscovered in 1944, and so were not the subject of explicit policy proposals.

There were, however, quite detailed plans for the development of the forestry and fisheries industries. The committee proposed stocking and restocking of suitable lakes, and providing more adequate facilities for 'processing, storing and marketing of all fish produced within our Province,'[26] along with an air transportation system to ship fish to market. It advocated a forest conservation program and revisions to timber regulations to prevent the unscientific exploitation of forest resources and to ensure proper fire prevention measures.[27] The committee did not propose the socialization of timber mills or the expropriation of timber operators; rather, it advocated compulsory marketing of timber,[28] which would have the effect of bringing timber and timber products under government control, so that a share of the profits would flow into the provincial treasury.

Few of these detailed plans were outlined in the 1944 *Program*, which contained a more general statement of policy. It quoted from a resolution passed at the 1943 CCF convention: 'The development of the vast northland so that the tremendous wealth in lumber, minerals, and water power which now lies undeveloped be brought into full production.'[29]

The second focus of the Committee on Natural Resources was the industrial development program, and in this area it was rather more unconventional. All the evidence suggests that the CCF thought of industrial development primarily in terms of public ownership. Certainly the philosophy of the party would lead the members in this direction. Still, there were undoubtedly conflicting points of view. While the theory upon which social ownership was based provided a broad rationale for the national ownership of monopolies, it provided a much shakier foundation for the provincial ownership of the small businesses to be found in Saskatchewan. Indeed, some provincial leaders had already spoken out against complete socialization. Given these conditions, it would be surprising if the Planning Committee considered seriously all of the proposals it received for public ownership of small industries.

Despite these apparent contradictions, the CCF's ideological foundation did provide some guidance for a provincial program of industrial development. The Natural Resources and Industrial Development Committee, influenced by the Regina Manifesto, held that 'industry should be socialized not for the sake of socialization, but only under certain defined circumstances.' One of these was familiar – where the industry is a monopoly that displays a tendency to restrict output or inflate prices.[30] A second reason that seems periodically to have brought the committee to favour social ownership was because it would enable the public to enjoy the profits of industry. George Williams had advocated this point of view in the 1930s, when he spoke of converting private monopolies into 'state monopolies and turning the profits from the sales of these commodities into the Treasury to be used for social purposes.'[31] But by 1943-4, this rationale for public ownership seems to have been applied largely to resource industries.[32]

A third reason for advocating development by public rather than private means was a very pragmatic one. Industrial development in Saskatchewan during the 1930s was negligible, and it had improved very little during the war. Understandably, therefore, there was little confidence in the possibility of industrialists and financiers 'in the East' doing much to assist the province in any program of industrialization. The prevailing view was that the interests of those industrialists lay in the central Canadian provinces, and that they simply refused to believe that there was a case for industry on the Prairies. The Industrial Development Board had stated this view bluntly in its 1944 report: 'We would be well advised to devote our energy to the development of our own resources and to the utilization of our own facilities ... it is becoming increasingly apparent that if Saskatchewan is to have industries, it will have to assume much, if not all, of the responsibility for their development.'[33]

The CCF reflected this point of view. After a member of the Industrial Development Board had addressed the CCF provincial convention in 1943, the membership resolved:

> That in our opinion the increasing tendency on the part of the Government of Canada to further centralize industrial development in central Canada is not in the public interest ... that consideration be immediately given to [establishing] those [war] industries that are logical for Western Canada in the processing of agricultural products ... and [which will] give encouragement to the development of sound and natural secondary industry in Western Canada.[34]

The convention resolved further: 'That the industrial facilities and the necessary power developments should be socially owned – i.e., either publicly or co-operatively controlled – to the end that production shall be for service and not for profit.'[35] This was a clear indication of the CCF's concern about industrial development, and an expression of the belief that it *should* take place under public auspices. Indeed, the CCF members seemed to believe that industrial development *would* only happen as a result of government initiative.[36] The Natural Resources Committee gave this as a prime reason for socialized industry.

Thus, the reasons for public ownership were both ideological and pragmatic, and party members were not unwilling to shift from one reason to another in defending their position. If social ownership were desirable, *per se*, then the case for government industry was unequivocal. But if industrial development was the primary goal, then public ownership was only one way of achieving it. To compound the uncertainty about first principles, the committee failed to subject its theories to any test of practicability. It did not collect evidence as to the capital the province would require or the profits government would earn if one policy or another were followed. Nor did the committee consider the limitations their policy might encounter, such as difficulties in borrowing capital from the 'Eastern financiers' or engaging management personnel, or finding markets for the products. Unhappily for the incoming government, these uncertainties were carried into the cabinet when it assumed office.

In this context, not surprisingly, people proposed a wide variety of industries or categories of industries to be developed.[37] These included public utilities – a provincial electric power utility (at a time when only urban centres received electrical power, some by private and some by municipal utilities); transportation services, notably an airline to serve northern Saskatchewan; marketing organizations that would sell, at cost to the producer, natural products such as fish, timber, and fur; and processing industries such as a tannery, a woollen mill, a linseed oil plant, a coal processing plant, fish filleting plants, and a brick factory. At one meeting of the Natural Resources Committee, twenty-five industries were listed, and party members were asked to study their feasibility. Despite this seemingly unsystematic approach, a pattern of sorts did emerge, as observed above. The committee advocated public utilities (not at all unconventional), compulsory government marketing organizations (not unconventional for Saskatchewan), secondary industries designed to use the province's natural resources (more unconventional), and 'high profit' industries which would provide the revenue for public social programs (quite unconventional).

The Planning Committee and the Provincial Council, however, did not support all of these proposals. The 1944 *Program* contained some public ownership proposals – it mentioned natural resource industries and distributive enterprises, both of which were intended to finance social programs; but it did not pretend to be a blueprint for industrial development. In fact, industrial development and social ownership occupied quite a small part of the 1944 *Program for Saskatchewan*. But it represented an aspect of CCF ideology that had assumed major proportions in the national party program, and it was one of the more spectacular features of the provincial government's policy during the 1944 to 1948 period. It was also the aspect of CCF philosophy that was clarified, or rationalized, most dramatically during the next decade.

The Program for Agriculture

In contrast with the importance of agriculture in the Saskatchewan economy, agricultural policies and programs received very little space in the 1944 *Program*. But what did appear was significant. The first main focus was on farm security, a matter of major importance during and after the Depression, and the second was a statement of national policy.

With respect to farm security, the *Program* was both forthright and radical. It promised to 'stop foreclosure on and eviction from the farm home,' to 'introduce legislation to protect [farmers] from seizure of that portion of [their] crop that is needed to provide for [their] families,' and to 'use the power of debt moratorium ... to force the loan and mortgage companies to reduce debts and mortgages to a figure at which they can reasonably be paid at prevailing prices for farm products.'[38] The *Program* also promised to declare a moratorium on principal payments and to cancel interest payments in any year when farm income fell below six dollars an acre; to prevent municipalities from collecting on old loans for buying seed grain when the farmers were having difficulty maintaining their families; and to cancel the 1938 Dominion-Provincial seed grain loans – the almost colossal debt which had accumulated in providing seed after the 1937 crop failure.[39]

These were radical commitments, indeed, some of them seemingly unconstitutional, some of them offensive to the national government, and some of them totally unacceptable to the financial institutions that held mortgages in the province. But they were the product of the Depression, and no political party in Saskatchewan dared oppose them. Douglas reflected these agrarian attitudes when he said:

Farming is a partnership. The farmer invests his labour and equipment. The finance corporations invest their money ... If the mortgage companies want to stay in business in this province they will have to start taking the good years with the bad, and begin shouldering their share of the losses.[40]

Naturally, these were the words and the position of a party that had not yet experienced the responsibilities of office, nor encountered the constitutional and credit limitations that confine a provincial government. The party had not yet been forced to reconcile conflicting goals: the desire to legislate in the interests of its people, as it saw them, and the need to obtain capital from financial institutions that are influenced in their lending decisions by their approval or disapproval of a government's policies. At this stage, however, a radical commitment seemed both warranted and appropriate.

The second major aspect of the 1944 *Program* for agriculture was a statement of national policy. The CCF advocated closing the Winnipeg Grain Exchange and setting parity prices for farmers ('those which will bring them their fair share of the total national income').[41] The party also advocated marketing boards with producer representation, regulation of the livestock industry, an agricultural bank, a farm implement board to manufacture and distribute farm implements, government grain storage facilities, import and export boards, and a vast soil and water conservation program.[42]

Beyond the 1944 election program, the party's policies for agriculture were far-reaching and based upon an understanding of the challenges to the agricultural sector as that sector had developed to the 1940s – the size of holdings, the difficulties of transportation and communication, and the isolation of farm families. The CCF advocated converting the subsistence farm to an economical farm unit,[43] preserving the family farm, and providing more adequate services to farms, including rural electrification. But the party also recognized that these policies could proceed only as farm security, new settlement patterns, and higher farm income were achieved.[44] In the same discussions of agricultural policy, the party considered measures to increase agricultural production, to extend agricultural education, and to settle new farmlands. While these policy ideas were not captured in the 1944 *Program*, they were certainly part of the new government's total commitments that emerged over time.

To complete its economic program, the CCF made a very few statements about transportation and communication. It advocated more extensive use of the Hudson Bay Railway for the shipment of grain through Hudson Bay. It made some harsh comments about freight rates. And the Economic Planning Committee 'agreed that no additional expenditures (over those budgeted by the Provincial Government in 1943) would be required for highways'[45] – a prediction that turned out to be more sanguine than far-sighted.

The Program for Health, Education, and Welfare

The amount of attention paid to increasing potential revenues from industrial development in order to finance social programs was a measure of the importance of social policy in the CCF's *Program*. The commitments made with respect to health and education and social welfare polices were comprehensive and exhaustive; after all, these policies lay at the heart of the CCF's beliefs. The party believed that higher standards of social security and equal access to good health and good education would permit the individual to develop to the full extent of his or her potential.[46] Nationally, the party advocated the highest possible standards in health care 'without regard to the economic status of the individual,'[47] and a comprehensive national social security scheme that would insure everyone against loss of income due to 'sickness, disability, widowhood and old age.'[48]

This philosophy and these positions were the starting point for the Social Services Committee. In an interim report in December 1941, the committee advocated gradual 'socialization' of health services (in other words, creation of a universally accessible health program), with emphasis on preventive medicine. It suggested maternity grants as a first step and proposed that the CCF should 'increase Mothers' Allowances to provide a decent standard of living for all widowed or deserted mothers.' The committee also proposed that the CCF should 'endeavour to induce the Federal Government to increase the Old Age Pension (a shared federal-provincial program), and to have the age qualification lowered to 60 years.' Finally, it proposed the inauguration of 'scientifically approved' agencies for the prevention of crime and delinquency.[49]

The words of Tommy Douglas capture the approach to the creation of the party's policy with respect to health:

We believe that by extending our present socialized health services ... to cover more and more kinds of illness, we can ultimately give our people a completely socialized system of health services. This would have to be done in a series of stages. The first might be to make the hospitals available to all who require hospitalization. The second might be to set up cancer clinics and gradually to extend them to cover other ailments and diseases. Other stages will include the steps by which the doctors, dentists and nurses, through some form of health insurance, would make their services available ... irrespective of ... individual ability to pay ... when we [consider] that a properly planned health system would place the emphasis on preventive medicine rather than curative medicine, we can see why the cost should be less than what we are now paying.[50]

Proposals for education were the largest part of the CCF *Program*. The Saskatchewan CCF had always emphasized the importance of adequate educational facilities, one reason being, no doubt, that education had suffered so seriously during the Depression. As early as 1932, the Farmer-Labour Party had called for 'the equalization of educational opportunity.'[51] In the 1944 *Program*, the CCF issued the same clarion call:

We cannot afford, in a democracy, to put education on rations if we want to give our boys and girls an adequate chance to develop their talents and make their full contribution to society. We must pay well for their training. We talk a great deal about developing our natural resources but the most precious of our nation's resources are the children and young people. If we fail to give them opportunity for development, we are guilty of the most appalling waste.[52]

The specific proposals for the education program emerged over several years. In 1941 the Education Committee recommended to Provincial Council that top priority should be given to improving rural education, and that special attention should be paid to children in difficulty.[53] In 1942 the CCF issued a pamphlet which called for additional measures, including improved 'status' and income for teachers, free textbooks and school supplies, larger units of school administration in the rural areas, the removal of income barriers to higher education, and the introduction of adult education. It also proposed regular consultation between the Saskatchewan Teachers Federation and the Association of School Trustees.

When the CCF held its three-day national policy conference in 1943, the party reiterated these points but with two notable changes. One was a considerable elaboration of the proposed policies, and the second was a new emphasis on the 'philosophy of education.' A confidential memorandum to the delegates suggested that curricula should be examined to determine what social values were implicit in the instructional materials, and that moral values stressing co-operation should be included, while the emphasis on competition should be discouraged. In more concrete terms, the proposed educational program included target figures for teachers' salaries, the number of school superintendents that Saskatchewan required, and a five-year program for implementing new school units. It even included a budget for the Department of Education.[54]

The Education Committee reported again, in April 1944, with a further elaboration of its program. The Planning Committee added only two items: a scholarship plan for assisting high school students, and provision for a provincial library program.[55] Thus the 1944 *Program* for education was a very detailed plan. It acknowledged the province's responsibility for 'providing educational opportunity for all children,' and outlined the proposals: larger school units, higher salaries for teachers, consultation with teachers and trustees, health services in schools, free textbooks and supplies, special educational facilities for developmentally handicapped children, assistance for college students, an adult education program, and curriculum changes to 'equip the child with the information and attitudes of co-operative living with his fellows in the modern world' (a lecture to the Fabian Society by G.D.H. Cole is cited).[56]

Over time, the work of the Social Services, Education, and Health Committees became more specific. In January 1944, the Planning Committee discussed very detailed recommendations, including contributions by government to the municipal schemes for employing doctors,[57] grants to municipalities for public health services, and public health clinics especially for school children. The committee estimated that the cost of its program would rise from $2 million to $16 million per year. The Education Committee proposals included the expenditure of $2 million to establish a medical college and a university hospital at the University of Saskatchewan. And the Social Services Committee estimated the annual cost of increasing mothers' allowances and old age pensions, and also proposed a reorganization of the welfare services into a single government department. This was the nature of the health and welfare policies that appeared in the *Program for Saskatchewan*. The *Program* varied only slightly from the committee recommendations in promising to press the federal government for an increase in old age pensions ('if necessary, the CCF will act alone to raise the amount of the pension'), and in providing for pensions for the physically handicapped. It also advocated improved child protection services, a vocational guidance and training program, and reforms to the prison system.[58]

The Program for Labour

Like the health and welfare programs, the platform for labour followed closely the national policies of the CCF. In its first report to Provincial Council in 1941, the Labour Committee proposed a new industrial standards act, higher minimum wages, improved benefits under the Workmen's Compensation Act, equal pay for equal work, and 'fuller representation of labour on all government boards having to do with labour.'[59] In 1942 the committee submitted more detailed proposals: for example, it suggested a minimum wage of $25 a week and 100 per-cent (workman's) compensation in case of injury, and it proposed that 'collective bargaining be made compulsory by law.'[60] In mid-year, the *Saskatchewan Commonwealth* published these proposals as the party's labour program.[61]

In 1943 the annual convention adopted a similar platform, and added provisions for 'compulsory recognition of trade unions,' machinery for settling industrial disputes, and the establishment of a Department of Labour.[62] In the same year, the Provincial Council proposed that an apprenticeship system be established.[63] Douglas summarized the published *Program* in this way:

> A CCF Government in Saskatchewan could enact legislation making collective bargaining compulsory and thus enable labour to become organized as an equal partner in our economy. Hours of labour, conditions of work, and wages paid would all come within provincial jurisdiction. A CCF Government would see to it that labour was protected against exploitation and intimidation.[64]

Financing the Program

This was the CCF *Program for Saskatchewan*, a long-range and comprehensive plan for a future government – what in later years would be called a 'strategic plan.' The *Program's* significance for the future lay not only in its sweeping multi-year proposals, but also in its recurring influence on the CCF government. It was an authoritative statement of party policy, subject only to review at the party's annual conventions.

At the same time, the very process of developing the *Program* helped to strengthen the position of party leaders who were to become ministers. For in developing particular elements of this program, they had already begun to fill government-like roles – a new expertise – as opposed to a more traditional party role. Their policy formulation procedures resembled those which responsible governments employ: they were engaged in making their policies and programs more specific, and they were subjecting their plans to the hard discipline of 'the possible.'

Evidence of this approach is found in the deliberations on the budget and in the recommendations concerning the machinery of government. The Planning Committee had gone through the exercise of designing a provincial budget, with levels of expenditure for each of the major departments of government and with emphasis on the incremental costs should the plans of the CCF be implemented.[65] Having drawn up an expenditure budget, the committee then turned its mind to methods of financing it. Here the committee members encountered a familiar problem: the party's pronouncements on taxation were not entirely consistent with its desire to increase public expenditures.

An example of this conundrum was the discussion of the provincial sales tax. In 1942 the Provincial Council resolved that the province's sales tax should be abolished,[66] a position which enjoyed wide support in the party on the grounds that the tax was regressive. In 1943 the question was discussed again and referred to the Planning Committee. Early in 1944, this committee concluded that the sales tax would have to be retained, but that it should be made less regressive by exempting necessities from its coverage. If this policy were seriously to reduce the tax yield, a higher rate, particularly on luxury items might have to be considered. This point of view was presented to the Provincial Council in April, and seems to have prevailed.[67] Douglas promised in a radio broadcast that the 'tax structure would be made more equitable, notably by the exemption of necessities from the Education Tax' (as the sales tax was then called). However, he went on to say: 'Just as soon as a CCF Government can develop other sources of revenue I promise ... we will abolish the Education Tax.'[68] As a result of this statement, there were party members who felt committed to removing the sales tax and continued to press this point of view for four or five years.

The Planning Committee considered each of the existing sources of provincial revenue. The province had already 'rented' to the federal government its right to impose individual and corporate income taxes and succession duties – a wartime fiscal measure – so that no changes could be made in them. Similarly the province had agreed that for the duration of the war the gasoline tax would not be raised. The sources of increased revenue the Planning Committee agreed upon were liquor revenues (to be raised by $1 million), resource royalties, and the provincial property tax (unusual at the provincial level). The latter, although many people in Saskatchewan opposed it, 'should not be abolished, but should be used for equalization and social services at the local level.'[69]

The committee considered, as well, new fields of taxation, including a tax on property for education and a tax on 'interest payments on Saskatchewan debt' (although members doubted the constitutional validity of this measure). It rejected suggestions for a 'flat rate social security tax,' which had already been described by the 1943 provincial convention as 'a poll tax and as such [it] largely means a redistribution of the income of the needy among themselves.'[70] To the committee's proposals, the party added suggestions advanced by other committees, including pressuring the federal government for increased aid for social services and education, anticipated higher revenues from natural resources, and anticipated revenues from public enterprises.

Two other methods of financing the *Program* were canvassed. One was to 'save money by the elimination of graft and inefficiency in the public service,'[71] a standard opposition proposal but one which held some promise in a province with a reputation for patronage in government operations.[72] The Planning Committee put no dollar amount on these economies: indeed, one member ruefully opined that there wouldn't be a saving anyway; it would simply be spent on welfare measures. The other method advanced was to refund the provincial debt at a lower rate of interest. This proposal was aimed at both bondholders and the federal government, to which the province was heavily indebted. While some committee members felt nothing would be saved, since the federal government would simply withhold an equivalent amount from its subsidies to the province, the committee finally agreed that 'the CCF Government would approach the bondholders and the Federal Government in an endeavour to get the public debt refunded ...'[73] In the end, the *Program* contained much blunter language, almost a belligerent promise to refund the debt, which was to harass the provincial treasurer in years to come.

The Program's Consideration of the Machinery of Government

Quite remarkably, the Planning Committee also approved plans for changes to the machinery of government and, less surprisingly, proposed reforms that would affect the public service. The committee proposed a new Department of Social Welfare, a move that had been advocated earlier by the provincial convention.[74] Along with the Provincial Council and the annual convention, the committee had also considered plans to include responsibility for industrial development in the mandate of the Department of Natural Resources, and to establish a Department of Co-operation and a Department of Labour.

The CCF also proposed the establishment of some kind of central planning machinery, presumably attached directly to the cabinet office and reporting to the premier. This proposal was a direct reflection of CCF economic theory. The Regina Manifesto had asserted that 'the first step [in social and economic planning] will be the setting up of a national planning commission,' and the *Program for Saskatchewan* reiterated that 'the CCF stands for the planned development of the economic life of the province ...' In 1936, George Williams had been quite specific about the organization of a central planning agency: it would be an advisory body and would report directly to cabinet.[75] In 1944 the CCF was less explicit, but the machinery constructed to prepare its election platform suggests the approach the leadership had in mind. For the party leaders, the Planning Committee was their 'cabinet,' and the sub-committees responsible for key aspects of government brought their recommendations to this committee for further deliberation and decision. The novel feature in this structure was a proposal for a central advisory body that would assist the cabinet in its responsibility for integrating departmental plans and for evolving an overall plan. But this novelty – as it was judged to be in 1944 – was not inconsistent with the cabinet system.

The party's plans for civil service reform fell well within British parliamentary tradition. And the party's intention to implement certain reforms was articulated years before it won the 1944 election. In 1937 the Provincial Council had pledged that 'when elected to power [the CCF will] remove the civil service from the influence of party patronage,'[76] and in 1939 the provincial convention affirmed this pledge.[77] Douglas himself said in a radio broadcast:

The time is long overdue for taking Saskatchewan's civil service out of politics. We believe that it is possible to hire men who are efficient and honest ... without recourse to patronage ... In the ten years I have been in public life in Saskatchewan, I have never had any supporter or friend approach me for a political job in the event of the CCF being elected – and I wouldn't advise anyone to start now.[78]

Nor was the party to engage in any patronage in government purchasing or other contracts: Douglas promised a 'Purchasing Board' which would award contracts entirely on the basis of price and quality.[79] Meanwhile the CCF newspaper quoted a CCF member of the Legislative Assembly as having said: 'None of us who are members of the Legislature looks forward to obtaining power in order to be a dispenser of patronage. The members of the CCF Party must recognize this, and refrain from asking for special favours. The CCF is a good party. We *must* not spoil it.'[80]

While the party and its leaders were prepared to take the civil service out of politics, they nevertheless expected their top civil servants to be loyal to the new government's programs. Douglas clearly reflected the party's views when he argued:

> It is most necessary for any government that those in charge of various departments and boards shall be competent and capable of absorbing new ideas and new techniques. No matter how good legislation is, if those in charge of administering it are unsympathetic to it or incapable of a new approach, then little good will come of it. The CCF will not demand that the men in key positions of the Government service shall be CCF, but it will demand that they be persons with some training and knowledge of the branch which they are managing.[81]

This statement embodies the two convictions about the top public service that recurred in party thinking: first that the senior public servants must not be out of sympathy with the programs they were administering;[82] and second, that there existed in the public service senior people who were not equipped for the jobs they were doing. One of the committees, for example, said of the department it was studying: '... a CCF Government will have to clear the deadwood out of [the department] and re-staff it with trained [professional] personnel who are in sympathy with the ... objectives outlined ...'[83]

The rest of the civil servants would be subject to civil service commission rules, and would be encouraged to form a union for the purpose of protecting these and other rights. In a radio broadcast, Douglas proposed a 'government employees' union with power to negotiate rates of pay, hours of work, and working conditions.'[84] Moreover, he and most of his colleagues endorsed the view held by many national CCF leaders that civil servants should enjoy complete political freedom.[85] This was a radical position in the 1940s and remained so in other parts of Canada for many years.

In sum, then, the CCF held a range of views on the public service that were, on the one hand, quite conventional and, on the other, quite radical innovations. Removing the civil service from politics was entirely within British and Canadian traditions, and giving cabinet the power to appoint top civil servants was in line with Canadian tradition. But giving civil servants complete political freedom and the right to unionize were positions well in advance of their time.

This statement of the CCF *Program* has been elaborated in some detail. Its importance lies in the comprehensiveness and interconnectedness of the program itself, as well as in the clarity of the vision and the strength of the party and in the government's resolve to implement its proposals. It will become clear as the story of the CCF government unfolds that the essence of this vision prevailed in most respects for nearly twenty years. While some aspects, notably the positions on social ownership, obviously changed with experience and economic growth and with growing development and availability of alternative policies, the whole was a remarkably consistent guide for the new government to enact.

3

The First Months of the CCF Government: Innovation and Ferment

Election day 1944 started a new phase in the life of the Saskatchewan CCF when ten years of planning and organizing came to fruition with a decisive electoral victory. The CCF had won forty-seven of the fifty-two seats in the Legislative Assembly, leaving the Liberals with only five. Only eight of the CCF MLAs had served in the legislature before. Fewer than half of them were known as active party leaders, and many were strangers to one another.

The next phase was to be a period of frenetic activity, as newly elected Premier Douglas formed a cabinet and with his colleagues began to exercise the responsibilities of governing. It was a period of intense innovation as the newly appointed ministers took charge of their portfolios and began to translate their *Program for Saskatchewan* into legislation and tangible programs. During its first eighteen months in office, the CCF government was preoccupied with the formulation and the creation of public policy. In the process, the ministers and the cabinet as a whole were finding their way to governing in practice.

The Challenges the Government Confronted in Policy-Making

The challenges and obstacles they confronted are difficult to imagine from the perspective of fifty years later. Recall, as earlier chapters have indicated, that the whole role of the state was changing – had to change – as the Depression and the war drew to an end. And the Saskatchewan CCF government was leading the way, provincially and, indirectly, nationally, as the first government to meet the challenge. With no model of policy development to guide the cabinet as it proceeded, the new government would have to develop its own model.

Secondly, the sheer magnitude of this task in a single small province was daunting. While the cabinet as a whole would be obliged to give shape and meaning to the new role of the state, in Saskatchewan, it could not straight off develop as a collectivity the constituent policies and programs for the new state. These would have to be developed by individual ministers. The scope and scale of the CCF *Program* made that inevitable.

A third challenge was how to go about the development of policies that would at one and the same time realize the ideals and the ideology of the CCF, and be both practical and implementable. How *does* one proceed in conceiving or imagining the kinds of policies that would be consistent with and advance the party's ideals? And how *does* one go about devising and designing programs – choosing the policy instruments – that would realize the policies? Having done that, how does one decide which programs will be financed in the next budget, and which will be deferred or implemented over time?

The ministers in the new government did have a start in their policy and program development, of course, by reason of the extensive policy planning that had gone into the formulation of the CCF platform. This was useful – indeed an integral part of starting to govern – even though the planning had proceeded in a political as opposed to a governmental context. So long as the policies or the programs in the platform were clear expressions of the CCF's beliefs and were internally sound and consistent, then the newly minted ministers would be working within an accepted framework. And this was largely the case in most of the major 'patterns' of policy development that emerged in the new government.

Where, however, the policies of the national CCF and those of the Saskatchewan *Program* were unclear, or ambiguous, or subject to different interpretations by different ministers, then the minister responsible, working without an accepted framework, would be prone to improvisation and 'ad hocery,' and to undertaking experiments that were not central to the government's goals. This was clearly the case with the CCF government's early policies and actions in respect of social ownership and its role in industrial and natural resources development.

This being so, or seemingly so, a discussion of the patterns of policy development is called for, and in particular a separate examination of the government's position on social ownership.

Establishing a Cabinet and Starting to Govern

Against this backdrop of the challenges confronting the new government, the premier selected his cabinet and they began to govern. The process by which premiers-designate select their cabinets, or whom they consult, has long been one of the undisclosed features of cabinet government. But the Saskatchewan CCF, rejecting tradition, had coined a clear party policy that a CCF premier was to consult the party's Legislative Advisory Committee with respect to the establishment of the cabinet. Douglas is known to have followed this procedure. The CCF MLAs met early in July following the election and selected their representatives to the Advisory Committee, and then Douglas met with the committee. However, it is further said that Douglas had pretty well made up his mind before he met the committee, for the meeting lasted less than an hour.

Nonetheless, Douglas did in fact consult others, notably Clarence Fines, who was president of the party and had been one of the prime movers in getting Douglas to take on the post of provincial leader. He consulted, too, with J.H. Brockelbank, who was the party's vice-president and former leader of the opposition, and with other members of the Provincial Executive of the CCF. A great deal of unsolicited advice flowed to Douglas as well, from constituency executives, CCF members, boards of trade, and trade unions: all pressing the case for a specific MLA.[1] Douglas sought and received advice on the portfolios he should establish too. Among others, he apparently consulted his trusted first appointee – economic advisor, Tommy McLeod – for McLeod wrote a long memorandum on June 28 outlining his suggestions. The premier determined upon fifteen portfolios, of which twelve already existed: Treasury, Attorney General, Health, Education, Provincial Secretary, Municipal Affairs, Agriculture, Natural Resources and Industrial Development, Telephones and Telegraphs, Highways and Transportation, Public Works, and Reconstruction and Rehabilitation. The new portfolios, created in November 1944, were Co-operation and Co-operative Development, and Labour; while Social Welfare was added to the Provincial Secretary.[2]

On July 10, Premier Douglas and his cabinet were sworn in. The new ministers were Clarence M. Fines, Treasurer; J.W. Corman, Attorney General; G. Williams, Agriculture; J.H. Brockelbank, Municipal Affairs; O.W. Valleau, Provincial Secretary (to which was added Social Welfare); Joe L. Phelps, Natural Resources; J.T. Douglas, Highways and Transportation; Woodrow S. Lloyd, Education; J.H. Sturdy, Reconstruction (later renamed Rehabilitation and Reconstruction); L.F. McIntosh, Public Works (later switched to Co-operatives); and C.C. Williams, Telephones (to which was added Labour), and of course Tommy Douglas himself as minister of health. Their average age was forty-six.[3]

A good many of these were familiar names, having held senior positions in the party and other public positions. Clarence Fines, a school principal, as we know, had become known as the key figure behind the scenes in the formation first of the ILP in Saskatchewan, and then of the CCF. He was to become, in the months that followed, Douglas's behind-the-scenes 'chief executive officer' and the government's spokesman for the program and policy mix combined in the annual budget. Woodrow Lloyd, the youngest minister at age thirty, had been president of the Saskatchewan Teachers Federation. He was to become the philosopher of the cabinet, whose principled yet practical approach was to be felt in all the key government decisions. J.H. (Brock) Brockelbank was a farmer and had been the leader of the opposition during the absence of George Williams abroad. He was to become the rock-solid pragmatist – and capital *P* politician – in the cabinet.

Joe Phelps was a farmer and had been active in the party's policy committees. He was to become, from its beginning, the wild card in the cabinet, fanatically loyal to the CCF platform and ideology, as he saw them. Jack Corman was not as well known in CCF circles, but he had a fine reputation as a solicitor and as mayor of Moose Jaw. He was, from the beginning, the wise – if not always assiduous – pragmatist, whose humour was as important to cabinet deliberations as was his wisdom.

Other ministers had strong local support and became familiar in and through their portfolios. But their presence was less notable on the provincial stage, and their influence in cabinet was not seen to be as substantial as that of the others. J.T. Douglas, like Brockelbank and Phelps, was a farmer and had been provincial organizer for the CCF and a member of the Provincial Council. He, again like Brockelbank, was known for his party work and his organizing abilities, as well as for the responsibilities he would assume as minister of highways. Oak Valleau, also a farmer, had been active in party planning committees and stood out in the war years as a pacifist. He became an able and dedicated minister of social welfare (and, like Phelps, he lost his seat in 1948). Lauchlan McIntosh was a prominent employee of the Saskatchewan Wheat Pool, who, after a brief stint in Public Works, became the first minister of co-operation and co-operative development. Jack Sturdy was another school principal, and, while not at the time a truly prominent CCF leader, his abilities had commended him to the premier and to the voters in Saskatchewan's second city, Saskatoon. Finally, Charlie Williams was a railway telegraph operator, but he was most noted – both when he was the mayor of Regina and when he was a minister – for his ability to run up huge electoral margins.[4]

This, then, is the cabinet Tommy Douglas chose, and which was duly endorsed by the party's Legislative Advisory Committee. The next step, again normally one of the undisclosed features of cabinet government, was the process by which the premier and ministers who had formed the new cabinet came to function as a coherent unit. In this case, as in so many others, the cabinet included a number of strong leaders. But the new premier occupied a strong position by reason of his person as well as his office. The power of a premier's office, or its potential, is well known. And the qualities of the man, Douglas – his intelligence, wit, sensitiveness, warmth, insight, eloquence – are equally well known, and well described in the literature about his time.

The important question, however, is the manner in which Douglas exercised the powers of his office: what was the essence of the man and what moved him? My sense of him – formed from the time I first met him in the late 1930s as an annual guest preacher in my father's church, through my sixteen years as an official in his government – was that the essence of Douglas lay in his idealism and in his capacity to inspire others with his sense of mission. 'Mankind has always been led by those who have dreamed dreams and seen visions,' said Douglas, and his dream, his goal, centred upon the right of the individual to dignity and to self-assurance, and on the realization of the brotherhood of man.[5] This was the value system that conditioned the way he looked upon and treated both individuals and social groups – with respect and trust, and with the optimism as to their response that is so much a part of idealism.

In government, and in the public service generally, these qualities – idealism, optimism, and trust – became the hallmarks of the motivation of ministers and public servants alike. Ministers shared these motivations, along with common political goals; public servants were animated by the same motivation, along with their dedication to the human cause embodied in whatever program they were engaged in. No other artificial or contrived motivations were needed – be they performance bonuses or the potential results of external evaluations of the effectiveness of their programs. A sense of mission, and a personal devotion to the public service, were enough to achieve good management in a merit-driven public service.

There is often, however, another side to the qualities of idealism, optimism, and trust, namely innocence. This quality, sometimes combined with deftness, was to be seen in Douglas's aversion to the harsh words of admonishment when they were called for, and even greater reluctance to remove or replace those unfortunates who were miscast. These unpleasant tasks he left to others – being sure they understood their roles.

In the public arena, too, Douglas believed the best of everyone – even those who differed with him. Give them the facts, give them the rationale for change, give them the human goal, and ultimately they will come around, at least to see your point of view. And thus agreement might be reached. Or at least a consensus could be achieved between the two sides – in the public interest. This belief in the goodness of human nature is important to an understanding of the new premier.

Having said all of this, it must also be affirmed that Douglas was a strong-willed man – some would say a stubborn Scot. The truly unusual quality of Douglas's leadership was his reliance on idealism and trust – not power or authority (or rarely so) – to achieve the humanitarian goals that were his life.

As for the other ministers, many among them were strong personalities too, and some had a longer history of leadership in the Saskatchewan CCF than did Douglas himself. But over time two bonds helped to bind the cabinet into a tightly knit group: the philosophy and platform of the CCF, and Douglas's unusual leadership qualities.[6] In the seventeen years of the Douglas government, it was impossible for even the closest confidants of cabinet ministers to get any admission of personal differences between ministers. People differed on policy, yes, sometimes vigorously. But they never attributed the differences to personal as opposed to policy motivations. Douglas ran the cabinet in a very democratic fashion; indeed, one or two of his more impatient colleagues felt that he was too democratic. Others, in the earlier years at least, were sometimes unable to recall that the whole cabinet had even taken a particular decision. But their loyalty to Douglas and to one another was extremely strong, and neither policy differences nor earlier party differences divided them.

A unified cabinet was vitally necessary during the first years of the CCF government. The ministers had set out to do an enormous job, and they encountered all of the difficulties inherent in it. They also confronted a special and particularly trying task, namely the necessity of modifying their theories when these theories were found, after some testing, not to be sound. While the ministers undoubtedly shared the same basic philosophy, they embraced socialist theory in varying degrees. Each of them, therefore, was inclined to interpret somewhat differently the results of the testing of theory in the crucible of practice. This meant they really had two jobs: implementing the programs that derived from the CCF platform and ideology, and modifying both the programs and the ideology if and when these seemed to be impractical.

The government approached its tasks with generally the same policy posture as that of the party when it was formulating the CCF *Program*. The first speech from the throne presented four main objectives: to guarantee 'at least a minimum degree of economic security' for both rural and urban workers; to provide greater social security for 'those, who, through no fault of their own, find it impossible to earn a satisfactory living'; to introduce legislation that would 'recognize the increasing importance of social enterprise in the life of the community'; and to create a 'governmental organization sufficient in scope to meet the needs of the post-war society.'[7] The government recognized the magnitude of its task but never doubted that it would succeed:

> We know that a cooperative commonwealth cannot be established at one jump. We know that it means moving forward step by step along many roads simultaneously – health, education, social services, development of cooperatives, and the establishment of socially-owned industries. These are the roads along which we propose to advance just as quickly as we feel that you will go with us ... We must go carefully but not slowly; we must go forward cautiously but resolutely ... I cannot promise you that we will never make mistakes, but I can promise you that we will never betray you ...[8]

Setting the Stage for Change

First, the party enjoyed a triumphant CCF provincial convention in mid-July. Then the government set about preparing for the first session of the legislature, which had been called for October 1944. During its first five hundred days in office, the CCF introduced the bulk of the new legislation and initiated the great bulk of its new policies and programs for the first term. During this eighteen-month period, the legislature passed 196 Acts. The government established four new departments and agencies and eleven government corporations. More than half a dozen royal commissions and special committees produced their reports.

Total government expenditures rose by over 20 per cent in the first term of office, and the emphasis within these expenditures changed as well. For example, the portion of the budget spent on health and welfare rose from 23 per cent to just over 30 per cent, and natural resources development from 5 to over 7 per cent. The proportion devoted to other expenditures rose marginally: for example, those on education, and on transportation and communication. There were reductions in provincial debt charges, and miscellaneous expenditures declined from 9 to 1 per cent of the budget. In all four years, the budgets were balanced. Investment in the capital plant, through loans to the public enterprises, notably the Saskatchewan Power Corporation and Saskatchewan Government Telephones, and in the newly established corporations, rose from $414,000 to $2.6 million.[9] (The financing of the entire CCF government program from 1944 to 1962, and the related developments in federal-provincial fiscal arrangements and in federal program funding, are related in the Annex on this topic.)

The new policies introduced into the legislature and then transformed into programs that were put into place during the first term of office were breathtaking in their range and scope. The 'banner programs,' from today's perspective, included the universal hospital services plan (1947), the equalization and enrichment of education through the reorganization of the school system (the school units of 1945–6), the establishment of a compulsory no fault automobile insurance plan (1946), the passage of advanced trade union legislation (1944), and the introduction of Canada's first Bill of Rights (1947). Others were precursors of the major programs that were introduced in later terms of the CCF government, notably the first steps toward universal public medical care – taking the form in 1945 and 1946 of free health care for pensioners, free hospitalization and psychiatric treatment for the mentally ill, free cancer treatment, and the establishment of the first comprehensive health services region. Then there were other policies of particular application in Saskatchewan: farm security legislation for the farmers, increases in resource royalties, and legislation to empower government to embark upon industrial and resource development enterprises.

All this activity required the articulation of new policies and programs in workable form. The cabinet as a whole groaned with overwork, but the individual ministers unquestionably were initiating this activity themselves. Indeed, they were so intensely involved in their new portfolios, that most of them later found it difficult to recall the rationale for many of the decisions that were made outside their own areas of responsibility. Nearly unanimously they said: 'I was so busy with my own department that I didn't really have time to investigate too closely what my colleagues were doing.' Indeed, some ministers felt that a few of their colleagues were inclined to take too much initiative: that some cabinet decisions were virtually predetermined. Those who were accused of committing their colleagues to a policy before it went to cabinet, however, found the business of getting cabinet approval both time-consuming and sometimes downright irritating.

Given this measure of individual ministerial responsibility – attributable to the inexperience of the government as a collectivity as well as to the lack of a proper 'cabinet office' – it is understandable that ministers would adopt different approaches to policy formulation. Thus, to describe policy development during 1944–5 is to describe the different patterns of policy-making that emerged, in the context of collective decision-making. The story of the first eighteen months of the Douglas government will be told around and within the three major patterns or styles of policy formulation that materialized. The first of these was the development of policy on the basis of *ad hoc* advice to the minister, as he sought and required it – a style exemplified by the minister of natural resources, Joe Phelps. Secondly, there was the development of policy through the advice and assistance of newly appointed officials in newly established agencies – a pattern exemplified by Tommy Douglas in his role as minister of health. The third was the formulation of policy through the advice and assistance of officials in an operating department, directed and led by the minister, as exemplified by Woodrow Lloyd, the minister of education.

The story begins with Joe Phelps, and how he went about the job of forming policy. But even this account must begin with the context of the problems the government as a whole was encountering in crystallizing its views on social ownership and reconciling them with the realities of governance.

The Government's Position on Social Ownership

From the earlier discussions on the background of the CCF and the content of the party's *Program*, it is clear that resources and industrial development were considered to be responsibilities of the state. But it is far from clear how much social ownership the CCF *Program* contemplated: and, indeed, government statements on the subject were equivocal. If the party had been less than precise about the amount of public enterprise involved in a mixed economy of public, co-operative, and private ownership, the government was equally uncertain. The throne speech of 1944 advocated a policy of protecting the public interest, with some 'social investment':

When resources that are rightfully the property of the community are being exploited, then the members of the community must be adequately compensated and protected. When enterprises that should be properly recognized as public utilities are being operated by private interests to the detriment of the general welfare of the people of the Province, then it becomes the duty of the Government to act on behalf of the people to make sure that these enterprises are conducted in such a way as to yield the maximum benefit to the entire community ... Attention is being given to the establishment of social investment on a planned basis.[10]

In contrast with this relatively moderate statement, the new Natural Resources Act, when introduced, empowered the minister to 'do all things he deems necessary to develop the resources of the Province which are the property of the crown,' including purchasing, constructing, and operating buildings, factories, research laboratories, machinery, equipment, or works. These powers suggested a wider social ownership program than did the throne speech, at least to the opposition.[11] One opposition member appealed to the premier 'to state definitely what the CCF Government stood for ... Premier Douglas objected when eastern magazines described his government as non-socialistic and he objected when western newspapers pictured the government as a socialist administration. The people wanted a clean-cut statement of policy.'[12]

Without a doubt, the government, like the party, was experiencing difficulty in articulating its position on social ownership. Some policy statements suggested that the government proposed a broad spectrum of public enterprises. The throne speech, for example, announced legislation to empower the government to enter the insurance business.[13] And the minister of natural resources was quite forthright about his view of the government's direction. He announced that the government was planning to own and operate a pulp mill.[14] He also said that some of the lumbering and fur trapping agreements would be cancelled when they came due, and consideration would be given in future negotiations to compulsory government marketing of natural products and to public ownership when it was in the public interest.[15] In September 1944, steps were taken to start a fur marketing service. The minister's view was that 'individual enterprise will no doubt continue to play a large part in the development of Saskatchewan's natural resources for some time to come. [But] eventually it is hoped to establish complete social ownership of key industries.' In December 1944 he also reported, to a national CCF conference, that 'several new industries are being considered and definite progress is being made. Some of these are – a woollen mill, a brick yard, a briquetting plant, a shoe factory, a tannery.'[16]

In contrast with these public ownership pronouncements, there were other indications that the government was not committed to any doctrinaire program. There was the throne speech, already cited, and there were specific examples of the rejection of social ownership – including a statement, in December 1944, by the provincial treasurer that the government did not intend to socialize the brewing industry. He pointed out that the province was the exclusive retail distributor of beer, wine, and liquor, and that it could therefore regulate prices and profits. Privately, the premier himself said of more than one industry – for example, oil drilling and coal mining[17] – that the government had no intention of intervening.

The differences within cabinet over private versus public ownership became more evident, particularly with respect to oil. The minister of natural resources made no secret of his belief that government should enjoy a larger return from the province's resources and that this might involve oil exploration by government, and even public ownership of oil refineries. On the other hand, the premier held the view that such ventures were both unnecessary and undesirable. He argued both that oil royalties and land rental regulations could be established to capture a fair share of the resources for the people,[18] and that the province could not afford an extensive exploration program. In the end, the government's decision on the petroleum industry favoured private ownership, as we shall see. The Department of Natural Resources drew up regulations governing private oil drilling and introduced a Mineral Taxation Act, which imposed a 3 per cent per acre tax on the 30 per cent of mineral rights that were privately owned, apparently in order to increase the public return from these resources.[19]

Given these uncertainties in the government's position on public ownership, it is not surprising that the topic occupied a great deal of time in cabinet. One minister recalled having the impression that one-third of the cabinet agenda was devoted to Joe Phelps's items and two-thirds to the rest of the government.[20] No record was made of these cabinet deliberations, but there is a fairly complete report of similar discussions at the CCF conference on provincial policy, held from 29 December 1944 to 1 January 1945.[21] In study papers likely prepared by Clarence Fines and by Joe Phelps, it is evident that the government was trying to define more clearly the fields where social ownership was appropriate. One such paper made a strong case for private ownership of resource industries:

We believe that some serious thought should be given to the possibility of allowing a certain measure of ... privately-owned and operated enterprise to continue operating ... We do not think we ought to socialize just for the sake of socializing ... We may be well advised to leave a substantial percentage of our primary production in private hands, as long as it is properly and efficiently regulated and steps are taken to safeguard the public interest.[22]

Even more bluntly, the case was made that 'the provinces cannot afford to alienate all private interests who will be performing 70 to 80 per cent of the economic tasks.'[23] The ministers went on, at the same conference, to say that the case for public ownership was clearer when it came to public utilities, such as electric power, telephones, transport, and insurance. They also felt that compulsory marketing of natural products through provincially owned marketing boards was appropriate, and Phelps mentioned his plans for timber, fish, and fur marketing boards.

When it came to manufacturing enterprises, the views were more mixed. Phelps made it clear that he favoured social ownership, both for ideological and practical reasons. It was the party's policy, and it seemed to be the only way in which Saskatchewan could get the capital to develop secondary industries.[24] Another reason was that the profits of government enterprises were necessary to finance new social services.[25] But the delegates wondered, and certainly many of the ministers wondered, whether the industries Phelps was proposing were the right enterprises for Saskatchewan, including, as they did, bricks, shoes, and a box factory. Others felt that the rationale for social ownership should be spelled out more clearly, being first for the purpose of developing the provincial economy and only secondly to obtain revenue for social programs. At least one delegate argued that if it was revenue the province was seeking, social ownership was only one way to get it, and perhaps one of the least productive ways at that.

In point of fact, it would have served the ministers well had they persisted at the conference, and after, in their efforts to differentiate between those industries that might reasonably be considered for public ownership and those which would not. For the industries they were discussing did in fact fall into different categories, on economic and public policy grounds. Public utilities, one category, could reasonably be considered for public ownership (the Saskatchewan Government Telephones already existed as an example), as did natural resources marketing boards, another category (e.g., the federal government's Wheat Board after 1943).[26] But the case for manufacturing and processing industries being publicly owned was different. However frustrated Prairie political leaders might be that 'Eastern interests' simply ignored – indeed casually rejected – the notion that secondary industries could be successful in sparsely settled and distant Saskatchewan, it still remained that public ownership would not change the economics of industry location. Moreover, there were other ways, as yet unexplored, of seeking to attract selected private industries to the province.[27]

As for natural resources industries, and in particular the as yet undiscovered petroleum and natural gas resources, the calculation of public ownership was different. Where government owned these resources themselves (the mineral rights), which they did, as we know, to the extent of 70 per cent in 1930,[28] then government simply had to decide whether the exploration for petroleum and natural gas reserves – and, when discovered, their exploitation – should be done by public or private enterprise.

In either case, the government would be extracting revenues from the resources it owned. But under the private enterprise route, government would reap its revenue through royalties (on production) or through the sale of rights, while private enterprise would raise the capital for and assume the risks associated with the finding of oil and natural gas in the first place. Under the public enterprise route, the government would be responsible for both the exploration and exploitation, and would be gambling that the profits from the latter would exceed the costs and the risks of the former – a rather perilous route, politically, though not seen to be such by the CCF's Planning Committee on Natural Resources and Industrial Development (a committee chaired by Joe Phelps). In January 1944, they had proposed that 'the CCF provincial government plan for the eventual and complete socialization under provincial administration of all natural resources now controlled by the province.'[29]

Policy Formulation through the Provision of *Ad Hoc* Advice to the Minister

This was the ideological milieu within which the minister of natural resources worked, an environment of ferment, change, and uncertainty. Joe Phelps sought advice wherever it was to be found without paying much heed to organizing his advisors, assessing their experience or their competence, or ordering the advice they gave. For him, the direction was clear: the province desperately needed economic development; the party had charted a course that involved social ownership; and his responsibility was to 'get things done.'[30] Certainly the results were dramatic.

Shortly after the government took office, the deputy minister of natural resources and four branch heads (today called assistant deputy ministers)[31] resigned or otherwise parted company with the new government. People who already worked in the department replaced them, although sometimes not for many months. The new deputy minister was not appointed until April 1945. That did not faze the minister, however. He admired innovators and felt that the civil service did not contain enough of the dynamism that is an essential attribute of innovation. So he personally would search out people with ideas, people with a taste for change, and people with the energy to bring change about. That did not mean that the advisors he chose were really innovators either – that they possessed the other attributes of innovation, other than energy and self-confidence. Indeed, Joe Phelps chose his advisors on an *ad hoc*, almost random basis: some were personal friends; some were new acquaintances since he had assumed office; some were federal civil servants; some were private consultants; and many were his own employees at various levels in the department. All of this was consistent with, or a reflection of, his impetuous personality.

The minister's major preoccupation was with resource development, and here he introduced radical changes. He quickly organized a northern administration district to oversee the affairs of Saskatchewan's vast and rich northland, and he sought advice on more effective and more scientific ways to develop the resources: timber, fish, fur, and minerals. He concentrated on the first three of these, not because they were the most important resource industries in Saskatchewan – altogether they accounted for some 1½ per cent of the province's commodity output – but because he believed them to be promising resources and the economic base for a large part of Saskatchewan's very poor minority people, the Aboriginals.[32]

He also announced changes in the forestry program, reducing the diameter of timber that could be cut, expanding the fire-guarding and fire protection programs, and raising royalties.[33] The minister wrote to sawmill operators outlining a plan for a lumber marketing service and asking whether they would favour a marketing board.[34] This initiative was postponed at the request of the Dominion timber controller, a federal government official involved in wartime economic planning. But the minister continued to consult his friends in the industry and to prepare to inaugurate the plan. The Saskatchewan Timber Board was established on 21 September 1945 and was empowered to buy, process, and sell timber and timber products.[35] It was also mandated to cut and log, but this was to be done by contract with private operators.

In a similar fashion, a fur-marketing agency was established. Minister Phelps had observed that a great deal of 'bootlegging' of furs occurred in the North, and that the fur buyers were in many cases exploiting the trappers. He gathered this evidence himself, through his flying around as a constant traveller in the North and through his rapidly multiplying contacts – both departmental staff and people he met on his travels.[36] The minister decided to circulate a questionnaire to trappers, dealers, and fur ranchers, and from the response he discovered that the majority did favour a government fur-marketing agency.[37] He then called a conference of fur dealers and other interested parties, and advised them of the government's intention to proceed. The dealers, of course, opposed this development, but an advisor to the minister 'sounded out' New York buyers to determine whether they would be prepared to come to fur auctions west of Winnipeg. When the answer was favourable, Phelps sought and obtained cabinet approval to set up a fur-marketing service. It was formally established in October 1945, as a Crown corporation (the form social ownership took, in practice).[38]

The minister also moved rapidly to establish fish-filleting plants in the North. The immediate rationale was to improve the quality of Saskatchewan's fish exports by removing sub-standard fish from the market, and thus to maintain access for Saskatchewan products to Eastern Canadian and U.S. markets. In this case, the minister was assisted informally by federal civil servants, and by a fish buyer who also operated filleting plants in the province.[39] Once the filleting plants were established, Phelps turned to marketing the fish. The fishermen were not prepared to assume responsibility for a co-operative marketing agency, but did favour a public marketing agency.[40] On 20 July 1945, Saskatchewan Fish Products was established as a Crown corporation to buy, process, and market fish caught in northern waters.[41]

It was becoming increasingly apparent, even to the ministry, that a more comprehensive examination of policy was necessary. Since neither the Department of Natural Resources nor the various advisors were equipped to undertake such a review, the minister established two royal commissions, one on fisheries (1945) and another on forestry (1947). Although it took some time for these commissions to prepare their formal reports, it was possible – if rather unconventional – for the minister to consult the commissioners informally during the course of their work.[42]

Much the same pattern is evident in the minister's efforts to establish secondary manufacturing industries. As noted earlier, he had already announced an interest in establishing a shoe factory, a tannery, a brick and clay plant, and a woollen mill. The first step was to establish, in September 1944, an Industrial Development Division in the Department of Natural Resources and Industrial Development. Its officials set out to examine industrial possibilities for the province, particularly those that had already been referred to in a report by the Reconstruction Council.[43] Established under the former Liberal government, the Reconstruction Council had been chaired by F.C. Cronkite, dean of law at the University of Saskatchewan, and had reported in early August 1944.

The woollen mill was a project promoted by the Saskatchewan woolgrowers.[44] Both the head of Phelps's Industrial Development Division and a consultant engaged from the United States favoured this initiative.[45] Subsequently, questions were raised about the adequacy of their investigations, since the quality of the wool was unsatisfactory, the costs had been underestimated, and the water supply was inadequate. At the time, however, the opportunity appeared to be a good one, and the government having advanced the money, the Saskatchewan Wool Products plant was established in June 1945.[46]

Similarly, the government purchased a previously unsuccessful brick plant in Estevan, Saskatchewan, and established Saskatchewan Clay Products as a Crown corporation.[47] And, one final example, the department studied 'the economics of the boot and shoe industry, and ... approved the establishment of such a plant in the Province.'[48] In this case, the chief advisor to the minister appears to have been a local distributor of leather products,[49] and he also recommended the establishment of a tannery to provide the raw material for the shoe factory. Saskatchewan Leather Products was established on 12 June 1945.[50]

Whether cabinet endorsed these projects enthusiastically or reluctantly was not entirely clear, although it was widely suggested that the cabinet was divided, and that indeed some of the projects were approved largely because of the uncertainty surrounding the proper role of social ownership – and partly because of Joe Phelps' aggressiveness. One story concerns a long cabinet meeting which discussed the proposed purchase of the brick plant. 'The meeting went on and on,' Douglas recounted to me some years later, 'and my colleagues were deeply divided. Finally I did something I didn't believe in doing: I called for a vote. When it became apparent that the weight of opinion was clearly opposed to the purchase, Joe expostulated: "But my gosh fellows. I've already bought it!"'

To understand Phelps' performance as a minister, one must reflect on his personality – what moved him. He was energetic and impetuous, and consequently impatient of any obstacle that impeded his race to achieve his goals. His goals, in turn, were the product of his beliefs, his ideology: he was not given to the rational process, and certainly not to what he would see to be ponderous research. He was, indeed, single-minded: not sensitive to nuances. It must be said that at least some of these qualities, or shades of them, would be required by anyone who sought to change the role of the state. But the ultimate paradox for Joe Phelps was that he was a supreme individualist bound by a collectivist ideology, and bound under parliamentary government to act as one of a collective.

Other Public Enterprises

The impression should not be left, however, that Phelps was the sole architect of the social ownership policies. Government had endorsed the principle of government marketing agencies and assumed that at least some industrial development would be achieved under government sponsorship or auspices. Indeed, other Crown corporations had also been developed.

One of these was an insurance company, sponsored by Ministers Fines and Valleau, whose objectives were to secure new revenues for the province's expanded health and welfare programs, to keep Saskatchewan savings in the province, and to force down the general level of insurance rates.[51] The company's mandate would be to write general insurance policies (other than life insurance), and later to operate a compulsory automobile insurance plan. The case for a general insurance company seemed very clear: 90 per cent of insurance in the province was being written in Eastern Canada, 'so [the] profits all went back East.'[52] A Saskatchewan Government Insurance Office (SGIO) would provide Saskatchewanians with low cost insurance. So early in 1945, with the arrival in Saskatchewan of newly appointed manager Michael Allore – an 'import' – the company went into business, writing thirteen classes of insurance, ranging from fire and accident, to machinery and harvest. From the beginning, it was a thriving enterprise, if not huge in size, catering both to the public generally and to public agencies that either did business with the SGIO voluntarily or were called on to do so by legislation.

In 1946 the government introduced a compulsory, no fault automobile insurance plan, the earliest of the Saskatchewan CCF's 'firsts' in Canada. The insurance was purchased automatically when motorists licensed their vehicles, and the plan was operated by the SGIO quite separately from its commercial insurance business. The introduction of this plan was far less controversial than might have been expected, and it quickly became a popular and a deliberately non-profit enterprise. The greatest appeal to the public, it seemed, was its equity: no longer were citizens penalized because of their inability to afford lawsuits or because of an offender's inability to pay. Nonetheless, the opposition derided the plan as 'the greatest hoax ever perpetrated on the people of any province under the guise of insurance.'[53]

An equally successful venture was undertaken in the public utilities field – an area of enterprise in which public ownership was clearly thought to be appropriate. Cabinet took the initial steps toward mandating the Saskatchewan Power Commission (later to become the Saskatchewan Power Corporation) to establish an integrated power system serving the whole province. The first step was to designate a minister responsible for the Commission; this was done in October 1944. The next step was to study markets and future sources of power. The minister of natural resources announced, in December 1944, the appointment of a firm of consultants to bring up to date the proposed hydro project at Fort à la Corne on the Saskatchewan River, and the minister of reconstruction and rehabilitation announced the appointment of a government committee to study the feasibility of rural electrification.[54] In February 1945, new legislation authorized the Power Commission to purchase the capital stock of private power companies. It then acquired the Dominion Electric Company,[55] and later the cabinet authorized Phelps to offer to purchase the Prairie Power Company as well.[56] The introduction in 1945 of legislation authorizing the corporation to distribute natural or manufactured gas was another important step, the wisdom of which was demonstrated through the 1950s.

To return to the 'Phelpsian' approach to administration, it must be acknowledged that while it was unorthodox, it enjoyed the distinction of producing the largest number of changes in public policy in the new government. And these changes occurred despite, or perhaps because of, the ambiguity as to the appropriate role for social ownership in resources and industrial development. Some would say that the minister contributed to that ambiguity. But out of this welter of activity, and out of the policy discussions it generated, a clearer policy began to take shape. Social ownership was appropriate for public utilities and natural products marketing, and private ownership was accepted for the exploitation of natural resources, subject to adequate government regulation.

The one very important unresolved area was whether industrial enterprises, in particular manufacturing, should be developed under private or public auspices. This question was not finally settled until the second half of the CCF's first term of office and on into the second term of office (1948–52), following changes in government's capacity for policy analysis and decision-making.

Policy Advice Provided by Experts in Newly Established Agencies

The second pattern of policy advice adopted by the new government is best illustrated by the work the premier initiated within the health portfolio, which he himself managed. If the government's social ownership program was the most spectacular, its policies on health were by far the most far-reaching and certainly the most expensive. The CCF was committed to the idea that a person's self-development and self-expression depended upon a minimum of economic and social security. Possibly the most important aspect of social security was hospital and medical care. If these were freely available to the individual, regardless of ability to pay, not only would people receive the best health care available, they would also be insured against crippling medical and hospital bills. As minister responsible for public health, the premier was able to ensure that the government devoted the effort, and the resources as they became available, to furthering the party's commitment to its social program.

The premier's approach to the work itself also encouraged the expansion of the health program. He preferred to choose the best advisors he could find – he was no victim of parochialism – and to provide them with an institutional framework in which to work. Whereas Phelps had chosen his advisors on an *ad hoc*, almost random basis, among people whose experience was largely limited to Saskatchewan, the premier sought the best advisors he could find from among people with very broad experience. The staff in the Department of Health had not been hired or encouraged to be innovators. The department's organization was characterized by small and specialized units, and the existing deputy minister was required to devote much of his energy to day-to-day administration. In any case, this deputy retired in January 1945, and the premier replaced him only after he had developed a highly effective planning organization outside of the department. The premier's advisors thus carried a double authority, both as international experts and as the incumbents of senior advisory positions.

The story of the first commission to review health services in Saskatchewan – the proposals it quickly produced, and the structured approach to health services reform then adopted – illustrates the more deliberate and organized approach to policy formulation which the premier created. His first step was to establish a special commission to review Saskatchewan's health services and to propose a course of action. On 8 September 1944 the government established the Saskatchewan Health Services Survey Commission[57] and appointed Dr Henry Sigerist the commissioner. He had an outstanding reputation as a professor in medicine at both Johns Hopkins and Cornell Universities.[58] Dr Sigerist set to work immediately and selected five people to work with him: two doctors, a dentist, a nurse, and a specialist in hospital administration. Mindel Sheps, a physician from Winnipeg, was made secretary to the commission. (Later, she became a professor of public health at Harvard University.)

Within a month, in October 1944,[59] the commission made a broad range of proposals, most of which Dr Sigerist felt could be implemented relatively quickly. He suggested, first, that the province should be divided into health districts, later called regions, to serve as the basic administrative units for both preventive and curative health services. Within the preventive services, public health nurses, sanitation officers, and other personnel would work under regional medical officers of health to provide child health clinics, dental clinics, mental health clinics, technical assistance to farms and towns for establishing sewer and water facilities, and other public health services. The regions would also establish a categorized system of medical and hospital services, including rural health centres with eight to ten hospital beds and simple laboratory and other facilities; district hospitals with a wide range of general and specialist medical services, which would be available by air ambulance; and tertiary hospitals (called base hospitals) in Saskatoon and Regina for the more complex and specialized medical services.

This basic structure, proposed the commission, would be the foundation for improved hospital services, including more beds, a number of regional homes for older people, and ultimately a universal, government-operated hospital insurance plan. Dr Sigerist also pressed for the development of free medical services, including treatment in mental hospitals and clinics, cancer treatment, services to pensioners, widows, and orphans, and treatment for venereal diseases. He proposed salaried dentists operating out of schools and travelling dental clinics, who would provide free dental care for children up to age sixteen. In addition, he proposed a new home for developmentally handicapped individuals and extensive improvements in the treatment of the mentally ill, expanded mental hospital facilities, and the establishment of mental health clinics.

The commission recognized that these improvements would require a significant increase in the numbers of health personnel, physicians, dentists, nurses, medical social workers, and others. To train these personnel, it recommended the establishment of a medical school at the University of Saskatchewan, and looked to improvements in the conditions of employment to keep the health professionals in the province. Finally, the commission recognized that its proposals would require extensive planning and, with the strong support of the premier's advisor, T.H. (Tommy) McLeod, recommended the establishment of a Health Services Planning Commission for this purpose.

On receiving this report in October 1944, the government promised that 'the spirit of this report' would be fulfilled as soon as 'the conditions of the wartime emergency become less stringent.'[60] In November, the government established the Health Services Planning Commission and appointed Dr Cecil Sheps as Chair and Dr Mindel Sheps as secretary (a husband and wife team, from Winnipeg), with Tommy McLeod as a member of the commission. All three were strong personalities and capable of exerting significant influence on the premier and the government.[61]

In February the next year, the commission submitted a detailed report on its work to date.[62] It estimated the cost of a complete system of 'socialized health services,' and proposed immediate steps that could be taken without worrying about financial limitations. These included planning the health regions, establishing experimental regions, and strengthening the existing medical services operated by the province and the municipalities. Further, the report addressed the machinery of government required for the gradual expansion of health services. It proposed strengthening the provincial Department of Public Health and assigning to it responsibility for both planning and executing the health program. It also proposed a division of responsibility between the provincial department and the health regions that would achieve a happy balance between 'the desirable principle of local control and autonomy, and the equally desirable principle of central supervision and co-ordination ...'[63]

The government also began to implement some of the specific recommendations of the Sigerist Commission. It extended the newly established cancer program to provide both free hospitalization and treatment for cancer patients. In the speech from the throne and the new legislative program, the government declared hospitalization and treatment for mental illness to be free services, and introduced a Health Services Act to provide a medical care plan for provincial pensioners.[64] The premier had begun to meet with representatives of the medical profession in August 1944,[65] and by the end of the year had negotiated an agreement with them. Thus, effective 1 January 1945, the government established a complete medical and hospital care plan for Saskatchewan's 29,000 pensioners and spouses.[66]

The provincial government also undertook, starting in 1945, some of the construction of new health care facilities. It agreed to provide hospital construction grants to local hospitals and provincial grants to support municipal doctor plans. The budget speech announced a new residence for developmentally handicapped persons[67] and the start of a college of medicine at the University of Saskatchewan. This project had long enjoyed support within university and CCF Party circles, and had come to be a top priority in the government's program.

Here, then, was a set of innovations that had been first proposed by the Sigerist Commission, and then endorsed by the Health Services Planning Commission as appropriate steps toward building the long-term plan it was developing. In this activity, the provincial Department of Public Health was generally seen as the 'administering agency' and the Planning Commission as the 'planning agency,' although the premier was prepared to receive advice from the department as well when it was proffered. Indeed, it is not clear that the premier was overly concerned with the organizational issues raised by establishing a separate planning commission. He wished to establish a formal centre of planning and innovation, and that goal superseded any organizational problems that might ensue. Attention to these issues came later, when he asked the Budget Bureau – a new budgeting and administrative management unit that will be described in the next chapter – to review both the department and the commission with a view to consolidating them.

The support of the party was another important aspect of the rapid development of the health services plan and program. The party's influence was strong and its objectives were unequivocal. Unlike the social ownership policy, there were no doubts or second thoughts in the field of public health. This meant that the job of the experts was clearly to translate party goals into specific policies and to make a plan for the gradual implementation of those policies. The government had acquired expertise, people of considerable distinction who were more than sympathetic to the development of public health care, and they were able to provide advice that was consistent with the goals of both the government and the CCF.

Policy Formulation through Structured Advice – The Case of Labour

The field of labour policy provides a second example of policy formulation directed by people with the same sort of outlook and the same kinds of expertise in their field, as the health reforms illustrated. The minister of labour also relied upon advisors designated by the premier's office, but drew upon people in other agencies in the labour field as well.

For the first session of the legislature, Douglas oversaw the preparation of a Trade Union Act, which was for Canada as revolutionary a piece of legislation as the Wagner Act had been in the United States. Indeed, the CCF consciously sought to follow that precedent. Andrew Brewin, a Toronto labour lawyer, working with the premier's staff, framed the Act. The premier also engaged Ken Bryden of Toronto, first as an advisor on labour matters, and then as deputy minister of labour. Bryden, in turn, consulted the leaders of the labour movement and employers within Saskatchewan, and may well have consulted informally with other labour lawyers outside the province. The *Regina Leader Post* reported these consultations and pointed out that the labour organizations had supported the draft legislation, while the Saskatchewan Employers Association and the Canadian Manufacturers Association (Saskatchewan Branch) opposed it.[68]

The substance of the Trade Union Act was to guarantee employees the right to organize into trade unions of their choice and to bargain collectively. It created the Labour Relations Board and gave it powers to make court orders and prohibit unfair labour practices. The Act empowered employees who wished to form a union to ask the board to conduct a secret ballot among employees to determine whether a union was wanted, and once the board had certified a union, required the employer to bargain collectively with it. The Act prohibited employers from interfering with employees in the formation of a labour organization or from requiring workers to refrain from joining a union as a condition of employment. It prohibited employers from engaging in industrial espionage, from threatening to shut down an operation during the course of a labour dispute, and from declaring a lockout while any matter was before the Labour Relations Board. To protect the individual employee, labour organizations were prohibited from using coercion or intimidation to encourage or discourage membership or activity in a labour organization.

The Act included three other central provisions. They were the 'compulsory check off' (deduction of union dues when requested by a certified union); 'union security' ('all new employees will within thirty days apply for and maintain membership in the union'); and authority for the minister of labour to establish boards of conciliation to investigate and conciliate labour disputes.[69]

The seven-member Labour Relations Board was given the authority to issue orders enforceable as orders of the Court of the King's Bench. In addition, if an employer were 'wilfully' to disobey an order of the board, the lieutenant governor in council could, on the recommendation of the board, appoint a controller and take possession of the business concerned.

Bryden, as deputy, was also responsible for drafting two other key pieces of legislation that affected workers. The Annual Holidays Act made compulsory a minimum two-week vacation, except for farm labourers,[70] and the Hours of Work Act provided for a forty-four-hour workweek. This latter bill was dropped when it encountered strenuous opposition both inside and outside the legislature. In all these innovations, the Department of Labour, as such, seems to have played little part; it was the premier and the special advisors who led and directed the work.

As in the health reforms, then, the labour policy initiatives drew upon formally designated advisors working outside of the operating department. They also drew upon people in other operating agencies for specific innovations. The Minimum Wage Board, for example, whose membership had changed in August 1944, raised the minimum wages from a range of $8–$14 per week to between $16 and $18.50 per week. The Workers' Compensation Board improved benefits and removed a waiting period for qualification. In both these cases, the Employers Association and the Canadian Manufacturers Association urged delay, but cabinet proceeded with policies that were fundamental to the government and to the party's *Program*.[71]

There were, indeed, allegations in Saskatchewan that the government's zeal to adhere to its *Program* caused it to commit its largest 'bumble,' the takeover of the Prince Albert box factory. Other people maintain that the action was necessary to uphold the rule of law. In any case, in June 1945 the employee's union in the Prince Albert box factory brought charges before the Labour Relations Board of unfair labour practices on the part of management. The board found the company guilty and issued the appropriate orders on 13 August 1945. When the company refused to comply with these orders, the union asked the board to appoint a controller to take over the plant. The board recommended this action to cabinet in September; cabinet debated the issue in early October and finally decided to invite representations from the company as to why such action should not be taken. The company appears to have requested some time to prepare its case, and then promptly transferred ownership of the plant to a newly created entity and fired all the employees. Cabinet responded promptly and on 3 November 1945 expropriated the box factory. Interestingly, the expropriation was made under the authority of the Crown Corporations Act, though the order in council also referred to the Trade Union Act.[72] The story illustrates both the difficulties of taking decisions in periods of stress, and the environment in which the new labour legislation was being introduced and implemented.

Policy Formulation through an Operating Department and Led by the Minister

The minister of education's initiatives in his portfolio illustrate the third approach to policy formulation. He relied very much upon the resources of the responsible operating department, strengthening them where necessary to achieve the desired results. Minister Lloyd was an outstanding practitioner of this approach, though in common with nearly all his colleagues he also checked the advice he was receiving with the views of interested groups. In this way, he made significant changes in the structures for delivering education services. While less politically appealing than the reforms going on in health and welfare, these changes were fundamentally important to long-term improvements in the quality of education in the province.

As with the health program, the CCF was determined to make education freely available to all citizens and considered access to good education fundamental to the fulfilment of the principle of individual self-development. In Saskatchewan, the provision of access to education was not just a financial matter, but also a problem of providing equal standards across a sparsely settled province.

The major change initiated in this period was to reorganize the school system by substituting larger administrative units for the very small school districts that had been created early in the province's history. This was a revolution not only in school administration, but also in local government. But the new organization was essential to the equalization of standards of education between rural and urban areas. The minister instituted other changes as well, increasing school grants with an 'equalization' factor built in, improving teacher training methods, creating a technical education division and a new adult education division in the department, and changing the governing bodies of the provincial university.

The minister played a leading role in making these changes – not surprisingly, given his already established reputation as an educational leader and his dedication to the associated causes of social democracy and educational reform. He was, like Douglas, an indefatigable idealist and a thorough believer in the inherent equality of human beings. But Lloyd was more of a philosopher by inclination, and more serious minded in his personality. His perseverance and his steadfast resolve in the pursuit of 'social goodness,' as he saw it, gave him the fortitude to pursue policies that represented fundamental change, in the face of concerted opposition. As Allan Blakeney, the third CCF premier of Saskatchewan, put it: 'He [exemplified] what ... one man with a great spirit and a warm heart can do to make the world a better place.'[73] These qualities were demonstrated in the course of education reforms in the early years of the government, and much later in the introduction of medicare.

Lloyd's leadership qualities enabled him to use his officials as advisors and critics, and to strengthen the parts of the department that were underdeveloped. Fortuitously, several positions fell vacant shortly after the election, and he was able to choose a number of key new officials to serve him, including a new deputy minister, Allan McCallum, selected from within the department, and other officials selected from among the teaching profession and school superintendents, several from the neighbouring provinces.

Immediately upon taking on the position, the minister established a special team to develop the reformed school units system that the CCF had promised. By early October 1944, he reported to the CCF Provincial Council with an outline of the changes proposed, and he consulted with the Saskatchewan Teachers Federation and the School Trustees Association on his proposals. On November 8, he spoke about the proposed statutory changes in the legislature.

The substance of the reform comprised four changes to the statute governing school districts. The minister proposed that it would no longer be necessary to have a petition and plebiscite among ratepayers in each area in order to form a school unit; rather, a vote would be conducted in each district after a five-year trial period of the new system, if such a vote were requested. Secondly, the new school units would include village as well as rural schools. Thirdly, the constituent school districts would be required to pool their assets and liabilities; and finally, provincial equalization grants would help achieve a minimum standard of education across the province. These changes aroused a storm of protest in the legislature.

The outcry against the proposals revealed the strong emotional reaction among people who felt that the 'one room school' was the institutional backbone of rural communities. Moreover, many of the advocates of gradual change as well as the advocates of 'direct democracy' were appalled at the thought of reforming the structure of local government, which was what the changes implied, without a plebiscite. The leader of the opposition described the legislation as the product of 'a typical socialist attitude,' and five members of the CCF caucus argued for the retention of the plebiscite. The School Trustees Association, an association of elected local government officials, supported both larger units and the retention of the plebiscite.

Woodrow Lloyd defended his position vigorously. The old Act, he said, imposed upon government a posture of neutrality where in fact there was 'no question of the government's neutrality in the matter. The Government is definitely in favour of larger units.'[74] He addressed the question of a plebiscite by saying: 'Democracy involves [more] ... than simply receiving petitions. We accept the principle of responsible government and the people of Saskatchewan are crying out for better educational opportunities and for more equitable distribution of the costs of education. Democracy implies equality of opportunity and requires equal [educational] opportunities.'[75] The minister wrote to the premier saying: 'The principle of the local option is one which ... should be used where the issue is ... easily interpreted and the results [are] of a local nature. Such is not the case in the matter of larger units ... Educational progress will not be clear until the whole province is in larger units.'[76]

The debate about the school units revealed a profound difference of opinion regarding the theory and exercise of leadership in a democratic society. Lloyd represented the tradition in which democracy is more nearly 'controlled leadership,' in which the cabinet is expected to lead for four years and then submit to the electorate's judgment. His opponents, of course, except those who simply opposed the larger school units, represented more nearly the Western Canadian notions of direct democracy. Reconciling these two traditions remained a problem throughout the Douglas regime, and such conflicts arose again when the government tried to lead a general municipal reorganization and when it introduced contentious social legislation, notably medical care insurance.

In the case of the school units, the minister and his colleagues decided to make a concession to the strong opposition they had encountered, and amended the Act to require a local vote if 20 per cent of the resident ratepayers were to petition for one within thirty days of the government's announcing its intention to form a school unit.[77] Despite this amendment – which was not acted upon – the school unit question remained, along with the social ownership program, one of the contentious political issues of the day. In retrospect, while only a small minority in Saskatchewan later questioned the enormous strides in education that were achieved as a result of the larger units, CCF MLAs still recalled that 'it was the school units that nearly beat us in the election of 1948.'

While the school unit legislation was the most spectacular change in education, the department formulated other legislation in much the same way.[78] For example, a team including the minister, the deputy minister, and several officials worked on the school grant formulas. These were raised by nearly 20 per cent in the first eighteen months, and, more importantly, the structure of the grant was changed to provide greater equalization in local educational revenues. The grants were also designed to encourage the reconstruction of schools, which was desperately needed after twenty-five years of depression and war and population movements.

The minister relied upon other departmental officials to pursue additional important objectives. One undertook a survey of educational facilities in the North, where the minister was concerned about the lack of opportunities for Aboriginal children. Several officials were charged to develop new standards and requirements for teacher training and certification and a new curriculum. The minister himself participated actively in discussions of these changes with the university and its College of Education. Yet another initiative was a comprehensive review of the high school curriculum, which involved extensive consultations in the province; by September 1946 the first phase of a new curriculum was ready for introduction.

Again demonstrating the style of personal leadership in concert with the public officials, the minister himself prepared legislation to increase teachers' salaries from a minimum of $700 to $1000 a year. He proposed changes to the structure of university governance with the leading figures involved, and took steps both to increase the size of the University of Saskatchewan board of governors and to change the composition of the senate to include representatives of local government and labour on that body. And he initiated the discussions that led to the granting of funds to build a college of medicine at the university and to a longer-term funding and building program for the university.

In the midst of this welter of activity and reform, one other new enterprise competed with the school unit question for publicity. That was the Adult Education Division in the Department of Education, which started innocently enough in October 1944 with the appointment of Watson Thomson, an adult educator from Manitoba, as its director. The new division's objectives were to be 'the activization of people in this Province, by the association of Adult Education with projects such as the local planning of [post-war] reconstruction in their community.' Thomson prepared a memo for the minister, explaining his theory of adult education. It concluded by stating: 'It is no business of adult education to recommend ... political programs or party doctrines. But it is the necessary business of socially intelligent adult education to ... promote full activization of the people, and encourage them to play a creative and responsible part in the affairs of the local and wider community.'[79]

The first ventures of the new division included the development of evening adult classes and community conferences designed to stimulate leadership in study areas such as the rehabilitation of veterans, the development of community centres, and so on. Early in March 1945, however, the premier and Woodrow Lloyd began to hear rumblings of discontent about the approach that Thomson was taking in his community conferences. When a 'Radio College and Living Newspaper Program' was established in the autumn of 1945, the rumblings became explosive. Designed to demonstrate how the news media influenced public opinion through the slanting of news, the program presented a decidedly 'leftish' view through a weekly radio program and newspaper.

As a brief personal note, the new division was also the location of my own first employment as a public servant. Having completed a Master's degree in public administration at the University of Toronto in 1945, I joined the Department of Education's new Adult Education Division, and soon found myself directing the 'Lighted School Program' (evening classes) and later drafting replies to the flood of letters concerning the Radio College and Living Newspaper Program.

But the premier and the minister became increasingly concerned, not just because of the program itself and the criticism it created (it was not planned as a permanent feature of adult education), but more because of the implied issue that it raised. This was the propriety of state-sponsored news programs on radio or in print. Despite a surprising and sustained body of support for the program, both from within and outside the province, the minister and the premier were not prepared to support a program that directly or indirectly raised the spectre of state broadcasting. At the end of the year, Thomson and the government parted company.

What the incident revealed was that in the burgeoning of new programs and policies in 1944 and 1945, there had not been time to develop within the administration adequate controls over the enthusiasms that are natural to new governments. Departmental structures and relationships, the relationships between ministers and civil servants, the integration of policies and programs through budgeting and planning – all these were rudimentary in the extreme. The unhappy experience of the Adult Education Division was merely a manifestation of the relative absence of the devices of cabinet and ministerial control. The problems of the machinery of government were, however, the next to be tackled, during 1946 and 1947.

Policy Formulation in Other Fields

The previous sections have related the three major approaches to policy formulation adopted by different ministers in different fields of endeavour: the development of natural resources and industry; the initiation of a comprehensive program of health reform focused toward a system of socialized health care; the process of new labour legislation; and the structural and program changes in the field of education. Other ministers followed patterns in their work similar to those already described.

For example, the minister of social welfare, Oak Valleau, adopted, an approach similar to his colleague the minister of education. The major difference was that he was put in charge of an entirely new department and therefore was able to appoint all the key officials required. His view seemed to be that the programs for which he was responsible required both sane and sensible administrators, and that a new and enthusiastic government needed the counterpoint of experienced public servants.

As a result, most of the staff for the new Social Welfare Department came from the old Department of Reconstruction, Labour and Public Welfare, and only one was a professional social worker.

However, the minister and his department introduced during the 1944–5 period a program very similar to that proposed by the CCF's *Platform*.[80] They made a number of changes to income support programs: increasing the old age pension by $3 per month; starting to eliminate the system of placing 'caveats' on the property of pensioners; increasing mothers' allowances by $10 a month, and extending them to unmarried, deserted, and divorced women as well as widows. In addition, free medical and hospital care were extended to all welfare beneficiaries under the program initiated by the Department of Public Health.

A new director of child welfare undertook a complete revision of the Child Welfare Act, aimed at vesting wardship of children in the minister, rather than in the voluntary agencies, where standards of performance varied greatly. The department proposed also to employ qualified social workers to supervise Crown wards, and to develop a more adequate adoption program. As well, the nucleus of a new youth corrections program was established when the government transferred the boys reform school from the Department of Public Works to the Department of Social Welfare, and through the new Child Welfare Act provided for immediate hearings for delinquency charges in a children's court.

Much like the minister of social welfare, the minister of co-operation and co-operative development, Lauchlan McIntosh, built a new department.[81] In this case, the deputy minister and key staff came from the co-operatives branch of the Department of Agriculture, and gradually they built an organization capable of serving the burgeoning co-operative and credit union movement in the province. One example of its programs was the provision of financial assistance, along with Manitoba and Alberta, to an inter-provincial farm machinery company. While the department did not run a spectacular program, it did establish the kind of research and inspection services that the co-operative movement was requesting.

In fact, the co-operative development project that generated the most public debate was that initiated by the minister of reconstruction, Jack Sturdy. His approach to policy formulation rather more resembled that of Joe Phelps in natural resources, with the major exception that Sturdy brought his advisors into the department and made them responsible for the new programs. The minister believed that one useful way of assisting in veteran rehabilitation was to provide veterans with land for co-operative farming, and he undertook a sizeable land development program. Some forty veterans became the pioneers in a co-operative farm experiment.[82] Unfortunately, both excessively wet weather and inadequate planning created problems for the new farmers. However, the debate centred, as might be expected, not on the effectiveness of the program, but on the ideological question as to whether this was the first step in the development of 'collective farms.' When the critics alleged that people were trying to introduce the Soviet principle of collectivization, the CCF supporters rejoined that co-operative farms were an answer to the problem of corporate farming and to absentee land ownership. Whatever the merits of the debate, the government did not expand upon this experiment.

These, then, were the major policies and programs that emerged during the 1944–5 period, the ones with the most lasting effect. There were other more controversial developments, such as the Farm Security Act and the seed grain dispute. The Farm Security Act fulfilled the CCF's promise of 'protection from eviction from the home quarter' and 'crop failure protection,' and was promptly challenged in the Supreme Court of Canada by both the federal government and the Dominion Mortgage and Investments Association.[83] The Court's decision essentially was that the province could not cancel interest or principal payments required under mortgage contracts. The seed grain dispute was an intense altercation over several issues, including whether the federal government should share in the cancellation of the debt that farmers had incurred after the 1937 crop failure. Before the dispute was settled, the federal government had emphasized its position by seizing the unconditional grants payable to Saskatchewan under the wartime tax rental agreement.[84] These episodes were of major importance in 1944 and 1945, but add little to an understanding of the processes of policy formulation in those years.

A Government Perspective

It would be misleading to leave the impression at this stage that there did not emerge during the 1944–5 period a 'cabinet view.' What I have written has described both the approaches adopted and the resulting policies and programs that emerged from the activities of individual ministers and of the premier. However, both the throne speech and the budget speech, which have been referred to in illustration of specific policy initiatives, provided very broad statements of policy and of the directions the government as a whole was pursuing.

The throne speech in 1944 set out the government's objectives. It gave first place to economic security for farmers and workers, second to social security, and third to 'the increasing importance of social enterprise in the life of the community.'[85] This third objective embraced the government's economic development policies. The second throne speech in 1945 referred explicitly to the need to diversify the Saskatchewan economy: '... if a repetition of the economic disaster of the 1930's is to be avoided, it will be necessary for this House to lend its untiring efforts to the creation of a more balanced economy.'[86] The emphasis still seemed to be upon government-directed, as opposed to market-directed, economic development.

The provincial treasurer came closest to stating the government's priorities as between social and economic development policies. In the budget speech in 1945, Fines said:

> I see my task, as Provincial Treasurer, to be a two-fold one. It is my duty so to administer the financial affairs of this province as to enable my colleagues and myself to plan a wide expansion in the fields of health, education, pensions and the like. Secondly, it is my task to tap the available investment resources for a planned and full development of old and new industries in this province.[87]

He added a strong note of caution:

> Government revenue, whatever its source, depends directly on the extent of economic activity. If the economy is functioning fully ... then, and only then, will government be able to find the necessary revenue to finance an adequate program of social services. There is no other way. Therefore it is government's direct obligation to ensure that the economy is functioning to its fullest capacity and that economic development proceeds ... in a planned way.[88]

The government's expenditures reflected this emphasis during 1944–5 and 1945–6. Expenditures on transportation and communication, agriculture and resources development, and trade and industrial development were about 20 per cent of the budget, while those for education, welfare, and health came to between 45 and 50 per cent of the budget. In addition, government invested about $5 million, the equivalent of 15 per cent of the province's revenues, in Crown corporations.[89]

In all of this, the government's fiscal policy was prudent, indeed orthodox, from the beginning. The treasurer seemed to set the target of balanced budgets, though he warned that he was not prepared to balance the budgets on the 'poverty or ... [the] misery' of the people.[90] He also discovered very early on that if he were to borrow money in any substantial amount, he would have to rely upon institutional investors. This meant going to the very insurance and mortgage companies that had protested against some of the new government's legislation, and were now challenging the farm security legislation in the Supreme Court of Canada. This was really the least of the problems; Saskatchewan had emerged from the Depression with its credit in a seriously damaged state. In early 1945, Fines warned his party colleagues that 'new money in [large] amounts cannot be raised outside of Saskatchewan, due to the sensitive credit position ...'[91]

Clarence Fines was a successful financial manager from the beginning. The province ended the first fiscal year under his stewardship with a surplus of $8 million, and a surplus of $9 million in the second year. He appreciated the seriousness of the province's credit position and saw no alternative to an orthodox financial course, including the reduction of the province's net debt and restoring its ability to borrow in the capital markets.

These, then, were the foundation-building changes introduced during the first eighteen months of the CCF government and the approaches to policy that the government used. Ministers engaged a plethora of advisors, advisory bodies, and consultants, and established planning groups such as the Health Services Planning Commission, the Library Advisory Council, and various royal commissions. For new ministers, this array of advice and influence was sometimes helpful and sometimes bothersome, sometimes sought and sometimes merely encountered. One pungent observation has been preserved, as one minister wrote of his advisors: 'I have at least twenty people advising me and all telling me our legislation is no good and suggesting something different ... It's a nice position for the advisors who can't be proven wrong and a hell of a one for me.'[92]

Of the approaches to policy development that the ministers adopted, the premier's use of special advisors who were 'institutionalized' in special agencies outside of the operating department was clearly the most successful. Mr Phelps' *ad hoc* approach was equally productive in the pure number of innovations, perhaps even more so, but it was less systematic and many of his programs failed to stand the test of time. The approach followed by the minister of education was nearly as effective as that of the premier, but it required that the minister himself devote nearly all his time to his own department – which a premier clearly could not do. The approach to policy formulation that was least productive of innovations was to rely on existing departmental staff. The Department of Highways, for example, did not begin to develop more scientific methods of road planning, design, and construction until there was an infusion of new energy later in the government's mandate.

What also emerges clearly is that the new government did not feel able consistently to rely upon the existing civil service for policy advice. Partly this was likely the result of mutual suspicion. And in some cases these suspicions were well founded. There were ideas in the CCF program that an experienced person could see were unworkable. And there was a tradition of patronage in the civil service that threw a cloud over the whole public service. Even so, it would have been surprising, indeed, if all senior officials in the province had possessed the skills and capacity to live up to the new ministerial expectations.

Beyond the immediate advisors to ministers, however, were the other important influences on the new government, including the party, the caucus, various interest groups, and both the federal and the local governments. The story of policy formulation must be extended, in the next chapter, to describe these external relationships and their effect on the cabinet as a whole.

4

New Wine in Old Vessels

Beyond the sweeping changes in policy during the first eighteen months of the CCF government, it became evident that important adjustments were called for in other aspects of governance. In particular, the role and the influence of the CCF Party and of its leaders had to be adapted to the new constitutional role of its elected leaders – now ministers in the cabinet and members of the Legislative Assembly. Simply put, the ministers were now responsible to the Legislative Assembly and through it to the public at large, and all of the CCF MLAs were responsible to their respective constituencies: what would or should happen, then, to their former and more formal responsibilities to the CCF Executive and Council and to the general convention, as CCF leaders?

At the same time, a veritable transformation was required in the machinery of government. As Tommy McLeod, then the premier's economic advisor, put it many years later, 'They [the CCF] inherited a governmental machinery almost totally incapable, in terms of its organization and personnel, of meeting demands made inevitable by the kind of governing that matched their philosophy and that they intended to provide ...'[1] The prime adjustment required was the enhancement of the capacity of the cabinet to function effectively in planning and assessing the policies and programs involved in creating the new role of the state, and in setting priorities. Cabinet also needed a budgeting system that would serve to reflect in annual and multi-year budgets the plans and the priorities settled upon. A further major and necessary adjustment was the capacity to develop effective organizational structures for the central agencies that would service the cabinet and an administrative management system designed to build an effective and efficient public service.

Equivalent planning and management capacity was required, too, in operating departments – some of which, along with newly created agencies, were early on playing a significant role in the development of policies and programs. And a key element of good governance in operating departments was the vitally important capacity for delivering new programs effectively.

But virtually none of this machinery of government as we know it today existed in Saskatchewan, or for that matter in any of the other provinces, when the CCF assumed office.[2] This is not surprising since all but one of Saskatchewan's earlier governments had their roots in 'classical liberalism' and its commitment to individualism and a generally limited role for the state.[3] That definition of liberalism was to change, as we know, with the widespread introduction of the welfare state in post-war years. In 1944, however, government in Saskatchewan was still 'minimalist.'

The need for new approaches to governance, it must be noted, had been forecast in the CCF government's first throne speech. Douglas asserted there that the CCF would 'create a government organization sufficient in scope to meet the needs of post-war society.'[4] But that was more easily said than done. In its early days, the new government was too unfamiliar with governance and its requirements – and too preoccupied with policy – to perceive the reforms that were called for. These reforms would be initiated during the second half of the first term of office.

Most of the ministers in Saskatchewan's new government, for example, were not inclined to ponder the relationship between what they were doing in one department and what may have been going on in some other department of government. Nor had many of them given much thought to the restraints that their programs might encounter because of budgetary limitations. They were more concerned with policy and program than with administration and finance, more accustomed to party than to administrative relationships. Moreover, the cabinet as a whole was necessarily engaged in two difficult processes. The first was the development of a sense of collective responsibility, to the legislature and the people, with a consequent adjustment of the relationship with the CCF Party and caucus. The second was the adjustment to new and unfamiliar pressures both from within the civil service and from interest groups outside.

Thus there were changes to be made in relation to elements outside of the government and the party. There were the interest groups that sought to advance their causes through influencing public policy. These had to be recognized and factored into the range of public policy forces confronting government – for experience in leading a new political party had not generally included consultation with a wide range of interest groups. The CCF had concentrated on the farmers' organizations, the co-operatives, and the labour unions. But now the number and range of interest groups was becoming more complex. Ministers could be expected to adjust readily to this aspect of governance, given their views on direct democracy. But changes in relationships were certainly under way.

Other important adjustments concerned Saskatchewan's municipalities and school districts, involved as they were in the delivery of services. Numerous functions of local government, including education, health services, and social assistance ('relief'), were part of the provincial reform program. The issue here was the institutional capacity of small local governments to deliver the level and quality of services called for in the CCF's new programs. True, these services were provided under provincial enabling legislation, and, true, one might consider it normal for the province to propose reorganizations where they were required to increase the level and quality of services. To do this, however, as we have seen in the story of establishing school units, was in fact to take on one or more of the larger and more powerful interest groups in the province: the Saskatchewan Association of Rural Municipalities, the Saskatchewan Urban Municipal Association, or the Saskatchewan School Trustees Association. Provincial-local government relations, in short, tended to go beyond reasoned discussions as to the role and financing of local governments, as creatures of the province, and to take the form of political confrontation. But that was part of the political system and of governance in Saskatchewan from its beginning.

Relations between the federal government and the provinces, in turn, were equally an integral part of governance in Saskatchewan – particularly given the province's status as a poor and not very populous or powerful province. It would be up to Tommy Douglas and his colleagues, once the post-Depression disputes between Ottawa and Saskatchewan had been settled, to develop a position in federal-provincial relations that would achieve essentially two ends: the maximization of the province's fiscal capacity through federal contributions to shared-cost programs and the federal equalization of provincial revenues; and, at the same time, support for a strong national government able and willing to share in the costs of nationwide social programs – equivalent to those to which the CCF was committed in Saskatchewan and nationally.

These were the elements of governance that the new government would have to integrate into its policy and political deliberations. These were the aspects of governance that would require both the forging of new relationships in the political system and the development of new capacities within the government and the public service.

The Government's Relationship with the CCF Party

The first and the most delicate of all these changes in the political system was the redefinition of the role of the party and the relationship between the party and the now-elected CCF leaders in the government and the caucus of CCF MLAs. Three adjustments were required. The first was the recognition by ministers of their role as ministers of the government, now constitutionally responsible to the Legislative Assembly and through it to the electorate at large. The second was the recognition on the part of the party that, while its power over the shaping of policies for the CCF platform had been supreme, the responsibility for policy-making under the CCF government had shifted from the party to the cabinet. The third adjustment was to be made by the CCF MLAs: while their assent to government policies was required to maintain a majority in the legislature, they would not be actively engaged in the policy-making process. This was the responsibility of ministers and their advisors.

Forging these new relationships would not be easy. No fewer than six cabinet ministers were also members of the CCF Provincial Council and its planning committees, and they were accustomed to a direct responsibility to the Provincial Executive and Council. For its part, the council seemed generally to expect that this relationship would continue undisturbed. For example, a motion was presented to council in July 1944, asking that the cabinet make known to council the legislation the government was planning for the fall session. The motion was then withdrawn, following a discussion of the government's responsibilities to the legislature and its members.[5] In August, the Provincial Executive suggested 'regular conferences of the ... Executive and cabinet members.'[6] In a similar vein, in September, the president of the CCF wrote to the premier to tell him that the party's planning committees had been disbanded coincident with the establishment of similar committees within the CCF caucus, and he suggested that these committees should report to the Provincial Council.[7]

For the party, it was obvious that because its elected members were pledged to support the CCF program they were also 'accountable' to the Provincial Council and Executive. Indeed, in 1943, the premier himself had seemed to acknowledge this view. Further, the advocates of 'direct democracy' had strongly influenced the formation of the CCF, and while many of the leaders were conscious that cabinet could not be responsible to the party, there was nonetheless strong pressure to establish some sort of 'accountability.' The president, for example, spoke of the need for some link between 'our Executive body in the legislature, and the Executive body in the movement,'[8] but just what sort of linkage this should be was not clear.

From the cabinet's point of view, the ministers were constitutionally responsible to the Legislative Assembly and through it to the people of the province as a whole. This responsibility was clearly incompatible with any formal responsibility to the CCF Party as such. The ministers were certainly subject to the influence of party views; it would be surprising if they were not. Yet as a government their first thoughts should be for the province, not the party. Responsibility to the legislature implied government consultations with the CCF caucus, rather than with the CCF Provincial Council, and this in turn suggested a change in the patterns of party organization.

The debate that took place within the party manifested itself in several ways. In October 1944, for example, the premier urged the council to keep in perspective the roles of the government, the convention, the council, and the caucus.[9] In turn, the council began to exercise greater caution in the resolutions it directed to the government: one resolution, for example, was reworded to read 'we suggest to the ... government' rather than 'we bring pressure to bear on the ... government.' As the months went on, the essence of the problem became clearer. At the inter-provincial CCF conference in December, there was a perceptive discussion of the whole question. One minister noted that those who were in the government were bound to be under some 'suspicion ... because they see problems that the rank and file cannot,' and suggested that the key problem was whether the movement should 'dominate' the elected members. A member of the Provincial Executive replied by acknowledging that the goal could not be party domination of the government, but rather a matter of offering 'helpful criticisms.' Another party officer argued that 'it simply is not possible for every MLA to report on each and every move to the Council ... [and] on the other hand the rank and file simply cannot be doing their ... full-time jobs and still expect to keep up on everything that is being done ... much less consulted at every step.'[10]

The leaders considered various methods of party-government consultation, including the existing means such as the premier's consultation with the Legislative Advisory Committee and the meetings between ministers and caucus committees. The discussions acknowledged that ministers had not been using the caucus committees as much as they might because of the pressure of work. There were also new possibilities, such as informal consultations between the premier and president, and more formal consultations between the caucus and council. The conclusions were typified in this comment from a party official:

> Some conflict between the Provincial Executive and the Cabinet is unavoidable because cabinet ministers assume new status while that of the Executive tends to recede in relative importance ... The members of a government have to act together as a team ... Confidence in a leader and the leader in his members and all members in one another is fully as important as any other consideration. Hence the leader must have considerable freedom of action ... Where a leader is elected by a majority vote he merits the full confidence of those who elected him.[11]

By mid-1945 a pattern of government-party consultations had begun to emerge which seemed to be satisfactory. It preserved the integrity of the government's constitutional position, but also provided that government seek and receive the views of the party through regular consultations. There would be 'frequent consultations' between the premier and the president of the CCF; the CCF MLAs would be invited to attend meetings of council; and the Legislative Advisory Committee would serve 'as a liaison ... between the Government and the Provincial Council,' and would 'be utilized to a greater extent than in the past.'[12]

As the party's executive bodies, the Provincial Council and Executive continued to maintain a strong interest in the government's performance, but they refrained from attempting to direct the ministers or the MLAs. They made suggestions on policy, on the machinery of government, and on the civil service. They endorsed, and sometimes criticized, government programs. The premier and the ministers explained both the impediments that some government actions confronted and the types of legislation being prepared for the legislature.[13] In 1945 the premier reported for the government on the 'boards and commissions abolished or created; ... economies effected; new services instituted; and changes in the policies of departments.'[14]

The Legislative Advisory Committee became, however, the formal liaison body between the party and the government. The committee consisted of three members of the Provincial Council, two CCF MLAs chosen by caucus, and the provincial leader, Tommy Douglas. There is evidence that the premier informally discussed with this group the government's policy proposals, the composition and size of cabinet, and the grievances that party officials reported.[15] For both the CCF and the government, this was the appropriate body through which to discuss the programs that were emerging from the party's policies.[16]

There was also the question of the role of the party's annual convention. Here, too, a new relationship with the government began to take shape. While the party's influence on the government was largely exercised through the caucus, the Legislative Advisory Committee, and the Provincial Council and Executive, both the government and the caucus looked to the annual convention for an expression of broad party views. The delegates commended or criticized the government for its actions, reminded the cabinet of basic CCF principles, and occasionally had sharp words of advice. Particularly in the first years of the CCF government, the convention made specific policy suggestions, ranging from the advocacy of co-operative farms to the promotion of a provincial art school.

The party established a new procedure for consultation and advice, as well. The cabinet ministers were invited to attend appropriate convention panels that were discussing their field of responsibility, and to listen to the policy debate and offer information and assistance to delegates. As long as the convention's views and the government's views were similar, or as long as any differences were over minor policy or administrative matters, there was no friction between the delegates and the ministers. But when a group of delegates was pressing for a policy with which a minister disagreed, tensions sometimes did develop. For example, during the convention debates of the government's oil policies in the later 1940s and early 1950s, when the government was opposing convention resolutions that advocated public ownership of oil exploration ventures, there were sharper disagreements. But in 1944 and 1945, the government's policies had not begun to stray from the party's approved positions. The convention's support of the government was enthusiastic, and the government accepted the policies it recommended as worthy of serious consideration.

The ability to establish the new relationship between the party and the government also depended upon the premier's skill in avoiding conflict between the various interests. After several years, Douglas described it this way:

In a people's government, the cabinet must work closely with elected members. They must also keep in touch with the Provincial Executive and the Provincial Council. Care must always be taken to see that the elected representatives of the people on the one hand and the CCF organization on the other, work together as a team ... In seeking to build a movement ... which is controlled from the bottom and not from the top, a great deal more care and patience must be exercised than is the case in a political party where decisions are made by a Political Leader and a small inner clique.[17]

The Executive's Relationship with the Caucus

Another important relationship that needed to be established was that between the cabinet and the caucus. Here again there were differences of opinion about the appropriate roles and about 'who governs.' Is it the government that formulates policies and programs or is it the legislature? Some CCF MLAs supported the traditions of 'direct democracy' and did not regard the cabinet as the body 'which controls Parliament and governs the country.' Nor did they feel bound to support all the government's measures, even if they had had an opportunity to criticize them in a meeting of caucus. They were quite aware that the CCF Provincial Council had resolved that 'any [CCF] member of the legislature ... shall be bound to uphold and support the CCF program, but is free to differ with the government on details of policy ... When a CCF member disagrees ... he or she should ... give notice to the caucus of his or her intention to vote against such measure.'[18]

Other CCF members, however, were readily prepared to accept the traditions of cabinet government, as they understood them. It was their responsibility to criticize government policies and to influence them when they felt it to be necessary, within the caucus. But once the government, which is to say the executive, had made up its mind, these members felt bound to support the program, except in the extremes of disagreement.

Aside from these mostly theoretically based differences, the CCF legislative group faced the very practical problems of any majority caucus. There were forty-seven CCF members of the legislature, all of them eager to take an active part in implementing the CCF program. And there were only twelve cabinet posts. It was very difficult for the remaining thirty-five members simply to wait for an opportunity to vote on government measures in the legislature. One member wrote to the premier about his concern over the ministerial-caucus relationships, and the premier responded:

> As you can well imagine, in the first two months of office most of the Ministers have been working long hours and have been mainly concerned with reorganization of their departments, and have had very little time to keep members informed as to what they were doing. I agree with you that it would be well to work out some techniques for an exchange of information.[19]

In fact, the premier had already taken steps to establish a formal relationship between the cabinet and the caucus when, in July 1944, he and his colleagues established eleven caucus committees, one for each department of government.[20] Four or five CCF MLAs were members of each committee, one of them acting as Chair; in no case was a cabinet minister named to the same committee as the portfolio he handled. The theory seemed to be that the minister should consult these committees, and they were to review and criticize ministerial proposals. Ministers were not to act as members of the committees, but to develop measures for cabinet approval and caucus consideration.

These committees, however, were not entirely successful. They seldom met, and when they did most members did not feel competent to engage in policy deliberations. Rather, it was the caucus as a whole that made an impression: it operated as both a sounding board (how will this sound to the 'grass roots') and as a conscience of cabinet (is this consistent with CCF philosophy). The sounding board role was very important. Remember that there were no polls in those years. Members might not feel equipped to criticize or suggest alternatives, but they did feel competent to judge whether a program would meet the needs of their constituents and what the public reaction might be. They were, in fact, better equipped in this regard than were the elected party officers, because the MLAs were certain to move around in their constituencies while party officers were more likely to speak with other party members. In the second role, that of conscience, the caucus served a function similar to that of the party itself; on the whole, though, it tended to be more pragmatic.

So, while there were vigorous debates and sometimes there were 'agreements to disagree' in the House, the caucus seems never to have tried to wrest the initiative from the cabinet. Not only did the cabinet have the advantage of its position as the executive, but its members were also acknowledged leaders in the party, and were becoming increasingly knowledgeable about their portfolios. Even so, after eighteen months, the caucus established a committee to discover 'ways and means for closer collaboration between the Cabinet and the MLA's.'[21]

While the relationship between government and caucus became more settled over time, this does not mean that the CCF MLAs settled for a minor or subservient role. The caucus exercised its influence with as much vigour as the members felt inclined to do. It was privy to virtually all of cabinet's secrets and even reviewed the annual budget without derogating from the authority of cabinet to govern.

The Public Service: At the Centre of Government

The machinery that facilitates cabinet planning, the evaluation of program proposals, the preparation of budgets, and the monitoring of implementation is now well established in Canadian government operations. But in 1944, as we have said, these functions in support of cabinet scarcely existed, and where they did, they were in the early stages of development. Certainly the CCF cabinet in Saskatchewan did not have them. There were no cabinet, as opposed to departmental, advisors; there was no planning or budgeting machinery, and no formal procedures to prepare agendas for cabinet or the minutes of meetings or to follow up the decisions.

From the start, the new premier seemed to sense the need for cabinet advisors. Indeed, his first action was to appoint his university colleague Tommy McLeod as his economic advisor. The two had met in Weyburn in church and political circles, before McLeod went first to study and then later to teach at Brandon College. Their association, maintained intermittently, was renewed immediately after the 1944 election when Douglas told McLeod he wanted him to leave academic life in favour of serving as the premier's advisor.

The importance of this appointment was indeed reflected in the fact that when Douglas asked the clerk of the Executive Council for a list of personnel in the Cabinet Office, the response was 'one,' the clerk himself, plus the occasional use of the assistant clerk of the Legislative Assembly 'when large delegations meet the government and it is deemed advisable to have a shorthand report of the proceedings.'[22] It was time to establish the Economic Advisory Committee that had been promised.[23] In November that year, the premier appointed three professors from the University of Saskatchewan to serve on the committee.

They were Professor George Britnell, head of political economy, F.C. Cronkite, dean of law, and Professor Vernon Fowke, an economist; Tommy McLeod served as the secretary.[24]

However the premier himself may have conceived the Economic Advisory Committee, it did not become an active advisor to cabinet on new policies and programs. In accepting the position of Chair, George Britnell noted his understanding that the committee would only be expected to advise upon matters referred to it by the government, and would not initiate or formulate plans or policy. This implied both that ministerial proposals might or might not be referred to the committee for its opinion, and that the committee would not advise the government on general policy directions or volunteer advice. Dr Britnell emphasized this view in a letter to the cabinet:

> The Economic Advisory Committee is upon no construction an economic planning board ... the initiation and formulation of policy – which is planning – must remain the duty and the function of the responsible Minister of the Crown ... the contribution of the Economic Advisory Committee must come through careful and judicious sifting, weighing and appraisal of the facts upon which policy makers are required to ... plan governmental programs.[25]

While this may have been a legitimate construction of the theory of cabinet government for this kind of body, in practice it left the government without general advisors. The committee limited its work to three main areas: advice on current and potential sources of revenue; the development of Saskatchewan's brief to the federal-provincial conference of 1945; and an examination of the theory of government in business.[26] It also recommended, on the advice of the secretary, Tommy McLeod, the establishment of an economic advisory and planning board.[27]

During 1944 and most of 1945, the premier looked to McLeod as his principal advisor and increasingly to Dr Morris Shumiatcher, whom he appointed in June 1945 as legal advisor to the Cabinet Office, which essentially meant to the premier. Douglas had confidence in both of these advisors, and consulted them on many cabinet matters. But they were more *ad hoc* advisors and confidants than planning officers. While their influence was very substantial, they were not equipped to undertake the evaluation of all the proposals being brought to cabinet, or to examine the whole of government policy.

By June 1945 the premier had decided to strengthen the planning capacity of cabinet. He approached George Cadbury, a British economist prominent in Labour Party circles and at that time a senior British official in Washington, to see if he would come to Saskatchewan. (The story of the recruitment of Cadbury and his influence on the government is described in chapter 5.) The premier spoke of 'planning and development of the economic resources of the Province ... with a view to development of new industries and relating them to the whole of the economic and social problems with which the Government has to deal,' and said Cadbury would be acting in 'an advisory capacity to the Cabinet as a whole.'[28] In August the cabinet discussed the establishment of the new Economic Advisory and Planning Board;[29] it approved the new agency, and Cadbury came to Saskatchewan as its first Chair on 31 December 1945. At that point, the Economic Advisory Committee was abolished and its members made 'fiscal and Constitutional' advisors, instead.[30]

In other circumstances, cabinet might also have been able to rely upon a functioning budgeting system to assist in the vetting and integration of proposals. But in 1944–5 the budget was not used for this purpose. In fact, the processes of budget formulation and control were rudimentary in the extreme. The ministers of each department submitted their budgets, through their deputies, to the deputy provincial treasurer, and through him to the cabinet's committee on budget and finance, called the Treasury Board.[31] The form for these budgets consisted largely of a list of the amounts required for each existing branch or division of the department. The budget analysis was equally rudimentary, consisting of some annual revenue estimates plus some general judgments as to the amounts that would have to be cut if the budget were to be financed and where the cuts could most likely be achieved. The scale of government until 1944 had been so small that it was within the capacity of one or two people, including the deputy treasurer, to keep in their minds what the whole government was doing, and where reductions could be made without seriously impairing the government's program.

The lack of established budget procedures, however, was not the whole problem. The new and inexperienced ministers thought of their budget strictly in financial terms at this point, as a necessary impediment to what they really wanted to do. Some of the ministers were openly hostile to the limits that the budget and budget control procedures imposed upon them. Joe Phelps, for example, insisted upon a single appropriation for 'conservation and development of resources,' without any breakdown of the activities that were involved. As a result, budget control became virtually impossible, as both the opposition and the treasurer pointed out repeatedly, in their own particular forums. More important, the cabinet was prevented from knowing the components of the policies of the Department of Natural Resources, and the premier and the treasurer were prevented from being able to take a broad view of all policies. (And the premier seemed reluctant to force the issue – a reflection of the fact that he was by nature slow to exercise discipline over or otherwise deal harshly with his colleagues.)

To compound these difficulties, cabinet itself was ill equipped for scrutinizing total government policy or for regular, day-to-day decision-making about the many proposals being brought by ministers. There was no cabinet secretary; the clerk of the Executive Council performed more clerical than executive functions. There were no cabinet agendas or minutes or documents. It had not occurred to the previous government, nor did it occur to CCF ministers, that the practices that the British government had developed to make cabinet more effective might be applicable in Saskatchewan. The Saskatchewan government was small and appeared not to need elaborate procedures. Cabinet was also constantly concerned about secrecy, especially in the early days of the CCF government, and this preoccupation seemed to rule out the use of a cabinet secretary.

In one of the first steps to rectify this situation, Douglas asked Woodrow Lloyd, the minister of education, to serve as cabinet secretary. The premier apparently did not want to admit anyone except ministers to the meetings. For some four or five years, Lloyd served in this role. However, his minutes were cryptic,[32] and he was not able, given his heavy ministerial responsibilities, to develop procedures for managing the decision-making. Ministers brought matters before cabinet at the last minute and without documentation. The cabinet minutes, such as they were, were not distributed or circulated to ministers; nor was there a system of follow-up to ensure action had been taken on the decisions.

Given all of these circumstances, cabinet depended almost entirely on the advice that individual ministers brought to the meetings. Occasionally, the premier used cabinet committees as a means for subjecting some of the problems or proposals to more critical scrutiny. There are records, for example, of a cabinet committee on the establishment of the Saskatchewan Government Insurance Office, a committee on the box factory, and one on social aid policies. But, like cabinet as a whole, these operated without staff assistance. As one minister put it, 'We found ourselves pooling our own inexperience.'[33]

Some ministers found this reliance on ministerial responsibility to be an appropriate arrangement. One of them even argued that there was too much of a 'cabinet view' and too little of the 'on the spot (departmental) view.'[34] Other ministers, though, freely acknowledged that they sometimes faced problems that they did not feel equipped to handle. Tommy McLeod later observed: 'Although it could be assumed that the normal restraints of Cabinet discipline and Cabinet solidarity would be adequate safeguards against frivolous exercise of the wide powers by an individual minister, there is evidence that the Government had not yet realized the strains which the rapidly expanding scope of government endeavours might place on the normal functioning of the Cabinet structure.'[35]

Undoubtedly the absence of support to cabinet did affect the adequacy of government planning. At the same time, many ministers were themselves assembling an impressive group of advisors, and most of the ministers were reasonably adept at assimilating new and perhaps more expert points of view. The public service was also small enough that ministers could meet and be influenced by advisors other than their own. The new civil servants who had come to Saskatchewan to help build the 'brave new world,' or as the leader of the opposition called them, the 'carpet baggers,' tended to move together socially and often in company with the ministers. As a result, the cross-fertilization of ideas and arguments and criticisms knew almost no limit. Every social occasion attended by ministers or senior civil servants was seething with shop talk. But this array of expertise and influence could not substitute for more formal and structured support to cabinet.

The Public Service in the Operating Departments

While the lack of adequate machinery in the centre of government was an impediment to the effective functioning of the cabinet as a whole, the capacity in the operating departments exacerbated the difficulties. It soon became evident to the new government that the civil service was not geared to the pace of innovation which the government had initiated or to the requirements for implementing the new programs. The structure of government was also a problem. The inherited structures had not been designed to encourage the evolution of new policies or the evaluation of old ones. Nor did they lend themselves to effective coordination between departments. There was no discernible pattern of decentralization of functions to regional units, or any general approach to establishing districts when regionalization had taken place.

The existing pattern was of departments with small branches administering a narrow range of programs; very few senior officials carried responsibility for whole 'functions' such as social aid and public assistance. The deputy ministers were not equipped with staff to help in program development or evaluation (there were no planning branches or budget officers), and they could not turn to their departmental branches for such expertise for it was not there. Departments were often characterized by fragmentation and semi-autonomous organizations in the same functions of government. Branches reporting to two different ministers, for example, were responsible for safety inspection.[36] Welfare functions had only recently been brought under the jurisdiction of a single minister.[37] The Treasury's functions were split among the department, a commission, and a board. The minister of public works was responsible for mental hospitals and jails.

Cabinet was similarly unable to find a clear pattern with respect to government corporations. Of the two existing Crown enterprises, the telephone system was organized as a department of government and the Saskatchewan Power Commission existed as an independent commission with some of the attributes of a Crown corporation. No statute existed to serve as a guide for future corporations, nor were there any systems to use in controlling public enterprises.

The patterns of government organization had determined, in a sense, the character of the public service. Senior officials had previously been recruited to fill narrowly defined roles, and their abilities had been judged in relation to the size of their jobs. Many officials, indeed, had been selected for reasons other than ability, and this knowledge tended to undermine the morale of the whole service. The Public Service Commission was not an active agency; it did not function, for example, in terms of recruitment or classification of personnel. Rather, the operating departments determined their own selection and payment criteria. This was the administrative machinery with which the government had to work.

The party had already expressed dissatisfaction with government organization and the quality of the public service, and the new cabinet rapidly made a number of changes. It created three new departments, for Social Welfare, Co-operation, and Labour, and substantially changed the Natural Resources and Development and the Reconstruction and

Rehabilitation Departments. It began to abolish boards and commissions that were not quasi-judicial or regulatory in function. Douglas had pronounced his opposition to 'government by commission' and promised to 'proceed to restore ministerial responsibility as quickly as possible.'[38] The government also immediately established a purchasing agency to buy equipment, material, and supplies on a professional, non-patronage basis, and made a start toward establishing an active civil service commission.

In addition to these structural changes, the government made some changes in personnel, mostly replacing the field staff that were known for their political activities (some eighty people) and the members of a few boards. But only four deputy ministers and fewer than a dozen other senior civil servants retired within nine months of 10 July 1944.[39] Going beyond this initial period, to the first two years in office, a total of 483 salaried staff members left the public service, which numbered about three thousand persons: 390 were recorded as resignations, 74 as retirements, and 19 as dismissals.[40] The Douglas government, in short, did not engage in any large-scale purge to make room for new and 'sympathetic' senior officials. It tended rather to rely upon the selection of a few key officials and advisors, many of them 'imported,' to lead in the launching of the new policies and programs, and to attract and develop over time new and promising younger people.

The so-called failure to bring in 'sympathetic' senior officials was to be a source of friction between the party and the government for some years.[41] But in many cases, the ministers were pleasantly surprised by the quality of the public service. One minister told his colleagues, for example, that after removing a few 'political heelers' he was 'delighted at the wonderful change in spirit of employees ... formerly they were meek, subdued and broken in spirit.'[42]

But the changes the cabinet made in the civil service still did not provide the machinery of government for the job that was expected of it. Some of the changes themselves exacerbated existing weaknesses. As an example, three ministers were concerned with industrial development: the minister of natural resources and industrial development had been assigned formal responsibility for industrial development, and the minister of reconstruction and rehabilitation had been authorized to undertake research into the industrial uses of natural resources. While the minister of co-operation and co-operative industrial development had a title that suggested involvement as well, he did not compete with his colleagues. And there were other examples of overlapping functions, frequently brought about by the mushrooming of new programs.

Not surprisingly, inter-departmental coordination was also faulty. Tommy McLeod discussed this problem with Premier Douglas early in 1945 and proposed that steps be taken to coordinate government policies. He suggested starting with cabinet committees to coordinate planning at the top policy level, then inter-departmental committees of 'permanent heads' (i.e., deputy ministers and heads of smaller agencies reporting to ministers), and finally special planning agencies where necessary.[43]

For the new Crown corporations, the government used makeshift devices. In 1945 the legislature passed the Crown Corporations Act, which provided for the corporate form of organization for public enterprises, but the structure remained relatively primitive.[44] The most important gap was the absence of any clear understanding as to the nature and character of the control that a cabinet needed over Crown companies or how it should be exercised.

The Influence of Interest Groups on the New Government

Going beyond the public service and the CCF Party, with whom the government had particular relationships, were Saskatchewan's interest groups, to which the government was either disposed or felt required to listen. In fact, the cabinet openly invited provincial associations and 'functional groups' to send their suggestions to government, and the groups were quick to respond. In July 1944, the premier said:

> We want you all to have some part in governing this Province ... some of you through your municipal and city councils, others through the local school board. We want your advice ... through your co-operatives or your trade unions, or through your local board of trade or vocational associations. We will welcome the assistance and advice of all organized groups and organized farmer bodies, retail merchants, the medical, dental and pharmaceutical associations ... we will welcome the help of all groups in the province, irrespective of their political, religious or occupational background.[45]

Such an invitation to public participation would no doubt have had its roots in the CCF's direct democracy theories and in the group representation theories of the United Farmers of Alberta. It was also a reflection of Douglas's personal tendency to be 'inclusive' – to seek a general consensus – as will be seen in the subsequent efforts to reorganize local government in the province. As Woodrow Lloyd made clear:

> Organizations of farmers, teachers and labour (professional or functional associations) are essential functional groups in the democratic society. Such organizations provide the opportunity of focusing collective thought and study on the important problems of definite and large groups of people, and on the general economic and social problems of their provinces. Such organizations provide a very essential liaison ... between the people and the government.[46]

As the public interest groups responded, cabinet soon came to devote a substantial portion of its time to hearing briefs from various groups in the province. It is not possible to say with any precision how much influence they had upon the government, but it was not insignificant. Cabinet's views came to be shaped not only by the party perspective, but also by an increasing appreciation of the problems and views of other organized groups. The interest groups exerted their influence on individual ministers and on cabinet as a whole. Chapter 3 has described the regular or periodic consultations that particular ministers held – for example, the premier with the organized health professions, the minister of education with the school trustees and teachers, and the minister of natural resources with primary producers. When the interest groups were seeking a broader influence or judged a policy to be a government concern, rather than a departmental concern, they approached the premier and cabinet directly.

It is important to consider the types of interest groups that characterized those times. These were far from homogeneous in character. They included national groups, such as the Canadian Federation of the Blind, proposing provincial homes for the blind,[47] and the Canadian Association of Social Workers, promoting improved provincial welfare practices.[48] Among the provincial associations, the Railway Transportation Brotherhood met annually with the cabinet,[49] and there were regular representations from the Saskatchewan Federation of Labour.[50] The cabinet made a point, too, of meeting frequently with the co-operative groups. In September 1944, for example, representatives of the co-operative movement met with cabinet to propose provincial assistance to establish the Canadian Co-operative Implements Limited. The Saskatchewan Employers Association and the Chamber of Commerce met annually with cabinet, and even more frequently when the government was introducing radical innovations in labour legislation during 1944–5.

Many more individual interests also found expression: a few examples will suffice. The Lumber and Pulpwood Manufacturers of Northern Saskatchewan urged the abolition of the Timber Board;[51] the operators of the lignite coal mines in Estevan-Bienfait opposed the mineral tax;[52] and the Flin Flon Board of Trade urged the government to locate its new fish filleting plant in Flin Flon rather than on Beaver Lake.[53] Individuals, too, made their interests known, proposing the establishment of a provincial art school, a medical college, and other initiatives.[54] The effect of these individual representations may not always have been perceptible, but taken together they introduced to the policy-makers the importance of foretelling the consequences of their policies and of anticipating the reactions of various groups to their proposals.

The Influences of Municipal and Federal Governments

Two other leading sources of influence on the government's plans and policies were the system of local government in Saskatchewan, including the groups that represented local municipalities, and federal-provincial relations. There is little doubt that the cabinet was influenced by the federal character of Canada's constitution and by the strong traditions of local government that existed in Saskatchewan.

The local governments tended in one sense to behave much like other interest groups. They were organized into associations: the Saskatchewan Association of Rural Municipalities (SARM), the Saskatchewan Urban Municipal Association, and the Saskatchewan School Trustees Association. They made representations to government and were consulted by government on a range of questions, from the proposed changes in local government organization via the new school units to the expansion of health services.[55] Individual municipalities made their views known too: for example, the mayors of at least two cities even wrote to the premier to advocate public ownership of natural gas distribution systems.[56]

But, in another sense, it was the local government system itself, and its capacity to deliver the services promised by the post-war welfare state, which most directly affected policy-making in the Douglas government. The system had been designed early in the twentieth century when it was arduous to travel even five miles to market. It consisted, for example, of rural school districts with an average of 120 persons, and rural municipalities with an average of 1,200 persons. These were the government units that in 1944 were responsible, under provincial legislation, for delivering education, health, and such social services as existed (not including income support programs such as old age pensions), and for providing the infrastructure so important to the economy and the quality of life in the country.

Obviously, changes needed to be made. The range of services now considered important demanded both a larger population base and greater financial equity between and among the local government units. Yet the local governments were reluctant to alter their existing structure in favour of a new one, and seemed to prefer either to maintain existing public services at a lower level or to shift programs entirely to provincial jurisdiction. For the province, the choice was difficult: to force reorganization in order to preserve local responsibility for the delivery of expanded programs, or to abandon local responsibility and provide the services provincially – likely through provincial regions or districts. These were the alternatives – or else the government's programs themselves would have to be abandoned.

In the first instance, the government did proceed and, as we saw in chapter 3, made substantial progress in implementing the larger school units. In the course of doing so, it compromised by permitting local ratepayers to vote on a new district if 20 per cent of them requested a plebiscite. None responded. In other cases, the province established entirely new local government regions based on function, notably health regions and library regions. In still other cases, the government abandoned local responsibility and provided the services in question provincially, creating its own departmental regions or districts.

As the story of the CCF government unfolds, in short, it will be clear that the issues of local government structure and the inability to achieve consensus around changing the structure had a significant influence on the design of provincial policies and programs in many fields. In the process of trying to change the local government structure, there was dislocation that in itself was disturbing to the province and the party.

In analogous ways, Canadian federalism equally influenced the new government. In this case, as we have said, the balance to be sought was between provincial responsibilities and provincial resources, and here the federal government was in a position to make a substantial difference to the CCF government's ability to realize its goals. Since its very beginning, the party had been prepared to assign greater powers to the national government in order better to ensure national economic planning and minimum levels of social security. Both the throne speech[57] and the first budget speech confirmed the government's readiness to do so. The treasurer argued that 'a comprehensive social security system must be a national responsibility.'[58]

Yet the government was also finding that the functioning of federalism could be an obstacle to provincial innovations. Several pieces of its legislation were challenged in the courts, as being *ultra vires*: for example, the Farm Security Act and the Mineral Taxation Act. And Saskatchewan became involved in a bitter dispute with the federal government over the seed grain debt. The problems stemmed from the fact that the government was trying to force the pace of social change, but it rapidly found that no matter how strong the inclination to change, the government of a province, and particularly a poor one, would experience very real limits in its capacity to effect change. Principal among these limits was the fiscal one. Constitutionally the provinces could impose direct taxes – on persons (poll taxes), on income, on sales, on property, on inheritances – but they could not improve, of course, their tax bases. This crippled the poorer provinces.

More, Saskatchewan like the other provinces had rented, as a wartime measure, its personal and corporate income tax powers and its inheritance taxes to the federal government in return for 'tax rental payments,' so that Saskatchewan could not raise its income taxes. The other side of the tax rental agreements, however, was that the federal 'rental payments' to Saskatchewan and other poor provinces greatly exceeded the yield of the provinces' income taxes. Thus, for Douglas, the extension and the enrichment of the tax rental agreements after the war was supremely important – a central goal of federal-provincial relations.

This was the position Douglas took at the first federal-provincial conference he attended in 1945, and one he was to maintain during his whole period as premier – adapted, of course, to changes over time that led to the explicit recognition of equalization payments to the poorer provinces and similar recognition of the 'provincial share' of the income and estate taxes. (The whole of this story, important both to Saskatchewan and Canada, is told in the Annex.)

Douglas's other central goal in federal-provincial relations – his prime goal, indeed – was, as we have said, the support of federal leadership in the construction of nationwide programs in the fields of health, welfare, and education. Again this was the position he took at the 1945 federal-provincial conference, where he supported vigorously Prime Minister

Mackenzie King's proposed 'charter of social security.' And it was the position he would continue to pursue when, in the face of opposition from Ontario and Quebec and other ideologically opposed provinces, the King government backed away from its commitment to nationally supported health and social security plans. Only now Douglas did so not only in the positions he took in federal-provincial conferences but by pioneering in Saskatchewan the very plans that had been dropped or deferred after the 1945 conferences – thus proving, starting with a universal hospital services plan (hospital insurance) in 1947, that they would work.

It was neither surprising nor difficult for a CCF government to establish for itself these goals of federal-provincial relations. They were expressions of the very ethos of the CCF Party. Here is what Douglas said with prescience in 1955:

> It seems to me that during the next few years, the battle in Canada is going to be between two opposing concepts – one which thinks of Canada as a nation in which the entire economy will be integrated so as to guarantee every citizen no matter where he lives, certain minimum standards of health, welfare and education, and on the other hand the concept that Canada is merely a loosely knit collective of provinces in which those provinces which have large corporations will be relatively fortunate, while those who lack this tax base will become depressed areas. This latter concept will certainly suit the business interests of Canada since they know they can exert sufficient pressure on provincial governments that are friendly to them to see that they are not taxed too heavily for social services.[59]

The story of the government in 1944 and 1945, then, was essentially one of introducing policy and program initiatives that created disequilibria both in the public service and beyond, and of testing the conventions and practices of cabinet government by introducing new and different interpretations of the democratic process. The province's machinery of government was strained; the party's ideology was being challenged by tests of feasibility and practicality; new patterns of authority and influence were being forged between the government and the party; new relationships between the government of Saskatchewan and the national government and the province's local governments were emerging; and more welcoming relationships were being developed with interest groups – all had begun to influence the government's thinking.

In the next phase, starting in early 1946, the government turned its attention more seriously to the creation of the machinery of government and processes that would suit its policies, and to the search for a new equilibrium or balance in program and administration. It also set about evaluating the whole complex of public policy to determine whether it represented the balance that the cabinet wanted and the province needed. And it reflected upon the amount of change the people of Saskatchewan both desired and could tolerate.

5

Transforming the Functioning of Government: 1946–1948

A virtual transformation in public policy characterized the government and the environment of governance generally during the CCF's first eighteen months in office, as the government introduced many of the policies and programs in the *Program for Saskatchewan*. In the same few months, the government engaged in many of the fundamental adjustments in relationships associated with becoming a government – notably the relationships with the CCF Party and the government caucus, with the public service, and with both federal and municipal governments. The experience the ministers gained during those months provided a growing understanding of the importance to governance of the organization and administration of government itself.

The Problem and the Remedy

In 1946 and 1947 the premier and his colleagues were becoming increasingly conscious of the need for greater coherence and order in their introduction of new policies. Some of their policies were under fire, notably the establishment of school units and the creation of Crown corporations. Some of the government's actions were seen by many to be errors in judgment, the most obvious being the expropriation of the Prince Albert box factory and the ill-fated news program of the Adult Education Division. Above all, the daunting scope and complexity of the challenges involved in changing the role of the state were becoming evident to ministers. Too, they were more aware of their own inexperience, individually and collectively, in running a government, tackling the questions of economic and social policy, and, on top of that, managing change. The existing machinery of government and the public service were not only inadequate to the task; they were themselves part of the problem that ministers would have to resolve.

Clearly, the government had only two avenues open to it. One was to 'ration' the energies of the ministers and the government through bringing the pace of change under control. The other, and more difficult, approach was to design new machinery of government that would assist the ministers in their enormous undertaking.

Reforming the machinery of government would require some pioneering, for there was no precedent to follow. No other government in Canada had undertaken what the CCF was trying to do. In the United States there was some experience in creating new agencies of government, and this came to be useful to the Saskatchewan government, as will be seen. In Canada, particular changes were emerging, notably the establishment of a cabinet office (Privy Council Office) in the government of Canada.[1] But the primary impetus to change had to be found within the CCF government. Premier Douglas himself determined to 'pull things together.'

The premier and his key ministers came to realize what they needed to accomplish, if not in each detail at least in general terms, to remedy the many shortcomings in the machinery of government and the outmoded qualities in the inherited public service and administration. They needed to design and establish the organization and processes of governing that would suit the demands of the expanded role of the state that they were actively creating.[2]

The government would need to establish central planning machinery to assist the cabinet in developing key policies and policy directions, and in devising a policy framework within which operating ministries could do their planning. In the process, they would achieve a better balance between policy-making in departments and policy-making at the centre of government. What 'better planning' in a provincial government involved was by no means self-evident. But there were some relatively predictable implications. First, the new planning machinery implied the development of rather more clearly articulated goals of government – a process the party had gone through in 1943 and 1944, but one that the government itself had not so far undergone. Secondly, it implied a re-examination of the policies that cabinet had introduced during the first two years, against the articulated goals. Thirdly, it suggested the use of planning in certain broad areas of government where none had been done before – fields such as economic development and public investment. And finally, it implied a more careful 'cabinet evaluation' of new ministerial proposals.

Beyond these elements, the development of improved planning machinery also had important implications for departments, which would have to look to the adequacy of their own performance if they were to retain the initiative in policy development.

Government also needed to design and introduce a budgeting system that could translate Cabinet's policies and priorities into reality through the allocation of resources, and that would manage the fiscal function generally. The budget could be used as a major – if not the major – device for discovering the government's real program. It could be the principal vehicle for making clear the policy choices that had to be made, and for forcing rational – or at least conscious – decisions between the alternatives. The budget could also be used to bring about an evaluation of administrative efficiency and effectiveness, including both an examination of the administrative machinery and of the resources being employed in given programs. Most importantly, it could give the premier, the treasurer, and the cabinet as a whole the facts they needed in order to bring about the balance in public policy they wanted, and the integration of the various programs that was required. Finally, the budget could give them a mechanism for control, to ensure that new programs could be introduced or old ones expanded only through cabinet decision.

Further, government needed to invent and to establish new machinery for the rationalization of Crown corporations and for their management within the mandate established by ministers and within the investment capital provided – but otherwise independently of political or public service direction.

Finally, it would need to develop a dedicated public service, based on merit and commitment, and one with structures and systems of public administration that would facilitate both policy and program innovation and the effective delivery of new services. Public service reform had been integral to the 1944 *Program*, and it was now time to design this reform.

In other words, the 1947–8 revolution in the machinery of government produced more than just improved techniques of planning and budgeting. It brought with it the first of a long series of changes in departmental and inter-departmental organization. It achieved a complete metamorphosis in the organization of Crown corporations. It wrought changes in the civil service that would make it a much more smoothly functioning body. And at the cabinet level it brought about a new emphasis on collective cabinet responsibility, as opposed to the earlier emphasis on individual ministerial responsibility.

This was the prime agenda of the Douglas government during 1946–8. But to say that this was the main concern of government does not mean that policy activity ceased or that no new programs were introduced during these years. As we shall see in the second half of this chapter, two of Douglas's banner innovations were introduced in this period: Canada's first universal and comprehensive hospital services plan and Canada's first Bill of Rights, both introduced in 1947. On the agricultural front, new policies did not emerge in the first year or more, owing to the serious illness of the first CCF minister, George Williams. Even after his death, and his succession by I.C. (Toby) Nollett, the changes introduced during 1947–8 were not radical in the scheme of things. In any event, there was the continuing and taxing job of implementing the policy innovations of the first eighteen months, including putting into place the first forty-five school units and six of the new health regions.[3] All of these were significant changes, alongside the reforms to the machinery of government.

The Establishment of the Economic Advisory and Planning Board (EAPB)

Reforming the machinery of government, however, remained the primary concern. The question was where to begin. Typical of Tommy Douglas, he looked for a key person (as he did as minister of health): someone who would be able to advise on the key issues of governance, and who would be capable of the innovation required to resolve them successfully. The central organization or authority for undertaking this work had already been proposed: the Economic Advisory and Planning Board, which Tommy McLeod had suggested in 1945. It was to be a cabinet committee, whose motive force for innovation and change would be its appointed Chair, and whose legitimacy would flow from its sweeping mandate and its status as the central cabinet committee.

The appointment of George Cadbury, late in 1945, was a singularly important step in creating the new board and the related machinery. Cadbury was a British socialist, who had studied under John Maynard Keynes and at the Wharton School of Business and Finance in Philadelphia. After a successful business career in England, he worked during the war in Washington for the British government; he was assisting in the procurement of materiel for the war effort. 'His interest in socialism led him to a meeting with Premier Douglas [in June 1945 in Regina] where they discussed the CCF's first year in government, its organizational problems, and its needs for reform, and led to an invitation to return to Saskatchewan after the War was ended.'[4] After George Cadbury moved to Saskatchewan early in 1946, his influence began to be felt immediately in all aspects of governance, from the organization of the centre of government to the policies being developed.

The Economic Advisory and Planning Board (the EAPB or Planning Board) came into being in January 1946, with George Cadbury as its Chair and four ministers and two cabinet advisors as members.[5] The ministers were Clarence Fines, Joe Phelps, Jack Sturdy, and Lachlan McIntosh; and the advisors were Tommy McLeod and Morris Shumiatcher. In early 1947, J.H. Brockelbank and Woodrow Lloyd were added to the board. The mandate of the EAPB was broadly conceived: it was to be responsible for 'advising the Premier on all economic, industrial and commercial matters affecting the province, co-ordinating all existing and future planning and economic study and research, and [receiving] for comment and action, where authorized, all plans and proposals relating to the government's existing or proposed participation in the economic, industrial and commercial fields in ... the province.'[6] Through the premier, the board was responsible to the cabinet.

The EAPB was given broad powers to achieve its mandate. It was authorized to engage personnel, to establish working groups to study various problems, to enter into discussions with any person in order to develop a plan for economic and industrial development, and to enjoy full access to the records of all government agencies. The Chair enjoyed a wide measure of freedom to exercise his duties. He was empowered to 'consult with and advise the members of the Executive Council individually and collectively on all ... industrial and economic development' and to 'participate actively in any ... industrial, commercial and public utility enterprise in which any branch of government possesses an interest.'[7]

George Cadbury possessed the talents to match this mandate. He was a formidable person – tall, imposing in his intelligence and his reasoning, confident in his knowledge of cabinet government (Westminster model), and particularly experienced in industrial development. Despite his almost magisterial presence and his obvious influence, he was, according to the senior people who worked for him, not arrogant – indeed, he was a 'pretty sensitive person.' His real problem would flow from the measure of the power he wielded and the confidence with which he wielded it.

Judging from the early records of the EAPB, cabinet was concerned with three major areas at this stage: to develop an economic plan for the province, both general and sectoral; to evaluate government policies in relation to cabinet's objectives; and to reorganize and bring under control the Crown corporations that had been established. This third function was different from the first two in that it obviously had implications for operations as well as planning. Cabinet assigned priority to it, giving the Chair special authority – in particular, the power to act as a director of any corporation and to assume managerial functions 'of any such enterprise as the Executive Council may from time to time direct.'[8]

The board's interpretation of its mandate, over time, gave it greater precision and force. The economic plan for the province came to comprehend the development of a blueprint for general economic development, and of plans and policies for particular sectors of the economy (natural resources, agriculture, energy, transportation, manufacturing, etc.). The evaluation of government policies was similarly extended to include the review and criticism of the allocation of the resources of the province as between the different functions of government (in the budget). And with the creation of the Budget Bureau in later 1946, the board became the government's principal advisor on organization and the machinery of government. Finally, the EAPB firmly directed and quickly brought under control the existing Crown corporations, and likewise subjected all proposals for new government enterprises to critical scrutiny.

One further change in the functioning of the EAPB came in the fall of 1946. In recognition of the difference between the economic policy and policy evaluation function, and that of rationalizing the Crown corporations, the board's organization was divided into two areas. Section A was to deal with economic planning and policy evaluation, with George Cadbury as its Chair, and section B was to deal with the Crown corporations – with staff assigned to each area,[9] and with Cadbury holding the post of chief industrial executive (a 'dual appointment,' so to speak). The EAPB continued to operate as a cabinet committee, dealing with both section A items and section B items until the creation of the Government Finance Office (a separate cabinet committee) in 1947. Yet the research staff of the whole of the EAPB grew to only some twelve to fifteen officers. And increasingly, both the cabinet and the individual ministers looked to this group of well-trained and dedicated young economists for advice and assistance. They advised on federal-provincial relations, on provincial-local government relations, on municipal taxation – on almost any subject that called upon the skills of an economist.

The leading people involved included Tommy Shoyama, whose presence is known throughout this biography, and who later became

Canada's deputy minister of finance, after having served as senior advisor to the Economic Council of Canada and then as deputy minister of energy, mines and resources in Ottawa. David Levin later became assistant deputy minister in Saskatchewan's Department of Social Welfare, and then a senior official in Canada's Department of Finance. Meyer Brownstone went on to serve as Saskatchewan's deputy minister of municipal affairs, and then became a professor of political science at the University of Toronto. Tim Lee was later the Saskatchewan secretary to the cabinet, and then a professor and administrator at York University. Jim MacNeill went on to become deputy minister of urban affairs in Ottawa, and then a prominent international environmental expert serving as director of environment at the OECD, as secretary general of the World Commission on Environment and Development, and as special advisor to the secretary general on the Earth Summit. And Charlie Schwartz also later moved to Ottawa as a senior official in the Department of Trade and Commerce.

The EAPB and the Organization of Crown Corporations

Between 1946 and 1948 the government almost completely reorganized its Crown corporations. The first step was to develop a different governance structure and to assume greater control over the corporations; the second step was to deal with several specific problem corporations; and the third was to alter the approach to financing the corporations.

First, the EAPB made a comprehensive proposal for reorganizing the Crown corporations, and cabinet adopted it. In February 1946 Cadbury became a member of the board of directors of several corporations,[10] and in March the EAPB recommended a board of directors for every corporation, with Cadbury to be appointed to each of them. Also in March, the EAPB proposed sweeping changes in corporation structure and in cabinet-corporation relations. Each corporation was to be independent of the department that had developed it (referring primarily to those created by the Department of Natural Resources and Industrial Development); each would be run by a general manager reporting to a board of directors; and each director would be equal in status, whether or not he was a minister. Further, the Chair of each board would be the minister responsible for the corporation. All new investment, including the use of reserves and surpluses, was to be approved by a central body, presumably section B of the EAPB itself.[11]

George Cadbury also recommended a process for the creation of any new Crown corporations. First, all proposals would be referred to the EAPB for consideration, and, if the board approved them in principle, they would then be submitted to the premier and cabinet. If cabinet gave approval in principle, it would designate a minister to chair a committee mandated to investigate the suggestions thoroughly; the Chair of the EAPB was a member of all such committees. This committee could then recommend for or against the establishment of the corporation.[12] Once a corporation was established, cabinet would also specify the limitations on its powers, the operations to be conducted, its objectives, and its marketing policies.[13] Cabinet accepted these recommendations as well.

In short order, the new policies took effect. During April, the Chair of the EAPB discussed with Joe Phelps the reorganization of several corporations that the government had established,[14] and the suggestions were soon implemented. The Saskatchewan Lake and Forest Products Corporation was to manage the Timber Board, the box factory, and the fish and fur marketing services. Saskatchewan Minerals was to manage the brick plant and the sodium sulphate plant, and Saskatchewan Industries was to manage the shoe factory, the tannery, and the woollen mill. The Insurance Office continued as an independent corporation.[15]

To complete the reorganization, the EAPB debated the wisdom of placing all corporations under the jurisdiction of a central body, possibly section B of the Planning Board.[16] It also considered establishing special machinery for financing capital investment in Crown corporations.[17] At the end of September 1946, the recommendations made to Clarence Fines, as provincial treasurer, were for a central corporation, or holding company, which would direct the disposition of all surpluses and reserves of the corporations, authorize and, if necessary, finance all capital investment, and generally oversee the financial affairs of the corporations. It would also supply them with technical assistance, notably accounting, industrial relations, and industrial research.[18] The cabinet approved this new organization and in the 1947 session of the legislature amended the Crown Corporations Act to establish the Government Finance Office (GFO).[19]

The GFO, it will be evident, was an interesting, and unique, example of the new machinery of government being developed. It was indeed a cabinet committee, whose purpose was to give coherence to the use of Crown corporations to achieve industrial development, and to act, in a sense, as the treasury board for 'the Crowns' (as they came to be called). Its members included all or most of the ministers who chaired Crown corporation boards, plus the head of the Planning Board and the deputy provincial treasurer. The Chair was the provincial treasurer.

But the GFO was also a holding company, as we have said, that advised and assisted individual corporations in legal affairs, in industrial relations, in accounting policies, and otherwise when called for. And for a time, the GFO was the arm of the government responsible for loans to industry from the Industrial Development Fund – until the creation of the Industrial Development Office.

But during the early months of the GFO, the Planning Board continued 'to be responsible for policy decisions relating to the operations of the crown corporations, with the Finance Office ... being concerned only with financial operations.'[20] This division of responsibility was found to be unclear and for some time there was a good deal of uncertainty as to the respective responsibilities of Planning Board B and the Government Finance Office. Ultimately, as the GFO staff developed, and as the treasurer, Clarence Fines, asserted his leadership as minister in charge of the Finance Office, Planning Board B dropped out of the Crown corporation picture, leaving the Finance Office responsible for both the planning and the management side of operations. But during 1946 and 1947, the dominant influence was that of Cadbury and his staff, who rationalized the whole administrative structure of the Crown corporations, including the two major ones responsible for telephones and electric power.

The key members of the GFO staff included George Tamaki – who was succeeded in 1950 by Allan Blakeney – Mike Kalmakoff, and Don Black. Tamaki, the first legal counsel to the GFO, had been forcibly moved from British Columbia in 1941. He had studied law at Dalhousie University and then at the University of Toronto, and was attracted to Saskatchewan in 1946. (Parenthetically, he and I studied constitutional law together under Bora Laskin during 1944–5. I first met Morris Shumiatcher in this seminar too.) Allan Blakeney, who succeeded George Tamaki in 1950, went on to become Chair of the Saskatchewan Securities Commission. After an interval at the Bar, he entered politics and served successively as minister of education, provincial treasurer, and minister of health in the Douglas and Lloyd governments. And then, in 1971, he himself became premier. Don Black, who had taken a law degree at McGill, was working at Dominion Bridge when he was attracted to Saskatchewan, by George Cadbury. When he left Saskatchewan he returned to McGill for a period, and then went to the Planning Branch of the Canadian International Development Agency.

Mike Kalmakoff, the treasurer of the GFO, came to Saskatchewan from the Wartime Prices and Trade Board; he later became the general manager of the Timber Board.

Work on both the telephone and power corporations was of long-term importance. In September 1946, the EAPB conducted a study of the telephone system,[21] and wrote a critical report on the structure of the Power Commission. The EAPB recommended converting the Power Commission to a Crown corporation in order to bring it under closer government control and to subject its policies to closer scrutiny. The board also suggested that the Power Commission might usefully assume responsibility for both natural gas and electricity distribution and transmission.[22] In May 1947 cabinet agreed to convert both the power and the telephone companies into Crown corporations and bring them within the sphere of influence of the Government Finance Office, but did not at this stage accept the suggestion that a single board should manage both gas and electrical utilities.[23]

However, the Planning Board's influence with respect to Crown corporations went beyond administrative reforms. It commissioned a twenty-year plan for the Saskatchewan Power Commission. The consultant engaged for this study, David Cass-Beggs, was a British engineer who had come to teach at the University of Toronto, and consulted with the new Saskatchewan government; he was later appointed as manager of the corporation. The plan called for using the province's coal, hydro, and natural gas resources to develop integrated sources of power supply, and for replacing 'the present hodgepodge of [transmission] lines inherited from formerly independent companies.'[24] The Planning Board also worked with the Power Commission in drafting a plan for rural electrification in the province.

Other examples of the EAPB advice on policy included proposals for the extension of the government's Insurance Office,[25] for containing the expansion of the government's bus company (which had been established in January 1947),[26] and for the integration into a single enterprise of the government's northern air services.[27]

The EAPB and General Economic Planning

While section B of the EAPB was engaged in rationalizing the Crown corporation activity, section A concerned itself with economic planning in a broader sense and with general policy evaluation. Operating at the highest level of policy, the board undertook three central tasks in the development of an economic plan: to postulate the goals of economic policy – essentially economic growth; to identify the contribution to that goal of the several sectors of the Saskatchewan economy, and which of them had the greatest potential for contributing to future growth; and finally to address the troubled question as to who should develop the high potential sectors of the economy – the private or the public sector. Within this context, the EAPB also undertook the ancillary task of evaluating the extent to which government policy was facilitating the desired development in the various sectors of the Saskatchewan economy – this being part of the board's program evaluation mandate.

The goals of economic policy were stated in 1946[28] and restated in 1947: 'Within the limited area of provincial activity, our four-year plan must embrace a rational approach to the problems of utilizing our resources to the full, of extending our utilities and services, and of providing for the minimum social [needs] of our non-productive groups [in the population].'[29]

The board's main concern was economic development. It acknowledged that Saskatchewan would not become a highly industrialized region. 'Any attempted move toward a completely self-contained economy,' it said, 'is foredoomed to failure in the face of growing and ... cheaper output of industries in other parts of North America.'[30] But it felt there was nonetheless room for greater economic diversification and a more rapid rate of economic growth. A special report to cabinet pointed to two principal 'growth' areas: resource industries such as petroleum, wood products, and industrial minerals; and market-oriented industries such as food processing and services.[31]

The EAPB seemed to conclude that resource development was the most promising area and concentrated much of its energies there. It established working parties, including personnel from the Department of Natural Resources, to examine each resource area. These groups studied the possibilities of potash mining,[32] sodium sulphate development,[33] natural gas production,[34] and oil resources and 'the problems of commercializing Saskatchewan oil,'[35] among others. The committee later evaluated the regulations that the Department of Natural Resources had prepared to govern oil exploration and development on Crown land. It is important to recall that early land grants in Saskatchewan (to the settlers, to the railways) did not necessarily carry with them the rights for any minerals that might be found beneath the surface of such lands. Indeed, nearly 80 per cent of the mineral rights in the surveyed areas of the province are 'Crown-owned.'[36]

All of the studies confirmed the view that the development of resources, and particularly of oil and mineral resources, should be given top priority. Having established this, the much more difficult question had to be answered: should this development be undertaken by the public sector or by the private sector?

The second sector of the economy to which the EAPB attached a high priority was industrial development. Here again the question as to the role of the public sector had to be posed – not this time whether the public sector should be directly involved in individual enterprises, but whether the government should contribute to industrial development by making loans to private industry.

The second of these two questions – both of which sparked sharp differences in the party and within the CCF caucus – was answered first.

It is important to pause here to observe that the debate that ensued centred on these two sectors of the economy – resources and industry – but that there was little debate in other sectors. In the energy, transportation, and communication fields, for example, public sector development was generally assumed (at least in CCF circles). The Power Corporation was responsible for the generation and distribution of electric power, and similarly, when it was developed, the distribution of natural gas. In the area of transportation, it was taken for granted that highways and roads were a public sector responsibility; and after little debate, the establishment by the government of a bus transportation system and a northern airline was similarly accepted.[37] Railways, of course, fell under national jurisdiction, and even here partial public ownership was not at that time being contested. Saskatchewan Government Telephones, in the communications sector, had been under public ownership since 1908.

Nor was there any debate about the agricultural sectors: private ownership – thought of in terms of 'the family farm' – was taken for granted (the notion of public ownership having only been flirted with in CCF circles in the 1930s). Similarly with the role of the private sector in industrial development: what was at issue was not whether government should own particular enterprises, but whether government loans should be made to facilitate private development.

First, then, the decision concerning industrial development loans. As early as January 1946, the EAPB had raised the question as to whether government would be prepared to establish 'a revolving fund to make loans to businesses on a repayment basis over a period of years.'[38] Shortly thereafter the EAPB established a working group 'to study the relationships between government and private enterprise,' and later that year cabinet decided to include in the draft Crown Corporations Act provision for an Industrial Development Fund.[39] The plan involved the government making loans to small industries that wanted to locate in Saskatchewan but that were encountering difficulty in obtaining the required capital. The loans would be financed from budgetary surpluses or borrowing.

This was a sharp departure from party policy. The CCF convention in July 1946 had expressed enthusiasm for the government's Crown corporation policy and recommended its extension.[40] And while cabinet had discussed the new policy of providing loans to private industry with both the caucus and the Legislative Advisory Committee, the ministers involved had apparently not understood a request for the matter to be debated by the whole CCF Council. As a result, the CCF president, Carlyle King, was surprised to find the proposal in the throne speech. He immediately wrote to the premier, who assured King that there was a misunderstanding, which he regretted, and requested a special meeting of the Legislative Advisory Committee before the legislation was introduced.[41] The committee was divided at this meeting, but the premier felt able to proceed with the legislation.

The division of opinion within the CCF continued into the Legislative Assembly. One CCF MLA, Myron Feeley, said the proposal to help private enterprise was contrary to the CCF's promise to eradicate capitalism, and he invited the premier to reconcile the two views. Douglas's reply was consistent with the approach he had advocated before the election, but its phrasing shows care to prevent a breach between the more doctrinaire party members and the more pragmatic ones:

> Premier Douglas said 'private enterprise' and 'capitalism' were not synonymous terms. The reference to capitalism meant monopoly capitalism where a small group of men were able to control the whole economy of a community ... The Government recognized three types of enterprise, public, co-operative, and private, and all had a place in the province's economy. It was the Government's intention to encourage private enterprise wherever it did not interfere with the welfare of the people.[42]

The private versus public development of oil and mineral resources was not settled as quickly. The EAPB had entered this debate, too, as early as 1946, pressing for a clear statement of public policy. The premier's position was clear, at least privately; he favoured private development of the province's oil and mineral resources. But the minister of natural resources, Joe Phelps, was not convinced of the wisdom or the necessity of a general policy, though he was prepared to endorse private development on an *ad hoc* basis. The debate over public ownership continued within the caucus and the party. In November 1946, Cadbury prepared a 'Statement of Policy on Oil, Gas and Mineral Development,' which advocated private development of oil, natural gas, metallic minerals, and, tentatively, industrial minerals (potash, for example). This paper represented a sort of focus for the discussion that lasted for a year or more.

The Department of Natural Resources and the EAPB proceeded, meanwhile, with plans to develop specific mineral resources. Cabinet agreed with the proposal for establishing a government-operated sodium sulphate mining (more accurately 'brining') operation. On the other hand, the EAPB endorsed private development of sodium chloride mining, a more expensive, underground operation.[43] The cabinet, apparently with caucus approval, authorized negotiations with a private firm for the development of this Crown-owned resource. Similarly, the government decided that potash would be developed privately, but only after more protracted study.

The best example of the Planning Board's role in resource policy is found in the development of the government's position on oil. The discovery of oil near Cabri, Saskatchewan, in March 1946 made it necessary for the government to develop a policy concerning the disposition of Crown-owned mineral resources. In this case, the minister of natural resources decided that private development was appropriate, and the departmental advisors prepared a lease plan that would reserve a 'fair share' of the resources to the people of the province, over and above the standard oil royalty. Leases for the new oilfield were negotiated on the basis of this plan, which reserved 15 per cent of the land (mineral rights) to the Crown.[44]

Meanwhile, the debate on a general oil policy unfolded. The Planning Board staff, with the participation of Vern Hogg, engaged in preparing a general policy for oil development. In March 1946, the board had decided that the 'Government should not at present enter the business of discovering and developing oil fields, but should for the present time, leave the field to private enterprise.' The CCF Party had also begun to debate the provincial position. The Chair of the caucus, for example, wrote the premier:

I feel many of our members have gained the impression we have only a wait
and see policy in regard to oil development: we are told, and quite properly, that the Government is not prepared to spend vast sums ... on wild-
catting; again that oil leases will only be granted on a checkerboard plan
[the Crown reserves being scattered throughout the lease]. This leaves the
matter most indefinite.[45]

The debate continued through 1947, demonstrating an area of real
disagreement between the government generally and elements of the
party. The Planning Board argued that this was not a favourable field for
public development, and that a combination of lease and royalty policies, plus the participation of co-operatives should they wish, would adequately secure the public interest. Natural Resources officials shared
this view. But a large number of party members held an opposite view.
At a Provincial Council meeting, for example, some members tried,
unsuccessfully, to pass a resolution 'instructing' the government to
engage immediately in oil drilling and processing.[46]

Again, in November 1947, the Planning Board recommended in
favour of private development. In December, cabinet authorized discussions with the co-operative movement to determine whether they would
be interested in participating in oil development; Cadbury reported in
March of the next year that the co-operatives had limited resources and
could not be an active element in the picture.[47] But by 1948 there was
still no unequivocal public statement of the government's oil policy,
although the Department of Natural Resources was actually leasing
Crown lands to private companies.

In fact, in January 1948 a joint committee of the EAPB and the
Department of Natural Resources drafted 'alternate proposals in
respect to the participation of private enterprise,'[48] which led to a crys-
tallization of the policy questions, including the general conclusion that
industrial minerals, except for sodium sulphate, should also be developed privately. In the end, Cadbury advocated the encouragement of
private capital in Saskatchewan, a conclusion that the premier and
the treasurer had reached earlier and independently. (This decision
is described in chapter 6.) Not until the government's second term in
office was a public decision taken against government participation in
oil development.

While the EAPB was participating in the difficult decisions concerning the economic development fund and the more difficult discussions

concerning the private and public development of mineral resources, the board's staff continued to initiate studies in other aspects of industrial development, agriculture, and transportation. Cadbury and his staff considered a variety of specific economic development suggestions in their role 'of continually studying ways and means of expanding Saskatchewan's industries.'[49] These included a rock-wool project, utilization of waste from fish filleting plants, the use of oil on Saskatchewan highways, and so on.[50]

The pattern that came to characterize resources policy-making was that the Planning Board, with selected departmental personnel, would develop broad policies into which the departmental programs would fit, and the departmental personnel would work out the programs required to meet the needs of the moment. For example, the department developed all of the conservation regulations, royalty regulations, and the plans for resources inventories. Following the suggestions of a (provincial) royal Commission, the department proposed a forest management program, a reforestation scheme, a fire prevention and control program, and a detailed forest inventory plan.[51] Day to day management of the province's resources required clear-cut policies, even if these were less than perfect at the time they were evolved.

Turning to agriculture, the board proposed a four-point plan aimed at increasing agricultural productivity in the province,[52] which was intended to serve as a guide to future policy development. As with the pattern of resources policy development, the Department of Agriculture developed specific program policies – for example, an expanded agricultural extension service, a system for veterinary services, a 'feed bank' program, a plan for developing community pastures, and policies for leasing of Crown agricultural lands, all of which were designed during 1946–8. The EAPB sought to evaluate these programs in relation to the longer-term agricultural outlook, and working parties studied irrigation, and reclamation and conservation projects, and formulated 'long range plans for land utilization, irrigation [and] water supply.'[53] The EAPB also conducted studies with respect to land tenure, farm credit, and machinery maintenance depots.[54]

Finally, another EAPB group wrote a detailed report on transportation policy and the budget allocations that should be made for provincial highways, resource development roads, main market roads, and municipal roads and streets.[55] It suggested a committee to study provincial air services,[56] the subsequent recommendations of which led to the formation of a Crown company to operate an airline in northern

Saskatchewan.[57] And it fostered the growth of the Saskatchewan Transportation Company, which operated a province-wide system of bus lines.[58]

In addition to these 'sector' studies, the board had a working party on physical planning, which concerned itself with population trends, settlement patterns, and community planning. A labour-policy working group concerned itself with government-labour industrial relations and with the broader questions of labour policies and their effect on the provincial economy. In addition, the EAPB gave *ad hoc* advice on a wide range of subjects – some of them clearly economic in character, and some of them less so.

The EAPB and Policy and Program Evaluation

The third major area of responsibility for the Planning Board was to evaluate government policies and programs. This involved defining and clarifying government's goals, assessing programs against these goals, determining whether total government policy was leading in the desired direction, identifying and reconciling conflicts between policies, and evaluating the effectiveness of individual programs. In short, it was the process of policy formulation in the broadest and most complete sense, as distinguished from the development of economic policies alone.

It is not clear that the government had anticipated how the board would fulfil this role. Economic planning it could envisage, including an evaluation of public policy in relation to economic goals, but the premier and his colleagues may well not have anticipated the inevitability with which these judgments were to lead to this more complete evaluation of the whole range of public policy, including health, welfare, education, even municipal affairs. In the end, Cadbury interpreted government direction very broadly and interpreted the planning function very broadly too.

The approach he developed to the task is an interesting study in public administration. First, he used the annual budget as a device for determining government's present program emphasis as between functions of government, and then compared this evidence with the general policy goals he believed the government was, or should be, pursuing. Secondly, he developed four-year plans, which were calculated to lead policy more surely in the desired directions, and he compared these plans with the departmental budget plans. Thirdly, he examined the program complex of each department and considered its effectiveness in achieving the broad policies that had been, or might be, enunciated. Then he studied individual proposals submitted by departments and commented on their relevance and potential effectiveness, and he made program suggestions of his own. In June 1946, only six months after assuming his position, Cadbury reported to the EAPB that

> [it] is becoming increasingly apparent that we cannot wait for a long-term plan of development to be prepared before this Board establishes some ratio between the various departmental and other activities which are utilizing the available resources of the province. I therefore suggest that we give immediate consideration to the relationship between the various major expenditures with a view to making recommendations to the cabinet for guidance on the next fiscal year or sooner.[59]

In September 1946, the board reported to cabinet, suggesting eleven objectives of government and assigning to each an index of relative importance. The objectives were the following: maintenance of capital and personal income, redistribution of income, maintenance of employment, development of resources, preservation of resources, improvement of scientific standards, attraction of capital, maintenance of government income, improved welfare standards, improvement of cultural and community services, and stabilization of population. The board then ranked the relative importance of the broad functions of government in relation to these goals. The order selected was as follows: first, resource and agricultural development, followed by transportation and communication; education and preventive health; industrial and utility development; curative health, social welfare, and labour policies; and finally physical and cultural amenities and community planning.

Having created these 'standards,' the board evaluated the province's expenditure patterns and pointed out the issues that emerged from this analysis. Even recognizing that levels of expenditure are faulty as a single index of the priority being accorded to a particular function of government, it was instructive, if not surprising, to see that a very small percentage of expenditure was devoted to agriculture and a very large percentage to public welfare. Moreover, there had been little change in the allocation of funds in the past seventeen years, nor 'any radical departure from traditional government programs since the CCF Government took office.'[60] Minister Brockelbank was moved to comment: 'There ain't been no revolution?'

One substantial reason for this expenditure pattern, of course, was the fact that certain programs were 'expenditure intensive' and others were not. A universal hospitalization program operating within the public sector, or a public education program, meant that all the expenditures involved in the health and education programs were part of the provincial budget. On the other hand, assistance to, or regulation of, the private sector or private enterprises required relatively small expenditures. So it was misleading to suggest that the scale of expenditures was a true measure of the priorities that were being attached to the government's several categories of programs. And, in any event, the CCF and the government were already committed to health and social policy initiatives.

The board's analysis did nevertheless make it clear that resources development should enjoy the highest priority, in order to help pay for social programs. This would be realized partly by the generous allocation of funds to industrial and resource development promotion (not an expenditure intensive function) and even more by according to the private sector a larger role in economic development.

The following year, at the premier's request, the board examined the estimates for 1948–9 with a view to recommendations on overall policy.[61] In the document titled 'A Four Year Plan,' the board reported:

> It is probably impossible to establish objectively scientific criteria by which to measure the value or necessity of expenditures as between broad fields of activity ... But, in general, it is submitted that a first concern must be given to the protection, maintenance and increase of the total productivity and real income of the people of the province. When this is established, it is possible to consider essential and desirable transfers of real income such as are involved in social service programs.[62]

In its report, the board sharply criticized the small percentage of the budget that was being proposed for agriculture and resources development, and argued against larger allocations to health and welfare 'until federal aid is secured.' It argued that choices had to be made: that 'to provide all of these very desirable [social] services is beyond the present resources of Saskatchewan.' The board proceeded to recommend specific budget allocations to the various functions of government and proposed, as a general guide for aggregate budgetary decisions, some general propositions regarding fiscal policy: '... in a period of low income, deficit financing is acceptable, but in prosperous times, accumulation of surplus either by debt retirement or actual cash reserve is desirable.'[63] The Four Year Plan, in short, was a program for achieving certain specific objectives over a limited period of time; one of these was an appropriate balance in the government's various programs. The means for achieving these goals would be budgetary and fiscal policy.

The influence of the Planning Board's advice was unquestionably felt in future policy deliberations. Certainly the government emphasized economic development much more during its second term of office. But an examination of the revised financial data, using current and capital expenditures, indicates that the percentage of the budget spent on transportation and communication, natural resources, primary industries, trade, and industrial development was already rising. The 'difficulty' was that the expenditures on health and welfare, education, and cultural services were rising nearly as fast. Except for the financing of the Hospital Services Plan in 1947, the growth was made possible by reductions in debt charges and in general spending.[64]

The board also assessed departmental policies as part of its mandate to evaluate the effectiveness of government's policies and programs. In 1946, for example, it criticized the Department of Highways for assuming that the only way to bring services to a widely scattered population was better road facilities. The EAPB suggested instead both lower road expenditures and a deliberate attempt to speed up population concentration (a revolution in itself!),[65] as well as changing the emphasis from expenditures on highways to expenditures on market roads. It urged the Department of Agriculture to embark on a resettlement program and to encourage the trend toward larger and more economic farms. The department was also criticized for its heavy emphasis on a provincial feed and fodder-growing program, and was urged to take an active part in planning an irrigation program.[66] In the social policy field, the Department of Public Health was pressed to give more emphasis to preventive health, and the Department of Education was urged to encourage the inter-provincial development of certain educational facilities, such as schools for the handicapped and specialized university colleges. Similarly, the Department of Social Welfare was urged to reduce costs through consolidating welfare institutions and through a revision of the penal system, with more extensive use of probation and parole.[67] In these and other areas, the board criticized departmental programs and made its own alternative suggestions to cabinet. None of which, it must be said, deterred the premier in the establishment of the Saskatchewan Hospital Services Plan in 1947.

In the Department of Natural Resources, the EAPB was less sweeping and more detailed in its policy assessments than it was in health and welfare and education. It centred more on the evaluation of specific departmental programs, reporting on the government's policies for forestry development; on the policies for and the potential of the fishing industry ('the history of the Saskatchewan fishing industry is not an encouraging one');[68] on the game and fur management procedures; on the department's geological surveys in the North; and on the encouragement of private mining companies in the Precambrian area.[69]

In fact, the board's involvement in resource development studies was so complete that, not surprisingly, relations with the minister of natural resources became strained. One consequence was that, in January 1948, cabinet felt it necessary to establish a committee on mineral development policy, involving both departmental and Planning Board staff, to consider 'overall developments.'[70] But even the use of joint working parties as a substitute for direct EAPB intervention was not acceptable to the minister. He saw EAPB participation in his department's affairs as a serious organizational problem. On the other hand, many officials in the department looked on participation in the working groups as a way of increasing the use of rational planning methods.

The board also extended its evaluation function and its role as a critic to providing comments on particular departmental proposals, though it performed this function more actively with respect to Crown corporations than departments. A proposed rate reduction by the Saskatchewan Power Commission, for example, was referred to the EAPB.[71] The Planning Board discussed a suggestion that the Insurance Office should enter the mortgage field,[72] and also examined the rent control measures being drafted by the attorney general.[73] And the EAPB made its own program proposals to cabinet – ranging from a tree planting program to a program to assist in providing sewer and water facilities in rural Saskatchewan, the development of a repertory theatre, and even the inauguration of a school camp program.[74]

Machinery of Government with an Emphasis on Budgeting

Cadbury and the Planning Board turned their attention very early to the machinery of government too. In September 1946, the board noted that

this Government inherited a certain type of administrative machine ... its main function ... was administration, with a bias toward regulation and restraint of abuses. Good administration is still needed but the emphasis should be on executive rather than merely regulative action ... A complete review of the whole framework on which various departments have been built may reveal that they are not suited to our purposes, and should be pruned, eliminated or expanded with our new concept in mind.[75]

A year later, the board was more emphatic; it argued that administrative inefficiency and overlaps were 'glaringly evident' and that sharp cuts should be made in administrative expenses. It made several specific suggestions, including the consolidation of research activities in the EAPB, consolidating industrial services, and coordinating scientific and technical research and educational services.[76] By 1948 the board was advocating even more substantial changes. It recommended that the premier give up the health portfolio, that ministers should withdraw from the routine duties they had assumed, that there should be a cabinet secretariat, that cabinet should meet more frequently, that the EAPB should be reduced in size and meet more frequently, and that Treasury should be recognized as the senior department of government, with greater responsibility for administration.[77] As for departmental organization, the EAPB advocated a variety of changes, including a review of the organization of departmental field staffs,[78] a study of the organization of government services in the North,[79] and a study of provincial parks organization.[80]

Of these suggestions, the one most quickly implemented was the creation of a Budget Bureau, fathered by Tommy McLeod. In September 1946, the cabinet agreed to extend the activities of the EAPB to include coordinating the budgeting practices of the departments, preparing the budget, and advising on the administrative techniques of all government agencies.[81] The Budget Bureau was formed in November 1946. It was modelled after the United States Bureau of the Budget, and was responsible for the budgeting function and for studies of government's administrative machinery. Cadbury recognized that budget analysis and budget control were key techniques of policy formulation and of cabinet control over policy:

Fundamentally [the budget] goes beyond [being a passive instrument of administrative control] and becomes an instrument of positive economic control. As such, it becomes an instrument not only of fiscal planning, but of economic planning due to the important position it holds in the economy of the province. As such, it is most important that the functions of this agency should be considered in close conjunction with the work of the government's economic planning agencies.[82]

The Cadbury perspective saw budget analysis as not simply being a matter of determining the resources needed to implement a given program, but also of being the process of determining how resources utilization could be optimized by the use of efficient administrative organization and methods, and by the most effective combination of programs.[83] This implied to the board the establishment of an agency that would prepare a budget capable of being analysed in this fashion, and that would include personnel skilled in administrative and budget analysis and perhaps program analysis. The new agency was staffed with this vision in mind. Early recruits included such political economists as Paul Byers, an 'import' from the United States, and, from Saskatchewan, Marjorie Allen (Haney), Jack Rowsom, and me.

The new Budget Bureau's first act was to introduce an entirely new system of budget preparation and control. Each department was required to submit for each activity or program within its responsibility a three-part document: a 'work program,' which outlined the objectives of the activity and the effectiveness with which the objectives were being achieved; a statement of the organization and administrative approach being employed by the agency; and an estimate of the resources required in the forthcoming year, classified on a uniform basis. The bureau used these documents as a basis for preparing a comprehensive budget document, capable of the analysis Cadbury and the EAPB had in mind, and as a basis, too, for an 'economy-minded' scrutiny of the resources requested by the departments.

The budget was then submitted to the Treasury Board for critical review. The Treasury Board was a ministerial committee chaired by the provincial treasurer, Clarence Fines, and including the premier and the attorney general, Jack Corman, with the deputy provincial treasurer as secretary. The minister of education, Woodrow Lloyd, later replaced Jack Corman. The Treasury Board was expected to examine the budget with four things in mind. The members must consider the aggregate fiscal policy of the government (that is, the balance among tax, expenditure, and borrowing policies); the program emphasis implicit in the budget proposals, with particular reference to the new programs or program expansions proposed; the administrative machinery being used; and the resources required for each program. During 1947 and 1948, the Treasury Board tended to emphasize the first and last functions, with the Planning Board and the whole cabinet exercising the second and third functions. But within two or three years, the Treasury Board became active in evaluating administrative machinery and over time became the most active cabinet committee in evaluating government's overall program emphasis and the aggregate of its policies.

From the beginning, the Treasury Board adopted the practice of holding annual budget hearings with each minister and his senior staff, to discuss the allocation of resources to each department and the policy and administrative questions that emerged from the budget analysis. After its budget meetings were completed, usually in early January, the board submitted its budgetary recommendations to the cabinet, which made the final decisions. The Treasury Board also adopted a budget control system, designed to ensure adherence to the budgetary plan.

Here was machinery that the government could use to assert cabinet control over departmental activities to an extent that had not been possible during the first two years of the CCF government. Moreover, this new machinery enabled the premier and the provincial treasurer to ensure that the 'cabinet view' prevailed over 'departmental views' whenever the two diverged. Clearly, any minister who was enthusiastic and ambitious for his program would seek to expand his area of government faster than others; it was for the cabinet to impose limits upon the total extent of government activity, and upon the extent of activity in individual departments. Without adequate budgetary machinery, the premier and the treasurer were almost helpless.

But there were organizational difficulties with respect to the Budget Bureau itself. From the beginning, its location as a branch of the EAPB created friction. The Treasury Department had been stripped of its traditional responsibility for developing the budget and relegated to a secondary role. Investment and debt management and tax collection, the remaining Treasury responsibilities, were essentially auxiliary functions; the department's policy role rested with its budgetary responsibility.

At first, the provincial treasurer himself seemed willing to accept the merger of the planning and budgeting functions outside of his department (perhaps because he was a member of the Planning Board). But over time, both he and the board looked upon the Budget Bureau as the treasurer's advisors. As early as December 1946, the bureau was instructed to report to the provincial treasurer in respect of its budget control responsibilities.[84] By March 1947, this perspective was formalized, when the EAPB decided the bureau should advise the provincial treasurer 'in all matters relating to ... the budget.'[85] In October an extended discussion about the control of the Budget Bureau took place, and it was agreed that Clarence Fines would study the possibility of transferring the bureau from the 'technical control' of the Planning Board to the Treasury Department. In January 1948, the responsibility for the Budget Bureau was transferred to the provincial treasurer, and there the matter rested until 1950, when the director of the Budget Bureau, Tommy McLeod, became the deputy provincial treasurer and the bureau became a branch of the Treasury Department itself.

Well before these changes, the Budget Bureau had turned its mind to its responsibilities for administrative management. As a personal note, the establishment of the Budget Bureau marked my own move from the Department of Education to this newly established agency (1946). At first I worked in the Administrative Management Division, and in 1948 was appointed its director. The division was intended to advise on the most effective organization of government departments, on the effective division of functions for administrative planning, and on administrative procedures, work scheduling, space allocation and layout, and office machinery. Its mandate, in short, was to 'assure that every dollar spent is, from the administrative point of view, spent with the greatest effect.'[86] The Planning Board's emphasis was on organization and on administrative or management methods. Only by implication was the Budget Bureau to concern itself with the machinery of government in its broadest sense – for example, cabinet organization, the use of boards and commissions, the development of advisory bodies, and so on.

During 1947 and 1948 the Budget Bureau undertook several major studies. The first was the question of organization of government programs in the North, undertaken at the request of a cabinet committee struck to examine this problem. The second was to assist in organizing the Hospital Services Plan (I was assigned to the Hospital Services Plan when it was being set up, in late 1946), which commenced its operations on 1 January 1947. And the third was a study of the government's accounting system, particularly as it related to the new budget procedures. Subsequently, the Administrative Management Division undertook studies of the Department of Reconstruction and Rehabilitation and the organization of health administration, including the Department of Health and the Health Services Planning Commission.[87] In 1948 it assisted the reconstructed Public Service Commission to develop recruitment and classification procedures and personnel regulations.

At this stage, too, the Budget Bureau influenced specific aspects of government organization. After a few years – from 1948 to 1950 – the changes in departmental structure brought about by the Budget Bureau's organization studies began to have a more general bearing on policy formulation and began to set a pattern for departmental organization throughout the public service.

Other important changes during 1946 to 1948 were emerging from the departments themselves. For example, the Health Services Planning Commission assumed responsibility for administering the Hospital Services Plan and the Medical Services Division of the Department of Health, and the Department of Social Welfare reorganized pensions administration. After a major row between the deputy minister and minister of natural resources, and the resignation of the deputy, there was a shake-up in that department too. But the Budget Bureau was the agency that embarked upon a systematic review of departmental organization and became the government's principal advisor on administrative and management methods.

Public Service Reform

One other major reform in the public service, apart from the creation of planning and budgeting machinery and the reform of governance of Crown corporations, occurred during the last two years of the CCF government's first term in office. This was the enactment of a new Public Service Act,[88] which had significant bearing on public administration in the province after it became operational in 1948.

The process of developing this reform had involved engaging a consulting firm, Public Administration Service of Chicago, to establish a classification and pay plan for the civil service and to recommend a new public service act. The government's aim was to introduce a merit system for the recruitment and promotion of personnel, to give 'a factual picture of the duties, responsibilities, etc. of each position ... [which] will provide the basis for scientific negotiation of wage rates ... a better basis for recruitment ... [and] for promotion on the basis of merit.'[89] When this preparatory work had been completed, the new Public Service Act was drafted and submitted to the Legislative Assembly in 1947.[90]

The new Act abruptly removed from departments and from ministers the freedom they had enjoyed to choose and select their own personnel. The Public Service Commission became responsible for 'merit examinations,' and for the 'certification' to departments of qualified personnel for nearly all positions, including promotions. Only deputy ministers and a limited number of other senior and central agency positions in government were exempted from this procedure (including the EAPB and the Budget Bureau positions, given their policy roles). In common with other governments in Canada, these postings were filled by Order in Council appointment.[91] Civil service reform had long been a plank in the CCF platform, and it was brought into effect with remarkable ease. One contemporary observer described the reform this way: 'In Saskatchewan ... probably the most dominant of these forces [in the elimination of patronage] has been the CCF Government which, out of deference to either principle, efficiency, or regard for the employee, had determinedly fulfilled its pre-election pledge of civil service reform.'[92]

This reform was, however, one cause of rumblings within the party about senior personnel being unsympathetic to the government and about the 'sabotage' of the party's program. The 1947 CCF convention resolved that

> whereas the Saskatchewan Government has given all its civil servants, regardless of political affiliation, every consideration, and has engaged new personnel without consideration of their political affiliations, which confirms the original CCF policy; and whereas there is good reason to believe that some of our civil servants have been sabotaging the government ... be it resolved that a thorough investigation ... be made of such instances of disloyalty and appropriate action taken.[93]

Most of the party's concern was with the alleged failure of the government to appoint people to senior posts who were sympathetic to the objectives of the government. Other observers, notably the opposition, argued that in too many cases government had appointed its supporters and that the government was not sincere in its civil service reform. In point of fact, the ministers who selected their deputy ministers and the cabinet that formally appointed them, while understandably seeking people who were sympathetic to the government's policies and programs, attracted some very able people. This can be seen in the influence these public servants came to exercise not only in Saskatchewan, but also, later, in the federal and other provincial public services.

The argument about Order in Council appointments occasionally took a humorous turn, too. This may be seen in one of Douglas's responses to a resolution, seemingly introduced annually at the CCF conventions in the government's early years, and demanding that all incumbent deputy ministers and all new ones should be CCFers. Impatient after a number of irascible interventions from the floor, Douglas ended his response by saying: 'And besides, it is easier to make a CCFer out of an engineer than it is to make an engineer out of a CCFer.'

Two other changes in the public service raised more political conflict than the introduction of the merit system. They were the unionization of the civil service and the granting of political freedom to all civil servants. The 1944 Trade Union Act had outlawed 'company unions,' and not long thereafter the Saskatchewan Civil Service Association, which represented most of the province's civil servants, declared its independence by becoming affiliated with the Trades and Labour Congress of Canada. This was one cause for concern: it might encourage militant trade unionism in the public service, including the use of the strike weapon. The greater political protest ensued when the new Public Service Act granted all public servants complete political freedom, including the authorization of thirty days' leave of absence to any civil servant who wished to seek election to public office.

The government seems to have been sincere in this reform. Certainly it gained no political advantage from its efforts: even the civil servants opposed the change.[94] The ministers, however, defended their position. One minister wrote to the provincial office of the CCF: 'I do not think we want to take away from civil servants their right to support any political party of their choice.'[95] The *Regina Leader Post* reported: 'Provincial Treasurer, C. M. Fines, said that while giving this right to civil servants might seem revolutionary, it was the Government's purpose to insure that this class of people had the same rights politically as others ... "Even if a deputy minister wanted to run against his own minister, under the act he would be entitled to do so."'[96]

Certainly this provision was not used with any great frequency. But it was part of the civil service reform to which the CCF was committed, and the civil service adjusted itself to its newfound freedom by exercising its rights with discretion.

Social Policy and the New Machinery of Government

Meanwhile, in the field of social policy, the government continued to introduce new health programs at a fairly brisk pace. The developments in this period included the implementation in 1946 of a medical care insurance scheme for the fifty thousand residents of the province's first health region, which was a further instalment on the CCF's commit-ment to a public medical care program. In February 1946, an air ambu-lance service was established to transport patients from rural areas to regional and central hospitals. The new health regions expanded as well: two were formed each year during 1945, 1946, and 1947. Mental hospitals were transferred to the Department of Public Health, and their staff began to work eight-hour rather than twelve-hour shifts. Four mental health clinics for treatment of 'out patients' were established during 1947–8 as part of the expansion of public health services.

Most significantly, on 1 January 1947, Saskatchewan introduced the country's first universal and compulsory hospital insurance program, accompanied by the rapid expansion of hospital facilities, with twenty-one new hospitals established over four years and the formation of forty-one union hospital districts.[97]

The Health Services Planning Commission or the Department of Public Health developed all of these programs. In particular, it was the Chair of the Health Services Planning Commission, Dr Fred Mott, and his deputy, Dr Len Rosenfeld, who developed the Saskatchewan Hospi-tal Services Plan (SHSP). Dr Sigerist had recommended Dr Mott to Douglas 'as the ablest man on the continent to implement the plan.' Douglas has said: 'His father was John R. Mott of the YMCA and a Nobel Prize Winner.' A winner in social gospel circles! Len Rosenfeld was a senior colleague of Mott's, and when the two left Saskatchewan they went to work for Walter Reuther and the United Automobile Worker's health scheme.[98]

The Hospital Services Plan was the first in North America to provide complete hospital benefits to all residents of the province. It included public ward care, X-ray and laboratory services, common drugs, and other hospital services. It also provided for the payment of a flat per diem amount toward the cost of out-of-province hospitalization for any Saskatchewan resident. The eligibility requirement for hospital services was that each person or family head must pay an annual insurance pre-mium; in 1947 it was $5 per person, to a family maximum of $30.[99] At the end of the year, each family received a receipt that, under Canadian tax laws, could be used to claim income tax deductions. The insurance fees collected covered nearly 50 per cent of the costs of the hospital plan, with the remainder of the costs being covered by general taxation. Over the years, the percentage of the costs financed from the per capita tax declined, and by 1958, when the federal government committed itself to cover 50 per cent of the costs of hospitalization under a national insurance scheme, only 39 per cent of the total cost of hospitalization was being financed by the insurance premium or per capita tax.

Once the administrative difficulties had been overcome, the plan operated very simply. The hospitals in the province admitted patients and simply recorded their hospitalization card number. The hospitals then billed the Saskatchewan Hospital Services Plan for the costs of public ward facilities. The hospitals and officials of the plan negotiated the cost per patient day annually, and the hospital administration specialists worked with hospitals to try to keep the costs under control.

To control the volume of care, the SHSP, in consultation with the Saskatchewan Hospital Association, ultimately developed a master plan for hospital facilities, establishing the number and location of hospital beds required to serve designated areas. It also established, in later years, a maximum occupancy rate of 80 per cent, beyond which the hospitals would not be paid on the per-patient day basis; this was intended to eliminate any incentive to overcrowd the hospitals.

In an important sense, the prime influences in developing these programs were the CCF's *Program* of 1944 and the recommendations of Dr Sigerist. But in another sense, Drs Mott and Rosenfeld, and Drs Cecil and Mindel Sheps before them and with them, brought the dynamism and professionalism that were so necessary to implement the hospital plan. They negotiated with the province's hospitals to obtain their co-operative participation,[100] and they wrestled with the many administrative problems for which there were no precedents in North America. The establishment of the Saskatchewan Hospital Services Plan ranks as one of the 'banner' firsts of the Douglas government, along with the establishment of school units and the introduction of compulsory automobile insurance and the Bill of Rights – all during the first term of the CCF government.

The Health Services Planning Commission was active in other aspects of health programming as well. It assisted in establishing the Swift Current Health Region, which of its own volition had decided to obtain provincial assistance to introduce a tax-supported medical care plan. The commission was directly engaged in the establishment of health regions. These new local government units, formed under the Health Services Act, provided a complete range of public health services. They were financed partly by local taxes and partly by provincial grants, and used staff assigned to them by the Department of Public Health. Finally, the Health Services Planning Commission continued its research function – on medical programs, health data, personnel requirements, and hospital facilities.[101] It became involved in negotiations for grants to the municipal doctor plans through which municipalities employed physicians directly. These plans required direct negotiation between the local governments and the medical society concerning the doctors' fee schedule. The commission necessarily became involved, especially when the Association of Rural Municipalities wrote to the premier in 1947 to urge a coordinated approach to their negotiations.[102]

The Department of Public Health led the reform of the province's mental health program, under the newly appointed director of psychiatric services, Dr S. (Grif) McKerracher, who had come to Saskatchewan from Toronto. The government had decided, in 1944, to make treatment and care of the mentally ill a free service, and Dr McKerracher developed the program. It ranged from mental health clinics in the health regions through to the conversion of mental hospitals from custodial institutions to treatment centres.

The driving influence in all of the health programs was, of course, the minister of public health, Premier Douglas. The Planning Board warned that expenditures on health should be contained, and that more emphasis should be placed upon preventive rather than curative services, and the cabinet 'registered' this point of view.[103] But the government's commitment to public medical and hospital care measures and the vigour of the premier and his advisors were too great to contemplate any substantial curtailment until the major innovations had been introduced.

In this period, the Department of Education was largely preoccupied with the new, larger school units. But it also found time to implement new teachers' salary schedules, a new high school curriculum, a reorganized superintendence service, and a new system of school grants. The larger grants to school units increased the department's budget markedly, and the minister found himself in disagreement with the Planning Board's recommendations concerning 'the appropriate allocation' of the budget to education. 'While agreeing with the principle behind the ... percentages,' he said, 'the percentages themselves are rather unreal as a basis for determining budget allocation. So far as my department is concerned, I can find no basis for the accepted percentages either in comparison with other provinces or as a measure of absolute need.'[104]

Woodrow Lloyd also succeeded in introducing a plan for regional libraries and in preparing plans to establish an Arts Board, despite the EAPB's view in 1946 and 1947 that 'cultural amenities ... must occupy a lowly place in the general plan.'[105] The Library Advisory Council mounted the effort to produce the regional library plan, while the director of adult education recommended the Arts Board be created and be made responsible for stimulating art, drama, and music in Saskatchewan.

Similarly, as I mentioned earlier, departmental efforts in the labour field produced the new labour standards legislation that was introduced in this period, including a forty-four-hour week, an act stipulating a two-week vacation with pay, and broader workmen's compensation benefits. The CCF Council endorsed the department's proposal for a forty-four-hour week,[106] undoubtedly aided by representations from the Saskatchewan Federation of Labour.[107]

The party had some influence, too, in the question of the pensions being paid by the Department of Social Welfare. In 1947 government raised the old age pension to $30 per month, but at the same time discontinued a provincial supplement to the federal-provincial pension plan.[108] This decision had been taken in the belief that the province could not afford to expand its social welfare commitments too much.[109] A storm of protest ensued. For example, the *Regina Leader Post* reported: 'Confirmation that the CCF Government has been severely taken to task by members of its own Party for withdrawing its supplementary old age pension payment ... came during a debate on a Liberal amendment in the House this week ... [Jake Benson] spoke his mind when he declared "I think the Government made ... a stupid mistake ..."'[110] Public, party, and legislative pressure combined, and in April 1948 the pension was raised to $35.

Finally, the attorney general, Jack Corman, produced Canada's first Bill of Rights, which guaranteed freedom of religion, speech, assembly, and elections, and made discrimination on racial and religious grounds illegal. The attorney general was known for his great wit, and his wry humour came to the government's rescue many times. On the introduction of this Bill, he wrote to the premier and Mr Lloyd to tell them:

> It would be appreciated if you would come to my rescue during the debate. Mr. Lloyd's ... excellent address [a recent radio talk] ... would ... rebut [the opposition's] suggestions that we are depriving people of their sacred liberties. If that is looked after perhaps the Premier would be good enough to answer ... the claim that free enterprise is a freedom that should be protected.[111]

These examples illustrate the nature of the new forces at work through the new machinery of government. A strong central planning agency and a new approach to planning and budgeting began to influence the overall formation of policy, and the operating departments began to reorganize and to assume their responsibilities with greater capacity. This process of adjustment, which began during 1946, continued through the next five or six years.

The other major adjustment that was occurring during 1946 through 1948 concerned party-government relations. This has been illustrated in the debate on oil policy, in the matter of social pensions, and in the establishment of a fund to make government loans to private industry. These are apt illustrations of one of the well-known challenges of governing – the necessity of finding viable policies to achieve the goals of the government, while at the same time reconciling conflicting views of strong influence. The cabinet had concluded that economic development necessarily implied a mixed economy. This was no departure for the premier, who had long advocated a mixed economy. Nor did the new policy cause any distress among the agrarian pragmatists, who constituted the majority of the CCF. But for those who interpreted the Regina Manifesto literally, in particular the last paragraph (which said that 'no CCF Government will rest content until it has eradicated capitalism and put into operation the full program of socialized planning which will lead to the establishment in Canada of the Cooperative Commonwealth'),[112] the new policy was a departure from first principles. Cabinet had to establish some kind of equilibrium among these views, lest the frictions of change were to remove the CCF from office altogether. The election results of 1948 reinforced this imperative.

6

Forging a New Equilibrium in Governance: 1948–1952

The first real test of the CCF government came when the electorate went to the polls on 24 June 1948 to express their satisfaction or dissatisfaction with CCF policies. The results startled both the party and the government. The voters, with a turnout of 83 per cent of the electorate, returned the government to power, but with thirty-one seats instead of forty-seven. Moreover, two members of the cabinet had been defeated, Oak Valleau and the controversial minister of natural resources, Joe Phelps. The Liberal opposition won twenty seats, and one Liberal-Progressive Conservative coalition candidate was elected. He was A.H. (Hammy) McDonald, later to become the leader of the Liberal Party. The CCF's popular vote declined from 53.1 per cent to 47.5 per cent. The only consolation was that the popular vote of the Liberal Party also declined, with the Progressive Conservatives, Social Credit, and Liberal–Progressive Conservatives picking up the balance.

These results lent new emphasis to what the premier and some of the cabinet ministers had already sensed: that change, and the turbulence which is the product of change, had to give way to some measure of stability if the CCF government was to remain in power. As Professor Harry Cassidy, dean of the School of Social Work at the University of Toronto, put it to Tommy Douglas after the election: '... the miracle is not that you lost some seats, but that ... [given] the extensive reforms you've introduced in the last four years ... you were elected at all.'[1] One minister commented: 'We have to realize that we can't do everything at once.' Some policy changes were called for as well: it was time to sacrifice the less popular policies, notably industrial development through public ownership. Other policies, which had cost some votes but which were fundamental to the CCF's program, for example the school units, would have to be allowed to develop more gradually.

The premier's first task was to reorganize the cabinet. He moved Brock Brockelbank from municipal affairs to the key natural resources portfolio. Jack Sturdy became minister of social welfare, into which the reconstruction portfolio was merged. Laughie McIntosh took the municipal affairs portfolio along with the co-operatives post. Jim Darling, a new appointment to cabinet, became minister of public works, and minister responsible for Saskatchewan Government Telephones. Charlie Williams dropped the responsibility for Telephones, but remained minister of labour, and Jack Douglas dropped the public works portfolio but remained minister of highways. A year later, when former CCF member of Parliament Tom Bentley was elected in a by-election to the provincial legislature, the premier relinquished the public health portfolio and gave it to Mr Bentley.

The premier's next task was to consolidate the policy gains of the first term in office and adjust these as necessary to achieve a more balanced policy, and greater stability. In fact, some of these adjustments had begun in 1947 and 1948, but they had not yet come to be recognized as part of the fabric of the CCF program.

A great many changes and adjustments were in train. The CCF's ideology concerning social ownership was undergoing a transformation. The government's policy of emphasizing social security, health, and education programs, so often the focus of Cadbury's criticism, was to be shifted, and the emphasis placed instead on economic development. Within the government, a new balance was to emerge between the two ever conflicting principles of cabinet government – individual ministerial responsibility and collective cabinet responsibility. As a corollary of this shift, operating departments were to achieve a new and more important status vis-à-vis central agencies such as the Planning Board. Changes were being made in their organization and personnel, and their planning methods were improving. A rationalization of the respective roles of planning and budgeting would also emerge – an adjustment made necessary by the recent restoration of the budgeting function to the provincial treasurer.

The transformation in government's external relationships continued as well. Party-government relations became more firmly and evenly established, partly as a result of more systematic consultation and partly because of the growing prestige of the premier and his cabinet. At the same time, the government became more responsive to influences other than the party and the 1944 *Program* that so dominated the first term of office. Interest groups, advisory bodies, and the opposition in the legislature were increasingly able to gain the ear of the government. With these adjustments, a new stability began to emerge.

Ideology and Policy in the Second Term

The major and early changes in ideology and public policy during the 1948–52 term of office centred on the clarification and rationalization of the place of social ownership in public policy, and on the shift in the priority to be accorded to economic development in the future. Both of these policy decisions were manifestly cabinet decisions, led by the premier, with central agency (EAPB) advice and, in respect of natural resources development, in association with the new minister of natural resources.

The shift in ideology had been in the course of fermentation and transformation well before the June 1948 election, but it had not been articulated and pronounced – nor would it have been accepted in some party circles if it had been. It remained for the premier and cabinet to enunciate their approach and to gain party support for this position.

The premier required no mental gymnastics; the government's position closely resembled the point of view he had held in 1944, when he said: 'The CCF does not want the Government to own everything ... [But] there are certain features of our economic life which by their very nature should be owned and operated by the people. [He mentioned public utilities, monopolies which in his opinion were abusing their powers, resource development, and banking.] ... This leaves a wide field for private ownership and private enterprise.'[2] In 1949 he said: 'I want to say, contrary to the statements of my honourable friends [the opposition], that private enterprise has not left this province except where they have demanded special privileges ... We think that private capital can play an important part in our industrial development ... at the same time we recognize that the Government has the responsibility of seeing to it that no group of individuals, because of its economic power, can exploit the community as a whole.'[3] This was still a fairly elastic position. Indeed, in practice, the Planning Board felt it necessary to retain a committee to discuss 'the respective spheres of private, co-operative, and public enterprise.'[4] But for all practical purposes the government had decided not to expand its industrial or resource development enterprises; rather, to leave these domains for private and co-operative capital. Utilities, on the other hand, would be developed publicly.

The government was not alone in wanting to clarify its social ownership policy. Many party members, indeed even some of the ministers, had from the beginning accepted social ownership really on pragmatic grounds, and when the practical reasons for establishing new Crown corporations did not materialize they were quick to reject further experimentation with them. The 1948 election results buttressed their position and demonstrated, they thought conclusively, the impatience of the people of Saskatchewan with social experiments of this kind.

Beyond the political and policy reasons for making this shift, very practical considerations drove the necessary clarification. It seemed obvious that if the uncertainty over the role of private enterprise in Saskatchewan were prolonged, private capital would not be attracted to the province. In addition, an uncertain social ownership policy increased both the difficulties and the challenge of borrowing capital to finance the utilities – which the government was determined to develop under public ownership.[5]

In addition to these difficulties, the government faced real embarrassment in having to admit that some of its experiments had not succeeded. Certainly the overall picture was good: net return on the equity capital invested in the 'new' corporations, excluding the power and telephone corporations, reached 6.4 per cent in 1949.[6] But in the premier's words, there remained three 'problem children' – the fish board, the shoe factory, and the woollen mill – and four industries that had yet to prove themselves. These were the bus company, the northern airline, the brick plant, and the sodium sulphate plant.[7] He went on to tell the legislature: 'We are not afraid of experiments, and we are not going to be afraid to tell frankly what the results of our experiments have been.'[8] This openness signalled the end of experimentation with Crown enterprises, except for the utilities and, in a minor way, in resources development.[9]

Policy Emphasis in the Second Term: Industrial Development

The shift in the government's policy priorities was more explicit and more definite. Both before and after the election, Tommy Douglas had announced the new policy emphasis in these words: 'We have now gone as far as we can go in terms of social security until we put a better economic base under [it].'[10] The objective, he said, was to 'lay the foundation work by which our gross provincial income would be increased, our productive capacity augmented, and the standard of living of our people raised ...'[11] He gave this as the rationale for relinquishing the health portfolio in favour of the lighter co-operatives portfolio, which would enable him to devote more time to the 'vital problems of industrial and business expansion.'[12]

This change in priorities was a triumph for the policy perspective of Clarence Fines and George Cadbury, though how real the shift turned out to be in terms of expenditure allocation is questionable. Certainly there was an absolute increase in expenditures on economic development, which rose from $13 million during 1947–8 to $17.5 million during 1951–2. But the expenditures on health, welfare, and education rose too, and by 1951–2 expenditures on economic development were a slightly smaller percentage of the budget than they had been during 1947–8 (25.7 per cent compared with 26.5 per cent).[13] At the same time, investment in the Saskatchewan Power Corporation and the Saskatchewan Government Telephones went up sharply.[14] Much more important than the expenditure numbers, however, was the *way* in which policy shifted, namely toward the positive promotion of industrial and resource development – occasionally through public expenditures, sometimes through royalty and rental concessions in respect of Crown-owned resources, and later through the public guarantee of private debt.

The government expressed its new policy most clearly when, in 1950, it established an Industrial Development Office (IDO). Until then, responsibility for industrial promotion had been divided between the Government Finance Office, which administered the Industrial Development Fund, the Department of Natural Resources, and the Department of Co-operation. This latter department, in fact, had begun to play a role in working with private industry (paradoxical as it may seem), even to the point of establishing a consultative committee of business and trade people.[15] At about the same time, the EAPB was recommending 'that all promotional work including that now being undertaken by the Trade Services Division of the Department of Co-operation ... should be placed under the Government Finance Office'[16] and that a Planning Board committee should review all industrial development projects before any final commitments were made.[17]

It was not difficult to remedy these multiple jurisdictions, however, for the new Industrial Development Office was made responsible to the premier, who by now was minister of co-operation. The Department of Natural Resources was relieved of its industrial development responsibilities.

The first director of the IDO was Don Black, formerly with Dominion

Bridge in Montreal, and now one of the key officials in the Government Finance Office.[18] He approached the new job with energy. He pressed for more active use of the Industrial Development Fund, urged the publication of an economic and business bulletin, and travelled through Canada and the United States to stimulate greater interest in Saskatchewan's industrial potential. He also supported the efforts of the Department of Natural Resources to gain funds to stimulate the oil and mining industries.[19] Thought was even given to establishing an Industrial Development Corporation, a joint government-business undertaking, but the idea was shelved.[20] With this activity, the IDO's influence soon became manifest. The number of applications for loans from the Industrial Development Fund increased. And both the government's purchasing agency and the co-operatives paid greater attention to the possibility of buying Saskatchewan products.[21] Executives of major Canadian enterprises began to visit the premier, partly as a result of Black's overtures to them.

There remained some uncertainty as to the sectors of the economy that the IDO should emphasize: whether the resource-based industries or the market-oriented industries were most promising. But whatever the uncertainty, the existence of an IDO provided a focus of energy and a symbol of policy that had previously been lacking.

New Policy Emphasis: Resources Development

Meanwhile, the Department of Natural Resources, under its new minister, Brock Brockelbank, a solid and balanced minister – a change from his predecessor – was aggressively stimulating resource development. To this end, the premier had announced:

> The Government is desirous of encouraging mineral and petroleum exploration development and production to the greatest extent possible, and to that end has embarked upon a program designed to lend technical assistance and advice to bona fide persons and organizations able and willing to proceed with this work.
>
> In addition it gives a firm undertaking that no steps will be taken to expropriate or socialize the mining or petroleum industry in the Province. At the same time, the Government will take all necessary steps to protect the public interest ... and royalties will be fixed guaranteeing to ... the Province a fair return from the mineral wealth produced.[22]

This announcement of government policy coincided with an investment boom that started in the late 1940s. By the end of 1948, exploration permits had been granted on three million acres of Crown-owned mineral rights and there were applications for a further five million acres.[23] In July 1949 the first really major oil company entered into an agreement with the provincial government, and more were negotiating with the minister.

During this time, too, the Department of Natural Resources revised the petroleum regulations, but only after consultation with the industry,[24] and revised them again in late 1950 to introduce a new Crown reserve pattern more acceptable to the industry. By 1951 oil development had begun in earnest, and exploration expenditures reached $25 million a year. The first major oil strike came in January 1952, and from then on Saskatchewan became an important centre of oil production. After extensive consultation with the industry, the government developed a new Oil and Gas Conservation Act 'to regulate all operations for the production of oil and natural gas.' The *Regina Leader Post* reported: 'The original draft of the regulations [under the Act] were submitted by the Department of Natural Resources to the Saskatchewan Committee of the Western Canada Petroleum Association for suggestions. The W.C.P.A. called in one of the continent's leading conservation experts ... for advice, and the act is understood to be the result of extensive study and talks between [him], the government and the W.C.P.A.'[25]

Other mineral developments followed a somewhat similar if less spectacular course. The department encouraged mining by making available large prospecting blocks, to attract larger companies,[26] and by assisting and training prospectors.[27] The government itself fielded six geological survey parties in 1948. The minister with his colleagues in the four western provinces pressed the federal minister of mines and resources for assistance in building mining roads – which came later to be called 'roads to resources.' By 1951 more than two thousand claims had been staked, and the discovery of rich deposits of uranium on Lake Athabasca sparked a 'second boom' after oil.[28] By the end of 1951, the Atomic Energy Control Board, which regulated the mining of radioactive ores, had issued forty-one development permits, and milling was expected to begin in the next year.[29]

Potash developments also began to show promise. In 1950 the rich potash beds of eastern and central Saskatchewan had been discovered, and the long struggle to develop them started. (Potash production would not begin until 1962.) The cabinet had already agreed to private development of this resource and in March 1950 approved the terms of the leases to be offered to private companies. They were very generous 'in view of the fact that the operation would be extremely hazardous' – as indeed it turned out to be.[30] The department submitted new potash regulations to cabinet that year, and it was agreed that the regulations should also be submitted to 'interested potash parties' for their comments.[31]

Another area for active debate was the government's policy concerning the transmission and distribution of natural gas. In mid-1950, the general outlines of the policy were settled upon by the EAPB: 'The official policy of the Government is to encourage the development of natural gas reserves within the Province by private capital, and to see the establishment of an equitable integrated system for the Province-wide transmission and distribution of natural gas, preferably under provincial ownership and in conjunction with the municipalities.'[32]

But three things needed to be clarified: the economics of transmission and distribution; the kind of financial obligations involved if the Saskatchewan Power Corporation were to become responsible for this phase of the gas industry; and the level of well-head prices necessary to encourage private exploration for natural gas. The Department of Natural Resources reported in 1951 that the problem was not one of speeding up the search for natural gas by providing drilling incentives, but rather one of guaranteeing markets for gas once it had been discovered. In short, the problem was not an issue simply for the department, but one for the government: should the Saskatchewan Power Corporation be given the power to proceed as the province's natural gas utility?[33]

The premier responded that he 'would not, without good reason, abandon this policy [public ownership of the gas utility], but was anxious to have the recommendation of the EAPB's (Natural) Gas Committee on the question of municipal operation of the distribution system.'[34] The committee favoured complete provincial ownership, but the cabinet was not yet willing to make a decision on the question. At this point there still had been no public statement of government policy, seemingly because some 'delicate negotiations' were in progress.[35]

Meanwhile, the Gas Committee proceeded to examine the economics of transmitting and distributing natural gas, and included this question within David Cass-Beggs's mandate for the development plan for the Saskatchewan Power Corporation.[36] Cass-Beggs recommended, among other things, that the province, and not the municipalities, should distribute natural gas, and that gas prices should be equalized for different classes of customer across the province.[37] By 1952 it seemed clear that the government would proceed with gas transmission by a provincial utility, but a decision concerning municipal distribution had not yet been taken.

It is not possible to assess the relative influence of government policy in the launching of all of these economic developments. Buoyant economic conditions and a rich resource endowment combined to make mineral exploration in Saskatchewan inevitable. The government's policies probably served largely as a catalyst to stimulate this activity. In areas where the potential was less promising, such as in the forestry industry, the efforts to attract investment were less successful. But the shift in policy had clearly been made and was being implemented.

New Policies and New Frictions

These measures to attract private industry to the resource field received their share of criticism, however. By the time the government's position on industrial development had crystallized, the cabinet not only had incurred the wrath of one wing of the party, but it had also spurred the opposition into action. The leader of the opposition, Walter Tucker, who had succeeded Billy Patterson in 1948, charged that the government was offering businesses terms that were too generous and, worse, that there was corruption in the granting of certain leases. The minister of natural resources replied by showing how much more generous the previous Liberal government had been in its treatment of the Imperial Oil Company, and arguing that the CCF government was protecting the people's interest in the wealth produced.[38]

The opposition also charged that a former cabinet advisor, Morris Shumiatcher, had obtained a lease on mineral rights while he was still employed by the government. Walter Tucker wondered: 'To what extent are these civil servants and former civil servants using information which prospectors in the North are forced to give the Government?' Brockelbank replied that mining companies were not required to file information (any they provided was given voluntarily) and that Dr Shumiatcher had left the civil service when he got the lease (admittedly only six days before). An offer to form an investigative tribunal was rejected by the opposition. Mr Tucker said he would not trust any tribunal set up by the CCF.[39]

This story of political wrangling does nothing to advance an analysis of policy formulation in Saskatchewan, but it was characteristic of the eleventh legislature and illustrates the context within which these shifts in policy were being made

New Policy Initiatives: Agriculture

Returning to the new economic policy initiatives during 1948–52, the Department of Agriculture also developed new programs during this period. The minister himself tended to take the initiative, yet increasingly the department's new organization provided the deputy with program advice that had formerly been more difficult to obtain. The major initiative was the establishment in 1949 of a branch for conservation and development, intended 'to initiate a broad program of irrigation and water conservation in co-operation with the [federal] Prairie Farm Rehabilitation Administration.'[40] The branch launched projects in reclamation, re-grassing, water development, irrigation, and drainage, and became responsible for the feed and fodder production program.

The Department of Agriculture undertook, as well, the classification of all crown lands, so that they could be leased for appropriate purposes.[41] This initiative was contentious, for every farmer in Saskatchewan considered himself to be an expert on the allocation of land. The government's main objective was to create 'economic farm units,'[42] but there were conflicting criteria for this, including residence in the area concerned, agricultural experience, veterans' preference, and co-operative versus individual farms.[43] The CCF Party complained that leases were being given to people who did not need land, and that those with the least land were not getting leases.[44] The department encountered still other problems when it tried to increase the land available by clearing and breaking virgin land in the northern parklands.[45]

The premier himself sparked the most ambitious projects of all. These were the South Saskatchewan River development project[46] and the appointment of the Royal Commission on Agriculture and Rural Life. The South Saskatchewan project was Tommy Douglas's favourite; it seemed to symbolize to him the kind of development that would stabilize Saskatchewan's agricultural economy. Negotiations on the project began informally in 1947 and continued until 1958, when an agreement with the federal government was signed. It was a spectacular engineering project, but equally spectacular as a feat of political negotiations. Something of the story is related in chapter 8.

The Royal Commission on Agriculture and Rural Life also seems to have been the premier's personal idea. To him, the many studies conducted on farm credit, crop insurance, economic family farms, and other issues such as the services required by a rapidly shifting rural population were but parts of a single puzzle, and he wished to see them put together. He apparently discussed the idea first in 1951 with the deputy minister of co-operation, for the deputy wrote him with suggestions for the terms of reference.[47] The cabinet then asked the EAPB to draft terms of reference for a 'Royal Commission on Rural Reconstruction,'[48] a task which the new secretary of EAPB, Tommy Shoyama,[49] found difficult since 'we have not been able to read the mind of the Cabinet very clearly on this question.'[50] Nonetheless, the terms of reference were developed and the proposal discussed with the caucus. The idea seemed a popular one: the premier's files were full of letters recommending commissioners or staff members (including some from correspondents who recommended themselves), plus letters suggesting how the commission should set about its task. The 1952 election intervened, however, before the commission members were appointed.

Initiatives in the Social Policy Field

Policy formulation in the social policy area was likewise characterized by departmental initiatives. The changes advanced consisted mostly of extensions and refinements to existing programs – changes that were largely the product of advice from departmental specialists.

In the Department of Public Health, the psychiatric services and preventive health programs expanded most during this period. The number of mental health clinics increased steadily to twelve in 1952 (five full-time and seven part-time): each provided general diagnostic services and some treatment facilities. The staff in the three mental hospitals had improved enormously, and the hospitals were now qualified as a training site for residents in psychiatry. Functioning as the organizational umbrella for providing public health, sanitation, mental health, dental health, and other related services, the number of regional health units also gradually increased. In addition, the government introduced a new grant program for diagnostic facilities. In all of this activity, the new federal health grants – started during 1948–9 – played a part. In some cases, the grants paid for programs that the department would in any event have started, but in other cases the grants brought about an allocation of funds to the health function that would not otherwise have occurred.

While some health programs were expanding, efforts were being made to control the costs of others, most notably those of the Hospital Services Plan. Several factors contributed to the rising costs of hospitals, including rising price levels and the wages of the usually underpaid hospital staff. There was also an increasing number of hospital beds,[51] and some abuses of the plan through a rather more relaxed approach to hospitalization, given the supply of beds.

The federal government's funding for health services that started during 1948–9 included hospital construction grants, available for individual hospitals, up to a maximum of one-third of the costs of construction, with the province and hospital board contributing the balance. This had the effect of placing enormous political pressure on the government – to permit hospitals to be built even when the government thought they were wrongly located.

The policy alternatives for cost control really narrowed down to two options, a payment formula for hospitals that would eliminate any incentive for crowding, or a 'utilization' or deterrent fee.[52] The first was easily adopted, but the second would require a payment that might indeed inhibit lower income people from going to hospital when they should, and the government could not impose this policy. In 1948 the per capita tax – or health insurance premium – was raised to $10 per adult and $5 per dependent, per annum, though the family maximum remained $30. At the same time, the sales tax of 2 per cent, referred to as the education tax, was raised to 3 per cent and was renamed the education and hospitalization tax. Two-thirds of the revenue was devoted to education, and one-third to the hospital plan

It was similarly difficult to control the costs of social welfare, partly because the pressure for higher allowances was so great and partly because the Department of Welfare itself was a strong advocate for certain programs. In 1948 the government increased social aid payments by 15 per cent.[53] Then in 1951 the federal government assumed responsibility for universal old age pensions for people over age seventy, a development that relieved some of Saskatchewan's costs. At the same time, it introduced a pension plan for needy persons aged sixty-five to sixty-nine, providing the provinces met half of the cost of the plan. For Saskatchewan, this meant assuming the new costs (half of the cost of pensions for those between sixty-five to sixty-nine years of age) in addition to the payment of supplemental allowances and the continued provision of health services for people over seventy years of age.[54] The net result was to increase provincial costs. In January 1953, after debating the extension of full health services for the new group of pensioners, aged sixty-five to sixty-nine, the government decided to give them free hospital benefits only.[55] In 1952 it decided to raise mothers' allowances as well.[56]

Other aspects of social programs were also changing. As a result of a Budget Bureau organization study, the Department of Welfare created a unified field staff, and this in turn created pressure to improve the quality of welfare services. The Public Assistance Branch continued to search for methods to unify the various categories of public assistance (although it could scarcely act independently of the changes being made in the 'categorical' programs controlled by the federal government). The department persuaded the government to build a new boys' correctional home, and to approve two new nursing homes for the aged.[57]

In other departments, too, there were gradual improvements in the programs that had been established during the first term of office, improvements produced partly through the advice of program specialists and partly through the sheer pressure of events – notably population shifts, increased school enrolment, and increased university enrolment in the post-war period. School building, for example, proceeded rapidly; school grants increased year by year; and a new elementary school curriculum was being developed. The government also established a million-dollar loan fund to help needy students.[58] The first regional library was established in 1950, and the promised Arts Board was getting under way.

This was the pattern of departmental initiative in policy formulation during 1948 to 1952. Two factors stand out clearly: the improved organization of departments and an increase in the number and the professionalism of people in senior positions in departments. But more subtle forces were also at work. George Cadbury and his EAPB staff, as well as the Budget Bureau, had set a new, and a high, standard of performance in planning and administration, and departments tended to measure their own performance by this standard. While some people charged that Cadbury did everyone's planning for them, it was more the case that when departmental planning achieved a certain standard, Cadbury stepped out of the picture, except to act as cabinet critic. His detractors would say he was forced out. But the pattern was too consistent to have been the product solely of competitive pressure. These pressures existed, of course. As ministers became more competent and confident, they wished to perform the responsibilities with which they had been charged. But this was simply part of a process of discovering a working balance between individual ministerial responsibility and collective cabinet responsibility.

Initiatives in Arts and Culture

This might be an appropriate place to say something about the government's cultural policies – broadly defined. The impression may have been created earlier on that the government shared the low priority originally ascribed by the EAPB to cultural policy. In point of fact, 'the government showed commendable interest in cultural matters in spite of pressing and urgent problems in the economic sphere.'[59] The government's support for the arts was firmly grounded: Premier Douglas himself said, 'I've always maintained that the people of the Prairies ... are hungry ... for things of the mind and the spirit: good music, literature, paintings and folk songs. This was why the Arts Board was established.'[60] The premier was not alone in this view. Woodrow Lloyd and his successor in the education portfolio, Allan Blakeney, at the ministerial level, and at least of couple of central agency deputy ministers, including myself, were strong proponents as well. This seems to be borne out by the policy initiatives in the first years of the CCF government.

The first of these was the creation of the Archives Board in 1945 – forty years after the creation of Saskatchewan as a province. The second – initiated by Woodrow Lloyd – was the opening of the first regional library in 1950. The major milestone came in early 1948 with the creation of the Saskatchewan Arts Board, said to be the first organization of its kind on the continent. Modelled on the Arts Council of the United Kingdom, the board 'was charged with making available to citizens greater opportunities to engage in arts, music, literature and handicrafts.'[61]

The story of the contribution made by the Arts Board extends over the years, and to tell it calls for a bit of a departure from a chronological recounting of the Douglas years. The board played a strong supportive role in all the arts – thanks in no small measure to its spirited executive director, Norah McCullogh. The board sponsored exhibitions of Saskatchewan painters, and it purchased art works from established Saskatchewan artists and from those emerging from the Art School in Regina College and the Art Department of the University of Saskatchewan. Both of these schools enjoyed the strong support of the board of governors of the university. This is the period when the 'Regina Five' – including Ron Bloore, Ken Lougheed, Art MacKay, Ted Godwin, and Doug Morton – emerged, after their 1961 exhibition at the

National Gallery in Ottawa, and when Saskatoon artists Wynona Mulcaster, Reta Cowley, Dorothy Knowles, and William Perehudof were flourishing.

With the support of the Arts Board, several important new arts agencies were created. The Emma Lake (summer) School was established and soon flourished with international names like Clement Greenberg, art critic of the *New York Times*, enriching the program. The writers' counterpart was the Qu'Appelle Valley Centre, which held workshops with such well-known authors such as W.O. Mitchell directing the courses.[62]

The Arts Board also contributed to the growth and development of musicians – providing scholarships to promising young artists and sponsoring tours of competition-winning musicians. Here, too, the board enjoyed the support of the university and its conservatories of music in Saskatoon and Regina. One thinks of many role models for the board and for Saskatchewan singers, always beginning with Jon Vickers from Prince Albert, one of the world's great tenors, and Irene Salemka, the celebrated soprano from Weyburn, both of whom had received earlier support from the CBC and the Canada Council.

The same kind of story could be recounted concerning the support of the Arts Board for drama and for writers. There was a veritable burgeoning of the arts. Other initiatives came into place as well. One small example: the deputy minister of public works, Jim Langford, and I (as secretary of the Treasury Board) engineered a requirement that all architects engaged to design and build buildings for the government or the university must set aside 1 per cent of the cost of the building for art works inside or adjacent to the edifice – one of the many smaller measures for supporting artistic endeavour and creativity in Saskatchewan.

One of my favourite anecdotes, indeed, has to do with just such a measure – arising from an exhibition at the Norman MacKenzie Art Gallery of works by the famous avant-garde sculptor Jacques Lipchitz. The Art School wanted, after the exhibition, to buy one of these sculptures, but because of the cost and because of a university regulation requiring the board of governors' approval of capital expenditures exceeding a specified amount, the school needed board approval for the purchase. Being a member of that body, I happily sponsored the approval of the acquisition. But my motion was defeated. The sculpture was both 'non-objective' ('expletive nonsense') and too expensive. So I waited until the next February when a couple of the dissenting members of the board were holidaying in the South, and moved once again that the

School of Art be authorized to make the purchase. This time the motion was approved. When the absentee board members returned, they were, in Saskatchewan fashion, not angry but wryly amused, and for some time I regularly received from one of them, on his travels overseas, post-cards of all the 'far out' sculptures he had seen.

New Developments in the Machinery of Government: The Cabinet Office

Throughout the CCF's second term of office there were continuing efforts to improve upon the machinery of government, given the deficiencies and disparities in public management that had emerged during the first term, and given, too, the side effects of the greater centralization of policy development that had been introduced to cope with this weakness.

A number of the elements of governance were at issue: in particular, the functioning of the cabinet at the summit of government; the role of individual departments of government in the development of policy and programs; the evolving roles of the central agencies in advising and assisting the premier and his cabinet colleagues; and the resolution of emerging tensions between the operating departments and the central agencies.

First in importance, if not in the chronology of change during the second term, was the action taken to strengthen the functioning of the cabinet and thus to contribute to decision-making. Cabinet was clearly overworked and understaffed, as the EAPB and the Budget Bureau emphasized in the course of their advocacy during 1947–8 of a cabinet secretariat based on the British and latterly the Canadian models.[63] George Cadbury put the case to cabinet:

> Good administration remains a primary duty of the CCF Government ... There can be no real advance toward a planned economy or an integrated administration unless the Cabinet operates as a supreme and continuing entity. It is therefore of prime importance to establish a Cabinet secretariat which will give the Cabinet permanent existence and undisputed authority by clear directives and good organization of its business.[64]

Two months later, in November 1948, this advice was heeded. The newly established cabinet secretariat was intended to serve five objectives: to facilitate the premier's coordinating function; to record the government's policies; to disseminate information to ministers on cabinet decisions; to provide a follow-up for cabinet decisions; and to secure advice for cabinet before major decisions were taken. The secretary was responsible to record decisions, not discussions, and to prepare agendas. He was also to receive, on the premier's behalf, 'comprehensive reports from departments submitted once a year immediately prior to the Legislative Session ... and continuous confidential reports ... quarterly.'[65]

The first cabinet secretary, Morris Shumiatcher, never attended cabinet meetings; he recorded the decisions at the end of each meeting on the advice of the premier or of a minister designated by the premier. But his successors, J.W.W. Graham and then Tim Lee, operated more in the manner of cabinet secretaries in Ottawa and the U.K.

The establishment of the secretariat greatly improved the functioning of cabinet. Its most important contribution was to collective decision-making: ministers had to give notice of their intention to introduce a matter in cabinet; and their colleagues were notified of their intention to do so. There was a tendency for the sponsoring ministers to come better prepared to discuss the item, and there was no dispute as to the decision that had been taken. The secretariat also greatly assisted the Treasury in its budget control responsibilities, so that it, in turn, could serve the Treasury Board and cabinet better. Tim Lee, in particular, developed close working relations with the secretary of the Treasury Board (the deputy provincial treasurer), so that both could be informed about the proceedings and decisions of both bodies.

Changes in the machinery serving the cabinet were not the only reason for an improvement in the functioning of cabinet. The premier and his colleagues were more experienced and they performed with greater efficiency, although they never during the Douglas government relieved themselves of the detailed decision-making that characterized Saskatchewan cabinets. The premier himself performed with greater assurance, perhaps because his leadership in the party was undisputed.[66] He was more precise in his directions to his colleagues when these were called for. At the same time, he maintained his view that cabinet decisions must be collective decisions. He told the cabinet secretary, for example, that he would like as a general rule to require that 'any items which are controversial ... should not be proceeded with unless at least six ... Cabinet ministers are prepared to give it their approval' (that being six out of twelve in 1950). He was similarly concerned that major policy decisions not be taken during the summer when many ministers were absent.[67]

The premier also began to make more systematic use of cabinet committees than had been the case during the first two or three years of the government. He used them, it seems, to compensate, to coordinate, and to contemplate. When a minister was apparently not coping with a problem that was concerning cabinet, Douglas was inclined to appoint a cabinet committee to deal with the question. He also struck a committee as a coordinating device, including all the ministers who had a departmental interest in the issues – notably the Committee on Rehabilitation. And he used committees, in particular, to consider more carefully some of the thornier problems that the government confronted. These ranged from one on oil policy to one discussing whether a new boys' reform school should be built – a controversial subject at the time.

Strengthened Operating Departments

However, neither cabinet committees nor the cabinet secretariat – nor, for that matter, central agencies – could act as a substitute for strong departments of government, upon whose advice the ministers and the cabinet must rely. And it became evident in reflecting upon the policy initiatives undertaken during 1948–52 that the operating departments and ministers were playing a steadier and more consistent role in the development of new policies and programs.

This stronger role for operating departments emerged partly from the increasing experience of departmental ministers, and in some places the departments themselves, but it was also the product of a conscious effort on the part of the government and its advisors to strengthen the policy and the administrative capacity of these departments. And whereas there had been no time to reorganize during the first three or four years of innovation, during the next four or five years nearly all of them did so. The Budget Bureau played a prominent role, as it produced organization surveys for many – ultimately most – of the departments of government: Public Health, 1948; Labour, 1948–9; Natural Resources, 1949–50; Social Welfare, 1950–1; and Treasury, 1951–2. It also consulted informally with the deputy minister of agriculture when he reorganized that department in 1949.[68]

From these management surveys there emerged an organization pattern that would have a significant influence on policy formulation and on the machinery needed for its implementation. At least four major changes in departmental organization were involved. First, the Budget Bureau recommended a grouping of functions that would provide a maximum of four or five major centres of operational responsibility in each department, each responsible for program development and operations in their respective fields. One of the reasons for poor departmental performance when innovation was expected had been the dispersion of responsibility among large numbers of divisions. Fragmented organizations had also been a barrier to recruiting outstanding new people, when there were no 'big jobs' in an organization.

Secondly, each department established a research and planning branch. Under the prevailing organization structure, no deputy minister had been provided with the specialized expertise required to perform the planning function. Put another way, the talents required for an operational or services delivery role would now be complemented by the talents required for the planning and evaluation role, per se. And the two would be in a position to function together to enrich both planning and program development and the services delivery function as well. More, the research and planning branch would provide a focal point for both the deputy and his branch heads.

This proliferation of departmental research offices appeared to be contrary to Cadbury's view that research and planning should be centralized in the EAPB. But in the end there was little difference of opinion. It had become evident by now that program planning, as distinguished from broader policy planning or from economic planning, could not be performed effectively in a central agency (except where the departments themselves failed to perform to cabinet's satisfaction). And equally it had become evident that program planning and broader policy planning could not be treated as separate and self-contained compartments. Indeed, Tommy Shoyama was to say years later, as secretary of the EAPB, that the creation of planning branches in departments was 'the genius part' of the new and collaborative approach to planning.[69]

The third change that affected all the departments in which organization surveys were conducted was the establishment of administrative services branches. These combined budgeting, human resources, accounting, procurement, and all of the housekeeping services of the departments. These branches became the departmental counterparts of central agencies, serving not only to assist the branches in their administrative tasks and the deputy in exercising whatever controls were needed, but also serving as a bridge between the departments and the central agencies. In fact, many departments came to look upon the Budget Bureau as the source of recruitment for their directors of administrative services.

The fourth major change in the structure of most departments was the establishment of a unified field staff. The size of the province and the sparseness of its population necessitated the use of field staff located around the province to deliver government services. But these staff units could not be allowed to proliferate in bewildering confusion. Consequently, the decision was taken to organize all the field staff into regional services branches with different departmental program branches exercising functional supervision over their work. The ultimate and ideal goal, it soon became apparent, would be the rationalization of all departmental field staff through the creation of common regions and with the provision for coordination of their work at the regional level.

The creation of rationalized departmental regions raised the question as to whether their boundaries could be made to correspond in some sensible way with local government boundaries. However, the steadfast determination of the rural municipalities to resist local government reorganization – one of the consistent themes of government in Saskatchewan – rendered this idea impractical. The result was that the regionalization of public services took place either through the creation by the legislature of new local authorities – hospital districts, health regions, school units – or by the creation within provincial departments of program delivery districts – conservation and development districts, for example, and later market road districts.

The Evolving Role of the Central Agencies

The increase in the effectiveness and the influence of operating departments did not imply that the roles of the EAPB, the Government Finance Office, and the Treasury became insignificant in any way. They simply changed. Where the Planning Board, for example, had initially devoted itself to planning, budgeting, organization advice, Crown corporation operations, and general advice to cabinet, it now concentrated on its policy advisory role. The direction and control of Crown corporations had been transferred in 1947 to the Government Finance Office, though the Planning Board continued to be involved in major policy questions. And the Budget Bureau had become the government's advisor on organization and machinery of government, and had assumed responsibility for budget analysis and control. The EAPB role became that which the premier and, one suspects, Cadbury conceived for it: general and sectoral economic planning, advice to cabinet on general and particular policies, and *ad hoc* advice to the premier, individual ministers, and departments. One caveat is important, though. When departmental planning was judged to be deficient, the Planning Board was nearly always called in, in some capacity.

While the functioning of the Planning Board during the second term of office has, in part, already been illustrated in the story of the shift in policy emphasis, there are other examples that provide an insight into its operations. One of the most significant was the creation of a periodic, at least annual, joint conference with cabinet to discuss the general directions of government policy. In effect, this was a meeting of full cabinet in a planning session which lasted generally five days, and which brought together both the ministerial members of the EAPB, plus George Cadbury as EAPB Chair (to 1951) and, after that, Tommy Shoyama as secretary and myself as deputy provincial treasurer. These sessions were used to review the government's overall program and its efficacy in achieving the government's goals; to consider four- or five-year plans from each department and Crown corporation (this being a cabinet committee, senior departmental/corporation officials could accompany their minister for the session on their program and plans); and to develop progressively more concrete programs for the next electoral period. The agendas for these conferences were broad: for example, in 1949 the discussion included the engaging and the development of administrative and professional personnel; the financing of government enterprises; the industrial development program and techniques of industrial development; mineral development policy; irrigation and land policy; rural electrification; and natural gas.[70] In this way, the annual Planning Board conference became an opportunity to discuss the general direction of policy as well as specific problem areas.

The EAPB's role in the budget was also significant. It provided the economic forecasts that were a prime element of the 'fiscal framework,' and its evaluation of general policy included its annual comments on the framework. Here the board played the role of cabinet's principal advisor,[71] though increasingly, through to 1952, the Treasury Board came to assume this task. Further, to ensure that the budget, including departmental plans, was viewed from a broad perspective, the EAPB introduced the device of 'five-year plans,' which required departments and Crown corporations to submit not only their annual budgets but also a projection of the shape of their programs over the next five years.[72] This was not so much a matter of preparing a blueprint, as a matter of getting a sense of perspective and some insight as to where government was headed.

In its role as economic advisor, the Planning Board tended to organize itself by economic sectors, with study groups active in areas such as mineral and natural resources (the Oil and Gas Policy Committee), agriculture (for example, the Irrigation Committee and the group working on the South Saskatchewan River project), public investment, transportation, and public utilities. It rarely conducted studies without the participation of departmental personnel; indeed, the board introduced the 'working party' approach, using representatives from the relevant agencies with staff support from the EAPB. The degree of intrusion into departments varied, as did opinion about when the point of intrusiveness had been reached. But the board was indisputably the acknowledged leader in inter-departmental questions – for example, the South Saskatchewan River project – and in these areas questions of 'departmental autonomy' rarely arose.

The Budget Bureau exerted its influence first in its organization studies. But its greatest influence in the longer run was exercised through its responsibility for the budgeting process. Through analysing the departmental budgets in preparation for budget meetings with departments, the bureau came to know more about the government's program, as a whole, than did any agency in the public service. Moreover, it was in an excellent position to provide ministers with an analysis of fiscal policy and of program emphasis.

An active Treasury Board, now consisting of the treasurer, the premier, and the minister of education, came to perform the budget function in its broadest sense. Between 1950 and 1955, the Treasury Board assumed responsibility for framing the recommendations to cabinet on broad fiscal policies. It held budget meetings at least once a year with all ministers and their senior officials, to arrive at a tentative budget. The board proposed to cabinet the annual budget, including the tax and borrowing measures needed. And during the course of the year, the Treasury Board exercised budgetary control. In these functions, the Treasury Board staff came close to doing the same things as did Cadbury and the Planning Board staff; indeed, budgeting, if done properly, is part of the planning process, and vice versa.

This is the role that cabinet and George Cadbury seemed to have in mind for the Treasury Board. In 1948 the Cabinet–Planning Board Conference argued for a strong cabinet committee to act as a 'co-ordinator of the administration of government policy on a ministerial level.'[73] The need and importance of integrating the two processes was evident. Moreover, Cadbury had said that he saw the planning and budgeting processes as one. Indeed, when the time came to replace him, he said that 'it would be quite logical for the Deputy Provincial Treasurer to hold such [an] office.'[74] But the line of demarcation between planning and budgeting – at least when it came to fiscal policy, expenditure evaluation, and administrative machinery – was difficult to find. The existence of separate centres for the two processes and of separate calls upon operating departments for planning documents – one-year plans versus five-year plans, for example – suggested that the harmonization of the respective responsibilities of George Cadbury and Clarence Fines had not yet been achieved. Not until 1952, when Tommy Shoyama and I took office as deputy ministers in the EAPB and the Treasury, respectively, was the integration of the planning and budgeting process fully realized.

The Government Finance Office, established in 1947 essentially as a holding company for all the Crown corporations, also developed rapidly in influence. The first stage of the GFO's work, as Cadbury described it, was to bring order into the operations of individual corporations and of the corporations generally.[75] The second stage was to create machinery for cabinet control of investment in the corporations. To be effective, this implied control over the creation of reserves and the use by a corporation of reserves or retained profit. The third stage was to achieve some coordination between corporations where this was desirable – notably in industrial relations, corporate structure, and accounting systems. In fact, the Government Finance Office, even though a holding company, was a cabinet committee that was to operate vis-à-vis Crown corporations much as the Treasury Board operated vis-à-vis departments. There were two differences: the GFO was to concern itself primarily with capital investment in the corporations, and through its staff to provide all of the central services for Crown corporations, while the Treasury Board concerned itself with budgetary revenues and expenditures as well as fiscal and financial policy.[76]

By 1950 the Government Finance Office and the EAPB had between them thoroughly rationalized the organization for Crown corporations and then the corporations themselves, and were engaged in rationalizing their corporate operations. After the 1948 election, and the defeat of Joe Phelps, the premier assigned new ministers to the corporations, and in a joint meeting of the cabinet and the Planning Board reviewed the operations of all corporations. This meeting identified the 'problem children,' as Tommy Douglas had come to call them. Their boards were told that if these corporations could not be rationalized with help from the EAPB and the Finance Office, they would be sold or closed. Even the operations of successful corporations were reviewed, and plans made for their long-run operations. This was particularly important for the Saskatchewan Power Corporation.[77]

Friction among Central Agencies, Crown Corporations, and Departments

All of these central agencies and the responsibilities they assumed were instrumental in defining and creating a new equilibrium in the policies and operations of government, so badly needed after the first hectic years in office. But just as the policy shifts described earlier created both greater stability and new frictions, the interventions of the central agencies – for example, in strengthening the operations of the Crown corporations – engendered their own difficulties. By 1950 some of the ministers responsible for Crown corporations, and certainly staff and managers in the Power Corporation and Government Telephones, were becoming restive under Finance Office control. Some of this restiveness had become apparent in 1948, when Cadbury wrote: 'An entirely new school of thought [has] developed along the lines that the Finance Office should relinquish control over the two major enterprises ... and that these should be dealt with directly by the Cabinet.'[78] But the Finance Office was a cabinet committee, and independence from it suggested independence from cabinet itself, argued Cadbury.

Nonetheless, the pressure mounted, and in 1950 the Power Corporation left the jurisdiction of the Finance Office, followed within a year by Saskatchewan Government Telephones. It is difficult to say why these frictions developed: whether it was a matter of personalities, or of aggressiveness on the part of the Finance Office, or aggressiveness on the part of the utility managers. Perhaps the structure itself was unsound. But, without a doubt, notions of ministerial responsibility were involved in the differences. The ministers who chaired the boards of the Saskatchewan Power Corporation and Saskatchewan Government Telephones simply could not visualize being controlled by a body below the cabinet level, particularly a body that they tended to identify as a group of officials, not as a cabinet committee, and particularly when their own officials were outspoken in opposition to the controls involved.

Other manifestations of friction between the central agencies and operating departments or corporations became apparent. The adjustment process was a delicate one. When the central controls were first implemented, they were recognized as being entirely necessary, a correction of the extremes of ministerial initiative during 1944–5. But as the processes of government became better integrated and the functioning of departments improved, some of the controls, and the advice and criticism, began to seem excessive despite efforts to maintain effective working relationships.[79] The role of the Planning Board sometimes created resentment, as for example when the Department of Co-operation battled to decentralize economic research. But more likely the problem arose from uncertainty as to roles. The EAPB felt responsible for the rural electrification study being conducted in 1950, and also directed the engineering study on natural gas transmission and distribution.[80] But the manager of the Saskatchewan Power Corporation felt these fields to be within his competence. It was not always clear, in other words, where the board left off and the departments and Crown corporations began. Indeed, the line could scarcely be clearly drawn, as sometimes the cabinet itself assigned work to the EAPB staff, and sometimes the departments were not competent to do the work in question.

Cadbury had predicted these problems of adjustment when he first came to Saskatchewan. He knew that the balance between individual ministerial responsibility and collective cabinet responsibility, facilitated through central agencies, was difficult to establish, and that when the time came for him to leave he would be unpopular in many quarters. And he was right about that. But he was also such an imposing figure – in stature and status and sheer intelligence and self-confidence – that without intent he intimidated others. Whatever the case, Cadbury left Saskatchewan early in 1951, to work for the Technical Assistance Committee of the United Nations.[81] But by the time he left he had built a central planning organization, a new budgeting organization, and a central agency for Crown corporations. Indeed, he left Saskatchewan just when some kind of balance was beginning to emerge. And this too may well have been one of the reasons for the timing of his departure: he enjoyed building, not administering. Cadbury was succeeded by Tommy Shoyama, who was appointed secretary of the Planning Board, and who was to imprint his own personality on the question of central versus departmental planning – one which was to generate harmonious and productive relations.

Adjustments in the Government's Relations with the
Party and the Legislature

Adjustments similar to those within government were in train in party-government relations. By the end of the first term in office, a pattern of consultation had evolved which, while useful, did not prevent occasional eruptions when party officials did not fully understand the nature of the relationship. For example, the party's Legislative Advisory Committee sometimes showed signs of wanting to do more than 'make its influence felt.' In January 1949 this committee urged the caucus to take more initiative in proposing the allocation of expenditures among departments, in controlling expenditures, and in deciding the policies for Crown corporation operations.[82] Sometimes the committee wanted to become involved in questions such as appointments to senior posts in departments.[83] Generally, however, there was a more mature understanding of the role and the constitutional responsibilities of the government and of the elected members. The Chair of the CCF caucus, a farmer from Kindersley constituency, John Wellbelove, wrote a classic statement on party-government relations in 1948:

> There is one thing in ... our CCF ... that is ... a little disconcerting; and that is the periodical request on the part of some of the elected officials [of the Provincial Council] for a review of relationships ... between the Government and the organization. To me this bespeaks a desire on the part of some individuals [for] recognition of equality of responsibility with the elected members on legislative matters ... [It may be that the] scope of authority will have to be very clearly stated. We as members have an elective responsibility on behalf of our constituencies, and a majority must therefore determine legislation ... A body [the CCF Council] that acts in a strictly advisory capacity is a source of strength to any governing body, but dual authority: never.

He added with a note of political realism: 'Go out and try to elect a Government on a platform of subordinated authority.'[84]

The premier understood the nature of the relationship too and acknowledged the important role of the CCF caucus. When a colleague was reluctant to have a matter discussed in caucus, he wrote: 'Neither the Minister nor anyone else has the power to prevent it from being discussed in Caucus ... If they decide that this is a matter which ought to be discussed, then of course the Minister will have to defend the actions of his Department in Caucus.'[85]

The government's willingness to consult the party is illustrated most clearly by the developments that led to an increase in the provincial sales tax in 1950. In 1949 it had become apparent that the hospital plan needed more money, and government began to discuss its options. The convention in July that year discussed the general problem, and the premier reviewed the alternatives with the Provincial Council to get its views.[86] In November the Cabinet–Planning Board Conference examined the alternatives and arrived at the same view as the council had expressed;[87] then the premier took the matter to caucus.[88] In the end, the tax change announced in the budget speech was lower than that which had been discussed, but the process of consultation had afforded all the bodies an opportunity to influence the decision. So conscientiously did Douglas consult party committees, that he was angered by any charge that he ignored the party and the caucus. He once wrote to the national leader of the CCF, M.J. Coldwell, about the complaints raised by CCF MP Ross Thatcher of Moose Jaw:[89]

> Ross Thatcher, who seems to be very disturbed about the proposed increase in the sales tax, wasn't at any of these meetings. I think it's about time Ross accepted some responsibility as a CCF member ... If he wants to have a voice in determining the policies of the Saskatchewan Government, then he should at least take the trouble to come to the meetings ... rather than rushing in at the eleventh hour to offer advice on matters to which he has given no thought and in which he has evinced no interest.[90]

During the first four years of office, the prime influence in the government's deliberations was the ideology and the program of the CCF. But by the second term in office, the government was also becoming accustomed to its 'exposure' – to the need to function in an environment where the problems and concerns of all citizens and groups, not just party members, had to be taken into account. A commitment to one's values and goals might well be a primary impulse to action, but a democratically elected government cannot ignore the wishes of the citizens generally. This was not a question of swinging to extremes, but of finding an appropriate balance if the government was to remain in power.

The best example of the influence of the Legislative Assembly and of public opinion generally is the case of the removal of the public revenue tax, a provincially imposed two-mill property tax. In October 1950 the Britnell-Cronkite-Jacobs Committee looking into local government issues recommended that this tax should be removed.[91] Extensive discussions ensued within the government and between the government and the local government associations as to the wisdom of this step. In the 1951 legislative session, the opposition was quick to suggest that the recommendation be implemented immediately. Cabinet, however, had two concerns: eliminating the tax would deprive the provincial government of $1.6 million in revenue per year; and abolishing a provincial property tax would be an inequitable way to give financial assistance to local governments.[92] The wealthier municipalities would benefit more than the poorer ones.

This reasoning led the government to an alternative course: to dedicate the revenue of the tax to school grants, there being an 'education fund' into which the tax proceeds could be paid. As school grants were already paid on an equalized basis, this would ensure that the wealthy municipalities would not benefit at the expense of the poorer municipalities. Moreover, there was no commitment to remove the tax within the three years, as recommended by the Britnell-Cronkite-Jacobs Committee. The government's decision was announced in the budget speech on 27 February 1952.

The reaction of the legislature was sharp and swift. The municipal associations joined the opposition in condemning the government for its decision. Since school grants should be increased anyway, they argued, there was no case for combining them with the public revenue tax issue. On the 1st of March, the minister of municipal affairs spoke during the budget debate and reversed the government's decision by pledging to repeal the provincial 'public revenue tax' within three years.[93] There seems little doubt that the government reversed itself because of the pressure it felt in the legislature. In fact, there was corridor gossip to the effect that the minister of municipal affairs reversed the government's decision without cabinet approval! Certainly, the reversal did not enjoy CCF Party approval; the 1952 convention passed this resolution:

Whereas the Provincial Convention of the CCF is our policy formulating body, and a directive body to our legislature, this Convention feels that the action of our Minister of Municipal Affairs in stating on the floor of the Legislature that the Public Revenue Tax was to be removed and thus committing the Government to a policy directly contradictory to that agreed to by the Provincial Convention of 1951, was an unwarranted breach of faith on his part and deserving of severe censure.[94]

Other illustrations demonstrate the government's increasing attention to the Legislative Assembly. It made more use of legislative committees: for example, a special committee to inquire into the high price of farm implements. It heeded the request of the legislature to establish a special committee to consider 'the purchase price of Crown lands on which veterans are settled.'[95] It avoided introducing legislation without prior notice in the throne speech. It also subjected the operations of Crown corporations to the scrutiny of a new legislative committee.[96]

This does not suggest, however, that government embarked on a program of reforming the legislative machinery. Except for establishing the Crown corporations committee, the Douglas government did not display a strong interest in reforming the functioning of the Assembly. But it did listen to the Legislature as a guide to policy formulation.

Government's Relationships with Interest Groups

Interest groups had a similar impact on the government during this period. In part, their greater influence reflected the fact that the government wanted to stay out of trouble, or wished to try to determine in advance the potential consequences of a decision. There had been a few notable examples in which failure to consult had led to real problems. For example, when the Honey Marketing Board was established, the price of honey rose and this was attributed, without investigation, to the marketing scheme. The Retail Merchants Association met the cabinet to complain;[97] both the retail and the wholesale merchants made statements to the press, and the Canadian Association of Consumers proposed to take 'public action.' The premier had worried about the possibility of this happening and had cautioned his deputy, but apparently no direct action had been taken to head off the potential difficulty.

There were other reasons for the growth of influence of interest groups. Government policies themselves led to an increasing range of relationships. For example, if the government were to encourage oil development, it would have to consult the Petroleum Association and the individual producers in order to obtain their point of view. The provincial treasurer was almost bound to be exposed to, if not to seek out, the views of financial and industrial interests. It was impossible to establish the province's credit in Canadian financial circles without encountering the attitudes and outlook of the business interests.

The more doctrinaire party members were suspicious of these relationships, but to the government the need to consult became a simple fact of life. And the consultations went on in nearly every field. For example, the premier told the minister of labour in 1951 that, 'as soon as legislation has been agreed to in principle by the Cabinet and Caucus, a general outline of labour legislation should be sent to both labour congresses and the Manufacturers' Association.'[98] The cabinet and all the departments of government continued to work closely with the local government associations. Perhaps the most outstanding illustrations of consultation continued to come from the Department of Education. In planning the new primary curriculum, the department consulted teachers, home and school clubs, business people, farmers, and school trustees. It did this in an organized fashion, through a general advisory committee and a summer school 'workshop,' because it believed its educational programs should reflect 'the values inherent in a democratic society.'[99]

Relationships with some associations, the farm groups, labour unions, and co-operatives, had always been close and continued to be so. Examples of consultation with these associations and interests abound. At times, though, the new outlook of the government strained relations with these older associations. For example, rumours began to circulate among trade unions that the government intended to amend the Trade Union Act. Nothing came of the incident, but it did become evident that some union organizers felt the government was obliged to interpret the Act as meaning that if a person applied for a job but was rejected by the union for membership, the employer could not hire him. Douglas made clear, as he put it years later, that he was 'in no one's back pocket' – neither the unions' nor any other organization's. In a letter to M.J. Coldwell, he said, 'I agree that if a man is going to get all the benefits of the collective bargaining that the Union does on his behalf he should be compelled to contribute to the maintenance of that Union. To go farther, however, and say that the Union should have the power of life and death over him and be in a position to deprive him of his employment ... is certainly abhorrent to me personally and I think would be repugnant to the entire CCF movement.'[100]

Despite the adjustments that came with the government's perceptions of new problems and new responsibilities, relationships between the cabinet and the farm, co-operative, and labour groups continued to be harmonious. And smooth relationships were being developed with other groups too. There were, of course, exceptions. The government and the medical society, for example, did not see eye to eye, and during 1950–1 when the College of Physicians and Surgeons was discussing health insurance planning with the government, it refused to meet the government's representatives in the Legislative Building, saying it preferred to meet 'on neutral grounds.' In another case, the doctors informed the cabinet that their agreement to treat pensioners under the public medical care scheme would end unless the government agreed to pay the physicians $15 per capita. In this case, the government agreed.[101]

By 1952 it seemed that a certain equilibrium had emerged in the functioning of government, at least a pattern for equilibrium. The pressures of intense innovation and those that developed when the political processes were adjusting to new requirements seemed largely to have subsided. The ideological and policy shifts had taken place. Within the government, a new balance was being achieved between the operating departments and the central agencies. Party-government relationships had become relatively systematized, and a better balance struck between party and other influences on policy formulation. Indeed, the political system had begun to assume a rather more stable and discernible shape.

In the 1952 election platform, *Program for Progress*, the Douglas government outlined its accomplishments. These were the hospital insurance plan; the automobile insurance plan; the partial health insurance plan covering treatment for cancer, mental illness, and the needy; the welfare program; the education program, including a 300 per-cent increase in school grants; new farm security provisions; reduction in the public debt; improvements in the highway and municipal road system; a province-wide power system and rural electrification program; a 'fair deal for labour'; and a rapidly growing economy in both resource and industrial development.[102] Describing the last two terms as eight years of 'the best government Saskatchewan has ever had,' it proposed a ten-point program for extending these achievements. And with this perspective, the government prepared to embark upon its third term.

7

A Mature Government in Its Third and Fourth Terms

The 1950s in Saskatchewan – Growth and Prosperity

By 1952, as we have seen, the government was reaching its maturity. It was more experienced, better integrated, and more proficient in the making of policy and the delivery of programs and services. Too, it was more cognizant of the impact of its policies and their effectiveness, not only in achieving the CCF's goals, but also in their effect on Saskatchewan society generally. At the same time, the fundamental values of the CCF remained unchanged and these values continued to be the wellspring of the government's policies.

The ideology of the CCF, however, and the articulation of that ideology, had been modified. It had become clearer and better – or more explicitly – balanced in distinguishing between the role of the public sector, including the services it should deliver, and the role of the private sector, including the extent of its regulation and support by the public sector.

These shifts in the 'positioning' of the government represented one feature of the government in the 1950s. A second feature was the character of the policies and policy changes that government introduced in these years. They were not the major policy innovations and initiatives deriving from the pioneering Progressives of the 1920s and 1930s or from the Depression and the war. Rather, the policy changes of the 1950s were largely incremental in nature. Most of the major or 'banner' programs – such as the hospital plan, the school units, and the automobile insurance plan – had now been introduced and would thereafter change more gradually. Other major shifts in policy in this period could only be achieved in stages: for example, the transformation of the mental hospitals from custodial institutions into professional treatment centres, and the improvements in pensions and other social assistance allowances. Thus public policy had become more incremental in character, and it would continue that way until the end of the decade.

A third feature of policy in the 1950s was the effect of Saskatchewan's changing social and economic environment, and the recognition of these changes and their incorporation into evolving policy formulation. One of the major changes of this period was the accelerated migration of the farm or farm-based population from the rural areas and the villages to larger and more widely separated towns and urban centres. By the mid-1950s, the automobile had made distances of twenty-five to fifty miles insignificant on Saskatchewan's plains. Agriculture had become mechanized: the number of combines grew from fewer than ten thousand in 1936 to some sixty-two thousand in 1956, and the number of tractors and farm trucks increased enormously too.[1] New needs and expectations emerged as a result: 'grid roads' to serve the farmers in these larger market areas; and within these larger areas, the concentration and consolidation of education, health, and other social services, along with retail trade and services. Indeed, new services (public goods and infrastructure, such as electricity, telephones, and sewer and water facilities) became more feasible when the population was more concentrated – all of which increased the appetite of those remaining on the farm and in the villages for the same services.

Associated with these developments was the ever-troubling question of the province's rural municipalities. If local government was to play a significant role in the governance of the province, especially in building the market or grid road system that was promised in the 1952 election platform, the municipalities would have to be greatly enlarged from their postage stamp size, just as larger school units were launched during the CCF's first term of office.

Another major characteristic of Saskatchewan's economic and social environment in the 1950s was the booming economy and a growing population – almost beyond the comprehension of people who had lived through the 'dirty thirties.' The population grew by some ninety thousand between 1951 and 1960. The crops were nicely above normal in five years out of ten, and below normal in only three years.[2] Farm cash income was on the rise, as was the size of farms – from an average of 551 acres per farm in 1951 to 686 acres a decade later. The result was that gross income per farm was more than sustained. Despite this abundance, there remained deep-rooted problems that nagged the farmers:

the inability to sell all of their wheat, and the rising costs of production in the face of steady and sometimes declining farm prices.[3]

The non-agricultural sectors of the economy were also booming during most of the 1950s. The problems that would emerge in these sectors did not become apparent until late in the decade. The value of construction, electric power production, and manufacturing grew, as did the resource industries. Developments in the oil industry were spectacular; the number of oil wells drilled rose from 124 in 1951 to a high of 1,258 in 1957, and then settled down at 600 to 650 wells a year by 1960. Natural gas production increased from less than one billion cubic feet to over 15.5 billion during the period 1951–60. Another spectacular – a 'uranium strike' – benefited Saskatchewan: at the peak of activity in 1953, ninety companies were exploring for uranium and other metals.[4] In 1958 the value of the uranium produced reached a high of nearly $60 million. Meanwhile, in the sedimentary basin in the south, potash was claiming almost as much attention. In aggregate, the value of mineral production grew from $51 million in 1951 to $212 million in 1960.[5]

Of greatest importance to the province was the diversification of Saskatchewan's economy. In 1945 the agricultural sector had accounted for 78 per cent of the commodity output of the economy, and the non-agricultural sector had accounted for the rest. By 1959–60 the situation was reversed, with non-agricultural industries accounting for some 60 to 65 per cent of commodity production.[6]

As a matter of pride, Saskatchewan people recorded that in four years out of ten their per capita personal income exceeded the national average.[7] The new affluence meant more households with electric refrigerators (from 135,000 households in 1957 to 203,000 in 1961), more with indoor toilets (from 85,000 in 1957 to 138,000 in 1961), and more with TV sets (from 65,000 in 1957 to 168,000 in 1961).[8] And with this affluence, the 'quality of life' expectations of Saskatchewanians grew too.

All of this economic activity and the related provincial prosperity were reflected in the government's financial position.[9] Revenues rose from $63.5 million in 1950–1 to $143 million in 1958–9, so that each year during the decade the Treasury recorded a surplus of revenue over current plus capital expenditures.[10] While expenditures also increased, the province's net debt fell, and in 1953 'Saskatchewan bonds, for the first time on record, [were] given an "A" rating in the [U.S.] investment markets.'[11] (A more complete review of the financing of the CCF's programs over the years is found in the Annex.)

At the end of the decade, the province's revenue growth began to slow, as the rate of economic growth in Saskatchewan and in Canada as a whole began to decline. The Canadian recession hit the oil and uranium industries especially hard, and this downturn in turn affected provincial finances. Specifically, mineral and natural resource revenues fell substantially in the last year of the decade, and were to fall yet again in 1960–1. But at the time of the elections of 1952 and of 1956, the economy was booming – auspicious circumstances for any government.

Government in Its Maturity

Paralleling the incremental change in the policies in the 1950s and in the environment affecting the development of these policies was the process and the performance of governing by this more mature, more seasoned government. We are speaking here, of course, of the people doing the governing, the premier and his cabinet, and in a certain sense the caucus, and the machinery of government, plus the quality of the public service available to assist them.

The CCF was blessed with strong leadership, as manifested best by Tommy Douglas, Clarence Fines, and Woodrow Lloyd. Other members of cabinet, of course, possessed their own measure and their own blend of leadership qualities exhibited in full by these men. But the CCF cabinet at its best is characterized by the leadership of Douglas and Fines and Lloyd – laced with the flat humour and unique insights of Jack Corman, the attorney general, and with the steadfastness and reliability of Brock Brockelbank.

Tommy Douglas was clearly the head of the government and of the party: immensely popular in his leadership of the humanitarian left; recognized and admired by his ministers and the caucus as their leader; and looked up to as a master craftsman by the public service. He was everything that has been said about him as an outstanding leader and a warm human being. He was quick and nimble yet retentive in intellect; possessed of a prodigious memory for people and facts and analysis; strong in energy, in speech, and in embracing ideas; sympathetic and thoughtful in his relations with people – though scathing in his criticism of what he found base or false in politics and very occasionally in persons; capable of relating policies and ideas to what his audience knew or had experienced; genuinely feeling for those who were weak or wanting; and correspondingly slow, if indeed almost unable, to inflict the penalties of displacement or dismissal that are a part of running a government – even though he often said himself he was cursed with a short temper.

This was Douglas the man. His leadership, in turn, was rooted in his vision for the people of the province – their individual and collective well-being – and in his vision of a state devoted to that cause.

Douglas found the roots of his vision in the Fabianism and the British Labour Party ideals to which he had been exposed in his home and in his political life, and in the values of the Christian ministry and the social gospel – as expressed particularly by J.S. Woodsworth. It was a vision that was fed by his empathy for people and what they faced in their personal lives. And it was expressed on the platform through blazing oratory, witty and eloquent and often moving, and in personal conversation through his human and very personal understanding.

These were the most visible and personal attributes of Douglas's leadership. Beyond them lay the other qualities that Douglas used to lead a government in the realization of its then-radical policies, within the constraints of governing that he faced.

Early in the life of the government, Douglas's leadership was tested and honed in the party and cabinet debates over social ownership, as we have seen. He moved artfully and openly – and with dexterity, his friends would say, or with cunning, his foes would say – from the political doctrines rooted in the Depression and expressed in the Regina Manifesto to a clearer definition of the economic and social role of the public sector and the role of the private sector. Effectively, he redefined 'socialism,' and indeed capitalism, in such a way as to discard earlier doctrine without rejecting the 'left.' He did so by transcending the arguments between 'left' and 'right' with the social gospel, with his belief in humanity and 'humanity first,' as the CCF platform expressed it. At the same time, he openly embraced individualism – he greatly admired individualists and was one himself – but within the context of equality and fairness and dignity for all.

When it came to policy-making, Douglas exercised still other qualities of leadership. On a range of issues and policy questions, he had to position himself and his colleagues somewhere between, on the one hand, acts of bold leadership that were in advance of public understanding and support and that count on the emergence of these sentiments over time, and, on the other hand, leadership that is exercised after, or concurrently with, the development of public understanding and support. The same positioning for the premier and the cabinet had to be achieved within the councils of the CCF – though more often expressed in terms of 'left' and 'right.'

Douglas did himself believe in acts of bold leadership, particularly in his early years as premier – witness the Hospital Services Plan, the school units, and automobile insurance – but always, it must be recalled, within the context of a four-year party platform and of the CCF's election on that platform, which presumably indicated a significant measure of public support for such measures. Beyond this rationale for bold action, Douglas really did believe – perhaps he did so more over time – that the public should be 'brought along' in advancing social change. And he equally believed that the public would be persuaded by reason, coupled with an appeal to the common good. Sometimes, of course, this belief brought him and his colleagues to compromise: to delay action in introducing certain measures, or to soften the hard edges of the measures proposed. And certainly Douglas's approach was reflected in his reaction to the proposals pressed upon him by delegations: the premier would express interest in the proposals, or even support them in principle. Then he would send them (the delegations and the proposals, or sometimes just the proposals) to Clarence Fines for an examination of the financial and political feasibility of what was being advanced. This, of course, had the added advantage that the treasurer would be the person who had to say 'no,' when that was necessary.

This belief that a social consensus should exist or be achieved before controversial legislation was introduced, or at least not long thereafter, led Douglas to announce on two occasions that the government would not proceed with a particular measure without the assent of those affected by it. I refer, of course, to the proposal that Saskatchewan's rural municipalities should be reorganized, and the reaction of the Saskatchewan Association of Rural Municipalities, and to medicare and the reaction of the doctors. Both are featured in the pages to come.

This 'seek a consensus' approach to public policy typified Douglas's relationship with his ministers, his legislative colleagues, and his party officials. But Douglas always remained the leader. He symbolized their common goals; he lent to their discussions his great gifts of clarity and synthesis; and he brought to bear in all he did his unique qualities of judgment, understanding, and persuasion.

Never did crass political calculations – patronage, polls (not being done in those days), political contributions, special interest groups, public relations exercises – threaten to eclipse the true goal of the CCF government: its humanitarian idealism. Douglas's relationships with his public service – which he valued very much – differed, as one would expect, from those with his cabinet and caucus and party colleagues. The 'political ingredient' was missing. He enjoyed spending time with the public servants whom he came to know, listening to and engaging in their discussions of policy and administration and of public affairs generally. For Douglas it was an occasion for intellectual discourse and for hearing different perspectives than he would normally hear in political circles.

For the most part, these discussions took place over lunch in the legislative building cafeteria, where the premier would take his tray in the line-up with others, order his poached eggs, and then join one of the tables of public servants. The conversation was always lively and often times contentious. Everyone felt free to challenge and to debate. This quality of freedom was characteristic of Tommy Douglas's relations with the public service generally: he extended to them in the discharge of their duties great freedom and trust. Their response was loyalty. As one deputy minister put it to me privately, 'I'm not a CCFer; I'm not even a Saskatchewanian. But I am fully committed to working with this government. I feel so free.'

Next in the trilogy of leaders in the maturing government of the 1950s was Clarence Fines. Unlike Douglas, Fines was more of a private person, and his interests more inclined to the 'how' of government as opposed to the 'why.' (Douglas, in talking about his colleagues, said: You've got to divide people in two categories: the people who are interested in "how" and the people who are interested in "why."')[12] Simply put, Fines was more of a pragmatist in addressing public policy issues than he was an ideologue. Indeed, Fines said of himself when talking about his role in the formation of the Independent Labour Party in 1929: 'Some people might call it socialism but neither [Coldwell nor I] was thinking about dogma or ideology. We were actually working in a vacuum trying to find some system to meet the needs of Saskatchewan.'[13] This was, of course, a huge understatement about the political ferment leading up to and surrounding the formation of the CCF, and, implicitly, about Fines's role in those years. But it was typical of Fines and his personality: no fluster, no bluster.

In fact, of course, his credentials in the formation of Canada's first socialist party (the Canadian version of socialism) were impeccable, as we have seen in chapter 1. There was his part in forming the ILP in 1929;[14] his role with J.S. Woodsworth and M.J. Coldwell in bringing the farmers' organization (the UFC-SS) to meet with the Western labour parties to discuss the formation of a Farmer Labour Party;[15] and his part as secretary and principal organizer of the Calgary Conference, where the CCF was formed in 1932.[16] In a less public way, one brief story illustrates his values and his approach. When Paul Robeson, the great African-American bass singer, visited Regina sometime in the 1950s, Fines was informed that the Hotel Saskatchewan had refused to give him a room in the hotel. Fines' response was to phone the hotel and inquire whether the hotel had a liquor licence, and whether it wished to retain the licence. Assuming that it did, a room should be found for Mr Robeson. It was.

Despite this record, and despite the part he played in establishing the Saskatchewan Government Insurance Company and in financing Saskatchewan Government Telephones and the Saskatchewan Power Corporation, as well as chairing the Government Finance Office (the 'treasury board' of the Crown corporations), Fines remained an enigma to his party – except for the left wing, which clearly regarded him as an enemy of true socialism. Yet, obviously, it was not Fines but the government and the party as a whole which made the decisions that most offended the left: for example, the decision that exploring and developing oil resources on Crown lands would be left to the private sector. So what was there about Clarence Fines that evoked such antagonism from the 'left' of the party, except perhaps that he refused to join the fray of left-right disagreements?

The answer to this conundrum became clear to me, I think, primarily in my job as deputy treasurer. It was that the provincial treasurer, Clarence Fines, was the minister responsible for recognizing and bringing into play all of the constraints on public expenditures and all of the limits on public revenues that fiscal prudence required. True, every budget was approved by cabinet as a whole, and vetted by the caucus and the Legislative Advisory Committee. But it was for Fines, the treasurer, to recognize and to invoke – or persuade his colleagues to invoke – the constraints. And it was for the treasurer to quantify what fiscal prudence meant, and then to persuade his colleagues to accept his definition of fiscal prudence.

To make the point, the provincial treasurer had the responsibility for coping with the constraints inherited from the economic failure of the 1930s and the accumulated debt of earlier Saskatchewan budgets. He had to accept the constitutional limits on a province's fiscal powers, to recognize the federal government's superior powers in the fields of fiscal, monetary, and debt management policy, and he had to cope with the constraints on revenues imposed by the rate of growth of the economy. Again, only Ottawa could manipulate the major economic policy levers. And only Ottawa could tailor trade policy in the interests of Western grain producers. Beyond that, Fines was the minister who had to cope with the constraints on the province's ability to borrow, emanating, particularly in the earlier years in office, from the prejudice of financial institutions against 'CCF bonds,' and from the province's low credit rating related to the sad history of the Saskatchewan economy. In the last analysis, Fines was responsible for grasping all these realities and designing a framework that would incorporate the constraints of fiscal prudence and that would resist the lure of borrowing and the consequential pain of rising debt – in short, the maintenance of a balanced budget.

How to explain all of this to a 'true believer'; how to understand the economics of constraint? For the layperson, it is virtually impossible: budgets are accepted, constraints are accepted, largely on the basis of trust. And, of course, the treasurer had to earn and maintain the trust of his colleagues. Perhaps, after all, it was Woodrow Lloyd's daughter who most aptly, if simplistically, explained the enigma of Clarence Fines: 'a dedicated socialist with the acumen of a tycoon.'[17]

But Fines was more than a fiscal manager; he was also the non-designated deputy premier, responsible for the 'management' of the government. Tommy Douglas said it best in the mid-1950s, after a federal-provincial conference in Ottawa, when I asked him, 'Why don't you act as your own minister of finance, as several other premiers now do?' 'Oh no, Al, never,' responded Douglas. 'As premier I am first of all responsible and accountable to the people of Saskatchewan and to the Legislative Assembly, and then to my legislative caucus, to the Legislative Advisory Committee and to the CCF Party. This is a full load. I don't have time to manage the government, day to day. That is Clarence's job. That is the arrangement we have between us. There is a price for that, of course, as you have witnessed: there are times when Clarence takes decisions that I personally would not have taken. But I always back him.'

This was evident in another unacknowledged arrangement: whenever during budget reviews at Treasury Board there developed an intractable disagreement, however rarely, between an operating department minister and Fines, Clarence would by a private signal ask me to get the premier to come to the meeting (recall that Douglas was a member of the Treasury Board). The premier always came and, after a few minutes of continuing disagreement, he would firmly 'suggest' a decision.

Having recounted the strong and responsible role of Clarence Fines in the government, I perhaps should add that he was the only minister in the government who was charged, through the leader of the opposition, Walter Tucker, with accepting kickbacks. Specifically, in 1953

Tucker tabled an affidavit from a Joseph R. Rawluk which alleged that Mr Fines, as minister in charge of Saskatchewan Government Insurance had, along with Mike Allore, manager of the SGIO, been accepting kickbacks from independent SGIO agents as payment for granting them their franchises. As 'evidence,' Fines was alleged to have arranged to meet Rawluk after dark, in a Regina street, to pay him a kickback of $100 or $200. To be recognized, Rawluk would be wearing a purple coat.

The alleged assignation was in itself so bizarre that it could scarcely be taken seriously. But it was all the more so given the widely accepted fact – certainly among opposition members – that Clarence Fines was a wealthy man. Why would a wealthy man risk his reputation for $100 or $200? To add to the cloak and dagger quality of the hearing before the Legislative Committee on Crown Corporations, where the charges were heard, 'Rawluk was discredited by his admission of various petty misappropriations of funds and passing bad cheques.'[18] He told the committee: 'I am here against my will.'[19] The committee found against the charges, and not long after Walter Tucker resigned. To me – and I attended all the hearings – the whole episode became simply a blot on the history of Saskatchewan's Legislative Assembly.[20]

To conclude this note on Clarence Fines, as one of the key ministers in the Douglas government, I should say a word or two about his personality. He was a confident man, professionally, but never advanced himself as a public or political person. Within the cabinet, he was respected, though sometimes suspected of underestimating the province's revenues, or the borrowing capacity of the province, in the interest of balanced budgets (what minister of finance is not?). But he had his human qualities too: he took almost childish pleasure, for example, in demonstrating his ability to almost instantly add, in his head, five columns of figures – up and down, or across. And he similarly relished the red carpet treatment he received in the East from the investment dealers with whom the Treasury dealt, and was hurt when they lost interest in him so suddenly when he ceased to be a minister. Whatever his foibles, however, Fines must be recognized as one of the Douglas government's greatest assets.

If Tommy Douglas was the brilliant and charismatic political leader of the trio of leading ministers in the government, and Clarence Fines was the master manager and financial wizard of the three, Woodrow Lloyd was the wise and thoughtful philosopher. Thirty years old when he became a minister, Lloyd had been a teacher and president of the

Saskatchewan Teachers Federation before his election. And he was, as we know, a co-architect of the CCF's education platform in the pre-1944 election period.

Lloyd was a product of the Depression. His early education was in a one-room school in rural Saskatchewan. He worked his way through normal (teaching) school, and then struggled to get his B.A. through summer school sessions at the University of Saskatchewan and correspondence courses at home. He then qualified for a principal's job – joining Coldwell and Fines in that profession. He became a councillor of the newly established Saskatchewan Teachers Federation in 1933 and president in 1941.[21]

Lloyd's political activism began when he campaigned for the Farmer Labour Party in 1934 and for the CCF in 1938. The driving force in his political life was his passion for individual self-realization, and for a society in which and through which this could be achieved for all. 'Our sensitivity to the rights and needs of others,' he said, 'is an ... excellent measurement of the maturity of the society in which we live.'[22] But it would take resolute action to achieve this goal: '... vision without courage,' he said, 'is as inadequate as faith without works [deeds].'[23]

Lloyd had given expression to these values through the education portfolio. There he pursued with vigour and persistence his twin goals of a higher quality of education across the province, and equality of access to it, for all students. The vehicle for achieving these goals, we know, was the establishment of larger school units. In doing this, he demonstrated other personal qualities for which he became known. He was resolute and determined – some would say stubborn and unyielding – in his belief that this course was the logical and the right one to pursue. He argued that public approval or disapproval could only be intelligently expressed after the school units had been tried. Otherwise, the choice for the public would be between the status quo and the unknown. 'How many things have been accomplished by waiting for unanimous approval?' he is said to have argued in cabinet.[24]

But he was broader in his capacity and his role in the government than in the education portfolio alone. Tommy Douglas said of him: 'Among my cabinet colleagues, I would go to Mr. Fines for financial matters and Mr. Lloyd for questions of basic policy. Mr. Lloyd has one of the best minds I have ever met ... his judgement when you get down to basic fundamentals is not easily equalled.'[25] Douglas used Lloyd accordingly in the councils of government. As the premier put it: '[Woodrow] had intellectual superiority that was apparent not just on education but on any topic that came up. The result was that Woodrow joined what became an inner Cabinet, the Treasury Board as it was called. We prepared most of the estimates and policies that go back to the Cabinet ... It was apparent right from the beginning that he had done a lot of thinking about these matters and that he had a very sound philosophical understanding about the application of democratic socialist principles to a given situation.'[26]

This was Woodrow Lloyd, as I knew him, while I was the secretary to the Treasury Board, when he became minister of finance in 1960, and most particularly when, as premier, he was seeing medicare through in 1962.

Effective and Creative Public Service

Just as the period of the 1950s saw the maturing of the CCF government as reflected in the qualities of its political leaders and public policies, so it was a period when the capacity of the public service and the operations of the machinery of government reached a more developed stage of performance. And this heightening of the professionalism in the public service and in the efficacy of the machinery of government was reflected in the increasing creativity and effectiveness of public administration as a whole.

Certainly this was true of the new machinery of government as designed and initiated in the first and second terms of the government. But the transformation in public administration that took place from 1946 to 1952 did not complete the process of reform, and during the period 1952 to 1960 there continued to be steady improvements. The combined changes to the machinery and processes of government resulted in greater integration of the planning and budgeting work of cabinet as a whole, as well as for departments, and in greater encouragement of departmental planning.

The most important changes were in planning and budgeting. As a first step, in September 1952, cabinet decided that the Treasury Board, as a cabinet committee, should assume responsibility for the preparatory work leading to the annual planning meeting of cabinet, that is, the Cabinet–Planning Board Conference. The Treasury Board was to meet with each department individually, along with representatives of the Planning Board and Budget Bureau staff, with the goal of bringing to the planning conference 'specific recommendations on program policy.'[27]

Shortly thereafter, the new secretary of the Economic Advisory and

Planning Board, Tommy Shoyama,[28] and I (also newly appointed as deputy provincial treasurer) decided to achieve a better integration of planning and budgeting. In essence, we determined to integrate ministerial-level planning and budgeting into a single process, and to use the staff of both the EAPB and the Treasury on joint working parties responsible for studies of individual policies and programs. This decision meant that individual departments would submit simultaneously their annual budgets to the Treasury for budget analysis, and their four- or five-year forward plans to the EAPB for policy analysis. Then, when the Treasury Board and then the cabinet met in their annual planning session, the members would be in a position to discuss not only individual programs, whether old or new, but also to consider the broad 'fiscal framework' for the forthcoming year and the forward plans for the next three or four years thereafter. To cement this integration, Tommy Shoyama, as EAPB secretary, would sit in on all Treasury Board meetings, and I would become a member of the Economic Advisory and Planning Board. Treasury Board approved this approach in September 1952.

A third major change to the budgeting procedures themselves followed shortly thereafter.[29] The newly designed procedures called for departments to submit their budgets in two 'compartments': the 'A' budget would provide for the administration of approved programs at the level of intensity the government had already agreed to, and the 'B' budget would include any new programs or program extensions that the departments wished to propose to government. This procedure would make it possible for the Treasury Board, first, and then the cabinet, to concentrate on policy issues raised in the 'B' budget and to delegate to officials in the Treasury's Budget Bureau the responsibility for reviewing the 'A' budgets with the operating departments. Officials were instructed to report to the Treasury Board any major reasons for increases in the 'A' budget, such as staff for increased workload, along with any problems that came to their attention. Issues that ministers encountered also would be placed on the agenda of the Cabinet–Planning Board Conference.

With these new procedures, the annual planning and budgeting meetings assumed a new shape. Each year the Treasury and EAPB staff reviewed the forward plans and budgets of departments and prepared memoranda for the annual cycle of planning and budgeting meetings. Concurrently, the EAPB staff prepared an economic review and forecast, to serve as the basis for estimating revenue and for ministerial evaluation of the budget as a whole. A report for the Treasury Board comprised the economic forecast, revenue estimates, a summary of expenditure estimates, and the forward plans of all departments.

The changes to the planning and budgeting procedures meant that the Treasury Board now had two major tasks. First, it formulated the 'fiscal framework' to be recommended to the cabinet for the forthcoming year. Against this, the board examined the spending requests of departments and Crown corporations, and framed in broad terms the revenue-expenditure-borrowing policies for the following year. Usually this involved limitations on 'B' budget expenditures, and often on 'A' budgets, and occasionally included a suggested tax increase.[30]

The Treasury Board's second major task was to meet with all major departments and Crown corporations to review with them their principal program proposals for forthcoming years, and in particular to examine their estimates for capital spending.

In the annual conference, the full cabinet and the non-cabinet members of the EAPB (who included two CCF MLAs, Tommy Shoyama as secretary, and myself) conducted a comprehensive review of the fiscal framework, the program proposals in the budget and forward plans, and the 'problem areas' that had been identified for the agenda. The conference also received reports on progress in fulfilling the last election platform. In some years, the conference put greater emphasis on forward plans – the year before an election, for example – and in others it placed more emphasis on special problems that had emerged in implementing earlier election platforms.[31] Whatever the emphasis, the cabinet devoted a full week, without interruptions, to appraising and reappraising its goals and programs.

These meetings produced three things. First, they established the fiscal framework within which the Treasury and Treasury Board would prepare the next year's budget. Secondly, they identified a policy emphasis to guide expenditure recommendations for the forthcoming year, notably with respect to the 'B' budget. Thirdly, they identified problem areas where special studies could be requested. And at some point after these meetings, the cabinet met with caucus to give a preliminary outline of its proposed program emphasis for the following year.[32]

The new planning and budgeting procedure was important for the new roles implied for the Treasury and Treasury Board, the Planning Board, and the operating departments. In his responsibility as secretary of the Planning Board, Tommy Shoyama had quite consciously set about encouraging departmental program planning. He had seen the 'legitimacy' of the Planning Board's efforts questioned, and he was prepared to develop a different approach – a three-pronged role combining inter-departmental planning, criticism for cabinet of plans and proposals as needed, and personal advice to the premier.[33] Congruent with the Budget Bureau's recommendations of planning branches for operating departments, he actively encouraged the development of this capacity in the departments, making it less likely that central 'criticism' would be needed.

The operations of the Planning Board altered accordingly. Its first role was that of 'co-ordinator in drawing up departmental long-term plans,' as the premier put it.[34] This was a matter of encouraging departmental planning. Secondly, despite the fact that the 'formal role of the Board proper has declined in importance with the Treasury Board and the Cabinet itself assuming greater responsibility in financial control and policy co-ordination,'[35] the EAPB staff continued to advise cabinet on supra-departmental matters. For example, during 1955–6, the staff appraised the report of the Royal Commission on Agriculture and Rural Life. The staff advised the premier on the South Saskatchewan Dam negotiations. They chaired working parties and provided staff for special economic studies in resource and industrial development. Gradually, the EAPB moved into population studies, income studies, and special analyses of various sorts.[36] The staff provided the day-to-day support to the Premier and government as a whole, and was developing a new kind of 'personal' authority, as Tommy Shoyama increasingly became the premier's personal confidante.

Meanwhile, the Treasury Department officials were becoming more and more involved in program and administrative analysis. There were increasing requests for organizational studies, usually requiring some degree of program planning.[37] These arose from the new role of the Treasury Board in the annual planning and budgeting process, and as a result of increased Treasury Board activity throughout the budget cycle. Cabinet had decided that 'all requests for projects or expenditures not provided for in approved estimates must be referred to Treasury Board,'[38] and this required work on program proposals during the year.

While these were the major changes in the functioning of the public administration during the period, others followed. For example, a new capital budgeting procedure was introduced during the 1956-60 term. The new procedure used the framework of a five-year plan and provided annual sums of money for construction, for engineering and architectural planning, and for property acquisition. This made it possible for cabinet, at any time, to speed up or slow down its capital expenditures.

And, as a result, departments and Crown corporations could follow a more rational process of planning, design, and contract-letting.

During this period, the Treasury also revised the province's form of accounts. For years, the consolidated fund had been a maze of funds, accounts, and reserves, meaning that only the initiated could determine what the province's financial position was or where it was headed. More, there was no perceptible relationship between the operating statement and the balance sheet. Clarence Fines authorized me to undertake a major reform of the accounts of the province, with the help of an advisor from the federal government, and I produced a paper on Saskatchewan's (new) form of accounts in December 1957. It was presented as a proposal from me, as the deputy provincial treasurer, for review by the Public Accounts Committee, and was approved.[39]

In the civil service generally there were improvements in organizational patterns and personnel policies. The Budget Bureau's influence through organizational studies and policy development was felt in the improved design of operating departments. Pretty well every department had established, in the late 1940s and the 1950s, a planning branch and an administrative services branch, as recommended by the Budget Bureau and supported by the EAPB. The planning branches, with program expertise, combined with the operating branches, with service delivery expertise, to improve greatly the departments' planning capacities. Similarly, the new administrative services branches increased the departments' professionalism in the fields of human resources, finance, administrative operations, and accountability.

Concern with departmental field operations led to a survey of provincial government district boundaries, the extent of decentralization of program administration, and the relationship between regional administration of provincial programs and local government units.[40] Given the complexities of local government reorganization, described in the next chapter, it was understandable that major changes could not be envisaged. Instead, field staffs were brought together in regional headquarters, and informal means of coordination would be developed.

Recruitment and Training

Along with these service-wide changes in the machinery of government and the organization of the public service, the government was engaged in plans for attracting, recruiting, and training professional and administrative personnel. Leading the field was the Budget Bureau with its training and development programs: a multifaceted, multi-year program designed to develop future senior officials, assistant deputy ministers, and indeed deputy ministers. The recruits to the Budget Bureau through this approach included a number of the senior officers mentioned in this history, plus others such as Grant Botham, Bob McLarty, and Jim Lynn.

It began with the recruitment of the most promising graduates (five or six per year) from the political science, economics, or commerce departments of the University of Saskatchewan, and from the University of Toronto, Queen's University, and Carleton University – plus, of course, applicants from other universities. Always we relied heavily upon the nomination or recommendations of professors known to us, and, of course, our own assessments of the candidates. If chosen, the candidates would be appointed for a one-year probationary period as administrative or budget analysts (mostly the former).

Those who successfully completed the probationary period automatically became part of a multi-year program of experience and training. After the first year or two spent as junior administrative or budget analysts, the officials would be eligible for a rather more senior job in the Budget Bureau, as supervisors of small Budget Bureau teams. In the course of these first few years, the participants also attended periodic training sessions and seminars to learn about the real-life functioning of ministers, deputy ministers, and other people engaged in the development and delivery of programs, and to discuss the various human, structural, and procedural facets of public administration.

After these first two stages, usually three or four years, the analyst would be eligible for the third stage – assignment either to an operating department as an assistant deputy minister of administrative services, or the equivalent, or as a senior analyst in the Budget Bureau. Operating department appointments were, of course, the prerogative of the deputy minister and subject to Public Service Commission requirements. But Budget Bureau recommendations were taken very seriously, and indeed the analysts themselves were well known to the departments.

Another alternative – a fourth stage in effect – would be for the analyst to take educational leave to study for his or her M.A. or M.P.A. – usually at Harvard or Carleton, whose public administration programs were highly regarded, and where other Budget Bureau people had been students (including, at Harvard, Tommy McLeod, Art Wakabayashi, and myself). The Treasury Board had approved, late in the government's first term of office, an educational leave program under which public servants could take leave of absence with partial pay. In return for the leave, the public servant would promise to return to the government for at least two or three years.[41]

This was the most ambitious recruitment and training program developed in the government, but other departments were developing similar approaches to increasing the professional capacity in their particular fields. Later the cabinet expanded the educational leave plan, which enabled public servants to take up to two years leave to pursue further university studies. It introduced a bursary plan for university students, such as social workers, which required that the beneficiaries work for the Saskatchewan government after graduation.[42] Ultimately, in 1959 government introduced a sabbatical leave program under which senior public servants were granted 'special leave' for a year, at 75 per cent of pay, to study or travel or both. This program was designed to stimulate and broaden the perspectives of key senior officials.

In all these developments, which extended over the life of the government, Saskatchewan's public service and public servants were becoming recognized across the country as among the most professional in Canada. This can be seen, by way of illustration, in the subsequent careers of some of the Budget Bureau 'graduates.' Several went on to senior positions in the federal government: for example, Arthur Wakabayashi was an assistant deputy minister in the Solicitor General's Department before he returned to Saskatchewan as deputy provincial treasurer; Del Lyngseth became an assistant deputy minister in Health and Welfare; and Grant Botham was the director-general of the British Columbia Region of the Department of Immigration. A trio became engaged in federal-provincial fiscal arrangements in the federal Department of Finance – Bob McLarty, Bill Haney, and Jim Lynn – plus David Levin from the EAPB. Other Budget Bureau graduates went to other provinces – notably Don Tansley as deputy minister of finance in New Brunswick, Paul Leger as deputy minister to the premier in New Brunswick, and Nancy Kenyon as a senior official in New Brunswick and then in the federal Department of Indian and Northern Affairs. Two others became deputy ministers to premiers in Saskatchewan: Wes Bolstad to Premier Lloyd and Mel Derrick to Premier Blakeney. This was quite a record for one agency in a small government.

The Government and the Party

By the 1950s, a mature pattern of relationships had been established between the government and the party as well – a pattern that amounted to an 'institutionalization' of party influence. The convention was the final party authority, and cabinet ministers were careful both to attend and to listen to the annual conventions. Over time, the conventions had become less likely to pass major policy resolutions that the government might find embarrassing. The inclination was to leave to the leadership the determination of such questions. But ministers also sought to explain to the conventions why, when they had not implemented a certain policy, it was not practical or reasonable to do so. Thus the conventions did have a significant influence, if not power. For example, it seems likely that the very vocal support in annual conventions for resource development by social ownership delayed the government's decision to look to private capital for oil and mineral developments.[43] This same concern no doubt contributed to the decision, after 1952, to grant substantial concessions to the co-operative movement in the development of Crown oil reserves. Conventions contributed in other fields too: for example, by promoting the agricultural machinery testing program and the introduction of an equalization feature into grants for rural roads. There are also examples of convention resolutions upon which the cabinet did not act, such as suggestions that the government go into the life insurance business, or that it take over all rural telephone companies.[44] But the influence of the conventions cannot be disputed.

The Legislative Advisory Committee, and to a lesser extent the Provincial Council, came closest to exemplifying a structural relationship between the government and the party. The Legislative Advisory Committee was more inclined to want to make specific suggestions and to examine the administrative details of government operations. Otherwise, the same sorts of issues were discussed with both the Provincial Council and the Legislative Advisory Committee. The latter, however, was in fact more able to engage in detail both because it met more frequently and because it included MLAs, who were more likely to make positive suggestions for legislative and administrative action.

For the party, then, the influence relationship was institutionalized, and party officials could engage as actively or passively as they saw fit. But the influence was not allowed to become direction. One amusing incident revealed the premier when he refused to listen to the party. The president of a constituency association wrote to the premier that his members wanted the government to 'curtail all work or activity on the... constituency for the remainder of [the Liberal member's] term in order to show people the foolishness of voting Liberal.' Douglas replied: 'You can be certain there will be no attempt on the part of the Government to adopt a mean or narrow attitude towards constituencies that are not represented by CCF members. Such a policy would be sheer stupidity to say nothing of being unjust and unfair. People in these constituencies pay their taxes and have as much right to any services we can provide as any other constituency.'[45]

The Government and Public Policy

Perhaps the most significant accomplishment of the maturing CCF government was the evolution and elaboration of a generalized framework of public policy in a welfare state (or, if you prefer, in a Canadian socialist state). Effectively, what the government had done, looking at the whole complex of its programs, was to define the essence of public policy and its elements in a socialist state, from the ground up. In doing so, it expressly articulated the value system upon which its policies were founded – in Tommy Douglas's speeches and in Clarence Fines' budget speeches. It was the same value system that had moved the founders of the CCF, notably Woodsworth and Coldwell.

The fundamental elements in the public policies that gave expression to the CCF's beliefs or principles may be found in the story we have told of the Douglas government thus far. They can be assembled and expressed very simply, if sometimes in somewhat different terms. The social policy of the government called for the provision through the state of education, health, and welfare services in accordance with three general principles: comprehensiveness of services, universal accessibility, and 'public administration' of the services. The modes by which these principles would be applied would differ as among the three main fields of social policy, as would the rate of progress in achieving them.

The economic policy of the government, within its constitutional competence, was the achievement of higher rates of economic growth in a market economy humanized where necessary by state regulation and a fair distribution to the people of Saskatchewan of the benefits of growth. The resources policies called for the development of publicly owned resources by the private sector, within an appropriate regulatory framework and with a fair share of the benefits going to the public. Exceptions to this policy were not ruled out, as the sodium sulphate mining by the province had demonstrated, and as the future role of the Blakeney government in potash mining was to demonstrate once again. But the basic policy was clear. Industrial development would be the responsibility of the private sector, with state encouragement and assistance where necessary. Co-operative enterprises would be encouraged to play a role in the development of industry and resources.

The 'essential services' policy of the government called for the provision by the state, where feasible, of services such as electric power, natural gas, transportation facilities, telephone services, sewer and water facilities, and (a special case, seemingly) compulsory automobile insurance.

These were the goals and principles of the Douglas government – representing, in a sense, a revision of the Regina Manifesto as it might have applied to a provincial government. That this had been achieved, and achieved via the route of actual policies and programs, was a noteworthy accomplishment.

Policies and Politics in the 1950s

The platforms for the elections of 1952 and 1956 were fundamentally the same, with variations that simply reflected the changing socioeconomic circumstances in the province. Essentially the government was largely promising incremental change, building on and expanding the policies and programs of earlier years. These election platforms reflected an established approach to governing, with refinements to existing policies and implementation of the directions charted.

The 1952 election campaign – entitled a *Program for Progress* – was a ten-point program that promised 'a $75 million highway and market road program, power to 40,000 farms and all towns and villages, continued development of Saskatchewan's oil and mineral resources, natural gas in larger cities and intermediate points, construction of the South Saskatchewan Dam in co-operation with the Federal Government, reclamation and resettlement of new Northern areas, [abolition of] the Public Revenue Tax ... [assistance to] municipalities on the basis of need, increased grants for education, extension of the medical care program, [and] extension of social welfare benefits.'[46] The program featured greater spending on physical facilities and economic infrastructure as well as on social capital and quality of life. With these commitments, the government was addressing both the economic and technological changes in the province and the well-being of citizens as the growing prosperity permitted. In essence, many of the developments accomplished both objectives. Rural electrification, for example, was an important economic investment and, at the same time, was undoubtedly a major enhancement to the lives of farm families.

It turned out to be a highly successful appeal. On election day, 11 June 1952, forty-two CCF members were returned and only eleven Liberals. The CCF had taken ten seats from the opposition and had acquired the one new seat. The Liberals had gained only one seat from the CCF. The government party also achieved just over 54 per cent of the popular vote. Premier Douglas and the party were jubilant: the election returns seemed to confirm their judgment in following the course that they had during the past four years. The premier did not change his cabinet, but he did bring in two new ministers: Joe Burton, who became provincial secretary, and Alex Kuziak, who became minister of telephones. He also split the natural resources portfolio, and made Brock Brockelbank the minister of mineral resources and Alex Kuziak minister of natural resources.

Following the election, the government began to implement its program, using the four-year plan that had been the guide to its development. The call for increased expenditures on social policy and for increased investment in infrastructure meant larger budgets, sustained by larger revenues. In the aggregate, expenditures rose by nearly $20 million – from $76 million in 1952–3 to $95 million in 1955–6. The call for heavier investments in the Power Corporation to finance rural electrification and the distribution of natural gas, and in Saskatchewan Government Telephones, for the extension and upgrading of the telephone system, meant more borrowing to finance their growth in capital plants – revenue generating though it would be. The net investment in the Saskatchewan Power Corporation more than doubled – from $40 million to $101 million – and the same was true of the investment in Saskatchewan Government Telephones – which rose from $19 million to $43 million.[47]

The election platform for 1956 was very similar. The government had promised a $100-million highway program, plus $3 million to be spent each year on municipal roads; a substantial increase in school grants; an expansion of the farm electrification program to 65,000 farms; a doubling of the electrical generating capacity in the province; and a plan for bringing natural gas to all cities, towns, and villages. It had also promised to improve, expand, or extend the development of oil, mineral, and forest resources and the drainage, irrigation, and land reclamation programs. It would expand the hospital plan to include outpatient and other services, expand social welfare benefits, and improve conditions for workers. More was promised in the way of industrial development. The final point in the 1956 platform was a commitment to 'fight for a fair share of the national income for farmers.' This would involve pressing the national government in the following directions: to 'establish parity prices for farm products,' to 'provide cash advances on farm-stored grain,' to expand international wheat sales, to establish a national livestock marketing scheme, and to begin immediately the construction of the South Saskatchewan River Dam.[48]

The response of the electorate, however, was very different on this occasion. After the relatively tranquil years of 1952 to 1956, during which the government had faithfully fulfilled its election program, the results of the 1956 election came as a shock to Premier Douglas and his colleagues. Support for the CCF had declined sharply. The *Regina Leader Post* summarized the results succinctly: 'Premier T.C. Douglas and his CCF Party were back in office [Thursday, 21 June 1956] for their fourth straight term, but they start the 13th year as Canada's only socialist government with a reduced majority, the lowest popular vote percentage since 1944, and minus one cabinet minister.'[49]

The CCF's popular vote had fallen, from just over 54 per cent in 1952 to 45 per cent. In fact, the popular vote of the Liberals had declined too, from 39 per cent to 30 per cent. Instead, the vote had swung to the Social Credit Party, although it had not been a force in Saskatchewan since 1938; it had gained 21 per cent of the total vote. The CCF retained thirty-six seats; the Liberals had fourteen, and the Socreds elected three members.

This decline in support called for reflection. It could not be explained as a fluke because 84 per cent of the eligible electorate had voted. Quite simply the vote seemed to have been 'against the government' and, as had happened before in Saskatchewan, the protest took the form of support for a splinter party.

Whereas the 1956 election platform had resembled that of 1952, it seemed the electorate was not satisfied simply with a continuation of past policies or even with the increase in physical facilities and infrastructure that had characterized the government's third term in office. There appeared to be other complexities in the on-going social and economic changes affecting the province. People wanted something more, or perhaps something different. Douglas and his colleagues recognized that somewhere they had gone wrong, and they resolved to try to determine over the next four years just where that was, and what the missing 'something else' was too. This was one of their main tasks, the other being, of course, to implement the programs they had promised.

Premier Douglas shuffled the Cabinet more extensively than had been done since the CCF first came to power, and resolved to

> reorganize the Cabinet, having in mind the need for preparing younger men to carry on the government of this province in the years ahead. [I also propose] making changes in the Cabinet periodically over the years as it becomes apparent that certain members are capable of assuming responsibility. We must look to the future and ensure that this movement will always have capable and experienced leadership at its disposal.[50]

Four new ministers came into cabinet, replacing three who had retired: Robert A. Walker became the new attorney general; Russ Brown, the provincial secretary and minister responsible for the Power Corporation; George Willis, the minister of public works; and Walter Erb, the minister of public health, while Thomas Bentley was shifted to social welfare.

The fulfilment of the commitments of these two elections now resided in experienced hands, and the government went on to meet its promises to the citizens. But the more difficult and the more preoccupying question was what the government had done or had failed to do that brought about the nearly 10 per cent drop in public support for the CCF. The next chapter picks up the story and describes the policy and program implementation of the period from 1952 to 1960, and the government's efforts to understand the attitudes and concerns of the people of Saskatchewan and to chart its directions according to this greater appreciation.

8

Policy Implementation and Reassessment in the 1950s

Having described the functioning of government in Saskatchewan through most of the 1950s – given the thoroughgoing changes that had been made or were in the course of being made in public administration and the machinery of government – I turn now to the policy and program changes during this same period, 1952–60. They were in no small measure incremental in character – whether in the development of infrastructure, or in the fields of health, education, and welfare, or in the field of resources and industrial development. But they were accompanied by a number of new and significant measures – even if these were dwarfed by Tommy Douglas's announcement of medicare in December 1959. They included the South Saskatchewan River development (in the field of infrastructure), the establishment of a cement plant and a steel mill (in the field of resources and industrial development), the initiation of a technical and vocational college (in the field of education), the extension of social assistance measures (in the field of welfare), aided by a new federal-provincial unemployment assistance program, and the establishment in Regina of Wascana Centre.

Building New Infrastructure

First, then, the building of new infrastructure. Rural electrification had been a long-term dream of the government. As early as December 1944, the minister of reconstruction had announced the appointment of a committee to study the possibilities of rural electrification,[1] but at that time the feasibility of proceeding seemed doubtful. In a brief to the national CCF conference, the ministers said that 'while we recognize the possibility and desirability of the program of rural electrification, we nevertheless must recognize that in an area so sparsely populated as Saskatchewan, such a plan of any extended nature ... could not, under existing conditions, be self-supporting.'[2] But after the war the conditions began to change, and in 1948 a joint committee of the Planning Board and the Power Corporation was charged with the responsibility for developing a program for rural electrification.[3] By early 1949 the cabinet had received the committee's report and had asked it to prepare enabling legislation.[4] The bill was enacted at the next session of the legislature.[5]

The plan called for electrification of fifty thousand farms in the first five years, and thirty thousand more farms in following years. The Power Corporation was to invite farmers to 'sign up' for power, and if there were sufficient demand (65 per cent) in any given area, the Power Corporation would install the transmission system. The corporation was to bear the costs of the system, and the farmer was to pay part of the cost of bringing the electricity from the 'road allowance' to the farm.[6] The program was immediately popular and, in order to increase the 'sign up' rate the Rural Electrification Act was amended in 1951 to provide for loans to farmers who were unable immediately to meet their share of the construction costs.[7]

In the 1952 election platform, the government promised to expand this work, and to bring electricity to forty thousand farms by the end of its next term in office. The Power Corporation prepared regular reports for cabinet on its progress in meeting this goal and in achieving the government's undertaking to have all Saskatchewan towns and villages connected with the power grid by 1956 or 1957. In 1956 the premier was able to announce success: the goal had been achieved. Moreover: 'In 1952 we had only 613 communities with power. We now have 750 communities served with power and 60 more communities will be added this year.'[8] This was substantially all the towns and villages in Saskatchewan. By the end of 1960, electrification had reached approximately sixty thousand farms, and the rate of signing up new farmers for electrification began to slow, as the program neared completion. To illustrate, the number of new farms receiving electricity fell from about 7,800 in 1956 to 3,775 in 1959.[9] The Power Corporation's electrical generating capacity more than doubled, as two new thermal stations were opened and a hydro installation was started on the Saskatchewan River, northeast of Prince Albert.

A second major aspect of infrastructure development was the introduction of natural gas as a source of energy in the province. By the autumn of 1952, the potential for natural gas development was clear, but the government had not yet made a firm decision as to whether gas distribution would be the responsibility of the province or of the municipalities. The Department of Natural Resources argued that gas reserves now being sufficient, a decision could and should be made.[10] The Power Corporation prepared a proposal to use in negotiations with the City of Saskatoon, the first city to be served with natural gas.[11] Cabinet approved the approach in November that year,[12] and agreed as well that it would *not* consider proposals from private companies to operate gas distribution systems in cities.[13] Toward the end of 1952, the minister of natural resources granted the Power Corporation a permit to build a pipeline from the Brock-Coleville gas field to Saskatoon,[14] and the City of Saskatoon agreed to permit the corporation to distribute gas to its residents.[15] By the end of 1955, three gas fields were producing, and three cities – Saskatoon, Prince Albert, and Swift Current – and fifteen towns and villages were being served.[16]

Discussions also started during this period on the future sources of gas supply for the Saskatchewan Power Corporation. The idea of a trans-Canada pipeline that would bring gas from Alberta had been mooted, but construction had not yet started, and, in any event, the price such a pipeline would charge was likely to be higher than locally produced gas. In October 1955, therefore, the Power Corporation began to propose the purchase of gas fields within the province and on the border with Alberta.[17] Cabinet approved a pipeline from a gas field in southwestern Saskatchewan to serve Moose Jaw and ultimately Regina,[18] and later the purchase of a gas field that straddled the Alberta-Saskatchewan border. By the end of 1960, the Saskatchewan Power Corporation had substantially fulfilled its part of the 1956 election platform, and the natural gas system had been connected in all cities, as promised, and to some eighty-three towns and villages as well.[19]

Meanwhile, Saskatchewan Government Telephones embarked on an expansion program of its own. It increased the number of telephones in service by nearly 30 per cent in the third term, installed numerous automatic exchanges, began a microwave system that would form part of the trans-Canada system, and – symbolic of Saskatchewan's boom – installed a telephone system in Uranium City, some seven hundred miles north of the U.S. border.[20] Investment in Saskatchewan Government Telephones continued to rise, from $44.5 million in 1956–7 to $73.5 million in 1959–60.

One more element in infrastructure development – in fact, quite a central one – was the expansion of the grid road system. It, however, was so closely intertwined with the issue of municipal organization and the difficulties of reforming local government that this part of the narrative will be resumed later, after developments in social policy and in economic and resource development have been recounted.

Building Social Programs

Developments in social policy were even more important than the government's emphasis on infrastructure during this period. The third and fourth terms were characterized by the gradual implementation of plans and programs in virtually every field, with revisions and adaptations, extensions and elaborations, as the resources became available. Here the operating departments were better able to refine and expand programs, and to adopt new ones, as a result of their improved organizational design and capacity. The financial investment in social programs – in health, welfare, and education – was substantial. Education expenditures rose by 39 per cent, and those for health and welfare by 24 per cent between 1952–3 and 1955–6.[21] Education spending continued to rise, and became 29 per cent of the budget in 1957–8.

In the field of social policy, the government was also responding to economic change and addressing the new and different needs of Saskatchewan society. Certainly it built on existing foundations, either by expanding existing programs or by developing new ones that were 'derivatives' of older policies. The operating departments themselves provided the analysis of change and the forward-looking program proposals. And in doing so, they, like cabinet itself, worked more closely with the relevant interest groups than they had in the past: the school trustees and the Teachers Federation with the Department of Education, as one example; the Canadian Mental Health Association and the Council for Crippled Children with the Department of Public Health, as another; and the John Howard Society and the Department of Social Welfare, which had responsibility for corrections, as a third.

During the third term, the Department of Education conducted a complete reappraisal of the provincial education program. In 1952 it noted in a report to cabinet that, since 1944, the government had devoted most of its new education resources to essential changes to the structure of education – including the organization of larger school units, the school building program, and the 'centralization' of school population. Now the department's focus turned to the content of education. There had been some progress on the 'qualitative' aspects of education – a new high school curriculum, work on a new elementary school curriculum, improvements to teacher training, and so on. But much more needed to be done. The department proposed three ways to achieve greater quality in education. First, it urged the government to work toward the goal of financing 50 per cent of the costs of education – the rest of it being financed by local property taxes – and it proposed, second, that government should revise the school grants formula so as to equalize educational opportunities more adequately across the province, and so as to encourage the transporting of children to larger and better-equipped schools. The third strategy was to make teacher training more rigorous, along with higher salaries to ensure an increasing supply of well-qualified teachers.[22]

Over the third term, the government made good progress in raising the school grants. They rose by $1.6 million in 1952, another $1 million in 1954, another $1.5 million in 1955, and by $1.75 million in 1956.[23] The grants formula changed, too, as the Department of Education had proposed and the school trustees had requested,[24] to support bringing the students to larger centres and to introduce a greater measure of equalization (which the CCF convention had been urging as well).[25]

The same pattern continued in the fourth term. School grants increased from $13 million in 1956–7 to $25 million in 1959–60, and cabinet resolved that these grants should be increased so that ultimately the provincial government would be covering half of the cost of public education.

The teacher shortage was greatly relieved during the 1952–6 period – partly as a result of consolidating the schools and partly as a result of higher salaries. The higher salaries, in turn, attracted more students into the teachers colleges – in 1956 there were one thousand.[26]

To increase access to post-secondary education, the government not only increased its annual grants to the university – a regular practice – but it also announced in 1959 a scholarship plan to provide scholarships for some three hundred high school graduates each year, enabling them to attend university, teachers college, or the provincial technical institute.[27] The same throne speech reported a 'continuing improvement in the level of certification of Saskatchewan teachers, and an increase in enrolment at teacher training institutions.'[28]

A new development, in response to the economic changes in the province, was the initiation and creation of a provincial technical and vocational training scheme. Until 1952–3, technical training was focused in the apprenticeship branch of the Department of Labour and in courses sponsored by the Department of Education (funded under the Federal-Provincial Vocational Training Program, one of the earliest federal-provincial cost-sharing plans). In 1953 the department's officials warned cabinet that the diversification of Saskatchewan's economy was driving the need for a provincial technical institute to train more people in skilled trades.[29] In 1954 the minister proposed the creation of a provincial technical and vocational school to offer programs not then being provided in the technical high schools or university. Federal assistance was anticipated, but the Department of Education would be directly responsible for the administration of the new school.[30] Within the government there was some debate about when the project could be launched, but there was general agreement that the proposal had merit, and a year after the proposal was first mooted the department reminded the Treasury Board of 'recent statements by the Premier [which committed] the Province ... to the building and equipping of a central technical institute.'[31] The 1956 speech from the throne announced the establishment of the new institute.

During these two terms of office, the Department of Public Health concentrated on expanding its curative health program, on increasing mental health services, and on establishing a new program of physical restoration or rehabilitation. The health regions had continued to expand: by 1953 they covered half the province, excluding Regina and Saskatoon. With the addition of four more regions in the third and fourth terms, the coverage of the province was complete.[32]

To assist in financing these and other public health initiatives, the Department of Health concerned itself with controlling the costs of hospital services under the Saskatchewan Hospital Services Plan. With the completion of the University Hospital in 1954, the province had reached its target of 7.5 beds per thousand population, and from then on the government expected local hospital boards to concentrate on upgrading services rather than on building more beds.[33] The volume of hospital care had levelled off since 1950 as well; presumably, the 'backlog' of health needs had been met.[34] Nonetheless, there were three nagging problems. Costs continued to rise, driven by rising hospital staff salaries and improvements in the quality of service, including, of course, new medical technology. Secondly, too many hospital beds were being used for chronic care patients, in the absence of alternative and less expensive accommodation. And there was continuing political and community pressure for new hospitals. While the government did not attempt to check the rising salaries or improvements in service quality, it did agree to 'resist the pressure to build hospitals in communities that do not rate hospital facilities,'[35] and it did agree that alternative accommodation should be sought for patients who needed chronic care.[36] The cabinet considered the possibility of introducing a deterrent fee into the hospital care system but rejected the idea on the grounds that it would prevent people who needed care from going to hospital.[37]

In 1958 the province was relieved of the increasing financial pressure when the federal government announced its intention to proceed with a national hospital insurance plan. Even more to the point, Douglas and his government would now be able seriously to consider the introduction of its long-promised universal medical care plan, for some 43 per cent of Saskatchewan's hospital costs would now be borne by the federal government. (A fuller story of the introduction of hospital care across Canada is told in the Annex, and a much fuller account of the introduction of medical care insurance in Saskatchewan appears in the chapters that follow.)

During the two terms of office from 1952 to 1960, the mental health program continued to expand as it had done during 1948–52. The Psychiatric Services Branch, the Canadian Mental Health Association (in which government psychiatrists were very active),[38] and a sympathetic CCF convention, which urged the elimination of overcrowding in mental hospitals,[39] all contributed to an expanding program. Their efforts led to extended facilities at the two major mental hospitals, a growing number of mental health clinics, and a new school for the developmentally handicapped. The treasurer described the mental health program this way:

> Nor are the mentally ill any longer the forgotten men and women of Saskatchewan. Our expenditures on mental hospitals alone amounted to $6.25 per capita in 1954–55, as compared with the average of $2.95 per capita being spent by all other governments in Canada in the same year. Perhaps of even greater significance for the future is the expenditure ... on mental health clinics and community services, and on psychiatric research ... We have reached the point where the ratio of patients discharged from the hospitals, as compared with those admitted, has improved immeasurably over the unhappy pattern of a few years ago.[40]

Another significant development in health care in Saskatchewan was the emergence of rehabilitation medicine as a field of medical practice.

In the mid-1950s, this program had nearly every possible advantage in the expenditure allocation process. As a policy, it appealed to the heart-strings (helping crippled children, as they were then called), and it was an economic investment as well (preventing people from becoming a public charge).[41] The serious polio epidemic of 1953 encouraged the development of rehabilitation services, and the Department of Public Health, the Canadian Council for Crippled Children, and the CCF Party all supported the program. Moreover, the Canadian government was suggesting the possibility of a new federal-provincial rehabilitation program, thus holding out the promise of federal health grant money to support it.[42] The government assumed responsibility for the 'crippled children's centres' in 1953,[43] and signed a Federal Provincial Rehabilitation Agreement in the same year.[44]

Even as it was implementing these new initiatives and expanding existing programs, the Department of Public Health continued to look to the incremental creation of the full 'socialized' health care system envisaged in the CCF's first election platform. Each year it submitted a list of new programs or program expansions to the Cabinet–Planning Board Conference. This enumeration usually included proposals for making hospital outpatient services a benefit of the hospital plan; for extending the partial medical care program by adding child and maternity benefits; or for adopting a complete medical care program through the complete coverage of the province by health regions.[45] The government remained consistently committed to a complete medical care program: indeed, three of the four throne speeches during 1953–6 mentioned this as a goal of the government. But cabinet felt unable to afford the plan until federal assistance became available.[46]

In similar fashion, the Department of Social Welfare engaged in making plans that would achieve a more comprehensive and more integrated system of welfare. Its major objective was the rationalization of public assistance programs, with a view to establishing a 'single program geared to the needs of the recipients, along with case work [social workers] services.'[47] Such a program implied both a uniform and higher scale of benefits. The department's second goal was to expand the nursing home program – both 'housing' for the elderly and facilities for people who had become chronic patients.[48] The department's third objective was to develop a more adequate treatment program in jails and to extend probation and parole services,[49] again foreshadowing nationwide developments decades later.

As for the plan to develop an integrated social assistance program, there were difficult hurdles to be overcome. One was the recognition that public support for specific disadvantaged groups in society – the aged, the disabled, the single mothers – was likely to be much greater than public support for an amorphous group called 'low income families.'

Another and more decisive factor in the early 1950s was the fact that the federal government was busy with what they saw to be the building blocks of a more comprehensive social security system. In 1951 the Old Age Security Act provided federal old age security allowances to all persons seventy years of age and over; and in the same year, the government of Canada undertook to share with the provinces the cost of needs-tested allowances to persons aged sixty-five to sixty-nine. In 1954 the Disabled Persons Act provided for federal sharing with the provinces of allowances to disabled persons; and in 1956 the government of Canada undertook to share the financing of provincial social assistance to the rest of those in need – as determined by the provinces.

However, the Department of Social Welfare did make progress in increasing the benefits paid under provincial programs. Here it was supported by the Old Age Pensioners Association, which argued for increased supplemental allowances,[50] and by the CCF Party, which argued for higher pensions, higher mother's allowances, and increased payments to foster parents.[51] It was assisted, too, by a cabinet that was by nature inclined to increase social aid payments whenever it felt it could manage to do so. In 1954 the department was invited to submit to the Treasury Board proposals for increasing allowances, and after extended discussions, cabinet agreed in 1955 to increase the mother's allowances, the old age supplemental allowances, and the foster home boarding rates.[52] Shortly after these changes were announced, Saskatchewan entered into the Unemployment Assistance Agreement with the federal government, under which Ottawa paid 50 per cent of the province's social aid bills (over an agreed amount), and this new arrangement helped to finance the increased benefits.[53] Then in 1958 the federal government announced increases in the pensions and allowances that it 'cost-shared,' and the province followed with a $1 million increase in its pensions and allowances.[54] And in 1959 the minister of social welfare announced that the province, assisted by the federal-provincial shared cost arrangements, would bear the entire cost of social aid (except for a 7 per cent per capita contribution from municipalities),[55] thus establishing more uniform levels of social assistance in the province.

Other programs improved gradually as well. A new nursing home was authorized in 1953, and another was completed in 1954.[56] As an incentive for the establishment of still more nursing homes, the government initiated a system of grants to charitable organizations and municipalities; these grants provided organizations with 20 per cent of capital costs and operating grants of $40 per bed per year.[57] By 1956, the provincial treasurer was able to boast that, 'since 1944, the number of public and private nursing home beds has more than tripled.'[58] The number of beds in provincial geriatric hospitals and municipal and charitable homes rose again in the fourth term from 2,000 in 1957 to 3,400 in 1959, with more construction under way.[59] In 1960 government increased the funding for the homes from $40 per bed per annum to $60.[60]

And there were other investments in the fields of health and education and social services, as well. In the third term, the government completed the 533–bed University Hospital and built a nurses' residence, a library, and two other buildings on the university campus. It built a residence for the developmentally handicapped, a natural history museum, a courthouse, and an administration building. And the Treasury assisted local governments, as well. The provincial treasurer assured local governments that 'any municipality which shows evidence of need, and a determined local effort ... can count upon the Government for full co-operation in the problem of financing soundly planned, self-supporting projects.'[61]

Capital expenditures on health, education, and welfare institutions continued at a high level during the fourth term. Four new buildings were built, or construction started, on the university campus, including structures for arts, biology, animal husbandry, and cancer research (built by the Cancer Society with contributions by government). The new technical and vocational institute in Moose Jaw was completed. The 300-bed geriatric hospital was opened in Regina, and another 100-bed facility was planned for Swift Current. The first small community mental hospital was proposed; and a new office building for the departments of health and welfare and a new courthouse were completed.

Changes in the corrections program consisted of gradual improvements, including the addition of training facilities at the jails, the engagement of new professional staff, and an extension of probation and parole services.[62]

In the field of labour there had been no major changes over the past several years, except for gradual increases in minimum wages and workmen's compensation benefits. In 1958 the government introduced legislation under which every employee who had worked for his or her employer for five years or more would be entitled to three weeks of vacation, with pay, annually.

Finally, a series of loans to municipalities plus capital grants for roads, schools, and hospitals stimulated a vigorous public investment program at the local level too. The provincial treasurer announced in 1957 that he was setting aside $15 million

> as a revolving fund for the purchase of debentures from those needy local governments which are encountering genuine difficulty in marketing their bonds ... In undertaking to purchase up to 50 per cent of the debentures of such local governments, we are giving formal recognition to the fact that local governments are encountering, as we are, real difficulties in keeping pace with economic and population changes.[63]

Economic and Resource Development Initiatives

In economic and natural resources policy, the striking characteristic of the period was the productive relationships that emerged between government and business and resource industries as the government sought to diversify the provincial economy through the attraction of private capital. The thorny questions of social ownership and public enterprise had effectively been resolved, and the third term saw a shift to a 'new model' of development. It entailed both the encouragement of private enterprise and the recognition in provincial policies that a reasonable balance had to be struck between ensuring the profitability of development for private investors, on the one hand, and, on the other, assuring a reasonable public benefit from the exploitation of Saskatchewan's resources and/or from provincial assistance in the financing of new industrial ventures. As a measure of the government's determination to succeed in its economic development strategy, expenditures on agriculture and natural resources rose by 47 per cent in the third term and those on trade and industrial development by 50 per cent. And they continued to rise in the subsequent years as well.

Officials of the Industrial Development Office and those responsible for the Industrial Development Fund were authorized and encouraged to be flexible in their negotiations with private firms if this would help to attract industry to the province. For example, when a group of businessmen proposed to establish a cement plant in Regina, the cabinet increased the amount it was prepared to lend to the company beyond the original limits it had established.[64] Ultimately the government guaranteed the bonds of the enterprise, extending credit in this way for the first time, and further agreed to specify in public contracts that Saskatchewan cement be used where prices and quality were equal.[65] And cabinet authorized the Power Corporation to negotiate with the company as reasonable an industrial rate as it was able.[66] The Saskatchewan Cement Corporation was established in 1956.

In another example, the cabinet considered special measures to assist in attracting a steel pipe mill to the province.[67] It seemed on the face of it to be a quite improbable venture. A steel mill in Saskatchewan? But the basic ingredients were there: a supply of scrap iron available from the farmers and the scrap dealers, and a growing demand for steel pipe to transport across the continent the natural gas and the oil being produced on the Prairies. But the capital required was at once truly substantial and equally difficult to attract – given again the apparent improbability of the endeavour.

The entrepreneurs of the company, however, were energetic, tough-minded, and imaginative, and the government negotiators – led in the final analysis by Clarence Fines – were equally enterprising. Through the guarantee by the government of Inter-Provincial Steel Company loans, and other assistance, the steel mill was established. The venturesomeness of both IPSCO and of the government's team of advisors – from the GFO and the IDO – paid off, handsomely. IPSCO was, and continues to be, a huge success.

The most varied illustrations of programs to attract industry, however, were to be found in the development of natural resources. Here, in particular, the government sought arrangements that would balance the desire for royalties as a source of more government revenue with the goal of making resource development profitable for the enterprises concerned. For example, the government sponsored a feasibility study on forest industries in the province,[68] and was prepared to negotiate a special forestry agreement with interested pulp and paper companies, including an extended option on forest resources.[69] While this effort was unsuccessful, others were more effective. They included special royalties with the 'pioneering' potash companies, assisting rural municipalities to construct access roads to the potash developments, and liberalizing the conditions for exploring and developing Crown-owned mineral lands.[70]

The government financed new geophysical surveys in the Precambrian north in 1957,[71] and again in 1960,[72] and substantially increased expenditures on mineral and forest access roads. In 1959 it announced:

During the past decade the government has constructed more than two thousand miles of roads in the mineral and forest areas of Northern Saskatchewan. Plans are underway to exceed last year's construction record of over two hundred miles of northern roads. In addition, the Saskatchewan Government is co-operating with the Government of Canada in the construction of roads which will connect Prince Albert to Creighton-Flin Flon, Hudson Bay to The Pas, Buffalo Narrows to La Loche and Lac la Ronge to Uranium City.[73]

While the tempo of mineral exploration had diminished greatly with the general decline in the Canadian economy, 'during 1958 Saskatchewan rose to fourth place among all the provinces in the production of mineral wealth.'[74] Significantly, in 1958 the throne speech announced that work had begun on a potash concentrator near Saskatoon,[75] and in 1960 it announced the discovery of iron ore deposits and helium.[76]

Cabinet was prepared, too, to assist the oil industry generally and to extend the term of oil exploration permits.[77] The minister of mineral resources commented that 'our relations with the industry have been quite satisfactory and I consider it my responsibility to maintain that condition if at all possible.'[78]

This change in attitude and policy did not, however, always guarantee smooth relationships between government and industry. What was called for, to repeat, was a constant effort to achieve a happy balance between the government's commitment to retain a 'fair share' of the resources for the people of Saskatchewan, and its desire to create a satisfactory business climate. Another example of the sort of difficulties that arose is the story of the government's 'reserve' policies. Cabinet had set aside for the province a certain percentage of all mineral rights in every oil lease it granted to oil companies; these reserves were later to be developed or disposed of so as to maximize the public return.

At first no firm policy as to how these lands should be handled was required. But as oil production proceeded on lands adjoining the reserves, some disposition of the reserved lands became essential to prevent government's oil from being drained by production from adjoining wells. In 1953 there appeared to be four options: the government could sell or dispose of rights by auction; it could offer rights by tender to the company bidding the highest 'net royalty' over and above the basic royalty; it could retain the rights but allow a company to operate the field for the government; or it could develop the reserves itself.[79] The Department of Natural Resources established a special unit to estimate the possible worth of each oil-bearing parcel.

The debate within government was extensive. Neither the minister of mineral resources nor the Oil Policy Committee favoured government development of reserves, as this would both impair industry-government relations and require very large sums of capital. But they believed the government should remain flexible in its use of the other alternatives. This was the course the cabinet determined to follow. By 1953 it had already sold some reserves by cash auction, without having announced a firm policy for the future.

In December 1953 the cabinet met with the Oil Policy Committee (a committee of senior officials chaired by Tommy Shoyama) to discuss the general policy question and to make decisions concerning a particular oilfield where some parcels were to be disposed of. The decision at this meeting was to enter into negotiations with the Federated Co-operatives for a 'farm out' agreement for certain parcels of mineral rights, as an alternative to a cash auction.[80] The reasons were fairly obvious. The government was not bound by any of its undertakings with private oil companies to follow any particular method of developing the oil lands, and the co-operatives, which unlike the private oil companies were made up of Saskatchewan citizens, were seen to approximate public participation in the development of resources.

Unfortunately, the news of this decision leaked to the press before discussions could be held with the private companies, and there was an uproar.[81] The Canadian Petroleum Association protested the 'favouritism' being shown to the co-operatives and expressed its apprehension that this would set a pattern for the future disposition of reserves. In fact, it did not, as some early advertisements of cash auctions of other parcels soon demonstrated. Over time, it became apparent that the government favoured a combination of 'net royalty' auctions and 'cash' auctions.[82] But industry-government relations had been damaged, and the incident demonstrated the hazards the government faced in achieving the policy balance it was seeking.

In some areas of government, notably the new Crown corporations, the improvements and refinements of 1952–6 took the form of a rationalization of operations. From 1948 on, the government had determined to close the corporations that were unable to operate at a profit, and to make more efficient those that were profitable and those which provided a public service at least at a break-even level. The shoe factory and tannery had been closed, and the Fish Board dissolved and replaced by the Fish Marketing Service. The woollen mill was finally closed in April 1953, and after repeated discussions between ministers and officials, the box factory too was closed in 1957.

Meanwhile, the other 'socialist enterprises,' as the opposition described the corporations other than the Saskatchewan Power Corporation and Saskatchewan Government Telephones, were doing well under the rigorous regimen that had been set for them. By 1961 their net accumulated profit was just under $13 million. Still operating were the Saskatchewan Government Airways, Saskatchewan Transportation Company, the Timber Board, the Fur Marketing Service, the brick plant, the sodium sulphate plant, the Government Insurance Office and a satellite company, Saskatchewan Guarantee and Fidelity Company Limited, and the Government Printing Company. Two others – a northern trading company and the Fish Marketing Service – were purchased by co-operatives in 1959. In a sense, the saga of government in business – beyond public utilities – had ended, and it was now simply a matter of operating going concerns on a businesslike basis, bearing in mind, of course, their social and economic objectives.

In the field of agriculture there were two major changes in policy in the fourth term, one a temporary program and the other a permanent change. The first of these occurred in 1959, when the province urged the government of Canada to make special relief payments to farmers after a large part of the prairie crop was buried under an unseasonable snowfall. The federal government countered with an offer to make payments to the farmers providing the province shared in them. In this way, the province found itself, for the first time, contributing a kind of 'deficiency payment' to farmers. The total payments exceeded $5 million, and then, in the spring, most farmers were able to harvest the crop owing to unusually favourable weather conditions.[83]

The ongoing program was the creation of a limited farm credit plan. In this case, too, political pressure seems to have contributed to the adoption of the program in Saskatchewan. First, the federal government was operating the Farm Credit Corporation, which was meeting a substantial part of the need for farm credit, and would meet more of that need as the new national government liberalized the terms of credit. The CCF Party itself had pressed for many years for a farm credit plan, and the farm organizations were now urging action that would force the federal government to liberalize its plan. The Royal Commission on Agriculture and Rural Life had also recommended a limited provincial credit plan.

In 1959 the government undertook to assist the Co-operative Trust Company to establish a plan that would make credit available 'to meet the problem of the transfer of the family farm to the younger generation.'[84] Provincial assistance took the form of a guarantee of Trust Company securities that were sold to raise the required capital, and an undertaking to purchase for provincial pension and trust funds as many securities as the company sold to the public. The resulting farm credit plan never did grow very large, however, for the federal government did what the government of Saskatchewan had hoped it would do: 'improve the provisions of its farm credit legislation' so as to make its credit terms similar to those in the Saskatchewan plan.[85]

Still within the Department of Agriculture, both extension services[86] and engineering services[87] were expanded in 1957 and 1959. A new Agricultural Machinery Administration was formed in 1958 to undertake the inspection and rating of farm machinery in a scientific and systematic way.[88]

A Special Note on the South Saskatchewan River Dam

One infrastructure project deserves special mention. The South Saskatchewan River project was more spectacular in both scale and complexity than all of the rest of the infrastructure projects combined. And it was a project with a long and thorny history.

The possibility of constructing a dam on the South Saskatchewan River, mainly as a source of water for irrigation on the dry prairies, had been mooted before the war. In 1946 discussions actually began when the federal Prairie Farm Rehabilitation Administration (PFRA) prepared a feasibility report on the project, which stimulated first governmental and then widespread public interest in the project. The proposal was for an earth-filled dam on the river that would make possible the irrigation of some five hundred thousand acres of land, would provide water for the cities of Regina and Moose Jaw, would give the province its first hydroelectric station, and would make possible the development of recreation sites.[89] What resulted is a tale of federal-provincial wrangling, and of failed communication and decision-making, over a ten-year period.

First, one must understand the positions of Premier Douglas and of the national minister of agriculture, James Gardiner, a former premier of Saskatchewan. Both were supportive of the project, and saw it as a means of providing a stable source of water for the irrigation of hundreds of thousands of acres of farmland. The searing experience of the drought of the 1930s and its disastrous consequences for the farmers and the society of Saskatchewan readily explain the deeply held rationale and the political importance attached to the issue of water and the promise of irrigation. But this view did not generally prevail in the cabinet of Prime Minister St Laurent, which helps to explain the protracted negotiations and discussions that ensued.

In 1947 the federal minister of agriculture, Gardiner, tabled the report of the PFRA in the House of Commons and announced an early commencement of the project – more than ten years before it actually did begin. Saskatchewan's minister of natural resources immediately asked for details of the project in order to plan a power development. Over two years, informal discussions took place concerning details of the project. These concerned the disposition of mineral rights in the reservoir area, the allocation of the water of the South Saskatchewan River, engineering problems, and the economic values of a power development. In 1949 the director of the Prairie Farm Rehabilitation Administration and the Saskatchewan minister of agriculture agreed that the PFRA would be responsible for construction and maintenance of the dam and for recommending the place for power production in the operation of the reservoir. The Saskatchewan Power Corporation would be responsible for distributing and selling 'residual power.'

Then, in 1950, the director of the PFRA suggested to Premier Douglas that the government make an offer concerning the use of power. Gardiner and Douglas then met, and the two men worked out a plan that made Canada fully responsible for the irrigation distribution system and for the hydroelectric installation. Despite these discussions, the government of Canada had not reached a clear decision as to whether it would proceed with the dam. Instead, in mid-1951, it established a royal commission to study the economics of the proposed development. In January 1953, the royal commission submitted its report to the federal government – a report that was not favourable to the South Saskatchewan River project.

The next five years were characterized by protracted debate and negotiations. Prime Minister St Laurent stated in the House of Commons that he was not convinced that the project made the best use of the water available. Nonetheless, Gardiner wrote to Premier Douglas in February 1953 indicating that the federal government would still consider an offer from the province. Premier Douglas requested from the prime minister an assurance that the Canadian government was prepared to proceed with the project. Even when this assurance was not forthcoming, he offered to pay $45 million toward the project costs, in effect committing the province to a contribution of $20 million toward the cost of the dam itself (to be paid in the form of rentals for water use in the generation of power). Still, no decision was forthcoming.

Some five months later, negotiations resumed and were pursued between officials of the PFRA and Saskatchewan's Irrigation Committee into 1954. Officially the federal position was that Saskatchewan should contribute $25 million to the cost of the dam and should, as well, assume responsibility for the cost of all power works. Unofficially, the impression was left that the federal minister and the PFRA officials thought the government of Canada should build the whole thing, but that there was a great deal of opposition to this point of view within the federal cabinet.

In April 1954, when Tommy Douglas and James Gardiner met, the premier made a new offer of $17.86 million to the costs of the dam. In effect, this meant that Saskatchewan would pay $73 million toward the total cost of the project, including irrigation and power works, while Canada's share would be $62 million. Nonetheless, Prime Minister St Laurent told the House of Commons on 3 June 1954 that 'I have not yet come to the conclusion that ... this project ... [is] an undertaking of value to the nation equivalent to its cost to the nation ...'

Negotiations dragged on until mid-1955, when Prime Minister St Laurent told Premier Douglas and Clarence Fines that he was adamant in his refusal to proceed with the project. The negotiations then came to a halt for nearly two years. This was the state of affairs when the St Laurent government was defeated in June 1957.

The new prime minister, John Diefenbaker from Saskatchewan, had promised that his government would proceed with the dam if he were elected. Negotiations about the costs and contributions of Saskatchewan resumed, with the federal government requiring still another increase in conditions. Finally, in July 1958, an agreement was signed.

This was really only the beginning, in the sense that the dam would take seven years to build. The power project had to be designed and integrated into the Power Corporation's plans for enlarging the province's generating capacity. The recreation potential and facilities had to be planned. The whole exercise had to be coordinated. At the provincial level, this was the responsibility of the South Saskatchewan River

Development Commission, made up of representatives from government and from the University of Saskatchewan. For the premier, however, the great dream for Saskatchewan agriculture was now being realized.

The Expansion of the Grid Road System and the Reorganization of Local Government

The story of the construction of grid roads in Saskatchewan is in one sense part of the investment in economic infrastructure that figured so prominently during the mid-1950s. But, at the same time, it was also a vivid illustration of one of the particular challenges of governing in an environment characterized by multiple levels of government, including local municipalities.

Recall that the 1952 *Program for Progress* had promised a $75-million highway and market road program. The magnitude of the public investment in roads and highways was an indication of the province's difficult problem with roads. Saskatchewan had over 100,000 miles of provincial and municipal roads serving less than a million people, and 8,200 miles of this were categorized as provincial highways – more miles per capita than Manitoba, Alberta, and British Columbia combined. This system had 'run down' very substantially during the 1930s and the war years, and much of it needed to be rebuilt. Even by 1953 only 956 miles were paved, and much of the remainder needed rebuilding. The Department of Highways was proceeding steadily to meet this challenge.[90] Gross provincial expenditures were $78 million for the period ending March 1956. And the government of Canada contributed some $10 million over a five-year period – most of it on the Trans-Canada Highway.[91]

Cabinet's principal concern, now, was the system of 'market roads' that was being proposed. For many years, the farmers and their municipal representatives had been pressing for provincial support for a network of market (grid) roads that would connect the major trading centres, and thus supplement the provincial highway system. There was no doubt as to the priority of such a venture, but the question to be decided was whether these roads should be the responsibility of local government or should be treated as a secondary provincial highway system. The difficulty lay in the fact that the individual municipalities were too small, by themselves, to plan or finance such a system. So they turned to the province for help. In 1944 and subsequently, CCF conventions resolved that the 'Minister of Highways inaugurate a program of road building designed to include the opening up and building of main market roads ...'[92]

By 1947 the government had turned its mind to this problem, and in that year, for example, the Planning Board proposed that the market roads branch of the Department of Highways should prepare for an acceleration of market road construction.[93] Then, periodically over the years, the cabinet revised the equalization formula for market road grants to municipalities and increased the amounts.

To understand the complications of the grid road question, it must be recalled that the basic municipal units in Saskatchewan had been established in 1909, that they were small rectangular units of 324 square miles, and that there were over three hundred of them. Add the urban municipalities, towns, and villages and there were some 785 municipal units. In 1909 there had also been some 1,700 school districts that requisitioned taxes from the municipalities.[94] By the 1950s, it was more than self-evident that these units were too small to carry out the functions of a modern state. The situation could only be resolved by creating larger and more efficient units. But while the urban municipalities favoured a reorganization of local government, the smaller rural municipalities were loath to accept such a solution.

Over the previous years, the policy and program developments of the CCF government had created a number of new local authorities instead. The health regions were responsible for hospital services, school units for education, veterinary districts for veterinary services, and conservation districts for land reclamation. A provincial department was responsible for social welfare services and care of the chronically ill. At this point, the logical remaining role for local government was for the most part roads – and specifically market roads. But even this prime remaining function of rural municipalities was weakened when the province began to plan and supervise the construction of the grid roads.

The story of local government reorganization, centring for the most part on grid roads, is a tale of committees, commissions, royal commissions, consultations, and conferences. The driving force for all of these bodies was the premise that local government reorganization was an essential reform. For the rural municipalities, however, the driving force was their continued existence.

One of the first committees to deal with the subject had been appointed earlier in the government's history and had reported in 1950. The Britnell-Cronkite-Jacobs Committee had not worried about creating new special function units of government. It only noted that 'this development has the disadvantage of weakening the municipal body by attracting many capable persons to ... such local authorities and overshadowing the achievements of municipal councils by the sheer magnitude of performance.'[95] The report appeared to condone the proliferation of local government units. Nor did it deal with the problem of equalization of services between municipal units. Rather, it reported: 'It is the considered opinion of your Committee that the equalization process cannot be accepted as an absolute principle, and that if applied to municipalities in a complete form it would result in the complete destruction of local self government.'[96]

This left the government pretty well where it had started, committed to an extension of social services, which should be provided equally across the province, but with a municipal system that could not administer them. Yet the municipalities continued to ask for and to receive more financial assistance. Conditional grants of all kinds, including grants in aid, increased from just under $5 million in 1945–6 to over $18 million in 1956–7.[97] The cost of services assumed by the province had risen from under $2 million to $8 million.

In 1952 the government tried again and appointed a Municipal Advisory Commission with Cronkite as its Chair. It reported to the minister of municipal affairs and soon became the principal advisor to the minister on the question of market roads. The commission immediately launched a study of market roads, arguing that the dilemma of the need for market roads and the capacity of local government to design and build these roads should be put clearly to the public, and that meanwhile no major revisions in provincial policy should be made – at least not before the commission's report had been submitted.

Meanwhile, the government had also established the Royal Commission on Agriculture and Rural Life with a comprehensive mandate. It too considered the problems of local government. At community hearings across the province, the royal commission was told repeatedly that there was a need for main market roads and that the present municipal structure was incapable of grappling with it.

While these two commissions were meeting, the government continued to be exposed to a good deal of pressure to 'do something': for example, the 1953 CCF convention passed a number of resolutions recommending increased provincial aid.[98] And the caucus was sympathetic. Cabinet finally decided to make no basic changes until it had heard both from the Royal Commission on Agriculture and Rural Life and from the Municipal Advisory Commission (suspecting all the while that the two reports would disagree).

In the meantime, the engineers in the Department of Highways were encouraged to speed up the design of a market road system, and the minister of highways was to give some thought to interim assistance for main market roads.[99] Late in 1954, the government received some intimation that the Municipal Advisory Committee would likely propose an eleven to twelve thousand mile system, costing $45 to $50 million, with a provincial contribution of some $2.5 million per year for ten years. Further, a very substantial contribution to the municipalities would also likely be suggested. But there would be no suggestion as to how the province was to finance these grants, nor any proposal for municipal reorganization.[100]

For the government, the fundamental issue was whether to reorganize local government into units that could assume larger responsibilities, not only for the road system but for other aspects of public programs; or, in the alternative, to maintain the existing local government structures while at the same time establishing special purpose regions, either as local governments (school units) or as regional entities within the provincial departments, including one in the highways department. Informally, the Chairs of both commissions advised the government that municipal organization should be changed. One said 'rural municipal government units as presently constituted have long since passed their usefulness,' and the other said 'grants to municipalities should not be substantially increased until such reorganization has occurred as to give reasonable certainty that an efficient use will be made of the money.'[101]

When, in October 1955, the Royal Commission on Agriculture and Rural Life submitted its report on 'rural roads and local government,'[102] it reported that 'the evidence conclusively indicates the urgent necessity of basic reorganization of rural municipal government in Saskatchewan.'[103] It outlined the alternative patterns of local government organization, which the government might consider, including the establishment of counties or modified counties to replace the rural municipalities. It also predicted a storm of controversy and urged a 'unified and non-partisan approach to [these] fundamental issues.'[104]

The predictions of controversy were certainly accurate. While the government was frank in saying it believed 'that some kind of basic reorganization, at least in rural areas, is an essential first step in meeting the problems of local government today,'[105] the opponents were equally frank in attributing the pressures for reorganization to the CCF. The president of the Saskatchewan Association of Rural Municipalities said:

Ever since this Government came into office, and to some extent before, whisperings and misgivings were the order of the day, even to the extent, at one time, that maps were already drawn, by those in authority, and it was anticipated reorganization of boundaries would become law. This ... undercover activity, I believe, has had a very detrimental effect ...[106]

The next step in the story was the provincial government's decision to call a major provincial-local government conference. To prepare for this conference, the government struck a committee of senior officials, including myself as Chair, Tommy Shoyama as secretary, and the heads of all the departments working with local government as members. The committee also included the cabinet secretary and Meyer Brownstone, who had been research director for the Royal Commission on Agriculture and Rural Life, and who was to become deputy minister of municipal affairs.[107] The conference was convened in December 1956 and brought together representatives of the Association of Rural Municipalities, the Saskatchewan Urban Municipal Association, the School Trustees Association, the Hospitals Association, and the health regions. Representatives of the Teachers Federation and municipal and school unit secretary-treasurers were present with the right to participate in discussion, and there was a large number of observers, including MLAs, MPs, and representatives of various provincial organizations.

In opening the conference, the premier made clear his views as to the need for local government reorganization. After proclaiming his belief that reorganization was necessary, he then added: 'I want to make it abundantly clear that the Government will not embark upon a program of municipal reorganization unless this program is assured of the co-operation of the local governing bodies and the widespread support of the general public.'[108] He also announced an immediate increase in provincial grants to local governments in the amount of $7 million.

With this commitment, the premier in effect gave the rural municipalities – obviously opposed to any change – a virtual veto over any plan for reorganization. Nonetheless, discussions at the conference proceeded and culminated in support for a continuing committee to study the issue yet further. Some time elapsed before the local government organizations endorsed the idea of a continuing committee, but in April 1957 the cabinet felt that it could proceed.[109] It appointed a committee[110] consisting of five cabinet ministers, three representatives each from the associations of rural municipalities, urban municipalities, and school trustees, and one representative from each of the health regions and hospital districts. Representatives of the Teachers Federation and the school unit and municipal secretary-treasurers were associate members of the committee.

The continuing committee went on to deliberate for four years.[111] One member of the opposition was moved to describe it as the 'continuing committee, which continues and continues and continues.' It examined the population of rural Saskatchewan, the trading and transportation patterns, and the optimum size of local government for each function of government. It considered alternative areas and alternative organization structures. It examined responsibilities and finances, and it consulted experts, interest groups, and the public generally. In the end, the committee recommended a general reorganization of local government and proposed regional boundaries for health, welfare, and other functions.

Throughout the exercise, Douglas maintained his earlier position: that he would have to enjoy the support of local government and the public before he would proceed with local government reorganization. But, despite the fact that their representative on the committee had signed the report, the Saskatchewan Association of Rural Municipalities vigorously opposed the committee's recommendations and argued that no county or modified county should be formed without a vote. There the matter rested. Only in 1962, after Woodrow Lloyd had become premier, did the provincial government announce a policy. It decided that counties or municipal districts (modified counties) would be established, but only following a favourable vote by the electors concerned.[112]

Why Douglas made such a firm commitment in the face of such intransigent opposition is puzzling. In retrospect, a number of factors may have influenced his thinking. One was the searing experience of transforming school districts into larger school units during the CCF's first term of office – a transformation that still was being blamed for the party's near loss of the 1948 election. Or it may have been a simple miscalculation as to the potential for reason, in the face of all the facts, coming to triumph over the emotions inherent in the status quo, admittedly an unlikely miscalculation for a canny if idealistic politician like Tommy Douglas. Another possibility, though there is no concrete evidence for this, is that ministers saw little point in taking on a battle they did not need to win: if they wanted or needed a larger unit of administration for market roads, they could always create one in the Department of Highways. And allow the municipalities to wither.

Beyond these speculations is perhaps the most likely – or deep-rooted – possibility. One must always remember the direct democracy roots of the western wing of the CCF. It was the responsibility of the member of Parliament, in this school of thought, to listen to and to heed the views of his electors. Witness the belief in the power of constituency initiatives and the power of recall. It is not at all unlikely that a person with this background would come deeply to believe in consultation and the search for a consensus in reaching truly enduring decisions. This is a consideration that must be borne in mind in reading the story of medicare in chapters 9 and 10.

Whatever the case, the government followed the course it had in the past, except in the case of the school units. It created regions in the provincial Department of Highways on a suitable scale and proceeded with grid roads on its own. By 1956 the planning work had in fact been done, and government was in a position to propose a 'Grid Road Plan,' announcing it even while the municipalities were still being consulted.[113] The substance of the plan formed part of the government's program for its next term in office.

The market road grants more than doubled between 1956–7 and 1959–60, and in 1959 the provincial treasurer was able to announce that, 'as a result of the enthusiastic co-operation of the municipalities the grid program is well ahead of schedule.'[114] The provincial contributions increased in relative terms as well; in 1958 the treasurer noted that the government's contributions now averaged 60 per cent of the cost of the grid road system instead of the 50 per cent originally agreed to.[115] Further, government increased its assistance to urban municipalities to construct streets that connected with provincial highways.[116] The election pledge of a $100-million highway program was fulfilled 'in less than the five year period originally proposed.'[117]

Wascana Centre

This is an opportune time, as well, to continue the story of the Douglas government's support for cultural programs and the arts. In my view, the government's most spectacular cultural achievement was the creation in Regina of Wascana Centre – a thousand-acre parkland surrounding Wascana Lake and comprehending four areas: the Legislative Building grounds, the lands dedicated to the newly created Regina Campus of the University of Saskatchewan, the lands to be dedicated to the arts and to cultural development, and finally the lands to be dedicated to recreation and family facilities.

The beginning of the idea was to be found in two existing dedicated areas: the Legislative Building grounds and, on the other side of the lake, the Regina College grounds. These were part of the far-sighted Mawson Plan for Regina in 1912, adopted at a time when Wascana Lake was only a creek, and when the whole surrounding area was farmland. But in 1960 that splendid vision was imperilled by an impending decision to move Regina College, as the newly created Regina Campus, to available lands to the east and south of Wascana Lake (the former experimental farm of the federal Department of Agriculture). This move would substantially vacate a large part of the area north of the lake and of the Legislative Building, and raise the spectre of later commercial development in the area – or so I feared as a member of the board of governors of the University of Saskatchewan, involved in the decision.

The possibility of averting that risk arose out of a personal conversation with a junior architect working on the design of the new university area – who knew of my apprehensions. Why not, he said, enlarge the vision of 1912 and create a 'park' that would encompass the whole of the area around Wascana Lake? The idea was exciting, and after some further discussions with a few artist and architect friends, I developed the concept of a four-part centre – dedicated to the legislature, the university, cultural institutions, and recreation. All the lands would be combined into a single entity, to be developed in accordance with a master plan, serving the four functions of the 'centre,' but always governed by the highest aesthetic standards. This would be the guiding principle for the governing commission, to be made up of representatives of the province, the city, and the university. These three parties would finance the centre, but the governing authority would enjoy virtually complete independence.

On 22 June 1960 I wrote a memorandum to Woodrow Lloyd, then minister of education, and proposed a 'Saskatchewan Centre of Arts, Education and Government' along these lines. I indicated that the first step toward realizing this vision would be to 'engage landscape architects to plan the whole development ... subject to the needs of each part of the Centre,' and that 'future construction and development within the area would have to be consistent with the master plan ...'[118]

Colleagues in government embraced the idea immediately. The evening after I sent my memorandum to Lloyd, a small group met at the home of Allan McCallum, the deputy minister of education, to discuss the whole concept. We were Woodrow Lloyd, minister of education, Minister Charlie Williams of Regina, Allan Blakeney, then a newly elected MLA from Regina, Marjorie Cooper, another MLA, and Allan McCallum, Burns Roth, and me – the latter three were deputy ministers and also members of the board of governors of the university. The group agreed unanimously to recommend the idea to Cabinet.

Reflecting the greatly increased capacity of government to get things done, a memorandum to cabinet was drafted on July 13, and on 2 August 1960 cabinet approved the recommendation and established a committee to proceed with planning the Centre. By now, Allan Blakeney, who was shortly to succeed Lloyd as minister of education, had clearly been designated, or recognized, as the government's leader in the realization of the Wascana Centre dream. And he truly fulfilled that role. Two tripartite committees were established – one at the ministerial level and one at the level of senior officials – to get on with the job. At about the same time, Blakeney engaged Allan Gilmore as the full-time executive working on Wascana Centre. The two committees had two goals: the first was to identify and to recommend to cabinet an architect, to be assisted by a landscape architect, to prepare a master plan; and the second was to attend to the complex legal and administrative arrangements needed to establish and operate this unique tri-partite agency – in addition, of course, to achieving harmonious working relations among the three 'sponsors.' Media relations were established and maintained through personal and often confidential sessions between Ted Davis of the *Regina Leader Post* – an arch-enemy of the CCF – and myself throughout the birthing period. (My minister, Clarence Fines, concurred.) A consistently favourable press was the result.

Less than one year later, in August 1961, the planners were named: Minoru Yamasaki, internationally known architect from Michigan, and later the architect of the World Trade Center in New York, and Thomas Church, an equally well known landscape architect from California. Nine months later, in March 1962, the master plan was unveiled and acclaimed. Legislation establishing the Wascana Centre Authority was presented to the spring session of the Legislative Assembly and was passed almost unanimously.[119]

Conceiving and creating Wascana Centre was a great achievement in urban park development, as can be seen today. Creating and managing such delicate tripartite administrative arrangements was an equally remarkable accomplishment. And it seems even more remarkable in retrospect, when one recalls that the whole of the development took place during the difficult deliberations, consultations, and negotiations leading up to the establishment of medicare.

I cannot forbear a personal postscript. On the last day of Yamasaki's many and lengthy visits to Regina – where he was both planner and instinctive public relations expert combined – I had lunch with him. I asked what had attracted him to Saskatchewan to do what he did for such a low fee (his charges were, in my view, miniscule for a man of his international stature). He readily replied (and I paraphrase): 'Al, when I first got off the plane in Regina all I saw was the thin straight line of the horizon. That and the colour of the sky. Nothing else. Then I met with all these vibrant, audacious people – from ministers to officials to educationists to artists – who so believed in the creation of a haven of beauty and enlightenment on these flat prairies. I was caught up by their enthusiasm and I wanted to help.'

Yamasaki had so aptly caught and described the spirit that moved and motivated the Douglas government and the public service.

9

Reflections on the 1950s and Renewal in the 1960s

Lurking behind all of these accomplishments in the last half of the 1950s were, as we have said, the election results of 1956. With a decline in public support for the CCF, it was clearly a time for self-examination, for reflection as to the underlying causes for this measure of discontent. Such reflections were indeed a kind of backdrop to political and policy discussions as the government engaged in the fulfilment of its 1956 election commitments. And clearly they were the focal point of the government's pre-election planning sessions in 1959.

A Protest Vote?

A number of hypotheses, or theories, were advanced as to the causes of the apparent public disaffection or discontent, and what could or should be done about them. One was suggested by the election results themselves: the 'protest vote,' which had played an important part in the election of the CCF in 1944 and during its early reforming period, appeared to have gravitated to the Social Credit Party. The evidence was clear, said the proponents of this point of view: both the CCF and the Liberals had suffered losses of nine percentage points in their popular vote, and the Social Credit, the third party, had captured 21.4 per cent.

There always is a 'latent' or built-in 'protest element' in voting shifts away from the ruling party, went the argument. Sometimes it is bigger, sometimes smaller, but it is always there. It is not necessarily against a specific thing; it is simply looking for something the government isn't offering. And the government in question, now, was the CCF. Implicit in this hypothesis was a certain inevitability: there was not much a government could do about 'inherent tendencies' such as this, except perhaps in equally general terms to attempt to renew itself.

A related argument was that the public had become accustomed to the major first-term advances, such as hospital insurance and automobile insurance, and had turned their minds to other and different issues. The most likely of these, of course, had to do with adjustments to economic and social change. Here lay the second and a more explicit diagnosis of the causes for public discontent: it had to do with social change itself. Social unease, or unrest, was occasioned by change, and that was feeding the protest reflected in the polls. This was possible despite the fact that the government was devoting so much of its policy attention to easing the adjustment to change.

But the problems of coping with change, for the average farm family or for the village or town dweller, embraced all of these developments – from the technological and the social through to the public infrastructure installed to cope with them. Bluntly put, even the expansion of economic and social infrastructure as counterpoints to the underlying technological and social changes involved adjustments. Some simple examples will suffice: the consolidation and specialization of hospital and health facilities; the location of nursing homes in relation to the families they were serving; the loss or change in the sense of community that accompanied the substitution of larger towns for smaller ones.

Alongside the problem of simply coping with change was the existence of an almost inherent asymmetry in the extension of new infrastructure and facilities to the rural, non-urban families, as opposed to those available to large town or city dwellers. Those who remained on the farm were aware of the amenities in neighbouring market centres – electricity, telephones, sewer and water installations – but knew they would have to wait. Even that was an adjustment to reckon with.

But these were changes and adjustments the government could do little about. At best, the province could increase the pace of investment in social and economic infrastructure, and thus reduce the period of adjustment in rural Saskatchewan. There was, in short, a certain inevitability, too, about change and adjustments to change. And the restiveness that went with this could understandably find its way into the polling booth.

An Aging Government?

A third hypothesis, or theory, as to the decline in support for the CCF was quite simply that aging governments tend to be cautious and stolid.

On the policy side, the excitement and the promise of deep-rooted change declines over time as the reforms are realized. This was not to suggest that there was something inherently wrong about the newer, emerging policies: it was simply that there was nothing magnetic about the recitation of statistics on the growing economy, on the number of oil wells drilled, on the government assistance that led to a new cement plant or even a steel mill, or the miles of grid road constructed, or even on the construction of university buildings or nursing homes. They simply lacked 'the magic with which to stir men's souls.'

Woodrow Lloyd was to say something akin to this in his personal diary, if expressed in more ideological terms: '1956 – another election year ... many of us feel that we should have preferred winning by emphasis on more worthy and lasting objectives. However, we do have to demonstrate our material achievements – no reason why we should not. But how do you motivate people to think and accept socialism and act like socialists in a period such as this? That is our No. 1 problem.'[1]

That was the policy side of the 'aging government' proposition. On the administrative side, the case was clearer and more explicit: the accumulation of grievances against the government or the public service. For the longer a government is in office, the more time there is for any given number of citizens to have been aggrieved at one time or another. And when the government is providing an ever-wider range of services, the greater is the likelihood of mistakes or errors or omissions, affecting any given part of a population of one million people. More, shortcomings in policy and administration that would have stood out in the early years of government tended twelve years later to escape attention. Ministers who had been in charge of departments over those years had become more understanding of the problems of their officials and quicker to defend their actions. And both ministers and officials, caught up with good governance within the public service, tended to lose touch with the perspective of the recipients of the public services.

Tommy Douglas himself was keenly aware of this and spoke frequently to the public service, directly or indirectly, of the importance of sensitivity to the public and its concerns, and equally the importance of timely response to these concerns. This was illustrated at a meeting of the Economic Advisory and Planning Board in 1956, when ministers were discussing 'public irritants' as one cause of public disaffection – one of these being the growth of bureaucratic language in public communication. In a rare display of temper, he said to the me and Tommy Shoyama: 'Let me give you an example,' and called his secretary to bring in a letter from a farmer, past whose land a new power line was being constructed. Douglas read it: '"Dear Mr. Douglas. Some bugger bust my fence." Perfect clarity,' said the Premier. 'Subject "bugger," verb "bust," object "fence."' Why,' he said addressing the two of us, 'why can't you public servants write like that?'

Douglas and his closest confidants recognized these problems of aging and determined to improve the government's performance and its public relations. The Cabinet–Planning Board Conference of 1957 agreed that special measures were necessary to improve departmental field operations and coordinate them more effectively, to improve governmental press and public relations, and to speed up public service and make it more obliging.[2] These were areas where it seemed the ministers themselves individually and collectively would have to assume direct responsibility for the job.

A final and more extreme manifestation of an aging government would simply be 'getting out of touch.' That would be something of a feat for a government whose policies were reviewed every year by a grass-roots political party, but nonetheless possible in respect of other 'public interest' interest groups – or private interest ones for that matter. But by 1958 the Douglas government, again, had already examined this question and had decided to increase its consultation with citizen groups in the formulation of policy. This was more than merely listening to interest groups. It took the form of a conscious effort to initiate and engage public interest and participation in policy formulation. In 1958, for example, following the recommendations of the Royal Commission on Agriculture and Rural Life, the government established the Rural Development Council to act in a consultative and advisory role to the government.[3] Made up of representatives of rural organizations and the public generally, the council was intended to meet periodically and to be an effective 'sounding board' for the evaluation of new and old programs.[4]

Other examples of the effort to engage public participation abound. In 1959 the government called a public conference to stimulate interest in the needs of the elderly and chronically ill, and to secure the voluntary co-operation of interested community organizations in research and program development in this field.[5] It established another body, the Rehabilitation Council, 'to advise both government and non-government agencies' on rehabilitation policies and programs.[6] Another conference was held 'to discuss the extension of the franchise to Indians and other matters affecting their welfare.'[7] Government consulted with the farmers concerning irrigation policy in the South Saskatchewan River development project.[8] And, of course, it had already established the Continuing Committee on Local Government. In all of these endeavours, the government's goal was to increase its own understanding of the public mind, to improve its perception of the problems that troubled various citizen groups, and to seek advice and support for policies and programs that might resolve the problems. In one sense, this collaborative approach to policy development was not new for the CCF, but its use at this stage marked a further step from the self-sufficiency of the younger government.

Program Reappraisal, April 1959

These were some of the reflections on public discontent as manifested in the 1956 election. The important question, of course, was what to do about them – beyond guarding against bureaucratic tendencies in the public service and widening the government consultative links with Saskatchewan's interest groups. What policies or policy priorities should be changed?

This, the government decided, could only be achieved through a comprehensive review of its policies and programs – one by one – and an examination of how successful they had been in realizing the government's fundamental goals. The goals were clear enough. The provincial treasurer spoke, in much the same terms as he had done fifteen years before of 'a sense of freedom, dignity and self-fulfillment' for the individual.[9] The premier spoke of 'the dignity of the individual ... the undeniable right of every person to health, opportunity and freedom,'[10] and of 'our passion for social justice'[11] (words to be echoed by Prime Minister Pierre Trudeau some fifteen years later). But how well did the priorities of the government, and its program, accord with these goals?

It was clear enough to the cabinet that it had placed, since 1952, a great deal of emphasis on economic growth. This was not just a matter of the balance in expenditures that had been established, but also a matter of preoccupation. The premier's speeches, like those of the provincial treasurer and other ministers, had increasingly become a recitation of statistics about Saskatchewan's economic progress. This had produced a certain attitude of mind, said some CCF supporters, which might be described as 'modern materialism.' This was surely not what the CCF was all about.

A second criticism was that the 1952 and 1956 election programs had

proposed – and delivered – a spectrum of social and economic infrastructure projects, each of which had electoral appeal, but the total of
which seemed somehow lacking in a comprehensive rationale. Again,
what relationship did these programs bear to CCF philosophy?

The third criticism was that the social programs – in education,
health, and welfare – had been extended and perfected, but they had
not been re-examined to determine how far they had gone toward
achieving the government's overarching objectives – that sense of
freedom, dignity, and self-fulfilment for the individual the provincial
treasurer had spoken of.

The premier had long recognized the dangers that beset a government that has been in office for a long time. Indeed, in 1952 he had
cautioned the CCF convention:

> A government which has been in office for eight years is always in danger
> of wanting to tread the safe and the known way and to be somewhat fearful
> of blazing new trails, especially if by doing so they are likely to infringe
> upon some special privilege ... There is a saying in the Scriptures: Take
> heed when all men speak well of you. Sometimes the fact that a govern-
> ment has aroused no opposition merely means that it has become apa-
> thetic and inactive. I am not suggesting that we should antagonize any
> section of the community for the sheer joy of arousing antagonisms, but I
> am suggesting that we never allow our desire for office to rob us of our pas-
> sion for social justice.[12]

Within this context, the cabinet conference proceeded with its program review, function by function. Cabinet believed that its education
programs had improved the standards of education and had made a
good education more equally available to all. But two principal problems were apparent. First, more had to be done to equalize the opportunity for higher education. Secondly, the increasing reliance on the
property tax as a source of revenue for financing the rising costs of education was an issue. The property tax was singularly regressive, compared with consumption taxes such as the sales tax. It seemed that the
government must contemplate both a bursary program for students and
an increase in school grants to shift more of the schools to the provincial tax base and out of the local property tax.

In cabinet's view, the welfare programs, too, had gone a long way
toward accomplishing the CCF's goals. The provincial government had
established a minimum standard of living for the unemployed and

unemployables, and was now developing an integrated program that would be based on people's 'needs' rather than their 'means.' The question now was only one of establishing the level of the minimum. And this was a matter of social attitudes: how much egalitarianism would society accept? The labour programs had established minimum wages and working conditions – legislation that still was in advance of most of the rest of Canada. Again, the question was one of degree – what additional assurances or benefits should the state provide?

For the farmers, a variety of agricultural programs had been designed to increase income, and certainly farm security was much better assured. Here, though, the problem was a national and even international one, and the CCF government as a provincial government felt frustrated in its efforts to improve the lot of the farmers.

The government's health programs, too, had gone a very long way to guaranteeing adequate health services to all citizens. Preventive health services were now provided throughout the province, and hospital care was available to all regardless of income and, as a result of better roads and of the air ambulance service, almost regardless of residence. Treatment for cancer, tuberculosis, and mental illness were provided through public programs, as were medical services for pensioners and social aid recipients. And those who could afford to pay privately had access, of course, to medical services. But at least one-third of the population, who had lower incomes and often experienced higher medical risks, did not have free and easy access to health care.[13] Clearly the next, and the most important, step to be taken was the establishment of a universal medical care plan for the whole province.

When it came to physical amenities, including roads, electricity, natural gas, telephones, sewer, and water services, the lot of the average Saskatchewan family had improved greatly. City residents enjoyed all of these facilities. And rural people had benefited from the rural electrification program and the grid road system, now being constructed. But the rural citizens still often lived in quite basic conditions, and perhaps the government could improve some of these – notably sewer and water facilities and telephone service.

In contrast with these more recent investments in infrastructure – in the physical comforts of life on the Prairies – was the consistent, if low cost, support of the arts and culture. The innovations of the early years of the CCF – the Arts Board, the Archives, the regional libraries, and the support of cultural programs at the university – were bearing fruit. But it had to be acknowledged that the proportion of the budget devoted to the arts and to culture was very small indeed, and should be increased.

The emphasis the government had been placing on economic growth was undoubtedly appropriate, as was becoming evident in resource revenues (see the Annex, p. 311). And recent developments, including the potash mines and the discovery of high-grade iron ore, were encouraging. Manufacturing industries were coming to the province at a more rapid rate, as the activities of the Industrial Development Fund testified. But the challenges of industrialization on the Prairies were and always had been deep-rooted. Beyond natural disadvantages, the province lacked the macro-economic policy instruments that were central to industrialization – in particular, tariffs and trade policy.

There was another dimension to the review of economic development programs, and that was a re-examination of the ends of economic growth. This had always been close to the consciousness of most cabinet ministers, but it remained to articulate the ends once again, after the achievement of a new measure of affluence in the province. The premier put the cabinet's views this way when he spoke in the legislature:

> There is a verse in the Bible which says that the measure of 'a man's life consisteth not in the abundance of things which he possesseth.' That is equally true of our province. The measure of abundance and greatness is not just its uranium mines, oil wells, factories, or its steel mills. These things are means to an end and not an end in themselves. In the final analysis the greatness of this province will depend on the extent to which we are able to divert a reasonable share of wealth production ... to raise the standard of living of our people, and to give them a reasonable measure of social security against old age, against sickness and other catastrophes.[14]

Here was a statement of goals markedly similar to the language Douglas had used in 1943 and 1944.

Planning the Program for 1960

Here, then, was the government's assessment of its progress in achieving its fundamental goals, and a sense of the direction to be taken in the future – both in the overall complex of policies, and in particular policies and programs. The next job was to translate this sense of direction into specific policy proposals for the cabinet's consideration in developing its 1960 electoral program. The responsibility for developing these proposals was assigned to a number of committees of officials, each chaired by the deputy minister of the department responsible for the function or policy area under review. Where multiple interests were involved, Tommy Shoyama, as the secretary of the Planning Board, or me, as the deputy provincial treasurer, chaired the committees. The committees were to report in November, in time for a second meeting of the cabinet planning conference, where cabinet would decide upon its electoral program.

One of these committees warranted – and received – particular attention. It was the Inter-departmental Committee to Study a Medical Care Program. Cabinet had decided at the April meeting of the planning conference that the time had come to establish the long-promised medical care program. The character of the intended program was clear in the mandate given to the committee officials: '[It] shall be a universal and comprehensive one ... [leaving] so far as practical, a maximum amount of responsibility to the [health] regions.'[15] The committee clearly understood its role: it was 'to translate the general directive of the Cabinet into a framework for a province-wide comprehensive medical care program with universal coverage.'[16]

It was equally clear that the government intended to be advised in the first instance by the Inter-departmental Committee of officials, but also that it expected to widen the planning process in developing the final blueprint for the Saskatchewan plan. Said the cabinet: 'If the Committee's proposals are acceptable, consideration will then be given to establishing a public committee to discuss a medical care insurance program for the province.'[17]

The premier acted quickly in informing the public of the government's intentions. Two days after the conclusion of the cabinet conference, on 25 April 1959, the premier announced the government's decision to a by-election audience in the village of Birch Hills, in these terms: the government is seriously considering the introduction of a universal and comprehensive medical care insurance plan.[18]

It was a momentous decision. Here was the ultimate expression of the CCF's goals and of its social (many still said socialist) values. Here, too, in rather more political terms, was the answer to the charges that after fifteen years in office the government had lost its gift of innovation and its enthusiasm for new programs.

It has to be said, at the same time, that the premier's announcement could scarcely be described as a total surprise. He had said repeatedly during the 1950s that the government would introduce a full health insurance plan as soon as the province could afford it. And that finally had come to pass. In 1957 the new prime minister of Canada, John Diefenbaker of Saskatchewan, had committed the government of Canada to share in the costs of any provincial hospitalization plan that offered universal coverage – thus annulling the earlier requirement that such federal funding would only become available when six provinces representing a majority of the population of Canada had agreed to establish such plans. (For the full story of these and other fiscal arrangements, see the Annex, p. 311.) Thus Saskatchewan became eligible on 1 July 1958 for federal support of the Saskatchewan Hospital Services Plan, amounting to some 40 per cent of the plan's expenditures. It was obvious to political observers in the province that Premier Douglas could and would now act to establish a full medical care plan.

Nonetheless, the status quo in public and private medical care arrangements, as it had been developing in the 1950s, was about to be challenged. Three days after the premier's Birch Hills announcement, the registrar of the College of Physicians and Surgeons, Dr George Peacock, wrote to say 'your planning could have considerable impact on the practice of medicine in this province, and as such we would be most appreciative if you could favour us with some indication of what your proposed plans consist.'[19] Douglas replied that the government fully intended to seek the advice of the doctors and of the public generally as soon as its studies had reached the point where specific proposals, or policy options, could be considered. In the government's planning schedule, this would be after the Inter-departmental Committee had reported to the cabinet planning conference in November. The college, for its part, would be holding its annual conference in October and could be expected to stake out there at least an opening position on the CCF's long-intended universal and comprehensive medical care insurance plan.

In keeping with established practice, the planning conference of November 1959 was to be used to develop the government's program for the impending 1960 election. But this time there were effectively two parts to the exercise: one was the development of the more or less conventional elements of the program, along the lines of the 1952 and 1956 election programs, and the other was to plan the final stage in the wholesale movement of the financing of medical care from the private sector to the public sector.

The Evolutionary Part of the 1960 Election Platform

The first of these two tasks might be considered the 'evolutionary' part of the CCF program for 1960. For the most part, the programs that emerged from cabinet's studies of the policy papers they had received consisted of elaborations or extensions – sometimes ambitious ones – of familiar programs or program areas. They appeared under the banner *More Abundant Living.*

First, there was the Family Farm Improvement Program. It complemented the advances already being made in rural electrification and the extension of telephone services. The FFIP was a farm sewer and water program, under which government would make a 15 per cent grant to farmers installing sewer and water systems. It would provide technical assistance in designing the systems, and make available at cost the equipment required outside of farm buildings.

Secondly, the government would make grants in aid to towns and villages where the installation of sewer and/or water systems would be economic. Supplementing the grants, the government undertook to buy up some 50 per cent of the debentures issued by towns and villages for financing such systems.

The third program was the provision of financial assistance to rural telephone companies, to meet one-third of the cost of telephone pole replacement and to pay an annual grant, per rural telephone subscriber, to assist in the maintenance of the system. An enlarged Department of Telephones would provide technical assistance to the rural telephone companies.[20]

To complete the initiatives for improving the physical facilities available to Saskatchewan residents, the government undertook a $125-million highway program and a $6-million annual municipal road program for the next term of office, and promised to connect at least one hundred additional communities to the Power Corporation's natural gas system.

The cabinet sought, too, to find some more substantial, perhaps more dramatic, devices for attracting industries to the province. It determined to establish a Department of Industry and Information, to bring together all the agencies presently concerned with industrial development. These included the Industrial Development Office, the Trade Services Branch of the Department of Co-operation, and the overseas office in London. In addition to the existing services, the new department was also to create a transportation branch and a new industrial research branch. It would provide a focus for initiatives out of which might develop new ways to attract industry. Further, legislation would be introduced to enable the establishment of municipal industrial development corporations.

The South Saskatchewan River dam and the detailed irrigation planning involved were a central part of the agricultural development platform. The major innovation was the establishment of a crop insurance program. The federal government had recently announced a federal-provincial crop insurance scheme, and this announcement accelerated the explorations of the subject that had proceeded sporadically since the late 1940s. It was a limited plan, providing for crop insurance in designated areas where a minimum participation of farmers was obtained. The provincial treasurer said that he had no 'illusions about Saskatchewan's ability to finance or underwrite an effective comprehensive crop insurance program' – this, he said, has always been and must always be a federal responsibility.[21]

This, then, was the evolutionary part of the election platform of 1960. The 'revolutionary' part was, of course, medicare.

The 'Revolutionary' Part of the 1960 Election Platform

The Inter-departmental Committee, which was to advise the government on medicare, was named immediately after the Birch Hills announcement. It was chaired by Dr Burns Roth, the deputy minister of health, and included two other public health doctors from the department, Drs Matthews and Acker. It included, as well, Tommy Shoyama and me, as representatives of the Cabinet Committee on Planning and Budgeting, plus David Levin of the Economic Planning and Advisory Board, and Meyer Brownstone and William Harding of the Local Government Continuing Committee. The committee was to report to cabinet in November 1959.

The committee undertook an ambitious task: a review of the current state of health services in Saskatchewan – in particular, of medical care. Its review included the cost of such services and the availability of medical manpower; an examination of the basic objectives and the scope of a comprehensive medical care scheme; and a survey of medical opinion in respect of such schemes. It would culminate in recommendations for a medical care scheme for Saskatchewan and its financing. The committee also recommended the establishment of an Advisory Planning Com-

mittee on 'the formation' of a medical care program and proposed
terms of reference for this committee.[22]

The heart of the committee's report is to be found in its review of the
basic objectives of a province-wide medical care program for Saskatchewan. There were ten of them:

1. The prepayment principle: the costs of medical care must be transferred from the private to the public sector if care for the sick and
   the disabled was to be made available without regard to the individual's ability to pay (universality) – with the costs being 'prepaid' year
   by year in the form of health insurance premiums and other public
   revenues.
2. The universal coverage principle: the inclusion of the entire population in the program is fundamental to its financing, and to the
   assurance of equal access to health services of all residents of the
   province, regardless of their circumstances.
3. The comprehensiveness principle: 'the health services of the future
   should be comprehensive and coordinated,' extending to the whole
   range of health care – preventive services, physician and diagnostic
   services, pharmaceutical services, home nursing services, special
   disease services (e.g., cancer, mental health), optical and dental and
   chiropody services, and rehabilitation services.

   The committee went on to recommend the immediate 'inclusion
   under the medicare plan of preventive services, provided under
   doctor or community programs, and of physician and diagnostic
   services; and the exclusion at the beginning of the program of optical, dental, and chiropody services.' Pharmaceuticals would be
   excluded too 'because of the extremely difficult problem of cost
   control.' Special attention was given, as well, to home care services,
   recognizing that 'some of these are really substitutes for hospitals
   and other institutions and include a whole range of activities such as
   medical care, nursing, housekeeping, physiotherapy, occupational
   therapy, etc.' The committee concluded that 'comprehensive
   [home care] services can best be developed on a hospital-centred
   basis ... [hoping] that the federal government might be prepared to
   consider sharing costs ... under the [federal] *Hospital Insurance and
   Diagnostic Services Act.*'
4. The preventive health priority: '[In] the design of a medical care
   program ... the preventive objective should always be kept at the
   forefront.' 'Medical practitioners ... must be encouraged to partici-

pate in preventive programs and apply preventive measures to personal health care.'

5. An emphasis on high quality of services: '... legislative and administrative measures should be designed to promote a high quality of care.' The committee added: '... modern diagnostic medicine with all its complexities demands a pooling of skills and professional knowledge coupled with up to date ... equipment ...' which suggested to the committee the consideration of group practice arrangements.

6. The principle of public and governmental responsibility: a universal publicly financed medical care program must in a democratic society be responsible and accountable to the legislature and the government.

7. The promotion of regionalization consistent with economy and efficiency: a province-wide medical care program demands provincial planning and unified general policies. At the same time, regional governments may have a role to play, such as 'assisting towards the integration of public health, hospital and medical care services on a regional basis.'

8. Promotion of professional education and training.

9. Measures to enhance research activities.

10. Promotion of health through public education.

The committee moved on from the objectives or principles of the proposed medical care plan to its financing and administration. On financing, the committee estimated the costs of the full, if not fully comprehensive, plan, and then looked to two sources of revenue to meet those costs: a medical care insurance premium (called a 'personal tax' in the report), plus general revenues – including now the federal contributions available to the Hospital Services Plan. The committee recommended that a minimum proportion of the total cost of medicare should be financed by the personal tax on the grounds that 'the public [should] always be aware that changes in utilization and remuneration of physicians ... have a concurrent [read, consequential] effect on each individual's cost [premium].'

On the management side of the proposed medicare plan, the committee found that the principles of universality and comprehensiveness were not compatible with private management of the health care financing system. The reasoning: first, a universal, comprehensive, non–'risk-tested' sickness insurance plan would require extremely high insurance premiums (individual and family taxes). Second, to make the premiums affordable to all Saskatchewanians would require very large public subsidies. And third, these high public subsidies would, in turn, call for – indeed require – a degree of public responsibility and accountability that could only be achieved through public management of the system. 'It, therefore, must be concluded that the only realistic way to design a program for medical care insurance is to vest the management in a public body responsible to the people in a direct way.'[23]

Here, then, was the essence – or the framework – of the medical care insurance plan recommended to the government. It remained for the committee to assess the likely reaction of the College of Physicians and Surgeons to these proposals, and to draft for government consideration possible terms of reference for the Advisory Planning Committee – the body cabinet had decided upon in April as the vehicle for 'sounding out' public and professional opinion on the draft plan, and for fleshing out the framework of principles upon which the plan would be based.

Where Did the Doctors Stand?

The Inter-departmental Committee recognized the 'prime importance [of obtaining] a clear appreciation of the official position of the organized medical profession on the question of health insurance.' [24] The committee first reviewed the evolution of medical opinion on this question in Saskatchewan, citing in particular the resolutions of the College of Physicians and Surgeons in 1948 and 1951, and then the college's brief on the report of the Health Survey Commission in 1953. The committee recognized that the profession had earlier supported or accepted universal and comprehensive medical care – coupled always with an insistence that the administration of any public plan must reside with an independent non-political body.

The committee of officials also recognized the fact that, alongside these policy statements, the college had demonstrated the willingness of the medical profession to participate in public medical care programs by accepting payment for professional services from public plans. Doctors were regularly being paid by municipal doctor plans, by the Swift Current Health Region, by the Cancer Commission, by the Workmen's Compensation Board, and by the Department of Public Health (in respect of pensioners). Indeed, it was estimated that in 1957 over 25 per cent of doctors' income came from the government – with another 28.7 per cent coming from the voluntary and commercial plans (mostly the

doctor-sponsored plans) and 45.8 per cent from direct patient payments.[25]

But whatever the earlier policy statements had said, and whatever the
past experience with public medical care may have been, the college's
pronouncement of October 1959 – a month before the committee's
report was due in cabinet – made it clear that the college now flatly
opposed any universal publicly funded plan. The resolution, passed
unanimously, said: 'We, the members of the College of Physicians and
Surgeons of Saskatchewan, declare ourselves in favour of the extension
of health and sickness benefits through indemnity and service plans. We
oppose a government-controlled, province-wide medical care plan.'[26]

How the government would or should react to such an unequivocal
response to public medical care insurance was clearly a question ministers would have to decide. What the committee of officials decided to do
was to try to put the resolution of the Saskatchewan college into a
broader context – which they did by recording the most recent position
of the Canadian Medical Association, as recorded at its 1955 conference. There the CMA had declared itself to be in favour of contributory
health insurance, available to all Canadians, and, more, had recommended the extension of voluntary prepaid medical plans, supported
where necessary by public funding, as the vehicle for achieving this
universality.

Later in its statement, however, the CMA did seem to contemplate the
possibility of public medical care insurance. It declared: '... in the event
of government participation in the universal extension of health insurance to all citizens ... the introduction of health insurance legislation
should be preceded by adequate consultation with the organized medical profession and [others] affected ... [and such] health insurance
should be administered by an independent, non-political commission
representative of those providing and those receiving the services.'[27]

Acknowledging that 'the position of the Saskatchewan College ...
appears adamant,' the committee noted 'on the other hand the CMA
statement visualized the eventuality of organized medicine backing
down on [the question of government participation]. The government
position,' added the committee, 'can be maintained intact if the provisions of the rest of the program prove acceptable and are demonstrated
to be in the profession's interest (as well as in the interest of the public
at large).'[28] It was, in retrospect, not a prophetic conclusion. But it
accorded with the prevailing view among ministers and senior officials
at that time: that an accommodation between the government and the

doctors could be reached. And this was to be the task of the Advisory Planning Committee.

The idea of an Advisory Planning Committee as a vehicle for achieving a consensus on a universal and comprehensive medical care plan for Saskatchewan had emerged at the April planning conference, and was very much the product to the premier's thinking. The Inter-departmental Committee was instructed to draft proposed terms of reference for Cabinet's consideration.

The committee advanced essentially four general propositions. The first was that the Advisory Planning Committee should be clear that the government had 'accepted' (one could equally have said prescribed) a number of cornerstones for the plan: that it must, for example, 'be operated under governmental auspices with direct responsibility to a Minister of the Crown who is responsible for reporting to the legislature'; that it must be universal in its coverage; that it would be 'financed partially by personal tax payments and partially from general tax sources'; and other designated principles. The second proposition was that the central mandate of the committee would be 'to advise the government as to the specific design of such a medicare program,' including such elements as methods of payment for services, the use of deterrents if any, and maintaining and improving quality control.[29]

Thirdly, the committee would be invited to serve as a sounding board 'for the views of the government, the health professions and the public in ... areas which are still indefinite and unresolved.' And finally, through bringing together and being informed by the diverse views and perspectives of people who were knowledgeable and interested, and in particular those who were experienced in medicare, the committee was to 'advise the government, the health professions and the public on rational program development.' In this proposed role for the Advisory Planning Committee, the officials also argued that each group would be forced 'to examine its premises and arguments ... which may lead to substantial modification of false assumptions.'[30] In other words, participation in the Advisory Planning Committee could help educate the representatives and thus contribute to a consensus on the design of a medicare program.

Tommy Douglas Reports to the People

The discussions of ministers on the committee's report, and on the likely public reception of their proposals, were intense and extensive.

But the decision they reached was unequivocally clear: the government would proceed – in the belief not only that Saskatchewan was capable of developing and delivering a universal, comprehensive, and quality medical care program, but also that it could be done in co-operation with the doctors.

Tommy Douglas announced the cabinet's decision in a radio broadcast on 16 December 1959. He began by reviewing the human case for medicare, and then the progress the government had made in the extension of hospital and medical services to the people of the province. In the case of medical services, he was proud of the partial programs the government had initiated and their treatment of particular illnesses and particular categories of persons. But even given these programs and the voluntary and commercial health plans that had come into being in the province in the 1950s, there was a sizeable proportion of people in the province that could not afford complete, lifelong medical care insurance.

'For these reasons,' said Douglas, 'the Government has come to the conclusion that it should embark upon a comprehensive medical care program that will cover all our people and will ensure a high standard of care to every citizen of Saskatchewan.'[31] Such a plan would be founded upon five principles:

1. *The prepayment principle:* 'general medical care should be paid for on an insurance basis.'
2. *Universal coverage:* 'The only way we can have a real insurance scheme is to cover the good risks as well as the bad, thus spreading the cost over the entire population.'
3. *A high quality of service:* 'Better distribution and availability of care' as well as 'the improvement of the quality of care' must be a major objective of the plan.
4. *Public administration:* 'This must be a government sponsored program administered by a public body responsible to the Legislature and through it to the entire population.' Douglas added: '... for that reason it is our intention to have this plan administered by the Department of Public Health and responsible to the Legislature through the Minister of that Department in the same manner as we do now with the Saskatchewan Hospital Services Plan.'
5. The plan '*must be in a form that is acceptable both to those providing the service and those receiving it* ... We have no intention of shoving some preconceived plan down doctors' throats. We want their co-operation

and from our experience with other health programs I am convinced we will get it.'

The premier concluded his radio talk with the announcement of the government's intention to appoint an Advisory Planning Committee on Medical Care, on which the government, the medical profession, and the public would be equally represented. Their job: 'to recommend to the Government the best method of developing a medical care program in keeping with the principles I have just outlined.' This would be done, Douglas hoped and expected, during the latter part of 1960 – one year hence – so 'that we can get ... the program started in 1961.'[32]

Two troubling questions were implicit in the plans the government was laying for the establishment of medicare. One had to do with the fifth principle. Was it possible that the proposition 'acceptable to the providers of the services' might encourage the doctors in the view that they had a right of veto even over a plan that had been decided upon by a democratically elected government – and, in particular, by a government that had been elected on the explicit promise of initiating such a plan?

The second question was implied in the establishment of a public advisory committee to design the details – if not the principles – upon which the plan was founded. Would the committee not supplant direct negotiations between the government and the doctors in the resolution of differences between them? More, could anyone but the premier (and colleagues), representing the government that was introducing the plan, and the president of the College of Physicians and Surgeons (and colleagues), representing the providers of service, wield the power, and the insight, that is required in the resolution of such deep-rooted differences? In the event, this is what ultimately happened, but not until the position of the doctors had hardened to the point of an active strike.

This, however, is a retrospective reflection. At the time Douglas was announcing the medicare plan, and indeed for a long time after, the premier and ministers still believed – indeed were confident – that a consensus could be achieved between them and the college. That they believed this, despite the early gulf of differences between the government and the college over medicare, is attributable, in no small measure, to two of Tommy Douglas's most endearing qualities. One was a profound belief in the qualities of goodness to be found in every person, and the other was an equally profound belief that reason and rationality would ultimately prevail in the fashioning of public policy.

Indeed, during the several months of controversy over the terms of reference of the Advisory Planning Committee, Premier Douglas persisted in his belief that the doctors would come to co-operate. In mid-February, he said in the legislature that it was not quite fair to the doctors to say they were opposed to the medical care plan, and he expressed confidence that the Advisory Planning Committee would resolve the problems over medicare in a way 'satisfactory' to all concerned.[33]

In December 1959, however, the reaction of the medical profession to the premier's broadcast was at first uncertain. The registrar of the College of Physicians and Surgeons, Dr George Peacock, said, 'I don't think you can quarrel too much with what the Premier said.'[34] He went on to add that 'he had a few reservations.' He did not like government control, but government sponsorship was acceptable. He noted, apparently with approval, that 'the envisaged control of the medical care plan [was] by some sort of commission responsible to the Legislature.' Two days later, however, the college itself reacted more vigorously: 'The medical profession deplores the fact that a question of so [sic] vital importance as the health care of our citizens is becoming the subject of discussion in the heated atmosphere of an oncoming election campaign. It should be pointed out that the medical profession of this province has recorded its unanimous opposition to a medical care program ... which is completely under government control.'[35]

The leader of the Liberal opposition, former CCF member of Parliament Ross Thatcher, asked in turn, '... why should a move with such far-reaching consequences and involving such huge expenditures be made by a few socialist planners without direct consultation with all citizens?'[36] The premier made it clear, in turn, that the people were to be consulted – in the forthcoming election. The press reported that 'Premier T.C. Douglas ... [has] laid the proposed medical care plan on the line as the issue on which the CCF Government is prepared to stake its future in Saskatchewan.'[37]

Thus, two lines had been drawn in the sand.

The College and the Advisory Planning Committee

The College of Physicians and Surgeons, for its part, proceeded actively to fight the government in its plans to introduce public medical care. Its first stratagem was to neutralize the proposed Advisory Planning Committee on Medical Care: the college sought both to deflect the committee from the medical care question, as such, into broader studies of health care generally; and, above all, to dislodge the government's five principles as the frame within which medical care deliberations and consultations would take place.[38]

This objective became apparent when the college first of all declined to participate in the committee and then later refused to name physicians to the committee unless a number of changes were made to the draft terms of reference proposed by the minister of health, Walter Erb. It took over three months of negotiations between the college and the government to achieve a schema for the Advisory Planning Committee with which the doctors would agree.

The college wanted to widen the terms of reference, to include the study of the whole of Saskatchewan's health system, not just 'health needs as they related to medical care' (the government's position). The government acceded to this, though not to the widening of the terms of reference beyond matters related to health care. The college also wanted to extend the time limit for the Advisory Planning Committee to report, beyond the end of 1960 – a date which the government had proposed. The government agreed that no arbitrary time limit should be imposed, but maintained 'it would seem fair to assume, however, that the people of the province will expect the committee ... to submit their recommendations as expeditiously as possible ...'[39] Above all, the college insisted on the removal of the five guiding principles from the terms of reference, and here the government was prepared to adjust its position in some measure, by placing the principles in the preamble rather than the body of the terms of reference. On a fourth demand, that the government would be precluded from naming public servants as members of the committee, the government held firm in its right to appoint the members of its choice. The government was quite happy to take up the college's suggestion that the Chamber of Commerce and the Saskatchewan Federation of Labour be represented on the committee, but was unwilling to give up its right to name public servants to the government's places on the committee.

Having seemed to accept the terms of reference, with these modifications, the college continued to object to the composition of the committee, and to demand other conditions prior to naming the physician representatives. These included a requirement that committee members would be free to express individual opinions on matters that fell within the terms of reference (a position already agreed to by the government), and that the committee would not hold hearings before the expected provincial election.

The exchanges on these issues took some three months. It was not until 26 March 1960 that the college met and finally agreed to select representatives to the Advisory Planning Committee, advising the government of their decision on March 29. The committee was then named on 25 April 1960.

Meantime, the second and central stratagem of the College of Physicians and Surgeons had taken shape. On 14 February 1960 a three-man special committee (later called the Information Committee) was established in the college's headquarters, equipped with a professional public relations officer and mandated to gather and disseminate 'information' to the profession and the public. All doctors were urged to 'contact the Special Committee ... prior to making statements on policy on medical economic matters.'[40]

The Doctors' Declaration of Rights

The next step by the college, taken on 2 March 1960, was to publish their own detailed statement of policy, thus to reinforce their earlier October declaration. It was intended as a response to the government's five principles but, in fact, took the form of a 'declaration of rights.' To cite the most salient of these 'rights,' the medical profession had 'the right to refuse to participate in any plan which in its opinion is not conducive to a continuing high standard of medical care ... and the right ... to evaluate the worth of its services and retain the principle of fee for service wherever possible.' Individual physicians 'must have the right to choose whether or not to become a participating physician in any insurance plan ... [and] the right to determine his method of remuneration.'[41] The people of Saskatchewan, the statement continued, 'have the right to determine whether or not they wish to prepay the cost of physicians' services [and] the insuring company or agency [and] the comprehensiveness of coverage.' Individual citizens 'must have the freedom to choose the method by which he will pay or prepay his medical care.'[42] No mention was made of the right of an elected government, as representative of the people, to establish universal and compulsory medical care plans, nor of the obligation of citizen participation in such plans.

As significant as these 'declared' rights were, in themselves, was the very fact that the college spoke of 'the rights' of individuals and groups, not of the principles or the fundamental ethos that should inhere in public medical care plans. That this was so was not only a measure of the gulf that separated the college and the government (rights versus principles) but also a measure of the mindset of an independent, self-governing professional body. This the college was: it had been established and empowered by the Legislative Assembly of Saskatchewan to license individual physicians, to discipline them, to oversee the granting of hospital privileges, and to act as the judges of any alleged malpractice. But by a curious – and questionable – turn of historical fate, the college had also come to be recognized, or to act, as the 'union' for physicians and surgeons, whereas in other provinces an entirely different body, the provincial medical association, served the latter purpose.

In Saskatchewan, however, the college not only presided over, or governed, professional competence and behaviour, but also protected the interests – economic and otherwise – of the doctors. Little wonder, it was easy to suppose, that the college had come to think of itself as the granter of rights and privileges to the doctors and the protector and promoter of those rights and privileges, and other interests. Little wonder, either, it could easily be suggested, that under these circumstances dissent within the ranks of duly licensed physicians and surgeons would be uncommon.[43]

The Campaign against Medicare

So it was that the College of Physicians and Surgeons geared itself up to do battle with the government of Saskatchewan over medicare. The council of the college assessed its members $100 each to finance its 'information program,' and the Canadian Medical Association contributed another $35,000 (after the election, to clear the college's bank overdraft).[44] Six hundred or so of Saskatchewan's nine hundred doctors paid the levy, which was declared by the college to be 'not voluntary and ... not compulsory – it is just an assessment.'[45]

The college emphasized that the 'information committee' was non-political.[46] But it soon became clear that the object of the exercise was to oppose public medical care. The literature produced by the college was vivid. Excerpts from the 'kit' sent to all doctors were quoted in the press: 'What will happen if British doctors pull out of the province en masse,' the circular read. 'They will have to fill the profession with the garbage of Europe.'[47] And elsewhere the pamphlet was quoted as saying:

A government-controlled plan offers a latent but potential threat to certain dogmas of the Catholic church relating to maternity, birth control, and the state.

Many times we have sat down in our office with a woman and discussed emotional situations which crop up during pregnancy or at other critical periods in a woman's life. We know under government administration we would be prevented in [sic] rendering these vital services.

The government of Saskatchewan says it is going to establish a compulsory program of prepaid medical care ... It is adopting the methods of an ancient tyrant.[48]

Another pamphlet elaborated: 'The concept of universal medical coverage is not new and the approach by government to seek support is just the same as it was when first enunciated by Karl Marx in his Communistic Theories of the last century.'[49]

The college had some things to say to the premier as well: doctors were reported as having appeared at his meetings to question and to debate with him. Nor did they hesitate to criticize Douglas. The president of the college, for example, was quoted as saying: 'It is deploring [sic] that a political leader should try and deceive the man on the street to believe that a large number of the medical profession is behind his medical care program ... everywhere doctors are adamantly opposed.'[50]

Douglas retorted during a television forum with a Regina doctor 'that if the people [want] to avoid medicare they should vote against the government. "The people of this province ... will decide whether or not we want a Medical Care Program. The [Public Advisory Committee] will determine the terms and conditions, the Schedule of Fees, and so on."'[51] Elsewhere, he decried the doctors' information campaign as 'abominable, despicable and scurrilous.'[52]

When the election was called on May 9, for June 8, it was clear that the contest was between the government and the CCF Party, on the one hand, and, on the other, the College of Physicians and Surgeons and the Liberal Party. It was equally clear that the Advisory Planning Committee would confront deep divisions. The government on one side had established the five principles upon which medicare was to be founded; the doctors on the other side had rejected the principles and published a contrary declaration of doctors' and citizens' 'rights.' The two were almost totally incompatible. The gulf between the two sides had been hardened by the odious campaign of the college against medicare and the government, and by the tendentious and protracted negotiations regarding the establishment of the Advisory Planning Committee.

Despite all of this, the government remained optimistic that a 'committee of reconciliation' (as it might be called in post-Mandela times) could achieve some middle ground between the two contending sides. The committee's membership reflected this hopeful view: it incorporated representatives of the two opposing views plus a 'third force' of independent public members. Representing the college's point of view would be its nominees, Dr J.F.C. Anderson, Dr E.W. Barootes, and Dr C.J. Houston, and (almost certainly) the representative of the Saskatchewan Chamber of Commerce, Donald McPherson. Representing the government's point of view would be T.J. Bentley, former minister of health, Dr F.B. Roth, deputy minister of health, and his colleague Dr V.L. Matthews, and a representative of the Saskatchewan Federation of Labour, Walter Smishek. Representing the public would be the Chair of the committee, Dr Walter P. Thompson, former president of the University of Saskatchewan, Mrs Beatrice Trew, and Cliff H. Whiting, while representing the university's College of Medicine was Dr Irwin Hilliard.

Short of divine intervention or a miraculous conversion of the government's and/or the college's supporters, it would be up to the independent/public members to serve as mediators or conciliators. In short, the Public Advisory Committee could scarcely be expected to accomplish the objective that the premier and his colleagues had envisaged for them: to achieve the assent of both the college and the government to a commonly agreed upon medical care plan. Certainly it could not be accomplished before the election of June 8.

Everything, therefore, turned upon the election and the electorate. Despite the dual opposition – the Liberal Party and the College of Physicians and Surgeons – Douglas and the CCF won the election of 1960 handily. There were many, indeed, in both the Liberal and the CCF Parties, who believed that the doctors' campaign had helped Douglas. Whatever the case, the CCF won thirty-eight of the fifty-five seats, a gain of two, with the Liberals taking the balance. In terms of the popular vote, the CCF won 40.8 per cent (down from 45.2 per cent in 1956), the Liberal Party won 32.7 per cent (up from 30.3 per cent), the Conservatives won 14.0 per cent (up from 2.0 per cent), and the Social Credit Party won 12.3 per cent (down from 21.5 per cent).

For a brief moment, it seemed that the election results had persuaded the College of Physicians and Surgeons to accept the inevitable. The press reported on June 10: 'CMA [executive director] Dr. A.D. Kelly said there could be no doubt the election result in Saskatchewan constituted endorsement for the medical care plan. The CMA was therefore dropping its opposition and offering to co-operate in setting up the best plan possible.'[53] But Dr Kelly was promptly contradicted by college president Dr Davies, who said the Saskatchewan college remained 'unalterably opposed.' Dr Davies added, 'Dr. Kelly was probably misquoted.'[54] Dr Kelly, in turn, declared he had not been misquoted, but acknowledged that his opinion was a personal one.

So began the fifth term of the CCF's twenty years in office. The abiding question confronting the province was clear: where would the room for accommodation be found when one side deeply believed in public medicare and the other side was equally determined to prevent its introduction?

10

Medicare

The story of the government during the CCF's fifth term of office in Saskatchewan – 1960 to 1964 – was the story of medicare. All the rest of policy and of administration seemed frozen in time. The medicare story began, after the June election, with a period of paralysis for the government, as it awaited a report from the Advisory Planning Committee (roughly June 1960 to June 1961). It was followed by a burst of renewed government activity culminating in the passage by the Legislative Assembly of the Saskatchewan Medical Care Insurance Act (introduced 13 October 1961, receiving royal assent 17 November 1961), and the establishment of the Medical Care Insurance Commission in January 1962.

There followed six intensive months of conflict and negotiations between the government and the College of Physicians and Surgeons seeking some reconciliation, or modus vivendi, as between the government's unwavering support for public and universal medical care, and the equally unwavering insistence of the doctors upon private medical care, supported by public subsidies to the extent that the government insisted upon universal coverage.

In the absence of agreement between the two sides, and despite growing public pressure on both the government and the doctors, the doctors withdrew their services on 1 July 1962. The doctors' strike lasted for twenty-three nightmarish days. Mediation efforts that had been initiated only days before the strike itself began, plus a unique external catalyst, finally brought the stalemate to an end.

This 'story line' provides only the guideposts of these two years in the development of medicare.[1] The drama is to be found in the fundamentals of the dispute: in the clash between two fundamentally differing value systems as embodied in opposing public policies in the field of

medical care; in the functioning of government and of the political system in the face of a challenge to the authority and the legitimacy of the
democratically elected government by a small but powerful private
body; and in the ultimate recognition that the harmonizing of different
value systems is achieved not by trying to make them congruent but
rather in finding a modus vivendi between them, out of which, in time,
reconciliation might emerge.

A Period of Paralysis: The Advisory Committee

The story of the Advisory Planning Committee was one of dissension
and delay. The committee had been appointed in April 1960 after
extended negotiations with the College of Physicians and Surgeons. It
began its meetings in May; it started its hearings on 12 January 1961;[2]
and it first turned its mind to the structure of a medical care plan in
May of 1961. All in all, it held twenty meetings for a total of thirty-seven
days, conducted thirty-three public and seven private hearings, received
one hundred briefs and staff papers, and visited seven foreign countries.[3]

From the beginning, it was apparent that the committee was deeply
divided. Two of the doctor members were well-known opponents of
public medical care, and one of them, Dr E.W. Barootes, was to become,
reputedly, the 'master strategist' of the doctors' strike. The trade union
member, Walter Smishek, was a well-known advocate of public medical
care, and during and after the strike was to assist in the development of
community clinics (which engaged salaried doctors). None of these
members attempted to hide his prejudices. The committee's deliberations were marred too by a whispering campaign against the chairman:
there were even rumours among some Regina doctors to the effect that
Dr Thompson was senile and therefore willing to do what the government wanted.[4] One doctor charged publicly that Dr Thompson was
prejudiced, and this brought a hot reply from the university faculty: 'As
members of the university faculty, we are grieved and shocked that igno-
ble motives can be ascribed to Dr. Thompson, a revered member of the
university community ... Unwarranted and prejudiced attacks of this
type are a grave disservice to responsible consideration of major issues
of the day.'[5]

There was no doubt in the public mind that there was a dispute within
the committee between those who wanted a medicare plan and those
who wanted to delay it by failing to report. In fact, Chairman Thompson

became so impatient with the delays that in the autumn of 1960 he informed the committee that he was considering resigning. Dr Thompson attributed the delays in the committee to three factors: first, a genuine interest on the part of members in current health services; secondly, an attempt to catalogue all conceivable gaps in health services with the objective of attaching a price tag which 'may scare the government and the public away from a medical care program'; and thirdly, an attempt to incur a delay that might frustrate the original objective. The chairman said he was prepared to resign, and was prepared to make public the reasons for his resignation. Premier Douglas urged Dr Thompson not to resign, saying, 'I am determined to proceed with the medical care program, but I do want to canvass every conceivable possibility of getting the cooperation of the medical profession.'[6] In the end, Dr Thompson decided to remain as chairman.

But the feuding went on. Indeed, in January 1961, the chairman publicly acknowledged the divisions within the committee. 'The political feuding [in the committee] was so obvious that committee chairman Dr. W.P. Thompson told a reporter that it would take a long time to write a report since there was so much disagreement.'[7]

It did, in fact, take the committee a long time to prepare its interim report. Early in 1960, the premier had abandoned any plans to introduce medical care legislation until he had received a report from the committee.[8] When the committee was appointed in April 1960, Health Minister Erb had expressed the hope that the committee would report fairly soon. 'It seems fair to assume, however, that the committee will make reasonable progress and submit their recommendations as expeditiously as possible.'[9] But in January 1961, Erb 'expressed doubts ... that next month's session of the legislature could pass enabling legislation for a medical care plan.' He added, 'Medical care insurance is important enough to warrant a special session.'[10] In April the cabinet noted with concern the need for an early report from the committee if legislation were to be introduced in 1961.[11] And later, Douglas instructed the minister of health to press the committee to issue an interim report.

The Doctors' Position Entrenched

During the same period (June 1960 to May 1961), the Saskatchewan College of Physicians and Surgeons repeated time and again its opposition to a public and universal medical care plan. The initial and most comprehensive statement of the doctors' position was articulated by the Canadian Medical Association at its annual meeting. On 14 June 1960 the CMA issued a statement of policy, or principles, on health insurance, arguing that 'a tax supported comprehensive program, compulsory for all, is neither necessary or desirable.'[12] But if such a program were to be established, the CMA went on to say, it would have to adhere to fourteen principles. Most of these principles were consistent with, or close to, the position of the government of Saskatchewan, but three of them were to become central to the medicare dispute.

The first of these provided that 'any board, commission or agency set up to administer any medical services insurance program [must have] fiscal authority and autonomy.' How the legislature and the government could impose taxes and 'premiums' and vote public money to finance a universal medical care program, without any responsibility or accountability to the Legislative Assembly for its actions, was far from clear. A high measure of independence for an administering commission would be no problem, but no responsible government could grant 'complete autonomy.'

The second difficult proposition provided 'that medical services insurance programs do not in any way preclude the private practice of medicine.' If this meant simply that any doctor and any patient could agree to function entirely outside the public plan, there would be no problem. But if it meant that participating doctors and patients could engage in privately financed services alongside or on top of publicly financed medical services, serious differences would arise between the government and the college.

The third problematic proposition was that 'the amount of remuneration is a matter for negotiation between the physician and his patient, or those acting on their behalf ...' If this meant that a public insurance commission could act on behalf of all participating patients in negotiating the fee schedule under which participating doctors would be paid, this is precisely what the government had in mind. But if this 'agency arrangement' was meant to apply to private insurers and not to the public agency, serious difficulties would, and in fact did, arise. This ambiguity was identified at the CMA meeting, and 'three separate motions [were introduced] to delete or amend the phrase 'or those acting on their behalf.'[13] All were defeated and the wording stood.

But there were no ambiguities in the position of the Saskatchewan college, and these positions were reiterated over the next months. On 13 October 1960 the College of Physicians and Surgeons at its annual convention 'reconfirmed its opposition to a "compulsory comprehensive government-controlled medical care plan."'[14] On 12 January 1961, in its brief to the Advisory Planning Committee, the college 'completely endorsed' the CMA's statement of principles.[15] In June 1961 the president of the college repeated to the CMA's annual convention the college's brief to the Advisory Planning Committee, 'categorically rejecting any [public financing] other than subsidized involvement in voluntary agencies.'[16] Then, on 9 July 1961, in a supplementary brief to the Advisory Planning Committee, the college recommended the implementation of the plan that had been suggested in its main brief of 12 January 1961.[17]

It was perfectly clear, in short, that the government's policy on medical care, and the value system upon which it was founded, were simply irreconcilable with those of the college. And there was no potential for seeking to bridge them, if not to reconcile them, by direct negotiations between the government and the college, until the Advisory Planning Committee had reported. The government had been paralysed, as it turned out, by its own well-intentioned decision to seek a consensus between the doctors and themselves through the committee.

The Premier and Federal Politics: A Backdrop to the Drama

During this whole period, it was gradually becoming apparent that Premier Douglas might be induced to leave Saskatchewan to become the leader of his national party. During 1959 and 1960, leaders of the CCF and of the Canadian Labour Congress had been developing plans for the formation of a new party of the left, a party that would enjoy formal trade union support as well as the continued support of CCF members, including the Western farmers, who formed the backbone of the movement. The new party was to be patterned after the British Labour Party, and it was hoped that with the fresh dynamic of new support, the CCF would become a truly national party.

It was obvious that a dynamic leader was as important as a forceful platform, and the founders looked to Douglas as that leader. But they had to persuade him to come, before the New Party's founding convention in August 1961.

Throughout 1960, Tommy Douglas persistently resisted their blandishments. To rumours that he was interested in the federal field, he replied: 'I am not at all interested in the federal field. There is plenty to do in Saskatchewan. I have started a big job here and I would like to finish it if the people will let me.'[18] By the end of 1960, however, he had begun to weaken under this pressure. Privately, he consulted a few of his intimates to obtain their views. Most of them encouraged him to follow the dictates of his conscience, which seemed by early 1961 to be leading him back into the federal field. Increasingly the news reports suggested that Douglas would succumb to the 'draft movement' – especially after March when CCF MLAs wrote individually to the premier to express their views.

On 23 January 1961 Douglas said: 'I will go wherever the movement thinks I will make my best contribution ... I think I will be of most use to the movement where I am.'[19] On February 7, several Saskatchewan CCF leaders formed a committee to draft Douglas for the leadership.[20] Finally, on April 21, Douglas confirmed that he was prepared to 'try for [the] leadership of the New Party if the provincial party is prepared to release him.'[21] Then 'on Saturday (27 May 1961) the CCF provincial council ... voted 36 to 16 in favour of releasing the premier.' And on June 17 the CCF members in Douglas's constituency voted 144 to 6 for letting him make up his own mind.[22] On 28 June 1961 he gave his decision: 'If those at the founding convention [of the New Party] feel that my re-entry into federal politics will advance the day when we shall have a people's government in Canada, then I am prepared to undertake that responsibility.'[23] On August 4, Tommy Douglas was elected leader of the New Democratic Party by an overwhelming majority. He announced that he would resign as premier of Saskatchewan in November.[24]

Thus the 'Douglas dynasty,' as some called it, began to draw to an end. And thus began, too, the suggestion that the premier's compelling desire to introduce a medical care plan in 1961 was simply a matter of his wanting the political credit for having introduced the first medicare plan in Canada.

It would be surprising indeed if Tommy Douglas had *not* cared about being identified as the father of medicare – his long-held dream. But there were other real and urgent reasons for pressing on with the design and the implementation of the medical care plan. First, the government was running out of the lead-time required to mount a new program of this magnitude. And secondly, to delay repeatedly the implementation of the program until it was too late in the CCF's fifth term of office to introduce it would be to acknowledge and accept the power of a small but potent group in society to overrule a democratically elected government. This no government in Canada could do.

Renewed Government Action

Here is what the government faced. It was clear to all those involved that the government would be reaching the mid-point of its term of office in twelve months or so (given the customary term of four years) and that no prudent government would risk launching a major new program during the last two years of its term. Before the start-up date, the government would have to complete the decision-making process (the legislation, regulations, and program guidelines, plus a financing plan); and it would also have to develop the structures and the systems required, and to engage and to train the staff required to make the program operational.

Clearly the government was running out of time. With a planned start-up date of 1 January 1962, at this point, and assuming a report from the Advisory Planning Committee by, say, September 1, the government would have four clear months for the decision-making and the preparatory work required. A 1 April 1962 start-up would give the government seven months; even a date of July 1 (not in ministers' minds at this point) would give them only ten months. Whatever the decision might be, and however much preparatory work could be done during the decision-making stage, the government was sorely pressed.

Early in June, in the face of the continuing inability of the Advisory Committee to reach some kind of consensus, and no sign that they would, the premier decided to seize the initiative. He directed his minister of health to ask Chairman Thompson whether the committee could produce an interim report, to permit the government to prepare 'enabling legislation couched in general terms to be ... introduced in the Legislature at the Fall Session.'[25] A special session was required, in any event, to enact provincial income tax legislation, as required under the new federal-provincial fiscal arrangements adopted for 1962–7. The committee responded favourably and, with the representatives of the College and the Chamber of Commerce dissenting, produced their interim report on 25 September 1961.

During the same period, the government had been turning its mind to other aspects of the proposed medical care plan, namely its financing and its organization and administration. As early as 16 May 1961, the Treasury reported to the Treasury Board on alternative revenue sources for the financing of medicare, and the board decided to invite the cabinet to express 'preliminary views on the relative weight that should be attached to the several alternatives ... particularly the family tax (premium).'[26] Further consideration of a financial plan would require a report from the Department of Health on 'the kind of programs which might be expected to be introduced, an estimate of its probable cost, and the time at which it would be most propitious to introduce such a program.'[27]

The Treasury Board was also concerned that plans should be laid for the kind of structures the Medical Care Insurance commission should adopt, and for the staffing of the commission, particularly at senior levels. The Department of Health was asked on July 18, August 18, and August 24 to prepare a report for the board on these questions, and as well to prepare some draft legislation that would conform with the trend of the deliberations of the Advisory Planning Committee. On 18 September 1961 the board reported to the cabinet that the department had failed to meet its deadline.[28] (It is well to recall that the deputy and the assistant deputy minister of health were also members of the Advisory Planning Committee.)

The Treasury Board was having greater success in the development of draft plans for the financing of medical care. This was not, it must be said, because the revenue requirements would be easily achievable. In fact, they were greater than had been expected after the government of Canada began contributing to the cost of the Saskatchewan Hospital Services Plan in 1958. But the expenditures on hospital insurance and on hospital construction had been increasing since then, and revenue yields had come under pressure as a result of the 1960 recession and the crop failure of 1961 (when wheat yields dropped from a ten-year average of 19.2 bushels per acre to only 8.5 bushels).[29]

Nevertheless, the development of a plan for the financing of medical care proceeded expeditiously. After the preliminary discussions at the Treasury Board meeting of 16 May 1961, the board met four more times, to examine Treasury Department reports on different tax sources and to assess the alternatives as they were emerging. On September 18 the Treasury's final report was received, analysing the incidence, stability, and 'collectability' of the tax sources being considered, and recommending a tax structure.[30] The Treasury Board made some modifications to the department's proposals and then submitted them to cabinet for approval. When the cabinet had made its decision, it consulted the caucus and the agreed tax structure was put into legislative form. Woodrow Lloyd, the provincial treasurer, submitted these tax changes to the Legislative Assembly on 20 October 1961:

Medical care insurance premiums of $12 for individuals and $24 for families.	$6,000,000
A 1 per cent increase in the personal income tax (1% of taxable income). (Under new federal-provincial arrangements, the province imposed its own personal income tax effective 1 January 1962.)	$3,600,000
An increase of 1 per cent in corporate income tax. (The same was true of Saskatchewan's new corporate income tax.)	$1,000,000
An increase in the retail sales tax of 2 per cent, with 1.5 per cent going to medicare and the rest to education.	$10,500,000

Lloyd was careful to point out that these contributions to the public treasury would not constitute an additional burden on family income; rather, they would replace the family payments then being made for medical care either directly or through private insurance companies. What was different was that all Saskatchewanians would be paying, year by year, the medical expenses of those who were sick, and all would be reassured by the knowledge that under this system no one would be bankrupted by 'catastrophic illness.'[31]

The Interim Report of the Advisory Planning Committee

To return to the debate over the medical care program itself, and to the interim report the Advisory Planning Committee had submitted in late September, there were few surprises in it.

It was no surprise that there was a majority report supporting a medical care plan that was universal, comprehensive, and publicly administered – endorsed by the public and the government representatives on the committee. It was no surprise that there was a minority report opposing such a plan – submitted by the representatives of the College of Physicians and Surgeons and the representative of the Chamber of Commerce.

It was no surprise either that the minority report, after rejecting 'a state monopoly plan,' went on to propose an alternative 'universally available' plan. Under such a plan,

(a) the self-supporting majority of our fellow citizens should be encouraged to cover themselves for the comprehensive range of medical benefits available through [private] medical care ... agencies ... these persons should have free choice ...

(b) public funds should be made available on application in the form of subsidy of approved carriers [the private medicare insurers] for: (i) those persons ... who are unable to finance the premium [set by the private insurers], (ii) self sufficient persons over 65 years of age [who] should [also] have some subsidy.[32]

There were other elements in the report that were more surprising, including the advocacy by the majority of limited 'utilization fees' and the payment of doctors on a 'fee for service basis.' There was also a separate minority report by the representative of the Saskatchewan Federation of Labour, which was pro-medicare, but more uncompromisingly so.

The most striking feature of the report, however, was the stark position taken by the doctors. After fourteen months, and after many compromises on the part of those who signed the majority report, the three private doctors on the committee had not budged from the original position of the College of Physicians and Surgeons. For the plan proposed in their minority report was virtually the same as that advocated by the college in its submission to the committee in January 1961.[33] It was not universal; it was not compulsory; it was not publicly administered; it was not to be financed on the basis of ability to pay; it involved unconditional government subsidies to private bodies; and it involved a means test. It violated, in short, virtually all of the principles that Premier Douglas had enunciated as being necessary elements in his medical care plan.

The government decided to proceed on the basis of the majority report, though it had to make haste if it was to prepare legislation between 25 September 1961, when it received the report, and mid-October, when the Legislative Assembly was scheduled to meet.

The Medical Care Insurance Act

After two weeks of intensive discussions in cabinet and among officials, the government was ready to submit its plan to the legislature: the Medical Care Insurance Act was presented to the Assembly on Friday, 13 October 1961. The Bill followed closely the majority report of the

Advisory Committee. It provided for a universal medical care plan, available to all residents of the province. The benefits were to include medical, surgical, maternity, diagnostic, and physiotherapy services, as well as specialist services upon referral. The patient was free to choose his doctor, and the doctor his patients. The plan was to be administered by a Medical Care Insurance Commission, appointed by the lieutenant governor in council.

The commission, in turn, was to consist of from six to eight members, one of whom was to be the deputy minister of public health, and at least two of whom were to be physicians (in addition to the deputy minister, who was a physician, and to the chairman – if he were a physician). The commission was to report to the minister through the deputy minister, but it was given powers that would make it, de facto, a very independent body.[34] Provision was also made for both an advisory council and a medical advisory committee of college-approved physicians.

The plan was to be financed from the four tax sources discussed earlier, which together represented about 1.4 per cent of personal income for the lowest income groups, up to 1.6 per cent for the highest income earners.[35]

The Act empowered the commission, subject to regulation, to administer the medical care insurance plan, to take action to improve the quality of the insured services provided under the plan, and to prescribe the terms and conditions for providing insured services. The doctors rendering services under the plan would be paid, it was presumed, on a fee-for-service basis, and would bill the commission directly. However, the Act left the method of payment to the commission. The Act was also silent on the question of practice outside the plan: however, it in no way prohibited purely private practice under which the patient would pay his doctor directly (although these payments would be in addition to the individual's tax payments).

The Bill was not presented to the College of Physicians and Surgeons for their comment before it was tabled in the Legislative Assembly. From the government's point of view, the college through its representatives on the Public Advisory Committee had been presenting their unchanging view for many months, culminating in their minority report. The college itself had also been presenting its views publicly, particularly in the nine months before the committee reported. Further consultations before the Bill was tabled in the legislature would contribute nothing to achieving agreement, but would certainly contribute to yet further delay. So the government concluded.

From the college's point of view, the failure of the government to consult the profession was a breach of faith: they insisted they had been promised such consultation.[36] Relations between the doctors and the government thus became angry as well as implacable.

The opposition, for its part, both supported and opposed the Bill. It voted for it on second reading (thus supporting the principles of the Bill) and voted against it on third reading (thus registering its opposition to the details of the plan). In their speeches, however, members of the opposition made it clear that they supported the position of the College of Physicians and Surgeons. Ross Thatcher, the Liberal leader, said: 'This whole attempt by the government to implement this legislation is just another example of the socialists trying to dispose of something that doesn't belong to them ... the doctors' services.'[37] On third reading, Thatcher made two additional points: first, that there should be a plebiscite before the plan was introduced; and secondly, that the government could not guarantee that doctors' services would be available.[38] This was to turn out to be an accurate prediction for twenty-three days in July 1962.

The College of Physicians and Surgeons, for its part, stood firm. At their convention in October, the doctors resolved 'that this College of Physicians and Surgeons and the Saskatchewan division of the Canadian Medical Association reiterates its refusal to accept a government controlled medical scheme as outlined in the legislative draft ... and declares it cannot co-operate in such a plan.'[39]

Such was the climate that surrounded the introduction of North America's first universal medical care legislation.

The End of the Douglas Regime

It was in this climate, too, that the Douglas government came to an end. On August 4 the premier had become the leader of the national New Democratic Party, and he had undertaken to resign as premier at the time of the Saskatchewan CCF-NDP convention.[40] The convention was held in early November 1961 – the legislature recessed while the convention was in progress – and one of its prime functions was to accept Tommy Douglas's resignation as the party's political leader, and to select his successor.

On Friday, 3 November 1961, Woodrow S. Lloyd was chosen to succeed Douglas as the CCF's political leader, and on the following Tuesday, November 7, he was sworn in as premier. Tommy Douglas had gone to the lieutenant governor to advise him of his resignation on Monday, after more than seventeen years as premier of Saskatchewan. It had been a remarkable seventeen years, but Tommy Douglas did not 'go out' in a celebratory blaze of glory: that is not Saskatchewan's way. More, this was a particularly intense time: the people of the province were troubled – they did not know where the bitter medical care dispute would lead.

But they had lived through – and were now living – the changes that Douglas and his colleagues had made. They recognized his achievements in their daily lives: an education system that provided a higher quality of education to everyone in the province's scattered population; a health system that provided to every person in the province, regardless of income, hospital and – now before long – medical services; mental hospitals that provided professional care rather than simple custody; a welfare system that provided income and services to persons in need; even telephones and electricity and natural gas to improve the quality of life. All of this was the legacy in the daily lives of Saskatchewanians that Tommy Douglas and his CCF government would be remembered for.

As for Douglas the man, it was Woodrow Lloyd, his successor, who spoke for the Legislative Assembly and for the CCF Party when he said to Douglas: 'Your profession has indeed been the public good, and no man has worked more assiduously or with more zeal at his chosen work. Your gifts have been recognized near and far. You have shown how wit may be allied with wisdom, humour with humanitarianism, sympathy with statesmanship. In you to an extraordinary degree are combined political skill and public morality, personal charm and persistent integrity.'[41]

From another, one might almost say unexpected, quarter came a different but similarly genuine tribute – one paid to him by his arch-enemy, the *Regina Leader Post*, upon his departure from office:

> Despite sincere differences over some of his government's policies, the people of Saskatchewan generally have respected Douglas while from his followers he has received their utmost admiration and adoration. He has stood forth during his 17 years which have seen premiers come and go in other provinces as one of the most dynamic to hold this office in the nation. He has been an indefatigable worker, a zealous crusader, and an inspired and inspiring leader. These personal attributes in the main have been responsible for his record of more than 17 years in office. His was a personal achievement which it is difficult to match elsewhere in Canada.

Certainly, it has no parallel in Saskatchewan's political history ... It is a sad-
dening thought to many ... the colourful 'Tommy' Douglas as of this day
ceases to be the Premier of Saskatchewan.'[42]

Woodrow Lloyd assumed office on 7 November 1961. He would complete the story of Douglas's medical care plan and, in doing so, become
its 'cofounder.' Lloyd's first act as premier was to change the cast of ministers who would play a central role in supporting and assisting him in
bringing the Saskatchewan Medical Care Insurance Act to life. The first
of these changes was to relieve Walter Erb of the health portfolio, and to
appoint him instead as the minister of public works – a move many
in government thought was long overdue. Simultaneously, Lloyd
appointed the former minister of public works, William G. Davies, a
former head of the Saskatchewan Federation of Labour, who was known
to have been an accomplished union negotiator in private life, to the
health portfolio. The third change was the appointment of Allan
Blakeney as provincial treasurer. By this time, Blakeney had moved on
from his position as legal officer and Secretary to the Government
Finance Office. In 1955 he had become chief officer of the
Saskatchewan Securities Commission, and in 1958 he left the public service and joined a private law firm. Then, in 1960, he had run for election as an NDP candidate, and following that success, he was appointed
minister of education, moving to the Treasury portfolio in 1961.

Bill Davies wasted no time in trying to establish a new and fresh relationship with Dr Harold Dalgleish, now president of the College of Physicians and Surgeons. Davies telephoned Dalgleish immediately after
the medical care bill was passed (November 28) to consult with him
about the Act generally and more specifically the three medical-doctor
appointments to be named to the commission.[43] Dalgleish replied publicly, '[making] it clear ... the doctors are not going to negotiate on the
basis of the medical care bill recently passed in the legislature.'[44]

Bill Davies made another overture in a letter dated December 4.
Dalgleish acknowledged the letter, met with his council, and then
responded on 12 December 1961. After reminding the government that
it had not lived up to its promise (as the doctors saw it) that the college
would be given a copy of the medical care bill before it was introduced
into the legislature, Dalgleish went on to say that the council was not
prepared to co-operate with a government-controlled plan. What they
were prepared to discuss with the government was 'the health needs of
the people.'[45] To the press, Dr Dalgleish was rather more pointed: 'We

have no intention of negotiating on the bill or any part of it, including the commission.'[46]

The situation facing the government, then, was clear: either they proceeded with their preparations to implement the legislation – which is to say, begin introducing their universal and public medical care plan – or they capitulated to the College of Physicians and Surgeons. There was, effectively, no choice: the government would proceed.

The Medical Care Insurance Commission

The first step in the implementation of the Act was the appointment of the Medical Care Insurance Commission. The premier acted on 6 January 1962. The chairman would be Donald D. Tansley, a leading 'graduate' of the Budget Bureau and indeed for a time its director, who was currently the executive director of the Government Finance Office. Tansley was also a member of the board of governors of the University Hospital and of the board of the Saskatchewan Power Corporation, and had served as the deputy provincial treasurer while I was on leave at Harvard University. The doctors named to the commission were Dr Burns Roth, deputy minister of health, Dr O.K. Hjertas, a medical practitioner who had played an active part in establishing the Swift Current Health Region, and Dr Samuel Wolfe, a member of the faculty of medicine at the University of Saskatchewan. The other members were Stuart Robertson, secretary of the Swift Current Health Region, A.V. Kipling, chairman of the Melfort Health Region, and G.J.D. Taylor, a Saskatoon lawyer. The fact that only one member of the commission was a practising physician was not lost on Dr Dalgleish: it showed, he said, 'how widespread and deep was the [doctors'] support of the College's stand.'[47]

Beyond the composition of the commission, however, the college and Dr Dalgleish seemed not to recognize that with the passage of the Medical Care Insurance Act and the appointment of the MCIC (the commission), the terms of the debate between the doctors and the government had changed. The college now had to challenge an Act of the Legislative Assembly to achieve their stated goals; and the government, in turn, had to find an 'operational mode' that would at one and the same time respect the basic principles of the legislation and demonstrate to the doctors that public payment for privately rendered medical care need not and would not compromise their professional practices and interests.

An opportunity to restate their respective positions was fortuitously provided by the hearings in Regina in late January 1962 of the federal

Royal Commission on Health Services – a commission that had been established by Prime Minister John Diefenbaker in June 1961 (and suggested by the Executive Committee of the Canadian Medical Association in December 1960).[48] In its submission to the royal commission, the Saskatchewan government centred on the values upon which Saskatchewan's medical care plan had been founded: that health services should be equally available to all citizens without regard to their means or their state of health, and that government was the only vehicle through which this universality and accessibility could be achieved. Certainly, argued the government, it could not be achieved through government subsidization of private health insurance plans. Medicare, as in the Saskatchewan model, should be available to all Canadians, not only those who lived in Saskatchewan. To achieve this universality, the federal government would have to – was urged to – act as it had done in respect of hospitalization in 1958.[49]

The College of Physicians and Surgeons in its submission to the royal commission reviewed the position it had taken in its brief to the Advisory Planning Committee and repeated, in the face of the Saskatchewan Medical Care Insurance Act, the college's resolution of 17 October 1961 affirming the refusal of the college to accept a government-controlled medical care plan. 'Therefore,' the college continued, 'we cannot agree to render service under the plan. We would, however, continue to treat our patients in accordance with our capabilities. We would presume that patients presenting receipts of payment would be able to obtain reimbursement from the insurance program.'[50]

Attempts to Implement the Act

It was evident from the two submissions that nothing had changed. This meant the government had no acceptable alternative but to proceed with its preparations for implementing the Medical Care Insurance Act – evidently without the co-operation, certainly without the participation, of the college. But one thing was seemingly apparent from the doctors' submissions: in the event of continuing disagreement, the doctors would continue to treat their patients and to bill them for their services. There was no talk of a withdrawal of services. So the big question was whether or how the doctors could be persuaded to accept reimbursement from the commission on behalf of the patients; or perhaps even, under appropriate circumstances, the patients could be reimbursed for their payments to the doctor.

The government, at this point, proceeded in the belief that the doctors could be persuaded to accept, or would come to accept, payment for their services through the MCIC. On February 8, Don Tansley wrote to Harold Dalgleish requesting a meeting to discuss with the college's council both the plan itself, and the regulations and actions required for its implementation. Dalgleish's reply fifteen days later reflected the depth of the anger and hostility of the doctors. After recounting a history of the college's grievances ever since Douglas's December 1959 announcement of the government's intention to establish a medical care plan, Dalgleish said:

> We regard this Act as a form of civil conscription of the profession of medicine and an attempt to put us under the control of government by political and economic pressure.
>
> The Saskatchewan Medical Care Insurance Act (1961) is quite unacceptable to the profession and we regret that since your Commission is an instrument of this Act, the Council of the College unanimously, with the widest support of the profession, declines to meet with the Saskatchewan Medical Care Insurance Commission.[51]

Tansley replied to Dalgleish that the commission deeply regretted the college's decision, but remained anxious and willing to meet with the college at any time. Copies of the exchange were sent, of course, to the minister of health. Then the commission decided to try another route to get from the doctors their views on how best to implement the Act: the direct route. Tansley wrote to all the physicians in the province, seeking their views (26 February 1961). A large number of them replied, but on balance the initiative was not helpful.

The minister of health then returned to the college. On March 2 he again invited them to meet with the government. But this time he offered to discuss changes in the Act that the college considered necessary in order to protect the profession's legitimate interests.[52] And on March 3 the minister announced that the starting date of the medical care plan would be deferred from 1 April to 1 July 1962. On March 9 the college replied with an acknowledgment. The minister then wrote to Dr Dalgleish saying:

> I find this lack of responsiveness most difficult to reconcile with the Council's expressed concern over the Medical Care Act. It is two weeks tomorrow since my letter was mailed. The failure of the College to reply suggests

one of two conclusions; either the Council's anxieties about the Act are not very great, or the Council's objective is simply to delay rather than to enter into any serious discussion leading to a resolution of the present problems.[53]

On March 15 the college replied, and Dr Dalgleish's letter evoked this response from the government:

> We conclude from your letter that the College of Physicians and Surgeons is not prepared to accept a public medical care plan but requests the Government to agree in advance of any discussions to abandon the Saskatchewan Medical Care Insurance Act in its entirety and consider instead:
> 1. Encouragement of voluntary medical coverage under existing private and commercial plans where each citizen pays his own fees or premiums.
> 2. Continuation and perhaps expansion of public means test medical assistance to depressed income families and the aged.
> Further, we understand from your letter that even this proposal would be subject to approval by doctors 'in the rest of Canada.'[54]

Davies, the minister of health, went on to point out that the college's position was unchanged from that which it had taken at the time of the Advisory Committee's report. Since that time, the Legislative Assembly had placed a law upon the statute books – this was now the law of the province. Nevertheless, said Davies, in an effort to resolve the differences the cabinet was suggesting a meeting with an 'open agenda.' He proposed March 28 – the latest date on which amendments to the Act could be considered (the legislature was likely to prorogue early in April).

The college agreed to this proposal, and meetings were held on March 28, April 1, and April 11. At these meetings, the government offered a number of concessions. The most important of these was the premier's undertaking to consider payment methods other than the existing commission-to-physician plan. It also undertook to remove from the Act any cause for concern as to professional independence (addressing the college's concern with the regulatory powers of the commission, which had been based on existing federal and provincial examples);[55] to provide for a special mechanism by which physicians' remuneration would be arrived at; to provide for appeal procedures in respect of differences between the commission and individual doctors; and to provide for regional bodies to assess accounts which came under dispute. The government also offered to enlarge the commission to provide for additional members to be selected by the college.

The college rejected these proposals – they did not meet its demand that the Act be rescinded. Instead, it offered a modification of its 'private plans' proposal:

1. That medical care insurance be province-wide and universally available to all Saskatchewan residents on the payment of a premium.
2. That this be made available through existing or new voluntary prepaid health agencies.
3. That a Registration Board function as an approval body for these insurance agencies.
4. That Government would pay the entire premium for persons presently deemed to be 'indigent.'
5. That the Government would provide, as a subsidy, a stated number of dollars for each contract offered by approved agencies.
6. That each approved agency would determine the amount of money required in addition to the subsidy, and would charge this additional amount as a premium to be paid by subscribers who enrol on a voluntary basis.
7. That patients would pay their accounts directly to their doctors, and would obtain from their approved agency a refund of a major portion of the expense incurred.
8. That the profession would not make charges to the indigent groups in excess of the amount of the refund to which the patient is entitled.[56]

This 'final concession,' as the college called it, did not represent to the government much of a departure from the college's original position. The doctors' plan was still voluntary; it still involved means tests; it still failed to assure coverage of the total costs of medical care (an unspecified percentage only of the doctor's bill would be refunded to the patient); and it still involved unconditional subsidies from the public purse. Moreover, it represented a retreat from the prevailing practices of the private plans: the patient would pay the doctor instead of the insurance plan, and the insurance plan would reimburse the patient – thus leaving open the possibility of 'extra-billing' by the doctor.[57]

Briefly put, the doctors were once again rejecting public medical care insurance in favour of private medical care plans – but now heavily subsidized by government, according to the doctors' proposals. In taking this position, the doctors were also rejecting the premier's suggestion that a kind of coexistence between these two poles of public policy could be achieved by providing that doctors could continue to bill their patients if they chose and that it would be the patient who, upon payment of the bill, would be reimbursed by the MCIC. In short, the public payment for medical care services would be visibly divorced from the private practice of medicine by the doctor. This was the essence of the patient reimbursement plan advanced in the April 4 meeting, included in the amendments to the Act on April 12, and subsequently, on April 21, proposed to the college by the Chair of the commission.[58] But all of this was irrelevant if there were no public medical care plan in the first place – the position which the college was insisting upon, and to which the government had to respond.

Again the government concluded that there was only one course to follow. The law of the province – the Medical Care Insurance Act – must be implemented. In making this decision, the cabinet had to consider the consequences, the doctors' probable response. The most likely course would be for the doctors simply to ignore the medical care plan and to continue to bill patients directly, as the college had indicated earlier.

Dalgleish himself confirmed this approach when, after the April negotiations adjourned, he 'advised the cabinet that the doctors would "deal directly with their patients," who would then "make arrangements with their insuring agency."'[59] If this insuring agency were to include the MCIC, which under the law it in fact was, then this fall-back position of the doctors was within hailing distance of the patient-reimbursement plan the government was prepared to consider – under the Medical Care Insurance Act. The sticking point, however, was that the doctors simply refused to accept a public medical care insurance plan as provided for under the Act.

So it was that on the morning of April 11 the premier abruptly adjourned the meeting, reading to the doctors a press statement he would be releasing to the media.

The Hazards of a Patient Reimbursement Plan

To proceed with the implementation of the Medical Care Insurance Act, as the government fully intended to do – but incorporating in it provision for patient reimbursement as one 'payment option' – would not, however, be trouble free. Aside from the political problems it would engender – some of the ministers had serious doubts about such a plan, as did a fair number of party members – there were technical problems. If the Act were amended to provide for the commission to reimburse patients for their doctors' bills, at whatever rates the patients may have been charged (and had paid), the government would technically have enacted an insurance plan with uncontrollable costs. Alternatively, if the commission were to reimburse the patient at fee schedule rates accepted by the MCIC, regardless of what the doctor had charged, this would be to sanction, or appear to sanction, 'extra billing' by the doctors, with the patient paying the difference between the fee schedule rate and the doctors' billing rate.

The most innocuous way of coping with these problems, it seemed to the government, would be to copy a provision already in Saskatchewan's doctor-sponsored (private) plans. These provided that an insured patient who was charged more than the accepted fee schedule rate could complain to the insuring agency (i.e., MCIC), and that agency would have the power to take legal action against the doctor in the case (acting for the patient), and no more than that. This method, dubbed the 'agency approach,' appeared to be less draconian than the possible alternatives: either to require the doctors simply to accept payment at MCIC rates, or to ban extra billing altogether. The government seems not to have contemplated these more sweeping measures (at least, not to my knowledge).

But the doctors' reaction to the government's 'agency approach,' put before the Legislative Assembly on April 13 – so early after the government-college discussions had collapsed – was as violent as if the government had instead taken the more draconian route.[60] What angered the doctors was that this amendment (there were others, as well) would confirm the MCIC as the sole 'paymaster' in the medical care plan, and one empowered, as the college interpreted the amendment, to disallow any billing beyond the rates set by the commission. In fact, the amendment actually empowered the commission to act for the patient only in respect of a particular billing and, moreover, gave to the patient (beneficiary) the right to cancel the agency provision at any time. Professor Tollefson, in his careful legal analysis, suggests 'the possibility of the commission suing doctors who had collected their fees directly from a beneficiary was, to say the least, remote.'[61] Nevertheless, given the political climate of the day, and given the deep suspicion on the part of the physicians regarding any publicly operated medical care plan, let alone its details, it perhaps should not have been surprising that the doctors would interpret the amendment as a further tightening of the noose of government-operated medical care insurance. Certainly that is how they reacted.

The president of the college, Dr Dalgleish, said the college might take the issue to court.[62] Leader of the opposition, Ross Thatcher, called the amendments 'peacetime conscription of the medical profession and the abrogation of its civil rights.'[63] Health Minister Davies replied that this was a standard clause in private insurance contracts for medical services (as we have said) and that a similar clause appeared in the Workmen's Compensation Act, under which the doctors were presently operating. This explanation did not quell the storm. Dr Barootes – who had been a member of the Thompson Committee and had emerged as a major strategist for the college – asserted that 'never since the days of Charles II [sic] has there been such legislation reversing the civil rights and liberties of the citizens.'[64]

Interestingly, no one in this debate referred to the continuing right of the doctors to operate completely outside the plan, with the consent of their patients. Perhaps it was because the patients would be obliged under this option to continue to pay the taxes and premiums that were levied to finance the public medical care plan, and no one in Saskatchewan could be expected to engage in such extravagance!

The Fateful Meeting of 3 May 1962

The next move in this troubled and uncertain period came a week after the bill to amend the Medical Care Insurance Act had been tabled in the legislature. The college announced that an emergency meeting of all doctors would be held in Regina on May 3 to discuss the current state of negotiations, and indeed the medical care issue as a whole. Premier Lloyd promptly requested an opportunity to address the assembly, and the executive of the college assented.

Lloyd knew that he would be addressing a hostile audience, but he was determined to review face to face with the doctors – calmly and dispassionately – the rationale for the public medical care plan and the history of the differences between the government and the doctors. His goal – typical of the man – was to bring both sides of the dispute to pursue the path of reason and reflection rather than that of anger and rhetoric.

What he did not seem fully to appreciate was the depth of the doctors' apprehension that public medical care insurance would 'governmentalize' their individual professional practices.[65] It would do so by effectively splitting the doctor-patient relationship into two parts: one part, the rendering of medical services, would remain in the hands of the doctors, but the other part, the payment for those services, would be 'nationalized.' How could any enterprise – and the doctors were fully conscious of the fact that their practices were businesses – operate that way? What the doctors were fighting for, in short, was the sanctity of their chosen profession, their chosen life. This, in my view, was the doctors' cast of mind from the beginning, and certainly at this deciding moment in the medical care dispute.[66]

The doctors were greatly buoyed about their ultimate victory at the very outset of the May 3 meeting – when it was announced, just before the premier was introduced, that former health minister Walter Erb had resigned from the government. His reason for leaving the CCF was even more cheering: the government had in its Medical Care Insurance Act, he said, violated one of the principles upon which it was founded, namely that the plan must be acceptable to both the providers and the recipients of medical services. That Erb had only just become conscious of this fact, or this argument – certainly he had never given any indication of his concern while he was a minister – did nothing to dampen the enthusiasm of the conference.

This, then, was the mood of the meeting when Woodrow Lloyd was introduced. But he was not deterred – either by the hostility of his audience or by its outright hissing (on three separate occasions). As Professor Malcolm Taylor described his speech:

> [It] was a low key review of the events to that date, an elaboration of the program, and a ... declaration by the Government to administer the plan in such a way as not to interfere with the doctors' professional freedom. He ended with an appeal to their rational judgment, hoping that a calm, unemotional assessment would conclude that the program, as proposed, would meet the objectives of both profession and public.[67]

Premier Lloyd's efforts were to no avail. At the conclusion of his speech, when the chairman asked those doctors who would refuse to co-operate with the government plan to stand, nearly all of them rose, to loud applause. And later, during the business sessions of the meeting, the doctors approved two major resolutions:

- To advise the government that if the Medical Care Insurance Act were implemented on July 1 the doctors would withdraw their services, and similarly,

- To advise the government that only the repeal of the Act would convince the doctors of the true intention of the government to meet their concerns.[68]

The doctors were fully aware of the import of their decisions: they were planning to use their power as the 'healers of the sick' in society to force the government and the Legislative Assembly to rescind the Medical Care Insurance Act. Indeed, the president of the college went even further when in a television broadcast two days later he was asked the question: 'Supposing the government had ... or was willing to conduct a plebiscite ... [on] a medical care plan, what would your thoughts be then if the plebiscite came to favour a compulsory government prepaid medical care plan?' Dalgleish replied: '... even if there was a vote, which might be overwhelmingly against us, we would think it would be in the best interests of our patients ... and the best climate for doctors if principles were the basis for our opposition to it.'[69]

Premier Lloyd's response to the doctors was already known. He had said that the doctors' resolutions and opposition leader Ross Thatcher's call for a general election were tantamount to a 'demand that the government capitulate to the Saskatchewan College of Physicians and Surgeons. It suggests,' he said, 'that a relatively small, powerfully entrenched group should be allowed to dictate the course of government.'[70]

Pressure on the Government

So the die was cast. And the pressures first on the government, and then increasingly on the doctors, began to mount.

The full import of the decision the doctors had taken was vividly expressed in the letter the college drafted for individual doctors to send to their patients, if they wished:

I cannot in all conscience provide services under the [Medical Care Insurance] Act and thus my office will be closed on July 1st. It will stay closed until the Government will allow me to treat you, as I have in the past, without political interference or control ... In the interval, our District Medical Society is setting up an Emergency Service so that qualified physicians will be available to treat any serious illness ... If you disagree with the action of

Government, you too should state your objection to your Elected Representatives. It is only in this way that Government will be forced to abandon the plan to institute political control of doctors and patients ...[71]

So the 'front line' of medical services – the doctors' offices – would effectively be emptied on July 1. An emergency service would be provided, yes, but what was meant by an emergency and how large and how extensive would the emergency service be? The locus of an emergency service would be the hospitals of the province, but if newspaper reports were accurate only 20 of them, out of 148, would be open.[72] (In fact, the number set by the college, on June 22, was 29, but that wasn't known through May and most of June.) Further, the emergency service would comprise about 240 physicians and surgeons – or about 25 per cent of the total 900 physicians in the province.[73] Equally important to the rural population was the location of these centres: how far would you have to drive to get medical care for your seriously ill or injured child, or spouse, or relative, or neighbour, or your pregnant wife?

All of these unknowns – and they were just that in May and June – were deeply disquieting. And even more disquieting was Dr Dalgleish's warning 'that the profession could not guarantee how long the emergency service would remain adequately staffed.'[74]

Out of this anxiety was born an organization known as the Keep Our Doctors Committees, whose objective was to press for an early settlement that would be acceptable to the medical profession and thus 'keep the doctors.' But the KODCs soon became, too, a rallying point for individuals and organizations that had a wider political objective: namely, to rid Saskatchewan of its socialist government. The committees and their adherents included 'opposition politicians, druggists, dentists, conservative businessmen, some clergymen, and everyone with a grievance against the government.'[75] The KODCs spread rapidly across the province, seeking and getting publicity for their cause, collecting petitions (forty-six thousand signatures were obtained), and organizing cavalcades – notably the May 30 cavalcade to Regina numbering nine hundred persons[76] (one hundred of them met with the premier to press their cause), and a second one on June 15, attended by some five hundred people.[77]

The pressure the KODCs brought on the premier and the government was supplemented by the campaigns of other groups. Druggists financed advertisements warning 'restricted and essential drug prescription(s) would not be refilled'; the imminent danger of doctors leaving the province was given wide publicity; and 'the Saskatoon Board of Trade warned tourists about possible dangers – "of a most serious nature" – if they came to Saskatchewan.'[78]

To add to these pressures, the press in the province was universally opposed to the government's position and favourable to the KODCs and the college. This was reflected not only in the editorial columns but in the news columns, as well. 'The General Secretary of the CMA [was to say] that Saskatchewan doctors should "be thankful for the local press."'[79]

Of course there was offsetting support for the premier and his colleagues. The leading force was the Saskatchewan Citizens for Medicare, backed by members of farmers' organizations, labour unions, co-operatives, and, of course, supporters of the CCF Party. A flood of letters to Woodrow Lloyd, numbering in the thousands, supported him and his position on medicare at a rate of twenty to one. But the manifestation of this support was less florid,[80] less strident, than that of the KODCs and their supporters. Lloyd strongly discouraged public and emotional demonstrations of support for the government or the plan. Public policy decisions, he deeply believed, must be taken by the democratically elected legislators, not by organized and potentially violent interest groups.[81] The strongest counter, indeed, was Woodrow Lloyd himself: his steadfastness and quiet determination, and his conviction of the rightness of public medical care and the values on which it was founded.

Pressure on the Doctors

If during May and June there were strong pressures on the premier and the cabinet – even to the point of some ministers urging Lloyd to withdraw the Act until an agreement could be reached with the college[82] – the doctors by June were themselves beginning to experience some pressures, at least some uncertainties. The first of these was very personal: the feeling on the part of some physicians that they had a moral, perhaps even a legal, obligation to continue to serve their patients. But for the great majority of the doctors, the pressures they experienced were mostly more tangible ones. The principal force was the MCIC's decision to develop a plan for the recruitment of doctors to serve in Saskatchewan in the event the strike were to proceed – a decision, by the way, that was made known to ministers, but was not made by them.[83] Before the end of May, the MCIC began to recruit doctors by placing advertisements in British newspapers, looking for doctors for rural practices generally and, when the strike was clearly imminent, for doctors to serve on a temporary basis. At the same time, informal contacts and inquiries were launched to seek doctors from other parts of Canada and from the United States.

It was a large and delicate task, undertaken largely by Dr Sam Wolfe, a commissioner of the MCIC, under Don Tansley's direction. Wolfe spent at least two weeks in London in June, assisted by Graham Spry, Saskatchewan's agent general to the United Kingdom, interviewing individual doctors who had responded to the advertisements. Discussions with potential recruits also took place in the United States, and elsewhere in Canada. The significance of this initiative lies not in the details, however, but in the fact that 110 doctors were recruited to the province in July – after the strike had begun – equal to about one-half the Saskatchewan doctors serving in the emergency service.[84]

A second pressure felt by the doctors was the gradual weakening of the impact of the KODCs. This ebbing influence was signalled first by the small attendance at the second rally in Regina, as we have seen, and then by the disappointing turnout for the third and major rally held on July 11. Far more influential than this indicator of trends in public support, however, was the recognition by the leaders of the college itself of the quiet but widespread public approval of universal medicare. Dalgleish himself recognized this in an address to the annual meeting of the Canadian Medical Association (June 17-18):

> Over the past two and a half years, the public [in Saskatchewan] seems to have accepted and approved of the fact that they will be provided with some form of plan for comprehensive, all-inclusive medical care insurance. None of the groups that have advocated delay, mediation and discussion of the disputed features of the Saskatchewan Medical Care Insurance Act have given any indication that this legislation should be completely withdrawn.[85]

At the very same time, however, the anti-medicare forces received an infusion of fresh optimism. On 18 June 1962 Tommy Douglas was defeated as the NDP candidate in Regina in the federal election. That the federal leader of the NDP and the father of medicare had been so defeated was surely a surrogate vote against medicare. So said the *Regina Leader Post*, as did the *Toronto Star* – 'a blow against medicare.' So indeed said the secretary of the national NDP, David Lewis, when he blamed the medicare battle for Douglas's defeat.[86]

The facts, however, spoke otherwise. The vote for the NDP in Regina rose from 27.6 per cent of the total votes cast in the 1958 election to 28.9 per cent in 1962, and the vote for the winning Progressive Conservative candidate declined from 54.4 to 50.4 per cent. If the electoral results proved anything, it was that Saskatchewan, including Regina, mirrored the cross-Canada, Progressive Conservative / Diefenbaker wave, not that the public had simply voted against medicare. The facts demonstrated, too, that the odds against Douglas in the Regina riding were powerful from the beginning: the PCs had won the riding with almost twice as many votes in the 1958 election as the NDP, and then won in 1962 by a slightly reduced majority.[87]

It was not the first time that facts had become the victims in the highly emotional medical care dispute, but on this occasion, when last-ditch efforts were under way, privately, to seek some resolution of the dispute through mediation, the stakes were very high indeed.

Efforts at Mediation, June 1962

The doctors and the government did not meet for seven weeks after the fateful meeting of May 3 – the two parties having been heavily engaged in coping with the pressures just recounted and in preparing for the implementation of a medical care plan that the doctors had said they would refuse to recognize. No one had had any experience, nor could they have had in Canada, with a powerful body of citizens refusing to comply with a law that the Legislative Assembly had enacted.

During this interval, however, efforts were being made, primarily by the Saskatchewan Hospital Association, to launch a mediation process through which some agreement might be reached. Indeed, the Hospital Association had written to the government as early as May 12, offering its services as mediator, and the government had agreed. They met on May 25 and again on May 31. On June 7, Woodrow Lloyd wrote to Dalgleish, offering once again to amend the Act to remove any hint of potential government interference in professional matters, and suggesting that the SHA be approached about serving as a mediator in their dispute. One June 10, representatives of the college met with the SHA, and the following day Dr Dalgleish replied to the premier's letter, telling him that he 'had taken the liberty of suggesting [that the] SHA should approach the Cabinet to discuss with them the feelings of the profession.'

On June 19, the day after Douglas's defeat in the national election,

Dalgleish called, publicly, for a meeting with the government. Minister of Health Davies promptly agreed, and, through the good offices of the Hospital Association, a meeting was arranged, beginning on June 22. It lasted for three days.[88]

Dalgleish went into the meeting demanding a 'complete rewriting' of the Medical Care Insurance Act and resolving 'not to compromise on 'basic principles.' Premier Lloyd, in turn, once in the meeting, offered to make major changes in the plan. He advanced three proposals: to guarantee the professional independence of physicians; to guarantee the right of a physician to practise outside the plan; and to provide for regional administration of the plan by health regions. The first proposal was designed to eliminate from the Act any implication that professional independence might be impaired. The third proposal was designed to meet the college's charge of 'government monopoly.' But the second proposal was the one that represented a major concession by the cabinet. The government was agreeing to permit the doctors to bill their patients directly and to authorize the MCIC to reimburse the patients at 85 per cent of the college's fee schedule. Thus the doctor 'will neither send his bills to the Medical Care Insurance Commission nor will he be paid by the Commission. He is free to practise completely outside the provisions of the Act.'[89] This was precisely the pattern of practice that the doctors had intended to follow when the government introduced its 'agency amendment' in April.[90]

Alongside, or consonant with, these proposals, the government proposed other specific changes in the Medical Care Insurance Act, having to do principally with two major and long-standing irritants: the power granted to the government to make regulations concerning the terms and conditions under which physicians and other persons might provide insured services to beneficiaries; and the 'agency provision,' which provided a safeguard against extra billing. Both of these clauses would be repealed, providing, in the case of the agency provision, that the doctors would agree not to discriminate between beneficiaries.

To the cabinet's surprise, the college rejected all these proposals. Apparently now believing that it could force the government to rescind the Act in its entirety, the college refused to accept even the patient reimbursement plan, which it had accepted prior to April 1962. On June 27 the cabinet proceeded, in any event, to implement its new payment plan by approving an Order in Council. Still, the college refused to call off the strike. It said the regulations passed by Order in Council 'would not be legal because [they were] contrary to the Medical Care

Insurance Act.'[91] It seems unlikely that this was the real reason for rejecting the government's proposals, for on July 6, when the government made explicit its willingness to ratify the Order in Council by legislation, the strike continued.[92] And on June 27 Dalgleish confirmed, 'We have a bad act on our statute books and the government must take immediate steps to remove it or alter it to make it a just act.'[93]

The Strike and Intensified Pressure

Eleventh hour efforts were made by Saskatchewan's municipal associations to avert the strike, but they were unsuccessful. The doctors began their strike on 1 July 1962. Dr Dalgleish said the issue was simply one of deferring the Act.[94] The premier said that delay would achieve nothing unless the doctors were prepared to make some commitment with respect to the plan: he pointed out that in twenty-six months the college's position had remained virtually unchanged.[95] Moreover, he said, Saskatchewan's doctors could continue to practise either inside or outside the Act.[96]

For twenty-three days, Saskatchewan was virtually in a state of shock. The people of the province knew – virtually everyone came to know – of the effect upon them, on their families, on their friends, of finding when struck down with some serious illness or injury, or when the birth of a baby was approaching, that their family doctor or some needed specialist had vacated his practice. And they recognized, too, the uncertainty as to how long even emergency services could carry on, with only some two hundred physicians and surgeons in place: even the college was warning about that hazard. Examples of the hardships suffered by people thus deprived of early and responsive medical services abound in the literature on medicare's beginning in Saskatchewan: we need not repeat them here.[97]

The issue now facing the people of Saskatchewan was no longer a straightforward division between those who favoured a universal publicly financed medical care insurance plan, and those who opposed it. That issue had been appropriated by anti-government partisans as a tool by which to rid the province of the socialist government they so hated. And this development, in turn, bred yet another issue: the legitimacy of a small but powerful group using the withdrawal of essential services as an instrument by which to force a reversal in a decision of the democratically elected Legislative Assembly. The room for division on these three inter-mingled issues – policy, politics, and democratic institutions – was enormous. And then, in addition, the vocabulary of the debate itself was becoming more and more emotional and extreme.

All of these forces found their focus in July 1962. The strike created divisions within families, between friends, and within communities – fissures that emerged before the strike and were to endure many months after. Saskatchewan, in short, became a house divided – analogous to the personal and social divisions to be found in Quebec at the height of that province's first referendum debate over separation from Canada (at least for those of us who in one way or another experienced both).

There was one countervailing force in all of this: extremism in a public debate such as this one contains its own contradictions. In a society that prides itself on its friendly, neighbourly, peaceful way of life, vitriolic debate comes at some point to be resented: sometimes to the point of silence, sometimes to the point of support being withdrawn from one side or the other, sometimes to the point of reciprocal extremism. Fortunately for Saskatchewan, the first two of these reactions tended to emerge, and they tended to moderate the positions of the extremists.

This, then, was the atmosphere that prevailed in Saskatchewan in July.

The KOD Committees

The Keep Our Doctors Committees intensified their efforts in July to put and to keep the government under pressure. At the extreme of their agitation, the KODCs sponsored a meeting at which violence was advocated. Father Athol Murray, a priest, was reported to have cried out, '... we must get off the fence ... this thing may break into violence and bloodshed any day now, and God help us if it doesn't.'[98]

But the climax of the KODCs' activities was a province-wide cavalcade to the Legislative Building in Regina to petition the premier. To ensure its success, the KODCs organized phone campaigns, purchased advertisements, arranged car pools, and even in some centres welcomed store closings for the big day. Leader of the opposition Ross Thatcher was to be a central figure at the event.[99] It was suggested that some fifty thousand people from across the province were expected to come.

As the hysteria mounted, various groups – particularly the clergy – called for calm. Woodrow Lloyd, too, repeated his plea for calm and order, invoking the entreaty of twenty-four prominent citizens – including the president of the Montreal Stock Exchange, Eric Kierans, editor of *La Presse*, Gerard Pelletier, and Canadian novelist Hugh MacLennan – who called 'in the name of humanity and of respect for democratic government ... [for] immediate resumption of normal practice and peaceful negotiation with the Government.'[100] Indeed, even the KODCs themselves called for public order at their rallies – though in their meeting with the premier on July 11, the leaders refused to repudiate Father Murray's call to violence.[101]

In the end, the demonstration fizzled out, relative to expectations. Only some four or five thousand people, instead of the forecast fifty thousand, turned up. This muting or moderating of the acrimony reflected more truly the Saskatchewan personality: what the people of the province, the great majority, wanted was a reasoned and reasonable solution, not hysteria. The politically minded members of the KODCs, and the doctors as well, were markedly affected by the event.

The Out-of-Province Press

The doctors were even more affected by the widespread criticisms of the strike, and of the attendant attempt to force an elected legislature to reverse its decision on medicare, that began to appear in the press outside of Saskatchewan. Some would argue, indeed, that this was the body blow that brought the doctors to back down on their demand that the Medical Care Insurance Act be revoked, or suspended, before negotiations could begin anew.

The main criticisms were expressed across the country, starting very soon after the strike had begun. The *Globe and Mail* opined on 4 July 1962:

> The doctors of Saskatchewan have taken an action which is not open to any individual or any group within a democracy.
>
> None has the right to set himself above the law. That way can only lie anarchy and the destruction of our democratic way of life.
>
> The doctors have not indulged in acts of violence in Saskatchewan; but the passive resistance they have instituted is the worst form of violence which could be perpetrated against the people of Saskatchewan.
>
> It is to be hoped that the rank and file of Saskatchewan doctors will ... end this massive and horrifying breach of the law by which an honoured profession strikes at the democratic foundation of its country.

In Montreal on July 3 *Le Devoir* commented: 'It is the medical profession that refuses to negotiate. It demands that the law be repealed. What government could obey a similar "dictat" without giving up as a government?' On July 5 the *Calgary Herald* said: 'The strike must end, and the doctors must end it ...' The *Winnipeg Free Press* of July 4 expressed the same opinion, blaming the impasse on the profession.

Outside of Canada, British newspapers expressed similar opinions. The *Observer* of July 6 commented acidly, '... the medical situation in Saskatchewan is more than a [doctors'] strike, it is a mutiny.' And the *Daily Mail* of July 4 added another British perspective: '... when doctors strike and neglect patients, the voice of humanity protests. That this could happen in Britain is so inconceivable that we regard Saskatchewan with astonishment and sadness.' Even the British medical journal, *Lancet*, said in an editorial on July 9: 'Withdrawal organized for political ends is, we think, wrong ... [The] doctors' action is an alien procedure, out of keeping with the character of any profession, and especially that of medicine.'

In the United States, The *Washington Post* (July 19) was scathing: 'Whatever the merits of Saskatchewan's new medical care act, the strike staged by doctors throughout the Province is indefensible ... A strike by the doctors is a betrayal of their profession. It reduces medicine to the level of a business. Worse, it desecrates the Hippocratic Oath which consecrates doctors to use their art for the benefit of the sick ... In every sense of the word, this strike is bad medicine.'[102] One of the most damaging articles was the coverage in the *New York Times* of July 3 of the death of a nine-month-old infant on the first day of the strike.

There were, of course, newspapers outside Saskatchewan that supported the striking doctors: the *Halifax Chronicle Herald* and the *Toronto Telegram*, for example, and others like the *Victoria Colonist* who blamed both sides, or took a neutral stance. But the great majority were critical of the profession. Yet in Saskatchewan the daily press was uniformly favourable to the medical profession and universally opposed to the government. Even so, the doctors knew that by and large they stood alone in Canada – outside of Saskatchewan – and similarly knew, or learned, that their stance vis-à-vis the province's elected government could never be sustained.

The Importation of Doctors

The unanimous support of the Saskatchewan press may have been comforting to the college, but not so the growing number of British doctors coming to Canada under the Medical Care Commission's recruitment program. And as the strike wore on, some of Saskatchewan's doctors began quietly to return to practice. On July 10 the commission began publishing data on the availability of medical and hospital services, and continued to do so through the rest of the strike. The information was revealing. The number of hospitals open and providing medical services doubled between July 10 and 23, from 59 to 121 (of a total 148 hospitals in the province). On July 10 the college's emergency services provided medical services in 58 per cent of the hospitals that were open, local medical services (full or partial coverage) covered 27 per cent, and MCIC doctors provided coverage in the rest – 15 per cent. By July 23, when the number of hospitals in operation had reached 121, the college's emergency services represented only 34 per cent of the total, community medical services (full or partial) covered 42 per cent, and 'MCIC doctors' provided the rest – 24 per cent.[103]

Even closer to home for the strikers was the number of doctors providing medical services. The number of practising physicians rose from 243 on July 10 to 316 on July 23 – even while the number of emergency services doctors provided by the college declined from 204 to 190. (None of these figures includes the 250 physicians thought to be on vacation.)[104] Seventy-nine of the 316 physicians in practice in mid-July were MCIC-recruited doctors – and this number rose to 110. Finally, the commission had made arrangements for the replacement, upon forty-eight hours notice, of all of the college's emergency services doctors (190) if that were to become necessary.[105]

A further threat to the doctors was the emergence in the province of community clinics – clinics established through community action, which engaged newly arrived physicians on salary. By the time the strike ended, five of them were in operation, ten more were nearly ready to begin functioning, and fifteen were under development. The college could not ignore the development of such salaried group practices.

First Efforts at Mediation in July

The first efforts to find some solution to the impasse came about late in the first week of July on the initiative of Regina lawyer (and active Conservative) Don McPherson. He called Allan Blakeney, a fellow lawyer and now provincial treasurer, to tell him that he (McPherson) proposed to enter into discussions with Dr J.F.C. Anderson, former member of the Advisory Planning Committee and former president of the Canadian Medical Association, to seek out ideas or possibilities that might open the door to an end to the strike. Would Mr Blakeney be willing to receive in confidence any such suggestions and promptly submit them to the cabinet? Blakeney agreed to the arrangement.

McPherson then spent several days at his cottage with Dr Anderson, analysing the MCI Act, and touching base periodically with Blakeney while Anderson did the same with the college. It emerged over time (the week of July 9) that the prime concern to the college was the retention of some role for the (private) doctor-sponsored insurance plans – Medical Services Inc. (MSI) and Group Medical Services (GMS). Would it be possible, for example, to designate these two bodies as agents for patients, to receive doctors' billings, transmit them to the MCIC (Medical Care Insurance Commission), and then in turn to receive the MCIC payments for such billings? Equally, would it be possible for MSI and GMS to collect from its subscribers any health insurance premium imposed by the government or the MCIC? These would be the doctors' proposals.

They went to the government and were discussed by a strategy committee of cabinet, around July 12 or 13 it would seem, along with other facets of potential dispute resolution. Ministers did not reach a decision on the proposals, but they did conclude that an 'informal negotiator' should be selected 'who would be authorized to discuss matters with McPherson and Robertson (the College's solicitor), but who would not be authorized to speak for the Government. If these informal negotiations resulted in a plan that was mutually agreeable, a mediator could be chosen who "miraculously" would come up with a proposal that was mutually acceptable.'[106]

As a footnote to this first effort at mediation, Allan Blakeney had come to the view that one essential ingredient was missing in the negotiation and mediation efforts to date. This was some purely personal contact between an official in government and someone in, or closely associated with, the college. This personal contact, reasoned Blakeney, would enable government to gain a better insight into the perspectives and the root concerns that moved the doctors, as they sought the means by which their personal and professional interests might be protected. The same held for the doctors vis-à-vis the government. It would be essentially a sympathetic 'intelligence operation,' not a part of any mediation or negotiation process.

Blakeney and I discussed this problem, and he asked me whether by any chance I knew anyone in or connected with the college. I did: Bob Robertson, the college's lawyer, was a university friend of mine. Blakeney immediately asked me to go to Saskatoon, where the college had its offices, and establish contact with him. There was to be no agenda: I was simply to talk with Robertson, with a view to getting a better insight and understanding as to what was 'moving' the doctors. Conversely, Robertson might, through me, come to a more personal understanding of what was moving the government. What might emerge from such discussions would remain to be seen. But it was worth trying.

At the same time, it was clear that an 'agenda' of the ingredients of a potential agreement had by now emerged. It consisted at this point of two principal elements. One was a system for paying the doctors for their services that would clearly and visibly insulate them from the government and the MCIC. Specifically, this entailed a patient reimbursement plan, to which the government had already agreed. It also entailed the designation of MSI and GMS as agents for the patients, to receive bills from the doctors for patient services and to be reimbursed by the public medical care plan (which plan, including the levying of any family premiums, would be financed by the government of Saskatchewan). GMS and MSI would collect these premiums from their subscribers. The government had received this approach and effectively deferred it.

The second major element of a potential agreement between the doctors and the government was unequivocal provision in the MCI Act both that the doctors would be free to operate entirely outside of the plan and that those who operated within the plan would be entirely free of any government influence or interference in prescribing and providing their medical services. Both provisions had already been agreed to by the government – including the elimination from the Act of the power of the government to make regulations concerning the provision of medical services by the doctors, and the provision that would appear to touch on the quality of medical services. As well, the famous 'agency provision' would be repealed.

One More Try at Negotiation

The question remained, however, as to the next step in the negotiations between the government and the doctors. What seemed to be 'on the table' had become somewhat clearer by the weekend (July 14 and 15), but who would initiate the next move?

It was Dr Dalgleish who contacted Premier Lloyd to request an invitation to speak to the annual CCF convention, which would be meeting in Saskatoon during the week of July 16. The premier agreed, as Dalgleish had agreed to Lloyd's speaking to the college's meeting earlier in May. On July 14 Dalgleish confirmed the arrangement by advising Lloyd what he intended to say to the convention. He would be withdrawing the college's prime condition to a further meeting with government, the revocation of the MCI Act, and proposing instead that the Act be suspended, by Order in Council, for a specified but limited period of time. Negotiations would then be resumed, and should they be successful, the necessary amendments to the MCI Act would be enacted by a special session of the Legislative Assembly. And the doctors would resume their practices.

The premier replied almost immediately, on July 17, rejecting the proposal. To suspend the Act for a limited period would provide no assurance that agreement would be reached within that period. Failure to agree would then generate a request for an extension of the suspension. Lloyd went on to emphasize that nothing prevented the doctors from practising outside the Act as it stood.

The CCF convention proceeded on July 18, with Woodrow Lloyd reporting to the delegates on his stewardship during his eight-month period as premier. Needless to say, his report was entirely about medicare. He said he continued to refuse any simple suspension of the Act, adding that the right of the doctors to practise outside the Act alone warranted their return to work. When they did return to work, a special session of the legislature would be convened to introduce any amendments to the Act that had been agreed upon. The premier spoke, too, to the affront to democracy inherent in the strike.

Dr Dalgleish spoke in the afternoon. He repeated the proposal he had made to the premier in his letter of July 14, but now added the amendments to the Act the college would be demanding. They included the right of the doctors to practise outside of the Act; the right of patients to assign to any agency (meaning really the GMS and the MSI) their rights to payments from the MCIC; and that these private agencies would be empowered to collect any premiums levied by the MCIC. All of these points had been among the ingredients of a potential agreement that had been developed by the McPherson mediation efforts (Blakeney and Anderson being the 'conduits').[107]

It was at this point that Lord Taylor appeared in Saskatchewan and came to dominate the medicare discussions.

Lord Taylor, the Mediator

Lord Taylor was a British medical doctor who had earned his (Labour) peerage through the role he had played in developing the National

Health Service in the United Kingdom. He also had some connection with Saskatchewan, having visited the province in 1946 just at the time the Hospital Services Plan was being fashioned, and had spent some time discussing Saskatchewan's emerging health policies with members of the Health Services Planning Commission. Lord Taylor was also known to Graham Spry, Saskatchewan's agent general in London, and through him had been helpful to Sam Wolfe when he was developing plans for the recruitment of British doctors.

So Saskatchewan was not foreign territory to Lord Taylor, and when Woodrow Lloyd went, secretly, to Toronto and Montreal on July 4 to talk with some of the national leaders of the NDP (CCF) about his strategy in managing the medical care crisis, he contacted Lord Taylor in London. His purpose was to invite Lord Taylor to come to Saskatchewan as a special advisor to the premier on medicare, emulating Tommy Douglas's readiness when required to seek the best professional advice available at home or abroad.

Lord Taylor immediately agreed, on two conditions – that he would not be paid and that he would be rewarded instead with a fishing trip in Northern Saskatchewan. However, he was unable to leave London before July 16. So he arrived in Saskatchewan in the middle of the most crucial days of the strike: when Premier Lloyd and Harold Dalgleish were preparing their respective speeches to the CCF (NDP) convention in Saskatoon on July 18. (Taylor did make time, too, between connecting flights in Toronto, to meet with George Cadbury for a personal briefing.)

So Saskatoon became the venue for the resolution of the medical care strike. The chief actors in the dispute were all there: the premier and his colleagues were there for the convention; the College of Physicians and Surgeons, whose offices were in Saskatoon, were represented by President Dalgleish and the executive of the college; and from outside the province came the president of the Canadian Medical Association, Dr Arthur Kelly, plus other senior officers. Even the emerging Saskatchewan Council for Community Health Services was meeting in Saskatoon at the same time.

From the very first day in Saskatchewan, Lord Taylor made it clear that he intended to act in the role of mediator between the cabinet and the college, not as the premier's special advisor. He said to the press on his first day in Regina (before going on to Saskatoon) that 'he has sympathy for both sides.'[108] He made a point of speaking to the doctors of the emergency service in Regina to get their perspective, as well as to ministers. On July 18 in Saskatoon, he attended the convention to hear Dalgleish speak and immediately after went to the college's Medical Arts Building to meet with Dalgleish and the college's council. At that meeting, he opined that he favoured the doctors' proposal that the privately owned GMS and MSI should be assigned some useful function in the new medical care system. He said he would personally try to persuade the government to accept this proposition – though, as a politician, he could not see how the government would agree to authorize the agencies to collect a governmentally imposed health insurance premium.

Thus it became clear to everyone that Taylor was taking on the role of mediator. He acted as such for the whole of the seven days with the government and the college (believing, all along, I personally think, that both sides knew they simply had to settle).

The Instruments of Mediation

It was equally evident all the way through those seven days – July 17 to 23 – that Lord Taylor possessed all the advantages and the attributes of a mediator:

- In his personality, he was perceptive, quick of mind, forceful, articulate, and, where needed, humorous or outraged. And yes, eccentric and dramatic.
- He was a doctor and a politician; so, as he put it, he spoke both of those 'two different languages.'
- He quickly ingratiated himself with the doctors, suspicious as they were at first, by supporting some version or other of a place for the two private, doctor-sponsored insurance plans in the new medical care payment system.
- He launched a whirlwind of meetings between himself and the doctors, and between himself and the premier plus a small group of ministers – who fortunately were staying at the Bessborough Hotel just a short walk from the Doctors' Building. And he maintained this pitch of activity, thus retaining the initiative – indeed, his position of leadership.
- He kept the ministers and the doctors apart – no meetings together – on the grounds, again, that they did not speak one another's language.
- He engaged in histrionics, when it served his purpose and always, above all, his 'sense of theatre.'

- And he amused everyone with his eccentricities – for example, his insistence on parking his car in the no-parking area in front of the hotel, with a piece of House of Lords stationery under the windshield wiper. And getting away with it!

It was essentially a one-man show, except that behind the scenes there were others at work. At the first level, there were the two negotiating and decision-making committees, one on the government side and one on the doctors' side. On the government side, the premier was very much in charge, with his close associates Allan Blakeney, perhaps the ablest policy thinker in the group, Brock Brockelbank, who embodied common sense and a feel for public views, the minister of health, of course, Bill Davies, and occasionally Bob Walker, the attorney-general.

Advising the ministerial committee was a committee of officials, including Tim Lee, secretary of the cabinet, Tommy Shoyama of the Planning Board, Bob Ellis, legal counsel of the Department of Health, and me, Secretary of the Treasury Board. In the wings, and always available to his minister and the premier was Don Tansley, chairman of the Medical Care Insurance Commission. These officials sat in on most of the meetings of ministers, and Bob Ellis and I were designated to oversee the drafting of the changes in the Medical Care Insurance Act in response to the decisions – indeed, the proposals – as they emerged from the government's and the college's meetings with Lord Taylor.

On the doctors' side, as I was told by Bob Robertson, equivalent advisory and decision-making bodies were at work. The discussions were tense and difficult. Indeed, on Saturday night, July 21, they seemed to be at the breaking point. I went that evening, in all innocence, to chat with Bob Robertson at the Doctors' Building (in a kitchenette next to the amphitheatre meeting room where Taylor was facing the doctors) when out came Harold Dalgleish for a break. He saw me there and came over. 'Al, what is it with this man Taylor?' he said. 'You guys didn't invite him as a mediator and we certainly didn't. Yet now when we won't agree with him on a particular proposal he says, "All right I'm simply going home," and we find ourselves begging him to stay on.'

Stay on he did, and by Sunday night the doctors were ready to sign an agreement. But Taylor advised them to sleep on it to be sure. Which they did. And on Monday morning they repeated their decision to sign, as did the premier and his colleagues. Lord Taylor, always given to good theatre, wanted to convene a joint celebrative press conference. But this was too much for either the ministers or the doctors: they were too bruised after their long battle. So Lord Taylor held a press conference, and the doctors and the ministers met to sign the agreement and to shake hands. It was an emotional moment.

The Settlement: The Realization of the Douglas Dream in Saskatchewan

The essence of the settlement was contained in two propositions. The first was the recognition by the doctors that Saskatchewan's medical care insurance plan simply transferred the payment for medical services from the affected individual or family to the community as a whole, financed out of public taxation. It had no mandate to intervene in any way in the diagnosis, treatment, and care of the ill.

The second was the recognition by the government that the continued existence of private 'medical care agencies' acting solely as conduits for the payment of doctors, with the agencies recouping their outlay through billing the Medical Care Insurance Commission, amounted to nothing more than a 'cluttering' of the billing system. The agencies could no longer be seen as private medical care insurance plans (and, indeed, were called 'voluntary agencies' in the revised Act).

Arriving at these respective acknowledgments required that the doctors accept the establishment by the legislature of a *public* medical care insurance plan, and that they give up on their efforts to protect and to preserve private sector medical care insurance. It required that the government, in turn, abandon the notion entertained by some of its supporters and advisors that this medical care legislation should leave the door open to a 'managed' health care system – which would call for greater government intervention in the system, if not in the diagnosis and treatment of individual patients. Different policy instruments would be required to achieve that goal in any event and would be developed as and when the imperatives of the evolving health care system called for their introduction.

The specific changes in the Act, as they were proposed by the college and agreed to by government, fell into four categories.[109]

Limiting the powers of the commission by narrowing the area in which the Commission might make regulations. This was achieved by:

- ensuring that the regulatory powers provided in the Act would be limited by the words 'pursuant to the Act' (in law this was the case in any event);

- removing any reference in the regulatory powers to regulations 'for the improvement of the quality of the insured services' or regulations 'respecting the maintenance and improvement of the quality of the services provided under the Act.'

Associated with these amendments was another to repeal the controversial 'agency provision,' already agreed to in June 1962.

Strengthening the presence of the medical profession in the Medical Care Insurance Commission by increasing the number of doctors on the commission from two to three, not counting the chairman and the ex officio deputy minister of health (at least one of the two would almost certainly be medical doctors). The total membership of the commission was increased to a minimum of seven and a maximum of eleven, instead of the former six and eight.

The elimination of the Advisory Council and the Medical Advisory Committee formerly provided for, presumably on the grounds either that the commission would not find more advice and representation helpful or because the college was fearful that the number of ideas and pressures for change in the provision of medical or health facilities might get out of hand.

Enabling the doctors to insulate themselves from the commission in the billing and payment for services process. The revised medical care statute would provide four ways in which the physicians and surgeons could bill and be paid for their services – listed here in the declining order of insulation of the doctors from the commission:

- First, the doctor could choose to operate independently of the Act altogether. Thus he would bill the patient at a rate of his own choosing, and the patient would not qualify for any reimbursement from the commission. Such an arrangement would require the prior assent of the patient.
- Secondly, the doctor could choose to practise independently of the commission and of any voluntary agency, and send his itemized bill to the patient. The patient would then claim reimbursement from the commission and pay any difference between the doctor's fee and 85 per cent of the approved fee schedule (the famous patient reimbursement plan).
- Thirdly, the doctor could choose to bill and be paid by a designated voluntary agency (being GMS, MSI, and the Swift Current Health Region, and possibly, in the future, other health regions). The proce-

dure: the doctor would bill the voluntary agency at the agreed rate of 85 per cent of the minimum fee schedule; the voluntary agency would submit the account to the commission, which would pay the agency; and the agency would in turn pay the doctor, who would accept the payment in full.

- Finally the doctors could choose to bill and be paid directly by the commission itself – whether the payments were based on fee for service or on salary.

This settlement enabled the physicians to return to their practices, and the government to complete the implementation of the Medical Care Insurance Plan. But it could not repair overnight the distressing rifts, and the distrust and the hurt, that affected so many who had participated in or sought to influence the negotiations. 'Woodrow Lloyd, the prime target of vilification, was the person most deeply affected. At the end of 1962 he said in the privacy of his diary "I doubt if anyone can go through a period of being lied about, hated, misrepresented and ever be the same."'[110] A longer period of healing was needed, indeed, for all Saskatchewanians to overcome the social cleavage and the personal hurt that were occasioned by the bitterness and the animus of the campaign against medicare. And it would take a longer period of time, too, for many, to recognize the realities of a public medical care system and to experience its social and personal benefits, as contrasted with the enormous fears attendant upon its introduction.

It did come: Saskatchewan regained its sense of community, its neighbourliness, and the value system of a co-operative and caring society.

EPILOGUE

The Legacy of the Douglas Government

In the final pages of this history of the Douglas government, I want to write in somewhat more personal terms, to address what I think to be the more important and lasting legacies of the Douglas government in Canadian public policy and in Canadian governance. I want, as well, to speak to some of the challenges we now face in maintaining that legacy.

The Legacy of Medicare

The first of the legacies of the Douglas government clearly was medicare. It was not long before the medical care model so painfully brought into existence in Saskatchewan was to become a model for medicare across Canada – the largest of all the many legacies left by the Douglas and Lloyd governments, and perhaps the earliest to be felt in the rest of the country.

There were three milestones in the development of a national medical care plan. First the Hall Commission on Health Services, appointed by Primer Minister Diefenbaker, reported in 1964, recommending 'that as a nation we now take the necessary ... decision to make all the fruits of the health sciences available to all of our residents without any hindrance of any kind.'[1] This went beyond even the medical care covered under the Saskatchewan plan.

Secondly, the Liberal Party of Canada, first through the Kingston Conference of 1960 with its 'Plan for Health,' and then in the party's 1962 election platform, promised that '[a Liberal government will] establish, in cooperation with the provinces, a medical care plan for all Canadians.'[2]

Then, when the Liberals were elected in 1963, Prime Minister Lester

Pearson set the wheels of government in motion to develop such a plan. The most difficult obstacle to the doing of it, however, was finding a vehicle through which the government of Canada could take the initiative in defining the kind of plan that it would be prepared to support (at a rate, say, of 50 per cent of total costs).

The traditional vehicle would formerly have been a shared-cost program, under which the national government would share the costs of any provincial program that met certain 'prescribed' conditions, incorporated in the shared cost agreement. But growing provincial opposition to these arrangements, led by Quebec and increasingly Ontario, on the grounds that they violated the exclusive jurisdiction of the provinces in the policy fields involved, had become a major obstacle to the launching of new shared-cost arrangements. This opposition reached a climax when the newly elected government in Quebec, led by Jean Lesage, a former federal cabinet minister, announced at a federal-provincial conference in 1960 that Quebec would never again sign a shared-cost agreement. Rather, it would demand unconditional fiscal remuneration for its 'share' of any new shared-cost program that might be undertaken with the other provinces. Of course, this would lead the other provinces to demand equal treatment. Who wouldn't prefer a totally unconditional fiscal transfer to one that was tied to a new federally inspired program?

So whether the provinces favoured universal medical care plans or not was effectively irrelevant, unless and until a new and acceptable vehicle for mounting federal-provincial programs was devised. With this in mind, the prime minister turned, not to the Department of Health for advice in shaping a national medical care plan, but to a small committee of officials which would include the deputy minister of health. The committee was chaired by Gordon Robertson, secretary to the cabinet, and the other members were Tom Kent, the prime minister's policy advisor, Bob Bryce, the deputy minister of finance, and me. (I was by then an assistant deputy minister of finance, responsible for federal-provincial fiscal arrangements.)

The committee met fairly frequently, if my memory serves me well. And over time the fundamentals of a new approach to federal-provincial arrangements for mounting nationwide programs became increasingly clear. First, we must find some kind of arrangement that would not require the premiers to sign agreements. Premier Lesage's 'refusal to sign in the future' made that clear. Secondly, we must find some way of prescribing the kind of medical care program the government of Canada would support, other than by expressing the requisites of the program in terms of conditions. (That is to say, 'federal contributions will be forthcoming providing certain program conditions and administrative conditions are met.')

What came to my mind, given my Saskatchewan experience, was the identification of the principles upon which the federal-provincial medical care programs would have to be founded. Casting my mind back, the pertinent principles from the Saskatchewan plan would be *comprehensiveness* (in respect of the elements of health care to be covered, such as physicians' services); *universality* (covering the whole population under the same terms and conditions); and *public administration* (ensuring provincial responsibility and accountability to the legislature). This being a nationwide scheme, one new principle would have to be added: *portability* (the benefits would have to be transferable between the provinces and territories).

The prime question, of course, was whether Premier Lesage would accept such an arrangement – it being entirely new to the federal-provincial relations arena. So I called Claude Morin, Lesage's deputy minister of intergovernmental affairs (after having advised my deputy Bob Bryce of my intent) and asked him to call me when he was next in Ottawa. We met a few days later at the Château Laurier lounge, and there I said to Claude, 'Look, your premier wants medicare, and my prime minister wants medicare, but we are blocked by Premier Lesage's repudiation of shared-cost programs. So how about this approach: the federal government would offer to contribute to any provincial medical care plan that was founded upon certain principles – no agreement to sign, no conditions, and federal contributions based, likely, on per capita costs of medical care across Canada as a whole (not shared cost, province by province).'

Morin saw this to be a potential solution to the dilemma and said he would speak to Premier Lesage. He did and called back to say that Lesage thought this to be an interesting approach to initiating medical care. We knew, of course, that this was said without prejudice to Lesage's broader and longer-term strategy, which called for the government of Canada to transfer fiscal capacity to the provinces via 'tax points' as opposed to program-related grants.

After this exchange, Bob Bryce advised the medical care advisory committee of the new approach, and the committee then fleshed out the bare bones of the proposed plan and satisfied themselves as to its practicability. We then advised the prime minister of our recommendations, and he approved this proposal for a national medical care plan.[3]

Prime Minister Pearson wasted no time: with cabinet's approval, he advised the federal-provincial conference of July 1965 of the federal proposal – in very general and diplomatic terms. Then legislation was introduced to authorize the introduction of the plan – with a start-up date of 1 July 1967, a date that was later deferred to 1 July 1968. The final vote in the House of Commons was 177 to 2 in favour of the Act.[4]

But there was vigorous debate over the plan, and over the very initiative, particularly among certain of the provinces (led by Ontario and Alberta). In the final analysis, however, all the provinces started medicare plans that conformed to the four principles, the last one being on 1 January 1971. The territories initiated their plans in 1971 and 1972.[5]

This was the legacy of the Douglas government – and the Lloyd government – that gained and sustained the greatest public recognition. It came indeed to symbolize Canada's proud and predominant social values – a humane and caring society.

The Legacy of the Government in Society

The second legacy of the Douglas government was its redefinition of the role of government in society, not in the radical way advocated by the CCF in its 1933 Manifesto, and in the party's associated program, but in the fashioning of a distinctively 'Canadian socialism,' as had been J.S. Woodsworth's lifelong dream. Medicare, of course, was central to this dream, but the legacy of a more positive role for the state in Saskatchewan – and in Canadian – society was broader than that.

The first, and to Tommy Douglas the fundamental, element of the role of government was to provide, through the public sector, services that would meet the basic needs of people in health, education, and welfare. It was the responsibility of the community to bear the costs of medically necessary health services and to promote public health in general. It was the responsibility of the state, too, to set a basic standard of income for all who were in need, whether because of unemployment or personal incapacity, and to provide social assistance when it was required. In the case of education, primary and secondary education should be available to all, paid for by the community. And university education should be accessible to all qualified students, with public support plus a fee structure that recognized the future benefits to the student of higher education.

Although it is not as frequently mentioned, the province also played an active role in the field of culture and the arts, which were not at all prominent in the Saskatchewan landscape even before the desolation of the Depression and the violent interruption of the war. But after the war, the Douglas (and Lloyd) legacy in the arts flowered: the creation of the Saskatchewan Archives (1945); the founding of the pivotal Saskatchewan Arts Board (1948); the establishment of the regional library system (1950); the long-standing support of the Regina Conservatory of Music and its Saskatoon equivalent; the art schools of the Regina and Saskatoon campuses of the University of Saskatchewan – strongly supported through the province's consistently generous grants to the university; the burgeoning of the art galleries of the two major cities; and more.

Beyond these social and cultural roles of government there lay the third, and more utilitarian, function, that of providing to the public – directly or through Crown corporations – basic public utilities. These included the provision of water supplies (municipal, in Saskatchewan), the production and distribution of electricity, the distribution of natural gas, and telephone services. Douglas well understood, in my view, that in recognizing this role of the state he was going a long way toward defining, and within the CCF Party resolving, the troubled issue of the place of social ownership in the economy.

The other part of the resolution of the place of social ownership came with the fourth role of the state – as Douglas saw it – namely the role of government in respect of the economy. Here it had come to be accepted – after Joe Phelps's experimentation with the woollen mill, the box factory, a tannery, and a brick plant – that economic development in the province would be better achieved through the attraction of private capital than through social ownership. That conclusion was clearly signalled by the establishment of the Industrial Development Office, but behind the scenes there was another compelling factor at work: the pragmatic recognition that government borrowing from private financial institutions to invest in the public development of industrial ventures was simply not on. That, in any event, is my view of the forces that were in play.

On the resources development front, where the CCF had been divided between public versus private development, it came to be recognized on equally pragmatic grounds that given the existing public ownership of resources – oil and natural gas, for example – the government could lease exploration and development rights to private companies and could extract from them – through royalties and other charges imposed through the lease – a fair return, which could then be devoted to social programs.

This was the provincial side of the role of the state in the economy – or the Saskatchewan side, so to speak.

But Douglas's thinking on economic policy generally – on Canada's economic policy – also matured and became more fully and clearly articulated. As expressed through his consistent positions in federal-provincial discussions and through his guidance of provincial policies, he accepted *de facto* that the market economy was the economic system of choice – but with important qualifications. First the state was and should be held responsible for 'managing' the economy – using its macroeconomic tools of monetary, fiscal, and trade policy, and its power to regulate banking and other financial institutions that play a key role in the functioning of the economy. Secondly, the state had a responsibility to ensure that the 'natural' regulator of the market economy, that is, competition, was operating effectively in stimulating industrial efficiency and in inhibiting exploitive industrial concentration or exploitive pricing. And thirdly, and perhaps most important generally to Tommy Douglas, the state along with industry had a responsibility to humanize the market economy – through the protection and the representation of consumer, worker, and social interests – ranging from labour legislation through to environmental protection.

This role of the state, these responsibilities of the public sector as I have described them, sound almost commonplace today. They have come generally to be accepted as elements in our definition of the role of the state. But in 1944 these were radical notions. How radical was vividly illustrated in the medical care saga.

Forty years later, of course, it is easy to forget how great the achievement was. For most readers, the conditions in Canada during the 1920s and 1930s, coupled with the nation's experience during the war – these being a wellspring of the vision of the Douglas government and the corresponding vision of the federal government's 1945 policy papers on economic and social policy – are a matter of distant history. But this very fact – that the role of government as it evolved in Canada during the post-war years has come to be taken as the conventional view – opens it up to attack. The public sector is less efficient than the private sector, goes the argument – without benefit of supporting data – so let's privatize this or that segment of the public sector. Public medical care or public education is not affordable, so let those who can afford to do so go to an extra-billing doctor or send their children to private schools, subsidized hopefully by the government. Canada's tax burden makes Canada less competitive than the United States, and we can ill afford the quality of life for all citizens we once thought important. My reaction to this perspective, and to its advancement without evidence or proof, will be evident. This disagreement, I must affirm, does not arise from the conviction that all of the functions of the state should or can continue to be fulfilled in a static and unchanging way. Far from it: it arises from a view of the role of the state embedded in a clear and certain system of values.

The legacy of the Douglas government, in short, is not founded simply in the programs and policies that it developed – and that have become part of the fabric of Canadian society. Nor is it to be found in the particular solutions to public needs and problems as these were understood and addressed in their time. The legacy is more fundamental than that. It lies in the values that the state should and demonstrably can embody in its policies. The starting point for Douglas and his colleagues, indeed, was the belief that the ultimate goal of the state was to enable every person 'to stand tall,' to live a life of dignity and confidence and decency. This is the goal that motivated the Douglas government in the establishment of a fundamentally new role of the state. And it was accompanied happily – some would say paradoxically – by another deeply held sentiment: respect for fiscal prudence and public integrity.

The Legacy of the Public Service

I come finally to the Douglas legacy in the field of public administration: the development in Saskatchewan of a first-class public service – in its quality, its professionalism, and its creativity. How this came about needs no recapitulation. It is enough to say that the public service of Saskatchewan came to be acclaimed in government circles across Canada; that its influence on the public service of Canada and in particular of New Brunswick, among the provinces – by way of the migration of the 'graduates' of the Saskatchewan experience – was exceptional; and that back home it was recognized that the government could not have achieved what it did had it not been for the support of such a strong public service.

Having said that, I would like to reflect personally upon some of the major, if little known, reasons for the success of Douglas's public service. They emerged from the qualities of the premier himself, and the climate he created in which the public service was built and worked.

The first reason was essentially this: that the dream of a better life that could be achieved by new policies and programs – often breaching the frontiers of the known and the familiar – would never be smothered by the mechanics of public administration or, if you will, public management. Tommy Douglas saw to that.

Students of government, and in particular public service practitioners, are aware of the huge number of activities that are involved in governing. They range from the creation of organizations and the engagement of people with the tools of their work, through the fashioning of budgets, and the reporting on their activities to parliaments and the public. We all know that. But beyond these functions there are a plethora of associated tasks that existed at the time Douglas was in office, but which have grown and multiplied over the years: activities associated with evaluating the effectiveness of programs and policies; tasks related to administrative efficiency; financial and program reporting; other activities associated with relations between different organizational entities; and competition for influence within and between these entities; tasks associated with the classification of positions and with hiring requirements (representational as well as professional); budget reports and financial statements and associated audits; the establishment of work plans and standards and work measurements; procurement rules and exemptions; and on and on. These tasks have become increasingly elaborate and 'professionalized' as an end in themselves, and now are subject to negotiation within and between the units of the bureaucracy. These tasks – rather than the objectives of policy – have for some become the substance of public administration.

I am by no means questioning the need for public management tasks that are essential in the context of policy and programs and that are essential in the support of good government. But the balance to be struck between these mechanics and the goals that they are supposed to serve is surely fundamental.

One enormous advantage that the Douglas government enjoyed was that it existed before this emphasis came to be placed upon the technical side of management – this and the simple fact that the government was small. Both contributed significantly to the success of the Douglas government.

The public service in Saskatchewan had the advantage, too, of a shared belief in the cause for which we laboured. This did not mean that public servants were, or were expected to be, political – that was never an issue in my entire career in the government of Saskatchewan. What it did mean was that the public service did not require contrived goals – contrived by management experts – as motivation. The climate of idealism, the belief in one's programs, and dedication to the service of the public were the really important incentives.

So also was the knowledge that the government of Saskatchewan was committed to a merit-based public service, that it was determined to recruit and promote the most capable people, and that it would support and encourage the further education and development of its public servants. The public service, in its turn, took pride in its professionalism, its expertise, and its effectiveness.

Finally, and fundamentally, there was the climate of freedom that was felt, I think, by most public servants. I have in mind, in particular, the freedom to engage frankly and openly in policy discussions among public servants and ministers; the recognition that the government encouraged innovation, and understood and accepted the risks associated with innovation; and the respect as between ministers and officials for the capacity of the public service and for the responsibilities of decision-making.

This climate, I repeat, was created and fostered by Tommy Douglas himself. And so, a final tribute must be paid to the legacy of the person, Douglas – the premier whose vision and commitment were dedicated to the citizens of Saskatchewan, to elected colleagues and the public service alike, but above all to the goal of putting humanity first.

Financing a CCF Program within the Canadian Federation

The story of the Douglas government from 1944 to1961 does not exist in isolation – a fact well known to the key participants in that government. The purpose of this Annex is to put this story of the introduction in Saskatchewan of a comprehensive social welfare system into the larger context of what the national government was doing at the same time and in similar social policy directions. It is also the place to address more comprehensively the question of how the government of Saskatchewan actually financed the creation of the new programs it developed, and thus to answer the question so often put in financial and political circles in Canada in those years: 'And how are the socialists planning to pay for all this?'

In fact, the two stories are related. To tell the story of the incremental social policy steps taken by the government of Canada in the 1950s – most of them 'shared-cost' programs, under which Ottawa contributed approximately 50 per cent of the costs of provincially delivered programs – is to explain the revenue source 'federal-provincial shared-cost revenues.' And to tell the story of the federal government's payment to Saskatchewan of the income and inheritance taxes it collected in that province, plus the equalization of their yield to levels that were set every five years, is to explain the revenue source 'federal-provincial tax agreements.'

These stories explain, in part, how a government in a poor province – because, for all the development of resources and the growth in related revenue, Saskatchewan did remain a relatively poor province – created its social, health, and educational institutions. The story explains as well how a fiscally conservative government, in today's parlance – witness the treasurer's insistence upon a balanced budget and even reducing the inherited debt – built block by block the vision on which it was first elected.

The story starts by recounting the federal and federal-provincial measures that contributed to the development of social policy in Canada as a whole. This account puts Saskatchewan's pioneering efforts into the broader Canadian picture, and puts into the Saskatchewan picture the emerging federal contributions to the costs of health and welfare programs, as well as the evolving equalization of provincial government revenues. From this beginning, the full picture of the financing of the CCF government's policies and programs can be told.

The Larger Context of Social Reform[1]

As we have said, Canada, like so many other countries, emerged from the war in 1945 with a determination never to repeat the experiences of the 1930s, and with a confidence that a different and better future was possible. It was clear politically that the public was ready for change. Saskatchewan had elected North America's first socialist government in 1944, and in Ontario the Co-operative Commonwealth Federation had elected thirty-four members out of ninety in the provincial legislature in 1943. Leading intellectuals in Canada had prepared reports on the kinds of reform that were called for: Marsh on social security; Heagerty on health insurance; and Cassidy on social security and reconstruction in Canada. But what was needed, nationally, was a vision, a design that the national government could commit itself to and convert into social and economic reality.

The Ottawa throne speeches of 1943 and 1944 affirmed this direction, promising a 'charter of social security for the whole of Canada.' The design itself emerged in two documents, the *White Paper on Employment and Income* and the *Green Book on Reconstruction*. The first described the new economic order, and the second promised a new social order.

In 1945, Prime Minister Mackenzie King convened a federal-provincial conference on reconstruction, where he tabled the government's economic and social policy proposals for the post-war era. The proposals were bold and sweeping:

High levels of employment and income would be assured [by the 'new economics' of that age]; the family income flowing from employment would be supplemented by the new universal Family Allowances Plan; social insurance plans would provide for the contingencies of sickness and unemployment; an income support plan would be established for the seasonally and longer-term unemployed; and the exigency of age would be provided for through a universal old age security plan. It was indeed a bold and broad blueprint.[2]

The government's proposals had four main elements. The first objective would be to maintain high employment levels and to ensure their stability. In turn, secure employment would assure people of stable income, the cornerstone of any system of social security. To ensure the adequacy of family income, there were both minimum wage laws across the country and now a universal Family Allowances Plan to supplement that income on the basis of family size.

The second main element was a system of unemployment insurance and assistance to support the income needs of people who were unemployed or whose employment was intermittent. Given the Unemployment Insurance Plan of 1941, what was needed was the third main element – a separate plan to support people who did not qualify for unemployment insurance, or whose benefits had run out. Such a plan would be financed from the government's consolidated revenue fund.

The fourth element was a nationwide health insurance scheme, covering both hospital and medical care. The national government's proposal contemplated that the provinces would legislate provincial health care plans and that the federal government would cover 60 per cent of their cost. It would be necessary for provinces to phase in these plans.

Here was the national foundation for the social policies to which the Saskatchewan government had committed itself: one that Premier Douglas, of course, supported.

At the same 1945 conference, the prime minister also proposed new federal-provincial fiscal arrangements, to replace the wartime tax rental agreements. Specifically, he proposed that the provinces should continue to forego the imposition and collection of personal and corporation income taxes, plus inheritance taxes (succession duties), as they had done during the war, in return for a new system of grants to the provinces, called, as before, tax rental payments. These would essentially be per capita grants, equal across all the provinces, and increased each year by the rate of growth of the population and the GNP. This meant effectively that the poorer provinces would be receiving more than they could collect by imposing their own income taxes at 'standard' provincial rates. In short, a form of equalization was built in.

Several of the provinces seemed ready to accept these comprehensive

social and fiscal proposals, with some bargaining. But Ontario and Quebec firmly rejected them, on constitutional grounds – federal government intrusion into provincial jurisdiction – and on policy grounds –
disagreement with some of the policies the charter of social security
called for. Moreover, many of the provinces considered the proposed fiscal arrangements to be insufficient: the per capita amount was too
small; the 'statutory subsidies' negotiated by each province upon its
entry into the federation had effectively been displaced; and other
detailed differences.

In the face of such implacable opposition, the conference was
adjourned, to be reconvened in the new year. The federal government
came to the 1946 conference with revised proposals on the fiscal
arrangements side, including higher per capita compensation, a back-
down on statutory subsidies, and other concessions. But again no agreement could be reached, and again the conference broke up, this time
not to be reconvened.

The next chapter in the reconstruction saga was the separation, or
'uncoupling,' of the two major elements of the federal proposals. The
minister of finance, J.L. Isley, took up the question of fiscal arrangements in his 1946 budget, where he advanced significantly revised proposals, but 'the welfare and public investment proposals were shelved,
presumably of necessity, until all provinces had made tax agreements.'[3]

In fact, however, the uncoupling of fiscal arrangements and social
policy carried with it more significant implications for the future of federal-provincial relations than that. It reflected two different views of how
financial resources should be made available to the provinces to enable
them to finance the programs involved in a charter of social security, or
indeed any program that provided services that had become, in the
public eye, essential to the public good.

One approach was, and is, that the federal share of income taxes, for
example, should be reduced and the provincial share increased (making room for higher provincial taxes), and that the national government should provide revenue equalization payments to the poorer
provinces whose per capita yield from these higher taxes was below
some accepted standard. Thus the provinces would have the revenues
required to finance their own 'charters of social security.' The harmonizing of these charters across Canada would then become a question
for inter-provincial and perhaps federal-provincial discussion.

The second view, held by the federal government through to the late
1970s and by premiers of Douglas's cast of mind, was that essential pub-

lic services, such as health, welfare, and education, should be available to all Canadians in equal measure and at equal standards. To this end, the nation's government should play a role, along with the provinces, in establishing the principles and the national standards that should prevail in assuring this measure of equality. And the national government should pay, say, half of the costs of what have become shared programs as its share in achieving the national goals.

While these two perspectives were reflected in the 1945–6 negotiations, this does not mean they could not be treated as complementary perspectives or approaches. In fact, they were treated as complementary through most of the 1950s and 1960s, though always with Quebec's dissent in respect of the second, 'co-operative federalism,' approach. Douglas's position, on the other side, was equally clear and unequivocal:

> The main argument for equalization lies in the concept that every Canadian citizen has an inalienable right to certain minimum standards of health, education and welfare, irrespective of where he may live in this broad Dominion ... no nation is truly great which has depressed areas whose citizens must content themselves with a standard of services far below the national average. Such a policy could only foment resentment and recriminations; such a policy would eventually destroy the fabric of national unity.[4]

As for the government of Canada, it was proceeding on the two-track approach: enlarging the provinces' fiscal resources both by making room for higher provincial income taxes accompanied by unconditional equalization grants, *and* by providing tied grants to finance particular social programs.

The Social Policy Side of Post-War Reconstruction

Turning first, then, to the social security side of the federal government's 1945 proposals, their detachment from the on-going federal-provincial discussions left Ottawa's social policy reformers with only one tool: the introduction of incremental reforms, which together, over time, would realize the promised social security charter. Paul Martin, Sr, minister of health and welfare, proceeded vigorously in this direction.

Three elements of a comprehensive income security plan were already in place in 1945. The first was designed for needy people aged seventy and over: the product of legendary negotiations between Prime

Minister Mackenzie King and J.S. Woodsworth in 1926, when Woodsworth was a member of Parliament. It was a federal-provincial shared-cost program. The other two elements of a nascent income security plan were designed for people who were of working age and able to work, the 'employable' category in the vocabulary of the 1950s. One was the Unemployment Insurance Plan (1941), and the other the universal Family Allowances Plan designed primarily to supplement the income of low-income families but paid to all, legislated in late 1944.

What remained to be done was to design a program or programs that would provide social assistance for all those in need who were deemed to be 'unemployable,' again in the vocabulary of the 1940s and 1950s, and to people who were 'employable' but whose UI benefits had been used up while they were still unemployed.

The easiest part of this job, in political terms, was to provide social assistance for the people who were not expected to work: the old and the disabled. The first step came in 1950 when the federal government announced its intention to legislate a universal Old Age Security Plan for people aged seventy and over, and undertook, as well, to participate in a federal-provincial, shared-cost pension scheme for needy people aged sixty-five to sixty-nine. A constitutional amendment was necessary to implement the OAS Plan, and was agreed to. Another measure addressed blind persons in need. They had been covered under the original Old Age Pension Plan (the costs of which were split 75/25 between the federal and provincial governments) but now would be covered under an independent Blind Persons Plan, legislated in 1951. These income security plans were extended in 1954 to disabled persons in need, the costs of which would be split 50/50 between Ottawa and the provinces.

In social policy terms, the social security charter as it applied to unemployed people was now in place – all governments having agreed, over time, to participate. In financial terms, the provinces were relieved of their 25 per cent share of the Old Age Pension Plan and assumed a 50 per cent share of the costs of the new Old Age Assistance Plan (for persons aged sixty-five to sixty-nine), along with the Disabled Persons Plan, already shared.

The remaining element of income security in the *Green Book* proposals of 1945 was social assistance for 'unemployed employables.' This would be a more difficult program to design: who, for example, would determine who was employable and who was not? Nevertheless, the federal government announced in 1953 its intention to establish such a program, and federal and provincial officials worked until October 1956 to design one. What eventually emerged was the Unemployment Assistance Plan, under which the body of eligible persons would be those who qualified for assistance under existing provincial plans of 'general assistance.' The government of Canada would contribute half of the costs, thereby relieving the provinces of some 50 per cent of their social assistance costs.

This is the essence of the income security plan that emerged in the ten years after the reconstruction conference of 1945. It was comprehensive, if highly categorical, and it was national in scope. More, it was very much the product of federal-provincial discussions with national government leadership. The position of the government of Saskatchewan in these developments needs hardly be recorded: its representatives were prominent in all the policy conferences, in support of the federal initiatives.

Health Policy

Accompanying the income security proposals of the *Green Book* and the reconstruction conference was a plan to establish a provincially operated health insurance plan, beginning with hospital insurance. The plan would be financed to the extent of 60 per cent by federal payments to the provinces. Once again, however, given the failure to reach agreement at the reconstruction conference, the federal government resorted to the incremental approach.

In 1948 the minister of national health and welfare, known to be a strong supporter of health insurance, introduced instead a new system of health grants, designed to contribute to the foundation of a full system of health insurance. There were ten separate grant programs in this system, four of them having to do with categories of illness (such as cancer and tuberculosis), four of them having to do with public health generally (such as health surveys and health records), and the largest of them all providing grants in aid of hospital construction (contributing about one-third of the costs of construction). The latter program was tied to provincial expenditures; most of the others were per capita grants.

But Premier Douglas had trumped these national developments. Without even waiting for the outcome of the 1946 reconstruction conference, the Saskatchewan Legislative Assembly legislated the Saskatchewan Hospital Services Plan, to be started on 1 January 1947. It was, as we have seen, a universal, comprehensive, and publicly administered plan, financed in part by family premiums (taxes) and in part by general revenues. By 1948 Saskatchewan had set a pattern that all provinces would later emulate. Indeed, British Columbia established its own Hospital Insurance Commission in 1949, followed by Alberta and Newfoundland.

In 1948, when a new prime minister, Louis St Laurent, took office, the prospects for an early introduction of hospital insurance dimmed. True, a committee of health ministers, led by the federal minister, plus deputy ministers and other officials, was established by the federal-provincial conference of 1955 to study health insurance. And, true, the proposals of that committee led the federal government to introduce the Hospital Insurance Act, which was approved by Parliament in April 1957 – ten years after the Saskatchewan plan had started. But at the insistence of the prime minister, that Act would not become operative until six of the ten provinces, representing a majority of the Canadian people, approved the commencement of a shared-cost hospital insurance plan. And that assent was not forthcoming.[5]

However, St Laurent and his Liberals were defeated in the election of 1957, and John Diefenbaker of Saskatchewan, leader of the Progressive Conservatives, became prime minister. One of his early acts was to remove the 'assent of the provinces' requirement, and federal financing of hospital insurance became available almost immediately to any province that was operating a qualifying public insurance plan.

For Saskatchewan, this meant that some 40 to 45 per cent of its expenditures on the Hospital Services Plan would now be recovered from the federal government. The larger implication was that a complete health insurance plan, full medicare, could be promised in the 1960 election.

The next major step in the story of national health insurance in Canada was, of course, the extension of medicare in Saskatchewan and from Saskatchewan to Canada as a whole.

Tax Sharing and Equalization[6]

The social policy story is the first part of the policy changes that flowed from the reconstruction conference. The second is the further development of fiscal arrangements between the federal and provincial governments – involving tax rental, tax sharing, and equalization. As I have said, the federal finance minister's 1946 budget speech proposed a significantly different set of fiscal arrangements than those that had been discussed in the 1946 reconstruction conference.

First, the per capita tax rental payment to those provinces that refrained from imposing personal or corporate income taxes or succession duties was increased to $15 per capita (from $12.50) minus the statutory subsidies. One tangible extension was made to this offer: the federal government would allow a deduction from corporate taxable income of provincial mining and logging taxes where the provinces did not own mineral or other resource rights and therefore could not charge royalties. More, the minimum payment to the provinces would not be less than 150 per cent of the Wartime Tax Agreement.

The proposals for the non-agreeing provinces, which levied their own taxes, provided for an abatement or credit of 5 per cent of the federal personal income tax, 5 per cent of corporate income, and a federal credit of 50 per cent of succession duties. In effect, the provincial share of the three tax fields would become '5/5/50.'

This offer having been made in the budget, a series of bilateral discussions with the provinces followed; these culminated in still further enrichment of the federal offer. At this point, all the provinces except Ontario and Quebec accepted one of the two tax rental options. The implicit equalization of revenues included in the per capita tax rental compensation would continue to be available only to the agreeing provinces; this qualification affected only Quebec, which refused to enter into a tax rental agreement.

In the interval between the signing of the 1947–52 tax rental agreements and the 1950 federal-provincial conference leading up to the 1952–6 agreements, a good many adjustments were made in federal and provincial taxation. The federal government withdrew from its special wartime taxes, which made 'room' for equivalent provincial taxes. Ontario and Quebec increased their corporation income tax levies to 8.5 per cent, without any corresponding adjustment in the federal 5 per cent abatement or tax credit rate. Both provinces refrained from imposing a personal income tax.

The 1950 federal-provincial conference saw few proposals for changes in the tax rental arrangements, the result in no small measure of the Korean crisis, which froze any impetus to reduce federal taxing powers. Technical adjustments were made to the escalation formula (the rate of growth of provincial population and the GNP) and to the guaranteed minimum payments, which together yielded a modest increase in the tax rental payments. And, significantly, Ontario signed a tax rental agreement after private discussions between the new premier, Leslie Frost, and the minister of finance, Douglas Abbott, and after a minor change in the standard rental agreement for Ontario's benefit.

The federal proposals for the 1957–62 fiscal arrangements were first revealed to a committee of federal and provincial finance officials in September 1955 and then presented to a federal-provincial conference in October. These were revolutionary by comparison with the tax agreements of 1947–56, though they revolved around the same three elements:

Tax sharing: the federal and provincial shares of the personal and corporate income taxes would be one of three foundation stones of the new fiscal arrangements.

Federal collection of provincial taxes would still be provided for, at the request of the provinces, but the yield to the individual province would be the actual yield of the provincial tax (provincial share), not a per capita grant as in the former arrangements.

Equalization of the shared taxes, formerly included in the per capita rental payments and thus conditional upon the province entering into a tax rental (collection) agreement, would now be paid unconditionally.

The federal-provincial conference met in October 1955 to hear the government of Canada's proposals, based on these three pillars, and to hear the proposals of the provinces. The various provincial positions included Premier Douglas's demand for the continuation of the rental agreements and some system of equalization; Premier Frost's advocacy of a larger provincial share of the personal and corporation income taxes, though not ruling out some kind of rental arrangements; and Premier Duplessis' implacable assertion that Quebec would continue to impose and collect its own taxes, without penalty.

The October conference adjourned to enable the premiers to examine the proposals at greater length. A Continuing Committee on Fiscal and Economic Matters, comprising federal and provincial officials, was established to meet from time to time to review federal-provincial fiscal and economic matters generally, and in particular to examine the principles and the technical implications of the proposed new approach to fiscal arrangements.

Early in the new year, Prime Minister St Laurent outlined his proposals in detail. The 'provincial share' of income tax would be set at 10 per cent of the federal personal income tax collected in each province and at 9 per cent of taxable corporate income (in the province). The provincial share of succession duties would be 50 per cent of the federal estate tax rates. These shares would be the same, whether the provincial taxes were collected for the province by the government of Canada or were collected by a non-agreeing province (where federal taxes previously had been abated).

The equalization formula, in turn, would provide that in provinces where the per capita yield from the provincial share of the three taxes fell below the per capita yield in the two richest provinces (Ontario and British Columbia), the government of Canada would make up the difference. These equalization payments would be unconditional. Stabilization measures were provided as well, to ensure that equalization payments in any province would not fall below, for example, the previous year's payment. These arrangements, too, would be totally unconditional.

Subsequent negotiations brought the government of Canada to make further tax concessions in other fields (though not changing the 10/9/50 share of personal income taxes, corporate income taxes, and succession duties) and, significantly, to offer to collect provincially imposed income taxes, providing the provinces adopted tax legislation that was identical to the federal tax laws, and providing the taxes they levied were at the 'standard rates.' It is noteworthy that the tax collection agreements as devised could equally have provided for the collection of provincial taxes at a higher rate than the standard rate. This would be recognized by a new national government in 1957.

Quebec rejected the fiscal arrangements proposed, though it agreed to accept the equalization payment for which it qualified. Ontario rejected the new arrangements too; but later, after imposing its own corporation income tax, it entered into a tax rental agreement in respect of personal income tax. All the other provinces entered into agreements, despite their belief that the federal government, enjoying a nice surplus, could afford to increase the tax share of the provinces, now suffering from deficits.

Normally the discussion of fiscal arrangements for the next five-year period, 1962–7, would have begun in 1960. But the new prime minister, John Diefenbaker, while campaigning in 1958 for the majority he had failed to win in the previous year, called for an earlier review of the federal-provincial fiscal arrangements. After he won his majority, a veritable marathon of federal-provincial conferences and meetings was launched – meetings of first ministers, meetings of ministers of finance, and meetings of their officials.

The first of these – a conference of the ministers of finance – was held in July and then October 1959 to prepare for a full federal-provincial conference sometime in 1960. The ministers were assisted in these preparations by the Continuing Committee on Fiscal and Economic Matters.

The first ministerial conference was called for July 1960. The prime subject on the agenda was the development of fiscal arrangements for 1962–7, including tax sharing, formulae for equalization and fiscal need payments, and a formula for stabilization arrangements. The last item on the agenda was 'the role in provincial financing of conditional grants and shared cost programs.' In between was a range of issues having to do largely with taxes other than the 'shared taxes.'

As events unfolded, there were actually three conferences: the July 1960 conference and two others in October 1960 and February 1961. In the course of these meetings, two things came to be better understood: the needs and the fiscal anxieties of the provinces; and the growing impatience of the federal government with taking the political blame for the taxes being collected on behalf of the provinces. Similarly, the alternative approaches to the financing of essential public services, notably health, welfare, and education, emerged with greater force than in earlier years. As before, the choice was between increasing provincial taxes (tax room) and the equalization of the tax yield, with the allocation of these funds being a matter for the provinces; versus federal financing of shared-cost programs through which reasonably equal levels of health, welfare, and education benefits could be assured to all Canadians.

In fact, the provinces had had a surfeit of shared-cost programs 'imposed' on them, as we have seen from the health and welfare story that preceded this one. Their growing impatience with 'federally imposed' conditional grants was evident at the conference. The underlying goal of shared-cost programs, the availability to all Canadians of relatively equal essential services, was eclipsed by that impatience.

The most dramatic statement on this question, by far, came from the newly elected premier of Quebec, Jean Lesage. He announced at the earliest conference that Quebec intended now to take advantage of all the shared-cost programs that the province had been offered but had eschewed until now; but that from that date forward, 'Quebec will never again sign a shared cost agreement.' This straightforward statement was to have a profound impact upon the shape and character of future nationwide programs, notably medicare and the federal financing of university and college education.

In the end, however, the central focus of the conference was on the federal government's proposals concerning tax sharing, tax collection, and equalization. Like those of 1955, they were quite dramatic:

- *The provincial share* of the personal income tax would be increased to 16 per cent of the federal tax, and increased by one percentage point each year up to 20 per cent. The provincial share of the corporation tax field would remain at 9 per cent of taxable corporate income, and 50 per cent of the federal estate tax collections in any province that did not levy such a tax would be paid to the province.
- In future, the provinces would be expected to *legislate their own provincial income taxes* and increase them as they chose (that is, increase the provincial share by provincial action).
- The government of Canada would be prepared to *collect the provincial taxes* through the federal collection system, providing the provincial tax laws (notably the tax base) were identical to the Income Tax Act of Canada.
- The *equalization formula* would be broadened to include provincial resource revenues, along with personal and corporate income taxes and succession duties. Given this broadening of the base of the equalization formula, the level to which the included revenues would be equalized would be the national average, rather than that of the two richest provinces. No province entitled to equalization would receive less than it had under the earlier arrangements. And the same '95 per-cent' stabilization guarantee would apply.[7]

Saskatchewan became a major beneficiary under the new arrangements, entitled to an estimated $42.5 million compared with $38.3 million.[8]

Aside from the financial benefit to Saskatchewan, there are several important conclusions to this story of federal-provincial fiscal arrangements. First, they effectively assured the fiscal autonomy of the provinces, within given political and constitutional limits. This was true, if in lesser measure, even in the poorer provinces, through the equalization (or 'averagization') of four major provincial revenues. Secondly, all governments in Canada were committed to this principle of equalizing provincial revenues in one measure or another. Thirdly, the belief that the national government should play an active role in equalizing essential public services for all Canadians – individual Canadians – was under a cloud, as was the constitutional tool for doing so, that is the 'spending power.'

There were two paradoxes or enigmas that stood out, as well. One, which we have referred to in earlier pages, was the relative emphasis that should be placed on the two vehicles for increasing and equalizing provincial 'revenue shares.' To the extent that federal-provincial fiscal arrangements were targeted solely to increasing and equalizing the 'provincial share' of public revenues, then the role of the federal government in the establishment of national standards in respect of nationwide health and welfare programs would become ambiguous, at best, or even non-existent. To the extent, on the other hand, that provincial revenues were to be increased by federal-provincial shared-cost programs, then the unqualified autonomy of the provinces (advocated by Quebec and over time by Ontario and other provinces) would be attenuated, but national standards in social security and national health and medicare programs would more likely be assured. This conundrum was never clearly and specifically addressed during the years of the Douglas government, or indeed after – though Douglas himself was clearly aware of it, and equally clearly supported federal-provincial shared-cost programs alongside revenue equalization.

The second paradox was the incompleteness of the revenue equalization formula. There had been a rationale, an economic policy rationale, for the central collection and equalization of income taxes during the war, but that had long since passed. What the rationale might be now, in 1961, for equalizing the revenues from only four revenue sources was far from clear.

Even here, however, the Douglas government was to have some influence in remedying this deficiency in the equalization formula – in a very indirect and personal way. While I was on educational leave at Harvard during 1957–8, I found myself puzzling about this anomaly in the formula, and about whether and how one might equalize all provincial revenues. I recognized that to do so one would have to find a measure for the base of every provincial revenue source, or at least a proxy for that base. I also recognized that a tax rate would have to be arrived at – likely the national average of the prevailing provincial rates. And so on. Finally, I developed a first approximation as to how one might go about equalizing all provincial revenues to the national average.

Back in Saskatchewan, in the fall of 1958, I consulted with Tommy Shoyama and another colleague, Robert McLarty, about the formula, and developed a model, which we then discussed with two leading economists at the University of Saskatchewan. The next step, with a plan on paper, was to consult with the premier about the possibility of Saskatchewan putting forward this new formulation to the prime minister or to a federal-provincial conference. After hearing more about it, he asked one question: 'How would Saskatchewan do under the formula?' The answer was 'in the long run, very well.' But unhappily in those particular years, by reason of bountiful revenues, Saskatchewan would be a marginal loser. Understandably, Douglas responded that while he thought the plan would be a great stride forward, he could not realistically be its sponsor. Not that year, anyway.

But the premier proposed an alternative approach: why not table the formula with the federal-provincial Continuing Committee on Fiscal and Economic Matters, on a purely personal and professional basis. This I did in early September 1960. However, it was not until 1964, after I had been appointed assistant deputy minister of finance in Ottawa, with responsibility for federal-provincial fiscal arrangements, that there was an opportunity to bring the proposal to the federal deputy, then Robert Bryce. His approval led to the further elaboration of the formula and its presentation to the minister.[9]

As a federal initiative, the plan was then presented to the Continuing Committee, where there were extensive discussions over several months. When these consultations were complete, and the formula had been improved by reason of other perspectives brought to bear on it, it was presented to and approved by the cabinet.

This was the equalization formula that was to inspire the constitutional amendment of 1982:

36(2). Parliament and the government of Canada are committed to the principle of making equalization payments to ensure that provincial governments have sufficient revenues to provide reasonably comparable levels of public services at reasonably comparable levels of taxation.

This completes the story of federal-provincial fiscal arrangements during the Douglas regime, and how they evolved as a major contributor to the financing of the Saskatchewan government's program. Together with the story of the emergence of the national and Saskatchewan programs of health and social security, from 1945 to 1960, the fiscal arrangements provide the background required to review the financing of the whole of the Douglas government's program over the years.

The Financing of the CCF Program

This biography of the Douglas government has centred on the policies and programs that were developed over its seventeen years in office –

that is to say, in financial terms, the expenditure side of the budget. The other side of the budget – the resources required to finance these policies and programs – has been alluded to as well, particularly when talking about the government's overall fiscal policy and about the more notable and more expensive programs.

To complete the picture, however, a more comprehensive account is needed of how the revolution in public policy was financed. This is what I have sought to do in this Annex. The story of federal-provincial fiscal arrangements is one part of the story. And to recount the revenue side of the Saskatchewan budget, I went back to the budgets and the estimates, comprehending both revenues and expenditures, and aggregated in five broad categories the revenues that the Douglas government relied upon, year by year and during each term of office, to finance the growing expenditures. It then was possible to calculate the 'percentage reliance' on each category of revenues during each term of office.

All of this is reflected in the three tables to be found at the end of the Annex. Through these tables it is possible to identify the key features of public finance as guided and directed by the CCF government, that is, how the cabinet and the minister of finance managed the finances of the province.

The budgets of the government of Saskatchewan increased nearly fivefold from 1945–6, when the first full-year budget was presented by Provincial Treasurer Clarence Fines, through to 1961–2, when Tommy Douglas left Saskatchewan to take on the leadership of the national New Democratic Party. Each of these budgets was financed entirely out of revenues, covering both current and capital expenditures, and not by deficit financing. The one exception was in 1961–2 when a $2.7-million deficit was estimated (less than 1 per cent of revenues), this being the consequence of the 1960 recession and of the crop failure of 1961.[10]

The reasons for this 'fiscal conservatism,' as it would be looked upon today, were many. The farmers knew from the Depression that to finance their operations by borrowing against their assets could well lead – indeed had led – to the possession of those assets by the lending institutions. And the CCF Party and government largely reflected that cast of mind. More, Provincial Treasurer Clarence Fines recognized that if the CCF government was to build and maintain its credit on the markets, balanced budgets were a necessity: even with them, the cost of borrowing for the government of Saskatchewan (for advances to Crown corporations) was one-quarter of 1 per cent higher than that, for example, of Progressive Conservative Manitoba, which did finance a part of its capital expenditures by borrowing.[11] As if that were not reason enough, why, asked Clarence Fines and his advisors, would anyone want to spend, say, 25 per cent of the revenues to pay interest on the debt instead of on social expenditures?

The second notable feature of the government's fiscal policy was the extent of its reliance upon its own major tax sources. It was, on the face of it, remarkably small. During the whole of Premier Douglas's seventeen years in office, Saskatchewan's provincially levied and collected taxes – the retail sales tax, the hospitalization tax or premium, gasoline tax, liquor revenues, motor vehicle licence fees, and so on – ranged between 45 and 49 per cent of total revenues. Even if one were to include miscellaneous revenues – all fees, licences, and permits, though not resource revenues – the total reliance on Saskatchewan-levied revenues of all kinds ranged between 53.5 and 58 per cent during the last three terms of the Douglas government.

The reasons for this apparently limited reliance on Saskatchewan's own tax sources are evident in Table 2, which presents an overall picture of the province's relative reliance upon five principal revenue sources: Saskatchewan levied and collected taxes; federal-provincial tax rental agreement revenues; mineral and natural resource revenues; federal contributions to shared-cost programs in Saskatchewan; and all other revenues. Why Saskatchewan relied upon these several revenue sources to the extent they did, starting with the province's own tax sources, becomes more evident as we proceed with this review of the fiscal policies of the CCF government.

The third notable feature of the government's fiscal policy was that Saskatchewan's 'own' taxes were not increased as much as might have been expected, given the magnitude of the policy innovations that were introduced.

Looking first at the taxes imposed to finance the hospitalization program, a family premium of $30 per annum was levied in 1947 (the hospitalization tax), and two years later the sales tax of 2 per cent was raised by one percentage point (thus becoming the education and hospitalization tax). The family tax, or premium as it was commonly called in those years, was increased three times over the fourteen years prior to the initiation of medicare, from $30 to $48, accompanied by larger increases in the rate for individuals. The hospitalization part of the sales tax, in turn, was not increased from the 1 per cent level until medicare was introduced in 1962 by the Woodrow Lloyd government.

In that year, to complete the picture, the estimated costs of medicare were made public, along with the tax increases required to finance them: a 2 per cent increase in the sales tax (1½ per cent for medicare) and a 1 per cent increase in each of the personal and corporate income taxes, now being levied by Saskatchewan.

Turning to the 'general' tax increases to finance the rest of the government's program, two principal revenue sources were involved: the gasoline tax and liquor profits (taxes under another name). This is aside from increases in licence revenues (notably motor licences) and in fees and permits, etc. The gasoline tax was increased three times during the Douglas years, from 8 cents per gallon pre-1947, to 14 cents in 1961–2 (while the tax on farm fuels was eliminated). How often and how much liquor prices and profits were raised was not disclosed (as in other provinces).

These, then, are the increases that lie behind the overall reliance of the Douglas government on its own tax sources – to repeat, between 45 and 49 per cent of total revenues. In assessing the measure of these tax increases, it is important to have in mind the fact that the value of the dollar declined from 100 cents to 58 cents between 1945 and 1961. (Data on revenue as a percentage of gross provincial product are not available pre-1951.)

On the other hand, it is equally important to remember that Saskatchewan was not levying or collecting personal or corporate income taxes or inheritance taxes during this period. Under the tax rental agreements, only the government of Canada was doing so. The result was that Saskatchewan was receiving and entering into its accounts only a tax rental payment that was composed of, but not split between, the Saskatchewan share of federally collected income taxes in the province and the implicit equalization payment. This being so, Saskatchewan's personal income taxes and corporate income taxes did not appear in the province's accounts, as such, but rather they appeared in the federal accounts. (One can understand the political restiveness this was coming to develop in the nation's Parliament.)

This anomaly, as it might well be called, was rectified only in 1962–3 when, under new fiscal arrangements, the provinces were obliged to levy their own personal and corporate income taxes, which the national government would then collect on their behalf (a kind of 'agency' agreement). From then on, these income taxes were included with the major tax sources reported in Saskatchewan's books, along with the retail sales tax, the gasoline tax, and so on. This meant, of course, that after these changes the proportion of Saskatchewan-levied taxes in relation to total Saskatchewan revenues increased – from 44.4

per cent in 1961–2 to 56.8 per cent in 1962–3. And the equalization payment, having become an explicit revenue for Saskatchewan, was recorded as such: it came to 10.3 per cent of total revenues in 1962–3. All of which illuminates, but does not alter, the facts of the fiscal story during the Douglas years.

The fourth feature of Saskatchewan's fiscal policy, it will be evident by now, was its heavy reliance on federal payments to the provinces: first and foremost the tax rental agreements, plus in most years federal contributions to shared-cost programs. The tax rental revenues amounted to between 22 and 30 per cent of total revenues during the whole of the Douglas years, while the shared-cost contributions ranged between 5.8 and 9.5 per cent in the 1950s and rose to 11.6 per cent when the government of Canada began sharing the costs of Saskatchewan's Hospital Services Plan.

Here again we see the two means by which the national government could, and in Tommy Douglas's view should, contribute to reasonably equal levels and standards of health, education, and social well-being for all Canadians. This belief was to become a quite universally held value system across Canada, but in inter-governmental circles there was disagreement as to the vehicles by which it would be realized. By the late 1960s the second of the two approaches – shared-cost programs – was under sharp attack, first by Quebec and then, following suit, certain of the other provinces, and finally even within Parliament and the federal government. But in the years of the Douglas government, the shared-cost program, as a vehicle for achieving this Canadian goal, remained not only institutionally sound (the constitutionality of the national government's spending power having been upheld in the courts),[12] but also politically viable.

It goes without saying that the CCF government in Saskatchewan would have been crippled, as would all the other poorer provinces, if these shared-cost contributions and equalization and tax payments had not become entrenched in the fabric of Canadian government. For they amounted, in Saskatchewan's case, to some 30 to 37 per cent of the province's revenues. Even in 1962–3, when Saskatchewan's income and corporation taxes were properly severed from federal equalization payments, as described above, the equalization payments alone amounted to over 10 per cent of Saskatchewan's revenues, and the federal reimbursement of hospitalization expenditures (shared cost) amounted to 13 per cent of the province's revenues.

The Saskatchewan story, in short, was both an example of and a precursor to the Canadian story, and the Canadian story, in turn, of fiscal and program equalization was an anchor for the Saskatchewan story.

The fifth feature of the Douglas government's fiscal policy was more conventional, which is to say, perhaps more widely understood and acknowledged, than the other features we have reviewed. That was the recognition that industrial and resources development was and would be a significant contributor to the public revenues that would finance social reform; and that reliance upon the private sector to achieve that growth and development – with some government help – was the surest way of realizing it. This is to say no more and no less than did Clarence Fines in his budget speech of 1945:

> Government revenue, whatever its source, depends directly on the extent of economic activity. If the economy is functioning fully ... then, and only then, will government be able to find the necessary revenue to finance an adequate program of social services. There is no other way. Therefore it is government's direct obligation to ensure that the economy is functioning to its fullest capacity and that economic development proceeds ... in a planned way ... It is my task to tap the available investment resources for a planned and full development of old and new industries in this province.[13]

Saskatchewan's success, after the earlier turmoil over public versus private sector roles, spoke for itself. Mineral and natural resources revenues, the measurable ones, rose from the 5 per cent range in the government's first two terms of office to 9.5 per cent in the third term, and to 16.3 per cent in the first half of the fourth term of office. From then on, through the rest of the Douglas regime, the resources revenues declined – an economic, not a policy, phenomenon – and declined even more noticeably as a percentage of total revenue, to some 11 per cent. (This was partly because the very large increase in hospitalization cost-sharing contributions reduced the relative contribution of other revenue sources, including resource revenues, to the whole.) It remains that resource revenues became a significant source of revenues for the province. This record of resource revenues helped to contribute to the recognition by the CCF that the market economy was in fact a major economic contributor to society and to social programs.

Tables on Sources of Revenue and on the Relative Importance of Each Source in Saskatchewan's Budgets

Departing, now, from the narrative of the Annex, I turn to an explanation of the three tables that follow. They set out the sources of revenue for the government of Saskatchewan and the relative reliance upon the five major revenue sources in the budgets of Saskatchewan. The creation of the tables – the sources and categorizations – is explained below.

Sources: Revenue estimates in Saskatchewan's annual estimates, and the 1962 annual report of the Saskatchewan Hospital Services Plan (the latter recording revenues from the hospitalization tax or premium from 1947 to 1952).

Adjustments: In the Saskatchewan estimates, the federal contributions under shared-cost agreements are shown as reimbursements, or deductions from the provincial expenditures on shared-cost programs. These figures have been rearranged to show the federal contributions as revenues of the province (and correspondingly the federal reimbursements shown in the expenditure estimates would be eliminated).

Categorization (see Tables 1 and 2): Five categories of revenue sources have been created, and the annual estimates of individual revenue sources have been allocated to, or grouped under, the appropriate category, as follows:

- Federal-provincial fiscal arrangements (tax agreement)
- Province of Saskatchewan revenues – levied and collected by the province or, in the case of income taxes from 1962–3 on, collected on behalf of the province by the government of Canada
- Natural resources and mineral resources revenues
- Federal contributions to shared-cost programs
- Other revenues

Grouping of data by terms of office of the Douglas government (see Tables 1,2, and 3): The revenues, in these five categories, have been assembled under six groups of fiscal years and for each of Douglas's four full terms of office as follows:

- 1944–8: The revenues estimated for each of the four budgets in this term of office, namely those for 1945/46 to 1948/49.
- 1948–52: The revenues estimated for each of the budgets in the second term of office, namely 1949/50 to 1952/53.
- 1952–6: The revenues estimated for each of the budgets in the third term of office, namely 1953/54 to 1956/57.

- 1956–60, plus 1961: The revenues estimated for each of the four budgets of Douglas's fourth term in office, plus the first budget brought down in Lloyd's term, namely 1957/58, 1958/59, 1959/60, 1960/61, and 1961/62. These five budgets have been assembled into two groups, in columns 4 and 5. The budgets for 1957/58 and 1958/59 reflected the status quo of cost sharing and tax rental agreements. In calendar 1959, the government of Canada began to share Saskatchewan's hospitalization plan costs, and this increased the province's revenue from shared-cost agreements by $14.2 million in the first full fiscal year. An increase of this size alters substantially the percentage figures for every category of revenue. This change is reflected in the budgets for 1959/60, 1960/61, and 1961/62. I chose to group the two 'pre-sharing years,' 1957/58 and 1958/59, and the three 'full sharing years' 1959/60 to 1961/62. In fact, the federal cost sharing of hospitalization costs affected the revenues of the last three months of 1958/59, which in turn affected the percentages of revenues from all sources for 1957/58 and 1958/59, but not significantly.
- 1962–3: From 1962/63, Saskatchewan began to levy its own income taxes (collected by the federal government). The data for this year reflect the 'real value' of the equalization payments, as well as the actual revenues from the personal and corporate income taxes.

The degree of reliance on the five categories of revenues (see Table 2): Having grouped Saskatchewan's revenue sources, first by fiscal year, and then *by averaging them, by 'terms of office,'* it is possible roughly to determine the Douglas government's 'degree of reliance' on each of the five categories of revenue.

Splitting the Saskatchewan income tax revenues from the federal equalization payments: As has been said in the text, the government of Saskatchewan began to levy its own income taxes in 1962 – collected and remitted to the province by Ottawa; and the equalization of provincial revenues was determined by a new stand-alone formula and remitted separately to the province by the government of Canada. This is shown in the data for 1962–3, where the figures for 'Saskatchewan levied and collected' revenues rise markedly, and those for federal-provincial fiscal arrangements decline substantially.

These explicit figures for 1962–3 – the income tax revenues at $23,464,000 and equalization payment of $22,236,000 – show how important it is to recall that the tax rental payments for earlier years masked the fact that a major component of those payments was federally levied and collected income taxes in Saskatchewan.

Table 1
Revenues of the government of Saskatchewan (in Canadian dollars) as estimated in the provincial budgets, 1944–62

Source of revenue	1945/46–1948/49 First term	1949/50–1952/53 Second term	1953/54–1956/57 Third term	1957/58–1958/59 Fourth term – first half	1959/60–1961/62 Fourth term – second half plus 1961–2	1962/63 W.S. Lloyd government's first budget
Federal-provincial tax arrangements	11,509,693	19,403,115	27,663,477	35,382,350	38,120,000	22,236,000
Saskatchewan levied and collected taxes	20,514,643	34,151,050	42,346,558	65,230,793	77,380,421	122,229,787
Mineral and natural resources revenues	2,392,325	3,264,017	8,833,905	23,648,040	20,747,353	21,786,160
Federal-provincial shared-cost revenues	3,566,916	6,616,733	5,655,290	8,419,665	20,165,463	28,221,910
All other revenues	7,443,372	6,294,705	8,404,680	12,536,350	17,566,260	20,882,030
Total	45,426,950	69,729,660	92,903,911	145,217,197	173,979,497	215,345,887

Note: The five major sources of revenue are shown for each of the four terms of office of the Douglas government plus one year of the CCF's fifth term of office. The first full year of the Woodrow Lloyd government, 1962–3, is also shown.

Table 2
Revenues of the government of Saskatchewan: the 'percentage reliance' on the five major revenue sources, 1944–62

Source of revenue	1945/46–1948/49 First term	1949/50–1952/53 Second term	1953/54–1956/57 Third term	1957/58–1958/59 Fourth term – first half	1959/60–1961/62 Fourth term – second half	1962/63 W.S. Lloyd government
Federal-provincial tax arrangements	25.3	27.8	29.8	24.4	21.9	10.3
Saskatchewan levied and collected taxes	45.2	49.0	45.6	44.9	44.5	56.8
Mineral and natural resources revenues	5.3	4.7	9.5	16.3	11.9	10.1
Federal-provincial shared-cost revenues	7.8	9.5	6.1	5.8	11.6	13.1
All other revenues	16.4	9.0	9.0	8.6	10.1	9.7
Total	100.0	100.0	100.0	100.0	100.0	100.0

Note: The five major sources of revenue are expressed as percentages of total revenues for each of the four terms of office of the Douglas government plus one year of the CCF's fifth term of office. The first year of the Woodrow Lloyd government, 1962–3, is also shown.

Table 3
Revenues of the government of Saskatchewan (in Canadian dollars): provincially imposed and collected taxes, 1944–62

Revenue source	1945/46–1948/49	1949/50–1952/53	1953/54–1956/57	1957/58–1958/59	1959/60–1961/62	1962/63
Hospitalization[1]	1,894,394	6,035,575	8,224,558	11,090,493	10,603,754	12,905,787
Sales tax[2]	4,175,000	9,150,000	15,500,000	17,650,000	21,666,667	35,500,000
Individual income tax						13,464,000
Corporate income tax						10,000,000
Gasoline tax	5,050,000	7,125,000	13,375,000	17,150,000	22,333,333	25,400,000
Mineral tax[3]	38,750			900,000	1,260,000	1,150,000
Insurance tax				625,000	648,333	850,000
Motor licences	2,556,250	3,275,000	5,188,250	7,653,800	7,516,667	8,100,000
Liquor revenue[4]	4,925,000	6,875,000		10,000,000	13,083,333	13,750,000
Public revenues[5]	1,837,500	1,650,000				
Wild lands tax	2,750	475				
Other taxes	35,000	40,000	58,750	161,500	268,333	200,000
Total	20,514,644	34,151,050	42,346,558	65,230,793	77,380,420	121,319,787

Note: Saskatchewan levied and collected taxes (estimated) are shown for each of the four terms of the Douglas government plus one year of the CCF's fifth term of office. The first year of the Woodrow Lloyd government, 1962–3, is also shown.

1 Also referred to as family tax.

2 Education and hospitalization.

3 Accounting practices in respect of mineral tax revenues varied: sometimes they were shown separately; sometimes they were lumped under mineral resources revenues. From 1957–8 on, the mineral tax revenues were consistently accounted for as such.

4 Liquor revenues (profits) in the third term of office were not taken into estimated revenues of the Consolidated Revenue Fund, as had been the practice, and was to be resumed in the fourth and fifth terms of office. Instead they were used to reduce the debt and some- times to finance investments in Crown enterprises.

5 A property tax.

Notes

The references in the endnotes fall into two general categories: those that pre-date 1963, which are almost entirely primary sources, and those dated from 1963 through 2002, which are for the most part secondary sources.

The citations of primary sources are drawn from my Ph.D. thesis, 'Biography of a Government: Policy Formulation in Saskatchewan, 1944–61' (Harvard University, 1963). Today, the following records may be found in the Saskatchewan Archives: Legislative Assembly documents – statutes of Saskatchewan, *Journals of the Legislative Assembly*, throne speeches, and budget speeches; government of Saskatchewan documents – minutes of Executive Council (cabinet minutes), ministerial reports to the premier, submissions to the Economic Advisory and Planning Board, minutes of the EAPB, budget submissions, and Treasury Board minutes (all consolidated in the T.C. Douglas papers); ministerial papers (T.C. Douglas, W.S. Lloyd, C.M. Fines); reports of royal commissions and Crown corporations; CCF Party documents – CCF Saskatchewan Section records, electoral programs, and other party correspondence/documents (to be found in the T.C. Douglas papers); and Saskatchewan newspapers and radio broadcasts.

Published works are cited in full in the first reference to them in the endnotes.

1: The Roots of the CCF in Saskatchewan and Canada

1 *Saskatchewan Commonwealth*, 28 June 1944. This is the CCF Party weekly newspaper, which began publication in 1936 and has continued since. Microfilm files of this newspaper are available in the Legislative Library, Regina.
2 *Regina Leader Post*, 14 June 1944, p. 11.
3 See the report by Sir William Beveridge (Great Britain, Inter-departmental Committee on Social Insurance and Allied Services, *Social Insurance and Allied Services* [New York: Macmillan, 1942]).

4 President Roosevelt's annual State of the Union Message to Congress on 6 January 1941 read in part: 'The first is freedom of speech and expression – everywhere in the world. The second is freedom of every person to worship God in his own way – everywhere in the world. The third is freedom from want – which, translated into world terms, means economic understandings which will secure to every nation a healthy peaceful life for its inhabitants – everywhere in the world. The fourth is freedom from fear – which, translated into world terms, means a worldwide reduction of armaments to such a point and in such a thorough fashion that no nation will be in a position to commit an act of aggression against any neighbor – anywhere in the world.'

5 Indeed, in 1944 the Liberals had been the governing party during thirty-four years of Saskatchewan's thirty-nine-year life as a Canadian province.

6 John H. Archer, *Saskatchewan: A History* (Saskatoon: Western Producer Prairie Books, 1980), 236. Much of the story in the next few pages is drawn from this book, from Gerald Friesen's *The Canadian Prairies: A History* (Toronto: University of Toronto Press, 1987), chapters 15 and 16, and from Walter D. Young, *The Anatomy of a Party: The National CCF, 1932–61* (Toronto: University of Toronto Press, 1969).

7 See Archer, *Saskatchewan: A History*, 259.

8 See ibid., 257.

9 Friesen, *The Canadian Prairies: A History*, 396.

10 Archer, *Saskatchewan: A History*, 232.

11 Ibid., 260.

12 Background on the province of Saskatchewan and its people is available from many sources. This study has drawn from Archer, *Saskatchewan: A History*; C.F. Conway, *The West: The History of a Region in Confederation* (Toronto: Lorimer, 1983); Friesen, *The Canadian Prairies*; David Laycock, *Populism and Democratic Thought in the Canadian Prairies, 1910 to 1945* (Toronto: University of Toronto Press, 1990); Dean E. McHenry, *The Third Force in Canada: The Cooperative Commonwealth Federation 1932–1948* (Toronto: Oxford University Press, 1950); and Young, *The Anatomy of a Party:* Earlier sources include *A Submission by the Government of Saskatchewan to the Royal Commission on Dominion-Provincial Relations* (Canada: King's Printer, 1937) and George E. Britnell, *The Wheat Economy* (Toronto: University of Toronto Press, 1939).

13 See *A Submission by the Government of Saskatchewan to the Royal Commission on Dominion-Provincial Relations*; and Seymour M. Lipset, *Agrarian Socialism* (Berkeley: University of California Press, 1950).

14 Lipset, *Agrarian Socialism*, 38.

15 *A Submission by the Government of Saskatchewan to the Royal Commission on Dominion-Provincial Relations*, 223.

16 See Lipset, *Agrarian Socialism*, 40.

17 W.L. Morton, *The Progressive Party in Canada* (Toronto: University of Toronto Press, 1950), 15.

18 Ibid., 15–16.

19 See L.H. Thomas, 'The Saskatchewan Society,' unpublished lecture delivered in Regina on 3 May 1962.

20 Morton, *The Progressive Party in Canada*, 46.

21 Laycock, *Populism and Democratic Thought in the Canadian Prairies*, 70.

22 Ibid., 287.

23 Friesen, *The Canadian Prairies*, 367.

24 These events are described fully in Morton, *The Progressive Party in Canada*, and in John H. Archer, 'The Political Development of Saskatchewan,' unpublished paper, n.d.).

25 John Richards and Larry Pratt, *Prairie Capitalism: Power and Influence in the New West* (Toronto: McClelland and Stewart, 1979), 30–1.

26 Archer, *Saskatchewan: A History*, 194.

27 Laycock, *Populism and Democratic Thought in the Canadian Prairies*, 64.

28 S.W. Yates, *The Saskatchewan Wheat Pool* (Saskatoon: UFC, Saskatchewan Section, 1947), 57.

29 Archer, *Saskatchewan*, 194ff.

30 For a full review of the complexities of the farmers' movement in Saskatchewan in the 1920s, see Duff Spafford, 'The "Left Wing" 1921–31,' in *Politics in Saskatchewan*, ed. Norman Ward and Duff Spafford (Don Mills: (Longmans Canada Ltd, 1968), 44.

31 Laycock, *Populism and Democratic Thought in the Canadian Prairies*, 150.

32 Walter Stewart, *M.J.: The Life and Times of M.J. Coldwell* (Toronto: Stoddart, 2000), 82.

33 See Archer, *Saskatchewan: A History*, 224. Walter Young (*The Anatomy of a Party*, 21) gives the year as 1926.

34 George Williams became the first president of the CCF in Saskatchewan.

35 See 'Farm Income,' in the *Report of the Royal Commission on Agriculture and Rural Life*, vol. 13 (Regina: Queen's Printer, 1956), 7.

36 See 'Farm Income,' 64.

37 See 'Land Tenure,' in *Report of the Royal Commission on Agriculture and Rural Life*, vol. 5 (Regina: Queen's Printer, 1956), 24.

38 Stewart, *M.J.*, 94.

39 Doris French Shackleton, *Tommy Douglas* (Toronto: McClelland and Stewart, 1975), 64; and Archer, *Saskatchewan*, 824–5.

40 Lewis H. Thomas, ed., *The Making of a Socialist: The Recollections of T.C. Douglas* (Edmonton: University of Alberta Press, 1982), 74.

41 See, for example, *The Commonwealth*, 4 Dec. 1957; M.J. Coldwell, *Canadian Progressives on the March* (New York: League for Industrial Democracy, 1945); M.J. Coldwell, *Left Turn, Canada* (Toronto: Duell, Sloan and Pierce, 1945); Co-operative Commonwealth Federation (Saskatchewan Section), 'How the CCF Got Started' (mimeographed paper, n.d.); Lipset, *Agrarian Socialism*; Grace MacInnis, *J.S. Woodsworth: A Man to Remember* (Toronto: Macmillan, 1953); McHenry, *The Third Force in Canada;* Kenneth McNaught, *A Prophet in Politics* (Toronto: University of Toronto Press, 1959); Morton, *The Progressive Party in Canada*; Dorothy G. Steeves, *The Compassionate Rebel* (Vancouver: The Boag Foundation, 1960); and Young, *The Anatomy of a Party*. I am also greatly indebted to Clarence M. Fines, former minister of finance in Saskatchewan, for his description to me of the events of the Calgary and Regina Conferences.

42 McHenry, *The Third Force in Canada*, 25.

43 MacInnis, *J.S. Woodsworth*, 268.

44 McHenry, *The Third Force in Canada*, 29.

45 William Irvine quoted in Laycock, *Populism and Democratic Thought on the Prairies*, 118.

46 See chapter 3 in Laycock, *Populism and Democratic Thought in the Canadian Prairies*; Friesen, *The Canadian Prairies*, 356, 374–81; William Kirby Ralph, *Henry Wise Wood of Alberta* (Toronto: University of Toronto Press, 1950); and chapter 2 in C.B. Macpherson, *Democracy in Alberta: Social Credit and the Party System* (Toronto: University of Toronto Press, 1953).

47 Quoted in Laycock, *Populism and Democratic Thought in the Canadian Prairies*, 121.

48 David Laycock holds that 'from 1926 to 1934, the UFC (SS) was dominated by the leftwing of the agrarian movement in the province, most notably by CCF leader-to-be George Williams' (*Populism and Democratic Thought in the Canadian Prairies*, 138).

49 Laycock, *Populism and Democratic Thought in the Canadian Prairies*, 193.

50 See chapter 4 in Laycock, *Populism and Democratic Thought in the Canadian Prairies*; Friesen, *The Canadian Prairies*, 424; Stewart, *M.J.*, 98; and Young, *The Anatomy of a Party*, 21–2, 30–1, 40, 54, and 76.

51 Tommy Douglas, as the son of a printer from Scotland, would have been influenced by the labour movement and would have been keenly aware of the Winnipeg General Strike and the issues raised by these events.

52 See chapter 10 in MacInnis, *J.S. Woodsworth*; chapter 7 in McNaught, *A Prophet in Politics*; and chapter 4 in Steeves, *The Compassionate Rebel*.

53 CCF (SS), 'How the CCF Got Started' (mimeographed paper, n.d.), J.S. Woodsworth, presidential address to Regina Convention, 1933.

54 Stewart, *M.J.*, 82.
55 Salem Goldworth Bland, *The New Christianity* (1920; rpt. Toronto: University of Toronto Press, 1973), 28.
56 McNaught, *A Prophet in Politics*, 51.
57 Adam Ulam, *Philosophical Foundations of English Socialism* (Cambridge: Harvard University Press, 1951), 24. See also Lord Lindsay, Introduction in *Lectures on the Principles of Political Obligation*, by Thomas Hill Green (London: Longmans, 1960), xviii.
58 Ulam, *Philosophical Foundations of English Socialism*, 24. See also Crane Brinton on T.H. Green in his *English Political Thought in the Nineteenth Century* (New York: Harper & Bros, 1962). For example: '... as Liberals we shall encourage labour unions, cooperative socialism, the various forms of social insurance ... and similar measures' (223).
59 Ulam, *Philosophical Foundations of English Socialism*, 20–1.
60 'The Regina Manifesto,' Co-operative Commonwealth Federation Program, adopted at the First National Convention, held at Regina, Saskatchewan, July 1933.
61 Lipset, *Agrarian Socialism*, 106.
62 Thomas H. McLeod and Ian McLeod, *Tommy Douglas: The Road to Jerusalem* (Edmonton: Hurtig, 1987), 55.
63 Archer, *Saskatchewan*, 254.
64 Shackleton, *Tommy Douglas*, 84.
65 McLeod and McLeod, *Tommy Douglas*, 62.
66 CCF (SS) Records, minutes of the Fourth Annual CCF (SS) Convention, 1939.
67 T.C. Douglas, 'The Candidates, 1944,' radio broadcast, 1944.
68 Archer, *Saskatchewan*, 255.
69 Shackleton, *Tommy Douglas*, 119–23.
70 T.C. Douglas, 'Religion and the CCF,' radio broadcast, 1944.
71 CCF (SS) Records, C.M. Fines, presidential address to the Eighth Annual CCF (SS) Convention, 14–16 July 1943.
72 Notes from the addresses of David Lewis, CCF national secretary, at the Regina CCF Winter School as reported in the *Saskatchewan Commonwealth*, 12 Jan. 1944.
73 T.C. Douglas, 'CCF and Education,' radio broadcast, 1944. See also T.C. Douglas, 'Religion and the CCF,' radio broadcast, 1944; and M.J. Coldwell, 'Monetary Policy,' radio broadcast, 1943.
74 T.C. Douglas, 'CCF and Co-operatives,' radio broadcast, 1944.
75 C.M. Fines, 'Equal Educational Opportunities,' a radio broadcast reported in the *Saskatchewan Commonwealth*, 10 May 1944.

76 CCF (SS) Records, report of the provincial leader (T.C. Douglas) to the Eighth Annual CCF (SS) Convention, 14–16 July 1943.

77 Laycock, *Populism and Democratic Thought in the Canadian Prairies*, 195.

78 George H. Williams, *Social Democracy in Canada* (Regina, 1936).

79 CCF (SS) Records, 'Economic Policy of the Farmer-Labour Group in Saskatchewan,' as adopted by the Farmer-Labour Convention, 1932.

80 T.C. Douglas, 'What Is the CCF?' radio broadcast, 9 May 1944.

81 Laycock, *Populism and Democratic Thought in the Canadian Prairies*, 169–70.

82 Young, *The Anatomy of a Party*, 114.

83 Ibid., 109.

84 T.D. Douglas, 'What Is the CCF?' radio broadcast, 9 May 1944.

85 T.C. Douglas, radio broadcast reproduced in the *Saskatchewan Commonwealth*, 16 Jan. 1944 (accompanied by an editorial article on the same subject).

86 David W. Slater, with two chapters by R.B. Bryce, *War Finance and Reconstruction: The Role of Canada's Department of Finance* (Ottawa: David Slater, 1995), 5.

87 Ibid., 236.

88 Ibid., 244.

89 Irving Brecher, *Monetary and Fiscal Thought and Policy in Canada, 1919–1939* (Toronto: University of Toronto Press, 1957), 27.

90 Allen Mills, *Fool for Christ: The Political Thought of J.S. Woodsworth* (Toronto: University of Toronto Press, 1991), 184.

91 Brecher, *Monetary and Fiscal Thought and Policy in Canada*, 55.

92 Notes from the addresses of David Lewis, CCF national secretary, at the Regina CCF Winter School as reported in the *Saskatchewan Commonwealth*, 12 Jan. 1944.

93 'Social Security,' in *Planning for Freedom*, sixteen lectures given by CCF notables in 1944, and published (mimeographed) by the Ontario CCF, 1944.

94 They were also explicit in their desire for a Bill of Rights, which would guarantee the rights of all citizens, and particularly of minorities. See CCF (SS) records for study papers for the CCF provincial program (1944) on a Bill of Rights, and the federal program advocated by the Provincial Council of the CCF (minutes of the meeting of the CCF (SS) Provincial Council, Regina, 18–19 June 1938).

95 CCF (SS), *What Is the Co-operative Commonwealth Federation?* (ca. 1935).

96 See CCF (SS) Records, minutes of the First Annual CCF (SS) Convention, 15–17 July 1936.

97 T.C. Douglas, 'Big Business versus the People,' radio broadcast, 14 Dec. 1943.

98 See CCF (SS) Records, minutes of the CCF (SS) Provincial Council, 10–11 Jan. 1942; CCF (SS) Constitution, 1944–5, s 17(2); and brief from the

Saskatchewan CCF members of Parliament to the retiring CCF (SS) Provincial Council, 1939–40.

99 George H. Williams, radio broadcast, 24 March 1936.

100 Douglas seems to have meant 'capable of being explained,' not 'responsible'; he had eight years in Parliament when he made this speech and well understood where cabinet responsibility lay.

101 See CCF (SS) Records, 'What Will We Do with Our Freedom?'; and T.C. Douglas, 'The Growth of Bureaucracy in Canada,' radio broadcast, 19 Jan. 1943.

2: Planning the Program for a CCF Government

1 CCF (SS) Records, Co-operative Commonwealth Federation (Saskatchewan Section), Constitution, 1944–5, Article 16, Section 1.

2 Ibid., Article B, Section 5(c).

3 Ibid., Article 16, Section 2. The council was made up of one representative from each constituency; three members elected by the provincial convention; the president, vice-president, and political leader of the provincial CCF; two MLAs elected by the provincial CCF caucus; and one MP elected by the federal CCF caucus. It met at least twice annually.

4 Ibid., Article 15.

5 Ibid., Article 17, Sections 1 and 2.

6 CCF (SS) Records, minutes of meeting of the CCF (SS) Provincial Council, 27–8 Sept. 1941.

7 CCF (SS) Records, minutes of meetings of the CCF (SS) Provincial Council, 14 July 1942, 9 Jan. 1943, and 9 Oct. 1943.

8 CCF (SS) Records, minutes of meeting of the CCF (SS) Economic Planning Committee, 15–16 Jan. 1944.

9 CCF (SS) Records, minutes of meetings of the CCF (SS) Provincial Council, 1941–4.

10 McLeod and McLeod, *Tommy Douglas: The Road to Jerusalem*, 111; and interview with Thomas H. McLeod, 19 Oct. 2000.

11 CCF, *Program for Saskatchewan* (1944).

12 CCF (SS) Records, T.C. Douglas, letter to David Lewis, national secretary of the CCF, 17 Dec. 1937.

13 T.C. Douglas, 'Saskatchewan's Place in a New Society,' radio broadcast, 1944.

14 The issue of 'fiscal balance,' or 'fiscal imbalance,' between the provinces' fiscal requirements, given their constitutional responsibilities, and their fiscal capacities, given the relative occupancy of direct tax fields by the national government, became a hardy perennial on federal-provincial agendas in the

post-war years. For more on this, during the years 1944 to 1962, see the Annex on financing the CCF government.

15 *Mineral Rights in Saskatchewan* (Regina: Saskatchewan Energy and Mines, 2000), 4–5. This figure represents 70 per cent of the mineral rights in the 'surveyed area' of the province in 1930. In the non-surveyed area – the northern 'half' of Saskatchewan – the province owned 100 per cent of the mineral rights.

16 CCF (SS) Records, report of the Committee on Natural Resources, January 1944.

17 CCF, *Program for Saskatchewan* (1944).

18 The Industrial Development Board had been established by the Saskatchewan Board of Trade and was supported by the provincial government. Undoubtedly the CCF had been influenced by the logic of the case (T.H. McLeod, 'Public Enterprise in Saskatchewan: The Development of Public Policy and Administrative Control' [Ph.D. diss., Harvard, 1959]).

19 CCF, *Program for Saskatchewan* (1944).

20 CCF (SS) Records, minutes of meeting of the CCF (SS) Economic Planning Committee, 15–16 June 1944.

21 CCF, *Program for Saskatchewan* (1944).

22 CCF (SS) Records, minutes of meeting of the CCF (SS) Economic Planning Committee, 15–16 Jan. 1944.

23 *Saskatchewan Commonwealth*, 1 March 1944, report of a speech in the Legislative Assembly by J.L. Phelps, CCF MLA for Saltcoats.

24 CCF, *Program for Saskatchewan* (1944).

25 C.A.L. Hogg, 'A Plan for the Development of Natural Resources of Northern Saskatchewan.' When T.C. Douglas resigned as premier, he turned over to his successor the administrative files pertinent to the office. However, he retained a number of personal papers referring to party matters and so on. These had not yet been turned over to the provincial CCF Party or to the Saskatchewan Archives at the time I wrote my thesis, and are hereafter referred to as Douglas Papers. The item by C.A.L. Hogg is in this collection.

26 CCF (SS) Records, confidential memorandum for delegates to the National Conference on Provincial Policy, Regina, 30 Dec. 1943 to 2 Jan. 1944.

27 *Saskatchewan Commonwealth*, 1 March 1944, report of a speech in the Legislative Assembly by J.L. Phelps, CCF MLA for Saltcoats.

28 CCF (SS) Records, minutes of meeting of Natural Resources Committee, 6 Feb. 1944.

29 CCF, *Program for Saskatchewan* (1944).

30 CCF (SS) Records, report of the Committee on Natural Resources, January 1944.

31 CCF (SS) Records, George H. Williams, letter to F.R. Scott, 20 June 1936.

32 *Saskatchewan Commonwealth*, 4 April 1944, report of a speech in the Legislative Assembly by J.L. Phelps, CCF MLA for Saltcoats.

33 T.H. McLeod, 'Public Enterprise in Saskatchewan: The Development of Public Policy and Administrative Control' (Ph.D. diss., Harvard, 1959).

34 CCF (SS) Records, minutes of the Eight Annual CCF (SS) Convention, 14–16 July 1943.

35 Ibid.

36 Interview with Clarence M. Fines, 1960.

37 CCF (SS) Records, minutes of the Natural Resources Committee and of the Economic Planning Committee. See also *Saskatchewan Commonwealth*, 1 March 1944, report of a speech in the Legislative Assembly by J.L. Phelps, CCF MLA for Saltcoats.

38 CCF, *Program for Saskatchewan* (1944).

39 The 1938 seed grain loan from the government of Canada to the government of Saskatchewan amounted to $16.5 million, about one half of the province's annual budget. See McLeod and McLeod, *Tommy Douglas: The Road to Jerusalem*, 135.

40 T.C. Douglas, 'Security and Debt Adjustment,' radio broadcast, 26 June 1943.

41 CCF, *Program for Saskatchewan* (1944).

42 T.C. Douglas, 'The Farmer and the World of Tomorrow,' in *Planning for Freedom*, sixteen lectures given by CCF notables in 1944, and published (mimeographed) by the Ontario CCF, 1944.

43 CCF (SS) Records, confidential memorandum for delegates to the National Conference on Provincial Policy, Regina, 30 Dec. 1943 to 2 Jan. 1944.

44 Ibid.

45 CCF (SS) Records, minutes of meeting of the CCF (SS) Economic Planning Committee, 15–16 Jan. 1944.

46 CCF (SS) Records, provincial platform adopted at the First Annual CCF (SS) Convention, 15–17 July 1936.

47 See 'Social Security' and Dr F.T. Nicholson, 'Socialized Health Services,' in *Planning for Freedom*.

48 'Social Security,' in *Planning for Freedom*.

49 CCF (SS) Records, interim report of the CCF (SS) Social Service Committee, 14 Dec. 1941.

50 T.C. Douglas, 'Socialized Health Services,' radio broadcast, 9 Feb. 1943.

51 CCF (SS) Records, 'Economic Policy of the Farmer-Labour Group in Saskatchewan,' as adopted by the Farmer-Labour Convention, 1932.

52 CCF, *Program for Saskatchewan* (1944).

53 CCF (SS) Records, report of the Education Investigation Committee, 11 Jan. 1942.
54 CCF (SS) Records, confidential memorandum for delegates to the National CCF Conference on Provincial Policy, Regina, 30 Dec. 1943 to 2 Jan. 1944.
55 CCF (SS) Records, minutes of the meeting of the CCF (SS) Economic Planning Committee, 15–16 Jan. 1944.
56 CCF, *Program for Saskatchewan* (1944).
57 A reminder that municipal governments had begun, in the 1920s, employing doctors to provide medical services within their jurisdictions, and this scheme had become widespread by 1944.
58 CCF, *Program for Saskatchewan* (1944).
59 CCF (SS) Records, first report of the Labour Investigating Committee, 1 Nov. 1941.
60 CCF (SS) Records, brief from the Labour Committee.
61 *Saskatchewan Commonwealth*, 13 May 1942, report of a speech in the Legislative Assembly by J.L. Phelps, CCF MLA for Saltcoats.
62 CCF (SS) Records, minutes of the Eighth Annual CCF (SS) Convention, 14–16 July 1943.
63 CCF (SS) Records, minutes of meeting of CCF (SS) Provincial Council, 9 Oct. 1943.
64 T.C. Douglas, 'Saskatchewan's Place in a New Society,' radio broadcast, 1944.
65 CCF (SS) Records, minutes of meeting of the CCF (SS) Economic Planning Committee, 15–16 Jan. 1944.
66 CCF (SS) Records, minutes of meeting of the CCF (SS) Provincial Council, 14 July 1942.
67 CCF (SS) Records, minutes of meeting of the CCF (SS) Provincial Council, 13 April 1944.
68 T.C. Douglas, radio broadcast, 12 June 1944.
69 CCF (SS) Records, minutes of meeting of the CCF (SS) Economic Planning Committee, 15–16 Jan. 1944.
70 CCF (SS) Records, minutes of the Eighth Annual CCF (SS) Convention, 14–16 July 1943.
71 CCF, *Program for Saskatchewan* (1944).
72 Escott Reid, 'The Saskatchewan Liberal Machine before 1929,' *Canadian Journal of Economics and Political Science* 2 (1936): 31.
73 CCF (SS) Records, minutes of meeting of the CCF (SS) Economic Planning Committee, 15–16 Jan. 1944.
74 CCF (SS) Records, minutes of the Eighth Annual CCF (SS) Convention, 14–16 July 1943.
75 George H. Williams, radio broadcast, 24 March 1936.

76 CCF (SS) Records, minutes of the CCF (SS) Provincial Council, 15–16 Nov. 1937.
77 CCF (SS) Records, minutes of the Fourth Annual CCF (SS) Convention, 12–14 July 1939.
78 T.C. Douglas, 'Saskatchewan's Place in a New Society,' radio broadcast, 1944.
79 *Regina Leader Post*, 17 June 1944, report of interview with premier-elect T.C. Douglas.
80 *Saskatchewan Commonwealth*, 26 Jan. 1944.
81 T.C. Douglas, 'What the CCF Will Do with the Civil Service,' radio broadcast, 1944.
82 CCF (SS) Records, minutes of the Fourth Annual CCF (SS) Convention 12–14 July 1939.
83 CCF (SS) Records, confidential memorandum from one of the CCF planning committees.
84 T.C. Douglas, 'What the CCF Will Do with the Civil Service,' radio broadcast, 1944.
85 G.M.A. Grube, 'Freedom and the CCF,' in *Planning for Freedom.*

3: The First Months of the CCF Government

1 Douglas Papers, various letters dated June and July 1944. See also McLeod and McLeod, *Tommy Douglas*, 120.
2 McHenry, *The Third Force in Canada*, 215
3 See McLeod and McLeod, *Tommy Douglas*, 121–4, for a review of the new ministers. There were two surprises. Many people expected that Jake Benson, a long-time Progressive and favourite among many CCF members, and Tom Johnston, who with George Williams had been one of the leaders in founding the Saskatchewan CCF, would be chosen. Johnston was made Speaker of the House. But Benson, perhaps because he was a relatively unpredictable member of the party and a less than energetic member of the Provincial Council, was left out. In fact, Benson frequently voted against his party in the Legislative Assembly, and finally left the CCF caucus and sat as an independent.
4 For other perspectives of the Douglas cabinet and its membership, see McLeod and McLeod, *Tommy Douglas*, chapter 12; and Shackleton, *Tommy Douglas*, 145–55.
5 Quoted in McLeod and McLeod, *Tommy Douglas*, 183.
6 The perspective and insights in this part of the story are derived from personal discussions with the various ministers over the nineteen years that I served in the Saskatchewan public service.

7 'Speech from the Throne,' in Saskatchewan, *Journals of the Legislative Assembly*, October 1944.

8 T.C. Douglas, 'Report Upon the Election,' radio broadcast, July 1944.

9 Saskatchewan, Treasury Department, *Financial Statements*, 1942–3 to 1960–1. Note that in Saskatchewan's accounts the budget is balanced when revenues equal or exceed the total of current plus capital expenditures. Borrowing was required only to finance loans to and investments in SPC and SGT, the return on which would generally exceed the interest on the borrowing. Thus the net debt of the province was not affected.

10 'Speech from the Throne,' in Saskatchewan, *Journals of the Legislative Assembly*, October 1944.

11 *Regina Leader Post*, 30 Oct. 1944.

12 Ibid., 26 Oct. 1944.

13 'Speech from the Throne,' in Saskatchewan, *Journals of the Legislative Assembly*, October 1944.

14 *Saskatchewan Commonwealth*, 6 Sept. 1944.

15 Ibid., 2 Aug. 1944.

16 CCF (SS) Records, brief to the National CCF Conference, Regina, 21 Dec. 1944.

17 Douglas Papers, letter from W.J. Lawless to T.C. Douglas, 12 Oct. 1944, and letter from T.C. Douglas to president of Eastern Collieries, 9 July 1945.

18 While in some areas more than half of the land had the mineral rights invested in the Crown and other areas had much less than half, an overall estimate would have been 70 per cent.

19 *Regina Leader Post*, 4 Nov. 1944. Originally a 5 per cent tax had been proposed, but after hearing representations from the major land companies in the province, this was reduced to 3 per cent.

20 Some insight into the dynamics surrounding these decisions may be gleaned from a story recounted by Premier Douglas's secretary, Eleanor McKinnon. Doris Shackleton relates: 'Eleanor McKinnon saw Joe Phelps as a fearsome presence. She recalled an occasion when Douglas became worried about interruptions during the serious planning sessions the cabinet was holding ... The ministers had gathered in the Council Chamber and Eleanor had instructions to hold all messages. "But Joe wheeled in, late, and hung up his coat telling me, 'I'm expecting an important call. Let me know the moment it comes.' So it came, and I went in and whispered to Phelps. Tommy beckoned to me and said, 'I told you not to call anyone out.' I just said, 'I know you did, but I'm much more afraid of him than I am of you'"' (Shackleton, *Tommy Douglas*, 148).

21 These records were made available through the courtesy of the Honourable C.M. Fines, provincial treasurer, 1944 to 1960.

22 CCF (SS) Records, brief to the National CCF Conference, Regina, 21 Dec. 1944.
23 Ibid., study papers for discussion of CCF provincial program, 1944.
24 Interview with J.L. Phelps, 1960.
25 *Saskatchewan Commonwealth,* 13 Dec. 1944.
26 Richards and Pratt, *Prairie Capitalism,* 107.
27 Ibid., chapter 5.
28 The figure of 70 per cent applies to the mineral rights in the 'surveyed area' of the province (Saskatchewan Energy and Mines, *Mineral Rights in Saskatchewan,* October 2000, 4–5).
29 Richards and Pratt, *Prairie Capitalism,* 101 (originally quoted in A.W. Johnson, 'Biography of a Government: Policy Formulation in Saskatchewan, 1944–1961' [Ph.D. diss., Harvard, 1963]).
30 Interview with J.L. Phelps, 1960.
31 In the Saskatchewan government, the principal divisions of departments were usually called branches, and the subdivisions were named divisions.
32 The total population of the north of Saskatchewan was some 10,000 people, and nearly all were 'Registered Indians' or Metis.
33 *Saskatchewan Commonwealth,* 27 and 30 Aug. 1944; and CCF (SS) Records, minutes of meeting of CCF Provincial Council, 8–9 Oct. 1944.
34 McLeod and McLeod, *Tommy Douglas,* 97–102.
35 Saskatchewan, Executive Council, Order in Council 1276/45 (hereafter referred to as O/C with appropriate number).
36 Interview with J.L. Phelps, 1960.
37 *Saskatchewan Commonwealth,* 20 Sept. 1944.
38 O/C 1525/45.
39 Interview with J.L. Phelps, 1960.
40 *Report of the Royal Commission on the Fisheries of the Province of Saskatchewan* (Regina: King's Printer, 1947).
41 O/C 1070/45.
42 *Report of the Royal Commission on the Fisheries of the Province of Saskatchewan,* and *Report of the Royal Commission on Forestry* (Regina: King's Printer, 1947).
43 'Report of the Reconstruction Council,' 2 Aug. 1944.
44 Interview with J.L. Phelps, 1960.
45 *Saskatoon Star Phoenix,* 8 Dec. 1944; *Saskatchewan Commonwealth,* 6 Dec. 1944.
46 O/C 71/45 and O/C 838/45.
47 McLeod and McLeod, *Tommy Douglas,* 117; O/C 661/45 and O/C 724/45.
48 Saskatchewan, Department of Natural Resources and Industrial Development, *Annual Report, 1944–45* (Regina: King's Printer, 1945).
49 CCF (SS) Records, J.L. Phelps, letter to J.M. Cantor, 18 April 1945.
50 O/C 870/45.

51 *Regina Leader Post*, 11 Oct. and 8 Nov. 1944.
52 Saskatchewan Government Insurance Office, 'Celebrating Our Fiftieth Year' (monograph), Regina, December 1955.
53 *Regina Leader Post*, 11 Oct. and 8 Nov. 1944.
54 *Saskatchewan Commonwealth*, 6 Dec. 1944.
55 O/C 373/45.
56 Saskatchewan, Executive Council, minutes of cabinet, 26 July 1945.
57 O/C 1013/44.
58 *Health* [Regina], Autumn 1944.
59 *Report of the Saskatchewan Health Services Survey Commission* (Regina: King's Printer, October 1944).
60 'Speech from the Throne,' in Saskatchewan, *Journals of the Legislative Assembly*, October 1944.
61 The Health Services Planning Commission was later headed by Dr Fred Mott, then the deputy surgeon general of the United States, who brought with him another outstanding U.S. expert, Dr Len Rosenfeld of the U.S. Public Health Service. Both provided distinguished direction in the establishment of the Saskatchewan Hospital Services Plan (1947).
62 'Report of the Health Services Planning Commission,' 15 Feb. 1945.
63 Ibid.
64 'Speech from the Throne,' in Saskatchewan, *Journals of the Legislative Assembly*, October 1944.
65 *Saskatchewan Commonwealth*, 30 Aug. 1944.
66 O/C 1571/44.
67 Saskatchewan Legislative Assembly, 'Budget Speech,' 15 March 1945, as delivered by the Honourable C.M. Fines (hereafter referred to as 'Budget Speech' with appropriate date).
68 *Regina Leader Post*, 8 Nov. 1944.
69 *Statutes of Saskatchewan 1944* (Second Session) c.69, s.25, ss (1).
70 This Act was passed in 1944, but because of federal wartime legislation did not come into effect until 1 July 1946.
71 See chapter 10 on labour reform, in McLeod and McLeod, *Tommy Douglas*, for a fuller account of the labour policies of the late 1940s.
72 O/C 1612/45.
73 Diane Lloyd, *Woodrow: A Biography of W.S. Lloyd* (The Woodrow Lloyd Memorial Fund, 1979), back cover.
74 *Regina Leader Post*, 8 Nov. 1944.
75 Ibid. See also Douglas Papers, Honourable W.S. Lloyd, memo to the premier, 23 Sept. 1944.

76 Douglas Papers, Honourable W.S. Lloyd, memo to the premier, 23 Sept. 1944.

77 *Regina Leader Post*, 29 March 1945.

78 Interviews with the Honourable W.S. Lloyd and Deputy Ministers A. McCallum and R.J. Davidson.

79 Watson Thomson, 'Memo on Adult Education Theory and Policy,' Regina, 1944.

80 CCF (SS) Records. The content is drawn from a report of the Honourable O.W. Valleau to the CCF Provincial Council, 8–9 Oct., 1944; and the 'Report of the Committee on Provincial Municipal Relations,' 1950.

81 Saskatchewan, Department of Co-operation and Co-operative Development, *Annual Report, 1944–45* (Regina, 1945); also an interview with the deputy minister of co-operation and co-operative development in 1962.

82 See *Report from Your Government* (Regina: Bureau of Publications, January 1948); and 'Speech from the Throne,' in Saskatchewan, *Journals of the Legislative Assembly*, October 1944.

83 T.C. Douglas, radio broadcast, 25 Sept., 1945.

84 T.C. Douglas, radio broadcasts, 14 Feb. 1945 and 6 Feb. 1946; and *The Seed Grain Dispute* (Regina: Bureau of Publications, n.d.).

85 'Speech from the Throne,' in Saskatchewan, *Journals of the Legislative Assembly*, October 1944.

86 'Speech from the Throne,' in Saskatchewan, *Journals of the Legislative Assembly*, 1945.

87 'Budget Speech,' 15 March 1945, p. 15.

88 Ibid.

89 Saskatchewan, Treasury Department, financial statements, 1944–61. 'Expenditures' included ordinary and capital expenditures, but not investment in government corporations.

90 'Budget Speech,' 15 March 1945, p. 18.

91 CCF (SS) Records, minutes of CCF Conference on Provincial Policy, 29 Dec. 1944 to 1 Jan. 1945.

92 Douglas Papers, letter dated 18 Sept. 1944.

4: New Wine in Old Vessels

1 Personal interview with T.H. McLeod, October 2000.

2 See J.L. Granatstein, *The Ottawa Men: The Civil Service Mandarins, 1935–1957* (Toronto: Oxford University Press, 1982), 198–207, for a description of the initiatives undertaken by Arnold Heeney, who was appointed clerk of the

Privy Council in 1940, as he began to introduce organization and systems into the functioning of the cabinet War Committee and to establish a cabinet secretariat. 'Almost single-handedly Heeney ... carried the Canadian government into the modern era' (207).

3 For a discussion of collectivist as opposed to individualistic principles in Saskatchewan, see Robert I. McLaren, *The Saskatchewan Practice of Public Administration in Historical Perspective* (Lewiston, NY: The Edwin Mellen Press, 1998), 92 ff.

4 'Speech from the Throne,' in Saskatchewan, *Journals of the Legislative Assembly*, October 1944.

5 CCF (SS) Records, minutes of meeting of CCF Provincial Council, 14 July 1944.

6 CCF (SS) Records, minutes of meeting of CCF Provincial Executive, 25 Aug. 1944.

7 Douglas Papers, CCF provincial president, letter to Premier T.C. Douglas, 20 Sept. 1944.

8 Ibid.

9 CCF (SS) Records, minutes of meeting of CCF Provincial Council, 8–9 Oct. 1944.

10 CCF (SS) Records, minutes of meeting of CCF Provincial Council, 10 Feb. 1945.

11 CCF (SS) Records, minutes of CCF Conference on Provincial Policy, 29 Dec. 1944–1 Jan. 1945.

12 CCF (SS) Records, minutes of meetings of CCF Provincial Council, 28–9 July 1945 and 8–9 Oct. 1944.

13 CCF (SS) Records, minutes of meetings of CCF Provincial Council, 1944.

14 Ibid., and memo to all ministers, 5 Feb. 1945.

15 CCF (SS) Records, minutes of meetings of CCF Provincial Executive, 1944–5.

16 CCF (SS) Records, minutes of meeting of CCF Provincial Council, 10 Feb. 1945.

17 CCF (SS) Records, report of the political leader (Premier T.C. Douglas) to the Twelfth Annual CCF (SS) Convention, 29–31 July 1947.

18 CCF (SS) Records, minutes of meeting of CCF Provincial Council 10 Feb. 1945.

19 Douglas Papers, Premier T.C. Douglas, letter to a CCF MLA, 7 Sept. 1944.

20 Ibid.

21 Douglas Papers, caucus chairman, letter to all CCF MLAs, 24 Jan. 1946.

22 Douglas Papers, report on the Executive Council staff, 12 July 1944.

23 'Speech from the Throne,' in Saskatchewan, *Journals of the Legislative Assembly*, October 1944.

24 O/C 1270/44.

25 G.E. Britnell, letter to premier, 4 Nov. 1944.

26 Douglas Papers, report to the premier from the Economic Advisory Committee, 1945, with respect to revenue sources. The committee examined motor vehicle fees (report to the premier on motor vehicles, 13 Feb. 1945), a gasoline tax (report to premier on the gasoline tax, 13 Feb. 1945), a tax on interest, which was judged to be unconstitutional ('A Tax on Interest,' 16 Feb. 1945), the incidence of the sales tax (report and recommendations on the education tax, 1 Nov. 1945), and the corporation tax (minutes of the seventh meeting of the Economic Advisory Committee, 10 July 1945).

27 CCF (SS) Records, report of the Economic Advisory Committee, 21 Aug. 1945.

28 Douglas Papers, Premier T.C. Douglas, letter to G.W. Cadbury, 14 June 1945.

29 Saskatchewan, Executive Council, minutes of cabinet, 14 Aug. 1945.

30 O/C 1131/45.

31 The members of the Treasury Board were its Chair, Clarence M. Fines, the treasurer, the premier, Jack Corman, and Tom Lax, the deputy treasurer.

32 Saskatchewan, Executive Council, minutes of cabinet, 1944–6.

33 Interview with cabinet minister, 1961.

34 Interview with cabinet minister, 1960.

35 T.H. McLeod, 'Public Enterprise in Saskatchewan: The Development of Public Policy and Administrative Control' (Ph.D. diss., Harvard, 1959).

36 Saskatchewan, Department of Labour, budget submission, 1948–9.

37 The CCF *Program* had referred to the Bureau of Child Protection reporting to the minister of highways.

38 T.C. Douglas, 'Report upon Election,' radio broadcast, July 1944.

39 This material is drawn from a series of ministerial reports to the premier, dated 6 Feb. 1945, and from records of the Public Service Commission.

40 The source for the number of public servants in 1944 is McLaren, *The Saskatchewan Practice of Public Administration in Historical Perspective*, 95. The source for the number of departing public servants during the period May 1943 to May 1945 is McLeod and McLeod, *Tommy Douglas: The Road to Jerusalem*, 129

41 CCF (SS) Records. See, for example, the demands of the Provincial Executive and the provincial convention that key officials be sympathetic to the CCF (minutes of meeting of CCF Provincial Executive, 23 Sept. 1944, and of the Tenth Annual CCF (SS) Provincial Convention, 4 Nov. 1945).

42 Douglas Papers, memorandum to premier, 6 Feb. 1945.

43 Douglas Papers, T.H. McLeod, memo to the premier, 1945 (exact date unknown).

44 Statutes of Saskatchewan, 1945, c. 17. See McLeod and McLeod, *Tommy Douglas, The Road to Jerusalem* for a complete story of Saskatchewan's Crown corporations.
45 T.C. Douglas, 'Report upon Election,' radio broadcast, July 1944.
46 W.S. Lloyd, radio broadcast, reported in the *Saskatchewan Commonwealth*, 29 Nov. 1944.
47 Douglas Papers, correspondence between the premier and the Canadian Federation of the Blind, June 1944.
48 Douglas Papers, Canadian Association of Social Workers, letter to the premier, 5 Aug. 1944.
49 Douglas Papers, minister of labour, memo to all cabinet ministers, 26 Jan. 1946.
50 Douglas Papers, Saskatchewan Federation of Labour, letter to the minister of labour, 12 Sept. 1944.
51 Douglas Papers, Harris and Nelson, Prince Albert, letter to premier submitting a brief from the Tie Contractors and Lumber and Pulpwood Manufacturers of Northern Saskatchewan, 13 Dec. 1945.
52 Douglas Papers, letter from an Estevan solicitor to the provincial treasurer, 2 Feb. 1946.
53 Douglas Papers, brief from the Flin Flon Board of Trade to Hon. J.L. Phelps, 30 July 1945.
54 Douglas Papers, correspondence, 17 Sept. 1945, 27 June 1945, 15 Aug. 1944, and 26 March 1945.
55 The premier wrote to the Urban Municipal Association on 24 November 1945, for example, suggesting a meeting to discuss the possible expansion of health services and the impact this might have on local government organization. See the Douglas Papers, letter from the premier to the Saskatchewan Urban Municipal Association, 24 Nov. 1945.
56 Douglas Papers, correspondence, 23 July and 28 Sept. 1944.
57 'Speech from the Throne,' in Saskatchewan, *Journals of the Legislative Assembly*, October 1944.
58 'Budget Speech,' 15 March 1945.
59 McLeod and McLeod, *Tommy Douglas*, 134.

5: Transforming the Functioning of Government: 1946–8

1 See Granatstein, *The Ottawa Men*, 198–207.
2 The Douglas government's initiatives in creating new machinery of cabinet government are characterized as the 'institutionalization of Cabinet' by Christopher Dunn in *The Institutionalized Cabinet: Governing in the Western*

Provinces (Montreal and Kingston: McGill-Queen's University Press, 1995), 23–40.

3 Ultimately there would be sixty school units: the forty-five established during 1944–6, another eleven by 1953, and finally another four from 1963 to 1966. See *Rural Education*, Report No. 6 of the Royal Commission on Agriculture and Rural Life (1956), 56; and Lyle Thorson, *Seventy Years of SSTA: A Short History of the Saskatchewan School Trustees' Association* (Regina: Centax of Canada, 1985), 39.

4 McLaren, *The Saskatchewan Practice of Public Administration in Historical Perspective*, 100–1.

5 O/C 158/46, as amended by O/C 1198/46.

6 Minutes of the preparatory meeting of the EAPB, 21 Jan. 1946. The Order in Council establishing the board was passed on 25 Jan. 1946 and was made effective 1 Jan. 1946.

7 EAPB, minutes of the preparatory meeting, 21 Jan. 1946.

8 Ibid.

9 EAPB, minutes of the 21st meeting of section B, 9 Feb. 1948.

10 EAPB, minutes of the preparatory meeting, 21 Jan. 1946; minutes of the meeting of 25 Feb. 1946.

11 Ibid., and EAPB, minutes of the 8th meeting, 29 June 1946. The committee that prepared this report on Crown corporations included Cadbury, McLeod, Shumiatcher, and the deputy minister of natural resources, Henry Lewis.

12 Douglas Papers, memo from G.W. Cadbury to Premier T.C. Douglas, 24 Jan. 1946.

13 EAPB, 'Report on Methods of Organizing Government-Operated Enterprises,' 15 March 1946.

14 EAPB, minutes of the 5th meeting, 22 April 1946.

15 EAPB, Memorandum on Crown corporations of Saskatchewan, Government Finance Office, 1 June 1962.

16 EAPB, 'Program Planning,' planning document prepared for the Executive Council, 9 Sept. 1946.

17 Ibid., and EAPB, Minutes of he 1st meeting of section B, 30 Sept. 1946.

18 Memorandum from Dr M.C. Shumiatcher to the Honourable C.M. Fines, 4 Oct. 1946. This item is from the papers of the Honourable C.M. Fines, provincial treasurer, 1944–1960, hereafter referred to as the Fines Papers.

19 'Speech from the Throne,' in Saskatchewan, *Journals of the Legislative Assembly*, 1947.

20 EAPB, minutes of the 10th and 11th meetings of section B, 7 April and 12 May 1947.

21 EAPB, minutes of the meeting of section B, 30 Sept. 1946.
22 EAPB, 'Program Planning,' planning document prepared for the Executive Council, 9 Sept. 1946.
23 EAPB, minutes of the meeting of section B, 19 Sept. 1946.
24 EAPB, 'A Four Year Plan,' report for discussion at the joint Cabinet–Planning Board Conference of 1 Dec. 1947.
25 Ibid.
26 O/C 168/46.
27 EAPB, minutes of the 14th meeting of section B, 28 July 1947.
28 EAPB, minutes of section A, 18 March 1946.
29 EAPB, 'A Four Year Plan,' report for discussion at the joint Cabinet–Planning Board Conference of 1 Dec. 1947.
30 EAPB, 'Program Planning,' planning document prepared for the Executive Council, 9 Sept. 1946.
31 Saskatchewan, Executive Council, minutes of special cabinet, 19 Sept. 1946.
32 EAPB, report on potash development, 14 April 1947.
33 Saskatchewan, Executive Council, agenda for cabinet meeting, 22 March 1946: recommendations from the EAPB re sodium sulphate development.
34 The history of the Natural Gas Committee is recounted in a memo of 18 Dec. 1952 from T.K. Shoyama (EAPB) to the Honourable J.A. Darling, minister in charge of the Saskatchewan Power Corporation in 1952.
35 EAPB, minutes of the joint Cabinet–Planning Board meeting, 21–6 April 1947.
36 The 'surveyed area' of Saskatchewan is approximately 80 million acres, of which 62.4 million acres of mineral rights were controlled by the province (Saskatchewan Energy and Mines, Mineral Rights in Saskatchewan [October 2000], 4–5).
37 See EAPB, minutes of the 14th meeting of section B, 28 July 1947; and minutes of the special meeting, 7 Aug. 1947. The Saskatchewan Transportation Company was established in January 1946 by O/C 168/46.
38 EAPB, Memorandum from G.W. Cadbury to the acting premier, J.H. Brockelbank, January 29, 1946. Minister Phelps had asked the Cabinet to discuss the same question. See Executive Council, agenda for Cabinet meeting, January 25, 1946.
39 EAPB, minutes of the 2nd meeting, 12–14 March 1946; and Douglas Papers, memorandum from Dr. M.C. Shumiatcher to Premier T.C. Douglas, 10 Jan. 1947.
40 CCF (SS) Records, minutes of the Eleventh Annual CCF (SS) Provincial Convention, 24–6 July 1946.

41 Douglas Papers, correspondence between Dr Carlyle King and Premier T.C. Douglas, February 1947.

42 *Regina Leader Post*, 1 April 1947.

43 EAPB, minutes of 8th meeting, 29 Jan. 1946.

44 Interview with C.A.L. Hogg, 1962.

45 Douglas Papers, correspondence between J. Wellbelove and the premier, 24 June 1947.

46 CCF (SS) Records, minutes of the CCF Provincial Council meeting, 1 Aug. 1947.

47 Douglas Papers, memo from G.W. Cadbury to the premier, 8 March 1948.

48 EAPB, minutes of joint meeting of the cabinet and the EAPB, 26–7 Jan. 1948.

49 EAPB, 'Program Planning,' planning document prepared for the Executive Council, 9 Sept. 1946.

50 EAPB, minutes in early 1947.

51 In other examples, the department's fisheries branch embarked upon biological surveys, the classification of fisheries waters, a propagation program, and a marketing survey. See the annual reports of the Department of Natural Resources, 1946–7, 1947–8, and 1948–9.

52 EAPB, 'A Four Year Plan,' report prepared for discussion at the joint Cabinet–Planning Board meeting, 1 Dec. 1947.

53 EAPB, 'Program Planning,' planning document prepared for the Executive Council, 9 Sept. 1946.

54 Ibid., EAPB, report of the Research Committee on Land Tenure, 20 Dec. 1947; and EAPB, minutes of the 4th meeting, 8 April 1946.

55 EAPB, 'A Four Year Plan,' report, 29 Nov. 1947.

56 EAPB, minutes of 14th meeting of section B, 28 July 1947.

57 EAPB, minutes of special meeting, 7 Aug. 1947.

58 The Saskatchewan Transportation Company was established in January 1946 by O/C 168/46.

59 EAPB, minutes of the 7th meeting, 3 June 1946.

60 EAPB, 'Program Planning,' planning document prepared for the Executive Council, 9 Sept. 1946.

61 EAPB, minutes of the 10th meeting of section A, 10 Nov. 1947.

62 EAPB, 'A Four Year Plan,' report prepared for discussion at the joint cabinet–Planning Board meeting, 1 Dec. 1947.

63 Ibid.

64 Saskatchewan, Treasury Department, financial statements, 1944–61. The EAPB was using ordinary expenditures only, in the calculation, whereas the revised series includes both ordinary and capital expenditures.

65 EAPB, 'Program Planning,' planning document prepared for the Executive Council, 9 Sept. 1946.

66 EAPB, 'A Four Year Plan,' report, 29 Nov. 1947.

67 EAPB, 'Program Planning,' planning document, 9 Sept. 1946.

68 EAPB, 'The Saskatchewan Fishing Industry,' report by G.W. Cadbury, 5 April 1947.

69 EAPB, 'A Four Year Plan,' report, 1 Dec. 1947.

70 EAPB, minutes of the 20th meeting of section B, 23 Jan. 1948.

71 EAPB, minutes of the 3rd meeting, 26 March 1946.

72 EAPB, minutes of the 2nd meeting of section B, 12 Nov. 1946.

73 EAPB, minutes of the 7th meeting of section A, 27 Jan. 1947.

74 EAPB, 'A Four Year Plan, Appendices 1–3,' 12 Dec. 1947.

75 EAPB, 'Budgeting and Administrative Planning,' planning document prepared for the Executive Council, 12 Sept. 1946.

76 EAPB, 'A Four Year Plan,' report, 29 Nov. 1947.

77 EAPB, criticism of the administration of the provincial government, apparently prepared by G.W. Cadbury, 1948.

78 EAPB, minutes of the Cabinet–Planning Board meeting, 26–7, Jan. 1948.

79 EAPB, 'Program Planning,' planning document prepared for the Executive Council, 9 Sept. 1946.

80 Saskatchewan, Executive Council, minutes of special cabinet meeting, 19 Sept. 1946.

81 Saskatchewan, Executive Council, minutes of special cabinet meeting, 17 Sept. 1946.

82 EAPB, 'Budgeting and Administrative Planning,' planning document prepared for the Executive Council, 12 Sept. 1946.

83 For a study of the relationship between planning and budgeting, see my 'Planning and Budgeting,' *Canadian Public Administration*, Sept. 1959.

84 EAPB, minutes of the 5th meeting of section A, 30 Dec. 1946.

85 EAPB, minutes of the meeting of section A, 12 March 1947.

86 EAPB, 'Budgeting and Administrative Planning,' planning document, 12 Sept. 1946.

87 Saskatchewan, Treasury Department, Budget Bureau, administrative management reports, volumes 1 and 2, 1947 and 1948.

88 'Speech from the Throne,' in Saskatchewan, *Journals of the Legislative Assembly*, 1947.

89 EAPB, 'Program Planning,' planning document prepared for the Executive Council, 9 Sept. 1946.

90 'Speech from the Throne,' in Saskatchewan, *Journals of the Legislative Assembly*, 1947.

91 This did not mean they were patronage appointments. Both the Budget Bureau and EAPB positions were filled by Order in Council appointment, but during all my years in the Budget Bureau, and later during my years as deputy minister, I never encountered political interference in the Order in Council appointments I recommended, nor was I requested to make patronage appointments.

92 Howard A. Scarrow, 'Civil Service Commissions in the Canadian Provinces,' *Journal of Politics*, May 1957, p. 245.

93 CCF (SS) Records, minutes of the Twelfth Annual CCF (SS) Provincial Convention, 29–31 July 1947.

94 The *Regina Leader Post* reported: '"Dangerous and retrogressive" summed up the reaction of most civil servants' (3 April 1947).

95 CCF (SS) Records, correspondence, 1947.

96 *Regina Leader Post*, 2 April 1947.

97 A union hospital district was a local government unit responsible for the provision of hospital facilities. The information regarding health programs is drawn from the 'Speech from the Throne' in 1946, 1947, and 1948.

98 Thomas, ed., *The Making of a Socialist*, 230.

99 The decision to implement a flat insurance premium per person was contrary to the CCF's earlier rejection of all 'poll taxes' or flat per capita taxation.

100 The Saskatchewan Hospital Association had grave reservations about the government's ability to put the plan into operation by 1 Jan. 1947.

101 Saskatchewan, Health Services Planning Commission, budget submission for 1948–9.

102 Douglas Papers, letter from the Saskatchewan Association of Rural Municipalities to the premier, 5 Nov. 1947.

103 EAPB, minutes of joint meeting of the cabinet and the EAPB, 1–4 and 9–10 Dec. 1947.

104 Saskatchewan, Executive Council, memo from the Honourable W.S. Lloyd to all cabinet ministers, 13 Jan. 1947.

105 EAPB, 'Program Planning,' planning document prepared for the Executive Council, 9 Sept. 1946.

106 CCF (SS) Records, meeting of the CCF (SS) Provincial Council, 3–4 Jan. 1947.

107 See, for example, 'Submission of Legislative Proposals to the Government of Saskatchewan by the Saskatchewan Federation of Labour,' 2 March 1946.

108 Saskatchewan, Department of Social Welfare, budget submission for 1948–9.

109 EAPB, minutes of joint meeting of the cabinet and the EAPB, 1–4 and 9–10 Dec. 1947.
110 *Regina Leader Post*, 21 Feb. 1948.
111 Douglas Papers, memo from the attorney general to Premier Douglas, 3 March 1947.
112 McHenry, *The Third Force in Canada*, 29.

6: Forging a New Equilibrium in Governance: 1948–52

1 Thomas, ed., *The Making of a Socialist*, 256.
2 T.C. Douglas, 'What Is the CCF?' radio broadcast, 9 May 1944.
3 Premier Douglas in debate on the speech from the throne, in Saskatchwan, *Journals of the Legislative Assembly*, 15–16 Feb. 1949.
4 EAPB, memo on industrial development for the Cabinet–Planning Board Conference, and minutes of the conference, October 1951.
5 It is important to understand that the government borrowed (sold debentures) for the purpose of investing in the public utilities (Saskatchewan Power Corporation and Saskatchewan Government Telephones). Thus, on the government's balance sheet, the indebtedness appeared as a liability, and the investment appeared as an asset (such investment being realistically expected to earn a rate of return higher than the interest being paid on the debentures). The province's net debt was unaffected by the transaction. For a further explanation of Saskatchewan's form of accounts, see Honourable C.M. Fines, *Changes in the Form of Accounts* (Government of the Province of Saskatchewan, December 1957).
6 'Budget Speech,' 2 March 1949, 10.
7 The three problem children were shortly closed, and the other four remained in operation in 1962, when the sodium sulphate plant had turned out to be enormously profitable, the bus and airline companies were 'break even' operations, and the brick plant was a marginal enterprise.
8 Premier Douglas in debate on the speech from the throne, in Saskatchewan, *Journals of the Legislative Assembly*, 15–16 Feb. 1949.
9 CCF (SS) Records. One very prominent member of the CCF is on record as having discerned this trend in policy. In April 1949 he wrote to the CCF Executive: 'Statements are being made which do not, in my opinion ... conform to our original policies and too much consideration is being given to moves on the basis of political expediency' (brief presented to the Executive of the CCF (SS), 1 April 1949).
10 Premier Douglas in a debate, Saskatchewan, *Journals of the Legislative Assembly*, 13 Feb. 1952.

11 CCF (SS) Records, report of political leader (T.C. Douglas) to the Fifteenth CCF (SS) Annual Convention, 2 Nov. 1950.

12 Press statement issued by the premier on 14 Nov. 1949.

13 Saskatchewan, Treasury Department, financial statements, 1944–61. Economic development expenditures included money spent on transportation and communication, natural resources and primary industry, and trade and industrial development.

14 The investment in the Power Corporation went from $2.5 million to $7.1 million, and in the telephone corporation from nil to $2.8 million (Saskatchewan, Treasury Department, statement of amounts advanced to Saskatchewan Government Telephones and Saskatchewan Power Corporation, 1944–45 to 1961–62).

15 'Speech from the Throne,' in Saskatchewan, *Journals of the Legislative Assembly*, 1949.

16 EAPB, minutes of the 37th meeting, 28 March 1949.

17 EAPB, minutes of the 35th meeting, 21 Feb. 1949. An Industrial Committee was established on 17 Oct. 1949, made up of D.H.F. Black (who later was appointed director of industrial development), C.A.L Hogg (deputy minister of natural resources), and George Cadbury, Tommy McLeod, and Tommy Shoyama, all of the Planning Board.

18 Don Black was recommended to Cadbury by Frank Scott, and he served in the same role throughout his career in the Douglas government. He left Saskatchewan in 1964 to take a Master's degree at McGill and then took a position in the Planning Branch of CIDA in Ottawa.

19 EAPB, memo on industrial development for the Cabinet–Planning Board Conference, October 1951.

20 Saskatchewan Executive Council, minute of cabinet, no. 2861, 29 Jan. 1952.

21 See, for example, letter from D.H.F. Black to the president of the Saskatchewan Federated Co-operatives Limited, Jan. 26, 1951, and memorandum from D.H.F. Black to the director of the Purchasing Agency, 13 June 1951 (from the files of the Industrial Development Office).

22 EAPB, policy statement by Premier T.C. Douglas toward the latter part of 1948, quoted in report on fuel policy, prepared by B. Sufrin for the 1949 Cabinet–Planning Board Conference.

23 'Budget Speech,' 2 March 1949.

24 Douglas Papers. One major company acknowledged the premier's invitation to discuss oil regulations in this way: 'You stated that ... if the present statutes and regulations ... were not satisfactory to us, you would appreciate the opportunity of discussing [them] with us' (letter to premier, 15 June 1948).

25 *Regina Leader Post*, 28 March 1952.

26 'Budget Speech,' 2 March 1949.
27 Saskatchewan, Department of Natural Resources, budget submission for 1949–50.
28 See 'Budget Speech,' 2 March 1949, and 27 Feb. 1952, as well as Department of Natural Resources, budget submission for 1949–50.
29 'Budget Speech,' 27 Feb. 1952.
30 Saskatchewan Executive Council, minute of cabinet, no. 672, March 1950.
31 Saskatchewan Executive Council, minute of cabinet, no. 1011, October 1950.
32 EAPB, second special meeting of the Industry and Resource Development Committee, 19 June 1950.
33 EAPB, memo from T.K. Shoyama to the Honourable J.H. Brockelbank reporting discussions between the premier, the Saskatchewan Power Corporation, and the EAPB, 11 Aug. 1950.
34 EAPB, memo to members of the Gas Committee, 27 July 1951.
35 Douglas Papers, memo from the premier to the Honourable C.M. Fines, 10 Aug. 1951.
36 Saskatchewan Executive Council, minute of cabinet, no. 2512, 27 Aug. 1951.
37 EAPB, memo from David Cass-Beggs on natural gas, 17 Sept. 1951. His full report on the costs and revenues of a prospective gas system was submitted in the summer of 1952.
38 Saskatchewan Legislative Assembly, *Debates*, Hon. J.H. Brockelbank speaking on 21 Feb. 1952.
39 Ibid., Mr Tucker speaking on 24 Feb. 1950.
40 'Speech from the Throne,' in Saskatchewan, *Journals of the Legislative Assembly*, first session of the eleventh legislature of Saskatchewan, 1949.
41 'Speech from the Throne,' in Saskatchewan, *Journals of the Legislative Assembly*, 1950.
42 Douglas Papers, letter from the premier to a correspondent in British Columbia, 10 Dec. 1948.
43 Saskatchewan Executive Council, minutes of cabinet, nos. 785 and 804, 1950.
44 CCF (SS) Records, minutes of the Fifteenth Annual CCF (SS) Provincial Convention, 2–4 Nov. 1950, and the Sixteenth Convention, 18–20 July 1951.
45 In addition to these new initiatives, the department extended older programs, including the veterinary districts, grasshopper control, weed control, and the agricultural representative service. There were forty-one 'Ag Reps' by 1952. See *Progress, 1952* (Regina: King's Printer, 1952).
46 This project called for the damming of the South Saskatchewan River to irrigate up to 500,000 acres of land and to install hydroelectric capacity of some 200,000 kilowatts.

47 Douglas Papers, memorandum from B.N. Arnason, deputy minister of co-operation, to the premier, 18 Dec. 1951.
48 Saskatchewan Executive Council, minute of cabinet, no. 2790, 1951.
49 George Cadbury left Saskatchewan in 1951, and for a short period of time Tommy McLeod was secretary of the Planning Board, as well as the deputy provincial treasurer. Shortly thereafter, Tommy Shoyama replaced Tommy McLeod as secretary, and chief of staff, to the EAPB.
50 EAPB, memo from T.K. Shoyama to the premier, 17 Jan. 1952.
51 By the end of 1951 there were 6.3 beds per 1,000 population compared with 3.9 per 1,000 in 1944. The agreed target was 7.5 beds per 1,000, but in the absence of a master hospital location plan some of the beds had been built in the wrong places. A master plan was not prepared until 1950. See *Progress, 1952.*
52 Chairman of the Health Services Planning Commission, memorandum to the minister of public health, 7 Sept. 1950.
53 'Speech from the Throne,' in Saskatchewan, *Journals of the Legislative Assembly*, 1949.
54 Ibid. There were two sessions during this year.
55 'Speech from the Throne,' in Saskatchewan, *Journals of the Legislative Assembly*, 1952.
56 Saskatchewan Executive Council, minute of cabinet, no. 2725, 6 Nov. 1951.
57 See Saskatchewan Department of Social Welfare, budget submissions, 1952–53 and 1953–54; Saskatchewan, *Journals of the Legislative Assembly*, 1949; and Saskatchewan Executive Council, minute of cabinet, no. 955, 1 Aug. 1950
58 EAPB, minutes of Cabinet–Planning Board Conference, 13–17 Sept. 1948.
59 Archer, *Saskatchewan*, 290.
60 Thomas, ed., *The Making of a Socialist*, 320–1.
61 Archer, *Saskatchewan*, 290. The Massey Commission, appointed by the government of Canada in 1949, proposed the creation of the Canada Council, which was to make, and continues to make, a rich contribution to the arts across the whole of the country.
62 Archer, *Saskatchewan*, 292.
63 Granatstein, *The Ottawa Men*, 200–7.
64 EAPB, memo for the Cabinet–Planning Board Conference, 13–20 Sept. 1948.
65 Saskatchewan Executive Council, minute of cabinet, no. 105, 30 Nov. 1948.
66 There had been a faction in the CCF Party that had been immensely loyal to George Williams, the former leader. After this death in 1945, these lingering feelings gradually disappeared.
67 Douglas Papers, memorandum from the premier to J.W.W. Graham, cabinet secretary, 10 Aug. 1950.

68 Saskatchewan, Treasury Department, Budget Bureau reports, 1948–52.

69 Interview with T.K. Shoyama, 11 June 2000.

70 EAPB, agenda for Cabinet–Planning Board meeting, 7–8 April 1949.

71 See, for example, EAPB, minutes of cabinet–Planning Board conference, 1–3 and 8 Dec. 1948.

72 Douglas Papers, memo from the Honourable T.C. Douglas to all cabinet ministers, 6 Sept. 1950.

73 EAPB, minutes of Cabinet–Planning Board Conference, 1–3 and 8 Dec. 1948.

74 EAPB, memo from George Cadbury to Premier Douglas, 21 June 1949.

75 EAPB, memo from George Cadbury to Premier Douglas, 23 Dec. 1948.

76 For more on the Government Finance Office, created in 1947, see Dennis Gruending, *Promises to Keep: A Political Biography of Allan Blakeney* (Saskatoon: Western Producers Prairie Books, 1990), 22–3.

77 EAPB, memo from George Cadbury to Premier Douglas, 9 Aug. 1948; and minutes of the Cabinet–Planning Board Conference, 13–17 Sept. 1948.

78 EAPB, memo from George Cadbury to Premier Douglas, 23 Dec. 1948.

79 An amusing example of trying to maintain happy relations between central agencies and departments is the following exchange between the Budget Bureau and the deputy minister of highways in 1948. Budget Bureau: 'A preliminary check of [your budget] ... would indicate the general excellence of the estimates with the possible exception of lack of work programs and explanations of large increases ... [in] the detailed estimates. Otherwise the format and general neatness are all that can be desired ...' Deputy minister of highways: 'Probably in the case of quite a few codes our estimates were not very close [last year], but we did the best we could under the circumstances and really in the end I cannot see that it will make a great deal of difference.'

80 First meeting of the Committee on Farm Electrification, 7 July 1950; and EAPB, minutes of meeting, 29 Aug. 1950.

81 Thomas, ed., *The Making of a Socialist*, 301.

82 CCF (SS) Records, report from Legislative Advisory Committee to CCF Legislative Group, 13 Jan. 1949.

83 CCF (SS) Records, letter from the president, Saskatchewan CCF, to the premier, 20 July 1950.

84 CCF (SS) Records, letter from John Wellbelove to Premier Douglas, 11 Nov. 1948.

85 Douglas Papers, letter in premier's files, 29 Nov. 1949.

86 CCF (SS) Records, minutes of meeting of Provincial Council, 22 July 1949.

87 EAPB, minutes of Cabinet–Planning Board Conference, 21–25 Nov. 1949.

88 Saskatchewan Executive Council, minute of cabinet, no. 476, 5 Dec. 1949.

89 Ross Thatcher was, first, a CCF member of Parliament, elected in Moose Jaw

in 1945. Ten years later, he left the CCF and ran as a Liberal candidate for Parliament twice. He was defeated both times. Finally, he was chosen the leader of the Saskatchewan Liberals in 1959. He was to become premier in 1964 when the Woodrow Lloyd government was defeated. See Dale A. Eisler, *Rumours of Glory: Saskatchewan and the Thatcher Years* (Edmonton: Hurtig, 1987).

90 Douglas Papers, correspondence between Premier T.C. Douglas and M.J. Coldwell, 25 Feb. 1950.

91 'Report of the Committee on Provincial-Municipal Relations,' 1950.

92 Saskatchewan Executive Council; see notes on cabinet meeting with Rural and Urban Municipal Association, 20 Oct. 1950. See also 'Budget Speech,' 27 Feb. 1952.

93 *Regina Leader Post,* 1 March 1952.

94 CCF (SS) Records, minutes of Seventeenth Annual CCF Provincial Convention, 16–18 July 1952.

95 Saskatchewan Executive Council, minute of cabinet, no. 2284, 27 March 1951.

96 This was the first such committee in the Commonwealth. See Allan E. Blakeney, 'Saskatchewan Crown Corporations,' in *The Public Corporation: A Comparative Symposium,* ed. W. Friedmann (Toronto: University of Toronto School of Law, 1954), 93–107.

97 Douglas Papers, correspondence between the premier and B.N. Arnason, deputy minister of co-operation, 23 Nov. 1950.

98 Douglas Papers, memo from the premier to the minister of labour, 19 Dec. 1951.

99 Douglas Papers, memorandum from the Honourable W.S. Lloyd to Premier Douglas, quoting speech by director of curricula, 15 Sept. 1952.

100 Douglas Papers, correspondence between Premier Douglas and M.J. Coldwell, 4 March 1950.

101 Douglas Papers, memo from the Honourable T.J. Bentley to Premier Douglas, 29 Dec. 1950; and Saskatchewan Executive Council, minutes of cabinet, no. 2768, 30 Nov. 1951, and no. 2888, 19 Feb. 1952.

102 *CCF Program for Progress* (Regina: Service Printing Company, 1952).

7: A Mature Government in Its Third and Fourth Terms

1 *Saskatchewan Economic Review* (Regina: Economic Advisory and Planning Board, March 1962).

2 Archer, *Saskatchewan,* Appendices F and G, 360–3.

3 *Saskatchewan Economic Review,* March 1962.

4 'Budget Speech,' 3 March 1954.
5 *Saskatchewan Economic Review,* March 1962.
6 Ibid., and 'Budget Speech,' 3 March 1954.
7 *Saskatchewan Economic Review,* March 1962.
8 Ibid. Earlier years are not available.
9 It is important, when talking about Saskatchewan's revenues, expenditures, and surplus or deficit, to understand what these terms mean in Saskatchewan's accounts (or, for that matter, in the government of Canada's accounts):
  - Revenues (technically, 'budgetary revenues') include taxes, transfers from the government of Canada, royalties and other returns from Crown-owned resources, fees for licences and permits, etc.
  - Expenditures (technically, 'budgetary expenditures') include (1) current or 'ordinary' expenditures, and (2) capital expenditures, that is, spending on physical assets which, while long-lasting, do not yield a financial return (e.g., roads, buildings, facilities).
  - Surplus or deficit is the difference between budgetary revenues and budgetary expenditures, either increasing or decreasing the province's debt.
  It is equally important to differentiate between loans and investments and capital expenditures. The former are expected to yield a financial return; the latter are not. Examples of loans and investments in Saskatchewan include, in particular, those to the Saskatchewan Power Corporation, to Saskatchewan Government Telephones, and to other Crown enterprises or entities. Such investments were/are included as assets in the government accounts; and, where they were/are financed by government of Saskatchewan borrowing (the issuance of Saskatchewan government bonds), such loans were/are entered in the accounts as liabilities (along with any other indebtedness).
10 Saskatchewan, Treasury Department, financial statements, 1943–4 to 1960–1.
11 'Budget Speech,' 3 March 1954. Only two Canadian governments had a higher rating, the government of Canada and the city of Ottawa.
12 Thomas, ed., *The Making of a Socialist,* 328.
13 C.H. Higginbotham, *Off the Record: The CCF in Saskatchewan* (Toronto: McClelland and Stewart, 1968), 7.
14 Stewart, *M.J.,* 88.
15 Ibid., 94.
16 Ibid., 94 and 100.
17 Lloyd, *Woodrow,* 62.
18 Shackleton, *Tommy Douglas,* 183.

19 McLeod and McLeod, *Tommy Douglas*, 189.

20 Lengthy accounts of the Rawluk affair are to be found in the works cited above, and in Thomas, ed., *The Making of a Socialist*, 304–14.

21 Biographical material on Woodrow Lloyd's life can be found, in particular, in Thomas, ed., *The Making of a Socialist*, and in Lloyd, *Woodrow*

22 Lloyd, *Woodrow*, 72.

23 Ibid., 73.

24 Ibid., 67.

25 Thomas, ed., *The Making of a Socialist*, 327.

26 Lloyd, *Woodrow*, 75.

27 Saskatchewan, Executive Council, minute of cabinet, no. 3194, 9 Sept. 1952.

28 The deputy provincial treasurer, Tommy McLeod, resigned in 1952 to become the dean of the College of Commerce at the University of Saskatchewan.

29 Saskatchewan, Executive Council, minute of cabinet, no. 3741, 24 April 1953; and memorandum from the deputy provincial treasurer to all department heads, 16 July 1953.

30 See, for example, the report of the Treasury Board to the cabinet conference in 1952, when in addition to revenue, expenditure, and borrowing proposals, the board proposed a one-cent increase in gasoline tax and a rise in the per capita hospitalization tax (EAPB, minutes of the Cabinet–Planning Board Conference, 17–31 Oct. 1952).

31 EAPB, minutes of Cabinet–Planning Board Conferences, 1952–55 inclusive.

32 Saskatchewan, Executive Council, minutes of Cabinet, nos. 5102 and 5104, 4 Jan. 1954.

33 In 1952, for example, Shoyama recommended that policy deliberations and administrative action on natural gas development should be transferred from the Gas Committee. The 'focus of responsibility,' he said, should be shifted to the Saskatchewan Power Corporation (EAPB, memorandum from T.K. Shoyama to members of the EAPB, 22 Nov. 1952).

34 Douglas Papers, memorandum from Premier T.C. Douglas to all cabinet ministers, 26 June 1952.

35 EAPB, budget submission for 1955–6.

36 EAPB, budget submission for 1953–4.

37 Saskatchewan, Treasury Department, Budget Bureau, budget submission for 1956–7.

38 Saskatchewan, Executive Council, minute of cabinet, no. 374, 3 Feb. 1953.

39 Endnote 9 describes the new form of accounts.

40 Treasury Board minutes, 25 Sept. 1952.

41 Saskatchewan, Executive Council, minute of cabinet, no. 3101, 16 July 1952.

42 Saskatchewan, Department of Social Welfare, budget submission for 1954–5.

43 CCF (SS) Records. See, for example, the meeting of the Provincial Council on 1 Aug. 1947 and the resolution concerning 'the Government's program of public development of oil resources' passed at the Fourteenth Annual CCF (SS) Convention, 19–21, July 1949.

44 CCF (SS) Records, minutes of the Twelfth Annual CCF (SS) Convention, 29–31 July 1947; and minutes of the Eleventh Annual CCF (SS) Convention, 24–6 July 1946.

45 Douglas Papers, correspondence, 2 March 1949.

46 *CCF Program for Progress* (Regina: Service Printing Company, n.d.).

47 Saskatchewan, Treasury Department, financial statements, 1943–4 to 1960–1.

48 *CCF Program for Prosperity* (Regina: Service Printing Company, 1956).

49 *Regina Leader Post,* 21 June 1956.

50 CCF (SS) Records, minutes of the Twenty-First Annual CCF (SS) Convention, 18 July 1956.

8: Policy Implementation and Reassessment in the 1950s

1 *Saskatchewan Commonwealth,* 6 Dec. 1944.

2 CCF (SS) Records, brief for the national CCF conference, 21 Dec. 1944.

3 EAPB, minutes of 26th meeting of section 'A,' 2 Aug. 1948.

4 Saskatchewan, Executive Council, minute of cabinet, no. 7 (49), 7 Jan. 1949.

5 'Speech from the Throne,' in Saskatchewan, *Journals of the Legislative Assembly,* 1949.

6 Farms that were farther than one mile from the line were not connected. The term 'road allowance' describes the property that has been set aside or allocated for roads.

7 'Speech from the Throne,' in Saskatchewan, *Journals of the Legislative Assembly,* 1951.

8 T.C. Douglas, 'Program Fulfilled,' a speech delivered in the budget debate, 16 March 1956.

9 'Speech from the Throne,' in Saskatchewan, *Journals of the Legislative Assembly,* 1957; and Saskatchewan Power Corporation, *Annual Report,* 1959.

10 Saskatchewan, Executive Council, minute of cabinet, no. 3231, 23 Sept. 1952.

11 EAPB, minutes of meeting of the Gas Committee, 25 Sept. 1952.

12 Saskatchewan, Executive Council, minute of cabinet, no. 3319, 4 Nov. 1952.

13 Saskatchewan, Executive Council, minute of cabinet, no. 3338, 14 Nov. 1952.

14 Douglas Papers, press release, 1 Dec. 1952.

15 Saskatchewan Power Corporation, *Annual Report*, 1952, 13.

16 Saskatchewan Power Corporation, *Annual Report*, 1955.

17 Saskatchewan Power Corporation, budget submission, 1956–7.

18 Saskatchewan, Executive Council, minute of cabinet, no. 6822, 24 Feb. 1956.

19 Saskatchewan Power Corporation, *Annual Report*, 1960.

20 Saskatchewan Government Telephones, *Annual Report*, 1952–3 to 1955–6.

21 Saskatchewan, Treasury Department, financial statements, 1943–4 to 1960–1.

22 EAPB, minutes of Cabinet–Planning Board Conference, 22–26 Nov. 1954.

23 'Budget Speeches,' 1953 to 1956 inclusive.

24 See resolutions of the Saskatchewan School Trustees Association at its annual conventions of 1954 and 1956.

25 CCF (SS) Records, minutes of the Seventeenth Annual CCF (SS) Convention, 16–18 July 1952.

26 'Speech from the Throne,' in Saskatchewan, *Journals of the Legislative Assembly*, 1956.

27 'Speech from the Throne,' in Saskatchewan, *Journals of the Legislative Assembly*, 1959.

28 Ibid.

29 Saskatchewan, Department of Education, 'Program Proposals, 1953–54 to 1957–58,' November 1953.

30 Saskatchewan, Department of Education, 'Some Considerations Respecting the Development of a Provincial Technical and Vocational School,' 22 Sept. 1954.

31 Saskatchewan, Department of Education, budget submission, 1956–7.

32 'Budget Speeches,' 1957 to 1960.

33 Saskatchewan, Department of Public Health, budget submission, 1954–5.

34 'Speech from the Throne,' in Saskatchewan, *Journals of the Legislative Assembly*, 1956.

35 EAPB, minutes of Cabinet–Planning Board Conference, 21–25 Nov. 1955.

36 The Saskatchewan Hospital Association was also pressing for this alternative, which was being met, to some extent, by the Department of Social Welfare's nursing home program. See Executive Council, minute of cabinet, no. 3547, 27 Jan. 1953.

37 EAPB, minutes of the Cabinet–Planning Board Conference, 21–25 Nov. 1955.

38 See the representations of the Canadian Mental Health Association in November 1953, and cabinet minute, no. 5012, 20 Nov. 20, 1953.

39 See CCF (SS) Records, minutes of the Twentieth Annual CCF (SS) Convention, 20–22 July 1965.

40 'Budget Speech,' 5 March 1956.

41 Saskatchewan, Executive Council, Treasury Board minutes, 7 Oct. 1952.

42 Saskatchewan, Department of Public Health, 'Next Stages in the Development of the Province's Health Programs,' a document supporting the budget submission for 1954–5.

43 The government approved a treatment facility and creation of a Physical Restoration Division. See Treasury Board minutes, 4 Oct. 1952, and O/C 1286/53.

44 Saskatchewan, Executive Council, minute of cabinet, no. 3946, 21 Aug. 1953.

45 For example, Treasury Board minutes, 7 Oct. 1952; 'Next Stages in the Province's Health Programs,' November 1953; and 'Program Proposals, 1955–56 to 1959–60,' September 1954.

46 EAPB, minutes of the Cabinet–Planning Board Conference, 16–20 Nov. 1953.

47 For example, EAPB, 'Program Proposals 1955–56 to 1959–60,' September 1954.

48 See Saskatchewan, Department of Social Welfare, 'Interim Report on Five Year Plan,' October 1952.

49 Ibid.

50 Saskatchewan, Executive Council, minute of cabinet, no. 3645, 3 March 1953.

51 CCF (SS) Records, minutes of the Eighteenth and Nineteenth Annual CCF (SS) Conventions, 1953 and 1954.

52 Treasury Board recommendations, approved by cabinet minute, no. 5898, 28 Jan. 1955; and 'Budget Speech,' 2 March 1955.

53 'Budget Speech,' 5 March 1956.

54 'Budget Speech,' 28 Feb. 1958.

55 'Budget Speech,' 27 Feb. 1959. This development followed the reduction in 1955 of municipal contributions to the costs of social aid from 50 to 25 per cent.

56 Saskatchewan, Executive Council, minute of cabinet, no. 3655, 11 Feb. 1953.

57 'Budget Speech,' 3 March 1954.

58 'Budget Speech,' 5 March 1956.

59 'Speech from the Throne,' in Saskatchewan, *Journals of the Legislative Assembly*, 1957 and 1958.

60 'Budget Speech,' 26 Feb. 1960.

61 'Budget Speech,' 3 March 1954.

62 Saskatchewan, Executive Council, minute of cabinet, no. 5567, 19 Aug. 1954.

63 'Budget Speech,' 6 March 1957.

64 Saskatchewan, Executive Council, minutes of cabinet, no. 6323, 22 Aug. 1955, and no. 6336, 25 Aug. 1955.

65 Saskatchewan, Executive Council, minute of cabinet, no. 6297, 14 Aug. 1955.

66 Saskatchewan, Executive Council, minute of cabinet, no. 6350, 2 Sept. 1955.
67 Saskatchewan, Executive Council, minute of cabinet, no. 5990, 8 March 1955.
68 Saskatchewan, Executive Council, minute of cabinet, no. 3422, 16 Dec. 1952.
69 Saskatchewan, Executive Council, minute of cabinet, no. 5577, 24 Aug. 1954.
70 Correspondence in the files of the minister of mineral resources, July 1953; and Executive Council, minute of cabinet, no. 6866.
71 'Budget Speech,' 6 March 1957, 25.
72 'Budget Speech,' 26 Feb. 1960, 19.
73 'Speech from the Throne,' in Saskatchewan, *Journals of the Legislative Assembly,* 1959.
74 'Ibid.
75 'Speech from the Throne,' in Saskatchewan, *Journals of the Legislative Assembly,* 1958.
76 'Speech from the Throne,' in Saskatchewan, *Journals of the Legislative Assembly,* 1960.
77 Saskatchewan, Executive Council, minute of cabinet, no. 3036, 16 June 1952.
78 Correspondence in the files of the minister of mineral resources, 12 May 1953.
79 EAPB, memorandum from the Oil Policy Committee, November 1953.
80 EAPB, minutes of joint meeting of cabinet and Oil Policy Committee, 23 Dec. 1953.
81 *Regina Leader Post,* 9 Feb. 1954.
82 Mr Fines said about the net royalty leases: 'Instead of seeking immediate financial returns from these resources, and making political capital out of the programs that could be financed in this way, the Government has been willing to accept instead an annual return in the form of a royalty over and above the regular royalty. In renting our resources in this way, we are not only benefiting future generations, but we are also making it possible for smaller independent oil companies, financed by Canadian capital, to participate in the development of our resources' ('Budget Speech,' 5 March 1956).
83 In the recollection of the author, only a few farmers then repaid the monies they had received.
84 'Budget Speech,' 27 Feb. 1959, 19.
85 Ibid., 20.
86 'Budget Speeches,' 1957 and 1959.
87 'Budget Speech,' 6 March 1957, 3.
88 'Budget Speech,' 28 Feb. 1958, 20.
89 Douglas Papers. This paragraph and those that follow are drawn from a report of the South Saskatchewan River Development Commission entitled

'Chronological Summary of Negotiations between the Governments of Canada and Saskatchewan on the South Saskatchewan River Project, 1944 to 1948' (1 Aug. 1962).

90 Department of Highways, *Annual Report*, 1952–3 to 1955–6.

91 Treasury Department, financial statements, 1943–4 to 1960–1.

92 CCF (SS) Records, minutes of Ninth Annual CCF (SS) Convention, 14 July 1944, and of the Eighteenth Annual CCF (SS) Convention, 4–6 Nov. 1953.

93 EAPB, 'A Four Year Plan,' report for discussion at the Cabinet–Planning Board Conference of 1 Dec. 1947.

94 Local Government Continuing Committee, *Local Government in Saskatchewan* (Regina: Queen's Printer, 1961).

95 *Report of the Committee on Provincial-Municipal Relations* (Regina: King's Printer, 1950), 19.

96 Ibid., 137.

97 Ibid., 18.

98 CCF (SS) Records, minutes of the Eighteenth Annual CCF (SS) Provincial Convention, 4–6 Nov. 1953.

99 Saskatchewan, Executive Council, minute of cabinet, no. 5227.

100 EAPB, minutes of Cabinet–Planning Board Conference, 22–26 Nov. 1954.

101 Douglas Papers, memoranda dated Nov. 1953. Despite the affirmation of these principles, the Municipal Advisory Commission advised the government, and the government agreed, to increase annual grants for municipal roads by more than $3 million.

102 Royal Commission on Agriculture and Rural Life, *Rural Roads and Local Government* (Regina: Queen's Printer, 1955).

103 Ibid., 264

104 Ibid., 268.

105 Opening statement by Premier T.C. Douglas to the Provincial-Local Government Conference, 11 Dec. 1956.

106 Presidential address to the Annual Convention of the Saskatchewan Association of Rural Municipalities (S. Duff Noble), March 1957.

107 Saskatchewan, Executive Council, minute of cabinet, no. 7016, 22 May 1956.

108 Opening statement by Premier T.C. Douglas, to the Provincial-Local Government Conference, 11 Dec. 1956.

109 Saskatchewan, Executive Council, Minute of Cabinet No. 7669, April 16, 1957.

110 O/C 1244/57.

111 *Local Government in Saskatchewan* (Regina: Queen's Printer, 1961), report

submitted to the government of Saskatchewan by the Local Government Continuing Committee, 1 March 1961.

112 Statutes of Saskatchewan, 1962, c. 56, Municipal Unit and County Act.

113 'Speech from the Throne,' in Saskatchewan, *Journals of the Legislative Assembly*, 1956.

114 'Budget Speech,' 27 Feb. 1959.

115 Ibid.

116 'Speech from the Throne,' in Saskatchewan, *Journals of the Legislative Assembly*, 1959.

117 'Budget Speech,' 28 Feb. 1958, 23.

118 Personal files, 'The Chronology of Wascana Centre, April 1960 to March 1962.'

119 Ibid.

9: Reflections on the 1950s and Renewal in the 1960s

1 Quotation from Woodrow Lloyd's diary in Lloyd, *Woodrow*, 100.

2 EAPB, minutes of the Cabinet–Planning Board Conference, 18–22 Nov. 1957.

3 Ibid., and CCF (SS) Records, minutes of the Twenty-Second Annual CCF (SS) Convention, 17–19 July 1957.

4 EAPB, 'Emphasis and Priorities in Program Development,' prepared for the 1958 Cabinet–Planning Board Conference.

5 Saskatchewan, Executive Council, minute of cabinet, no. 8985, 30 Dec. 1958.

6 Saskatchewan, Executive Council, minute of cabinet, no. 9039, 24 Jan. 1959.

7 'Speech from the Throne,' in the Saskatchewan, *Journals of the Legislative Assembly*, 1959.

8 Saskatchewan, Executive Council, minutes of the meeting of the Cabinet Committee on Land Control Policy, South Saskatchewan River Project, 8 Jan. 1959.

9 'Budget Speech,' Feb. 1960.

10 CCF (SS) Records, *More Abundant Living: CCF Program for 1960.*

11 CCF (SS) Records, report of political leader (T.C. Douglas) to the Seventeenth Annual CCF (SS) Convention, 16 July 1952.

12 Ibid.

13 This excluded the fifty thousand people who were the beneficiaries of a public medical care program in the Swift Current Health Region.

14 Speech of Premier T.C. Douglas in the debate on the speech from the throne, Legislative Assembly, *Debates*, 17 Feb. 1960.

15 'Proposals for a Medical Care Program for Saskatchewan' (a report to cabi-

net by the Inter-departmental Committee to Study a Medical Care Program, 20 Sept. 1959), 1 (in the author's personal files).

16 Ibid., 2.

17 Ibid.

18 Robin F. Badgely and Samuel Wolfe, *Doctors' Strike: Medical Care and Conflict in Saskatchewan* (Toronto: Macmillan of Canada, 1967), 22.

19 Quoted in Malcolm G. Taylor, *Health Insurance and Canadian Public Policy*, 2nd ed. (Kingston and Montreal: Institute of Public Administration of Canada and McGill-Queen's University Press, 1987), 277.

20 This information is drawn from the Economic Advisory and Planning Board's reports 'Water and Sewerage Development Program' (April 1959) and 'Municipal Water and Sewerage' (Sept. 1959); from the report 'A Summary of the Rural Telephone Study Interim Report' (April 1959); from minutes of the cabinet conferences on planning and budgeting, 20–3 April 1959 and 19–23 Nov. 1959; from the Treasury Board minutes of 4–12 Jan. 1960; and from the 1960 throne speech debate and the budget speech of 26 Feb. 1960.

21 'Budget Speech,' 26 Feb. 1960.

22 This review of the report to cabinet by the Inter-departmental Committee to Study a Medical Care Program, including the pages that follow on 'Proposals for a Medical Care Program for Saskatchewan (from the Committee),' is drawn from the report itself, a copy of which is in the author's personal files (75 pages).

23 'Proposals for a Medical Care Program for Saskatchewan,' 54.

24 Ibid., 45.

25 Ibid., 39.

26 Ibid., 50.

27 Ibid., 47–8.

28 Ibid., 52.

29 Ibid., 70–1.

30 Ibid., 70.

31 Premier T.C. Douglas, 'Prepaid Medical Care,' in the *Provincial Affairs* radio series, 16 Dec. 1959 (in the author's personal files).

32 Ibid.

33 Shackleton, *Tommy Douglas*, 236.

34 *Regina Leader Post*, 17 Dec. 1959.

35 Ibid., 19 Dec. 1959.

36 Ibid., 17 Dec. 1959.

37 Ibid., 22 Jan. 1960.

38 This chapter of the medicare story is told splendidly in E.A. Tollefson, *Bitter*

Medicine: The Saskatchewan Medicare Feud (Saskatoon: Modern Press, 1963). The pages that follow are drawn substantially from that book, along with others.

39 Tollefson, *Bitter Medicine*, 51.

40 Shackleton, *Tommy Douglas*, 236.

41 Taylor, *Health Insurance and Canadian Public Policy*, 278–9.

42 Ibid., 279.

43 Badgely and Wolfe speak in stronger terms about combining the powers of 'licensing, setting standards, and self-discipline [with the] trade union or negotiating role in economic matters.' They argue that 'the profession was in a much stronger position to control dissenters ...' under these circumstances (*Doctors' Strike*, 29).

44 C. David Naylor, *Private Practice, Public Payment: Canadian Medicine and the Politics of Health Insurance, 1911–1966.* (Kingston and Montreal: McGill-Queen's University Press, 1986), 185. Naylor says the $35,000 was paid after the election to clear the college's bank overdraft. He also points out that 'total College expenditures of $95,000 was invested in the College's campaign' and adds that 'exclusive of central funding, the Liberal candidates spent a total of $71,000; the CCF candidates $89,000.' See also Badgely and Wolfe, *Doctors' Strike*, 231, and McLeod and McLeod, *Tommy Douglas*, 198.

45 *Regina Leader Post*, 25 March 1960 (attributed to the president of the college, Dr A.J.M. Davies).

46 Ibid., 28 March 1960.

47 Ibid., 25 May 1960. 'British doctors' here presumably refers to the large influx of British doctors in the 1950s. See Aleck Ostry, 'Prelude to Medicare: Institutional Change and Continuity in Saskatchewan, 1944–1962,' *Prairie Forum* 30:1 (Spring 1995): 87–105.

48 *Regina Leader Post*, 26 March 1960.

49 Quoted in Badgely and Wolfe, *Doctors' Strike*, 31.

50 *Regina Leader Post*, 26 March 1960.

51 McLeod and McLeod, *Tommy Douglas*, 198.

52 Edwin A. Tollefson, 'The Medicare Dispute,' in *Politics in Saskatchewan*, ed. Norman Ward and Duff Spafford, (Don Mills: Longmans Canada Ltd, 1968), 243.

53 *Regina Leader Post*, 10 June 1960.

54 Ibid., 11 June 1960.

10: Medicare

1 In writing this chapter, I have benefited from three categories of source

material. First, I have drawn on the primary sources available to me at the time I wrote my Ph.D. thesis, 'The Biography of a Government: Policy Formulation in Saskatchewan 1944–61' (Harvard, 1963). Almost all of these sources antedate 1965. Secondly, I have drawn on and acknowledged particular books as secondary sources to verify, and in places to amplify, my narrative of a government under pressure. They are Badgely and Wolfe, *Doctors' Strike*; McLeod and McLeod, *Tommy Douglas*; Ken MacTaggart, *The First Decade* (Ottawa: Canadian Medical Association, 1958); Naylor, *Private Practice, Public Payment*; Taylor, *Health Insurance and Canadian Public Policy*; Tollefson, *Bitter Medicine* and Tollefson, 'The Medicare Dispute,' in Ward and Spafford, eds, *Politics in Saskatchewan*. Thirdly, I have drawn on my own memory of events, as deputy provincial treasurer, and on the memories of several other prime participants in these events, notably the Honourable Allan E. Blakeney, Donald D. Tansley, and Thomas K. Shoyama.

2 *Regina Leader Post*, 31 May 1961.

3 *Interim Report of the Advisory Planning Committee on Medical Care* (Regina: Queen's Printer, 1961), 10.

4 Personal conversations.

5 *Regina Leader Post* 30 March 1961.

6 Douglas Papers, Dr W.P. Thompson, letter to Premier T.C. Douglas, 7 Nov. 1960; and reply, 9 Nov. 1960.

7 *Regina Leader Post*, 17 Jan. 1961.

8 Ibid., 30 March 1960.

9 Ibid., 25 April 1960.

10 Ibid., 14 Jan. 1961.

11 Saskatchewan Executive Council, minute of cabinet, no. 714, 12 April 1961.

12 Tollefson (*Bitter Medicine*, 67–8) includes a statement of the CMA's position.

13 Naylor, *Private Practice, Public Payment*, 189.

14 Ibid., 190.

15 Tollefson, *Bitter Medicine*, 57.

16 Naylor, *Private Practice, Public Payment*, 94.

17 Tollefson, *Bitter Medicine*, 60.

18 *Regina Leader Post*, 13 May 1960.

19 Ibid., 23 Jan. 1961.

20 Ibid., 7 Feb. 1961.

21 Ibid., 21 April 1961.

22 Ibid., 19 June 1961.

23 Ibid., 28 June 1961.

24 Ibid., 4 Aug. 1961.

25 Taylor, *Health Insurance and Canadian Public Policy*, 283. Badgely and Wolfe

(*Bitter Medicine*, 38) suggest that the chairman himself recommended an interim report.

26 Treasury Board minute, no. 1591, 16 May 1961.

27 Treasury Board minute, no. 1652, 4 and 5 July 1961.

28 Treasury Board minutes for 18 July, 18 Aug., 24 Aug., 24 and 18 Sept. 1961.

29 Archer, *Saskatchewan*, 363.

30 Saskatchewan Treasury Department, *Financing Medical Care*, 1961.

31 Hon. W.S. Lloyd, 'Financing the Medical Care Program,' address in the Saskatchewan legislature, special session, 20 Oct. 1961 (in author's personal files).

32 *Interim Report of the Advisory Planning Committee on Medical Care*, 120.

33 *Regina Leader Post*, 12 Jan. 1961.

34 Statutes of Saskatchewan, 1961 (Second Session), c 1, ss.9 and 39. The commission was empowered to 'take such action as it considers necessary for the establishment and administration' of the plan – pursuant, of course, to the Act; it was authorized to manage its own funds and to engage its own staff, and the minister was obliged to submit directly to the legislature the annual report of the commission.

35 Treasury Board minute, no. 1694, 18 Sept. 1961.

36 Tollefson, *Bitter Medicine*, 63–5.

37 *Regina Leader Post*, 19 Oct. 1961.

38 Ibid., 18 Nov. 1961.

39 Ibid., 19 Oct. 1961.

40 The Saskatchewan CCF decided to operate as a 'hyphenated party,' at least until the end of the CCF government's fifth term of office.

41 Douglas Papers, W.S. Lloyd, 'T.C. Douglas – an Appreciation,' 7 Nov. 1961.

42 Quoted in Thomas, ed., *The Making of a Socialist*, 376–7.

43 Tollefson, *Bitter Medicine*, 88.

44 *Regina Leader Post*, 1 Dec. 1961.

45 Taylor, *Health Insurance and Canadian Public Policy*, 289.

46 *Regina Leader Post*, 21 Dec. 1961.

47 Tollefson, *Bitter Medicine*, 92.

48 Taylor, *Health Insurance and Canadian Public Policy*, 335, 341–2.

49 Ibid., 289.

50 Taylor, Ibid., 290.

51 Tollefson, *Bitter Medicine*, 92–3.

52 Chronology of discussions prepared by the secretary of the Medical Care Insurance Commission (in the files of the Medical Care Insurance Commission, 1962).

53 Ibid.

54 Ibid.

55 Taylor, *Health Insurance and Canadian Public Policy*, 286.

56 These points were recounted in the address by Premier W.S. Lloyd to the Saskatchewan College of Physicians and Surgeons on 3 May 1962, which subsequently was published by the Queen's Printer, Regina.

57 Ibid. See also the statement by Premier W.S. Lloyd in the Legislative Assembly, 11 April 1962 (in mimeo form).

58 Taylor, *Health Insurance and Canadian Public Policy*, 294–6.

59 Naylor, *Private Practice*, 201.

60 This part of the medicare story, as with other parts, is told well in Taylor, *Health Insurance and Canadian Public Policy*, 296; Naylor, *Private Practice*, 201–2; and Tollefson, *Bitter Medicine*, 99–101. The latter two authors look upon the 'agency amendment' as a huge mistake on the part of the government, while I tend to regard it as an amendment intended to complete the design of the patient reimbursement plan preparatory to proceeding with the implementation of the Medical Care Insurance Act. (The doctor's decision to strike was not taken until 3 May 1962.)

61 Tollefson, *Bitter Medicine*, 100.

62 *Regina Leader Post*, 1 April 1962.

63 Ibid., 14 April 1962.

64 Ibid., 3 May 1962.

65 Though it was, after all, Premier Lloyd who had advanced the patient reimbursement plan, which would 'insulate' the doctors from the Medical Care Insurance Commission.

66 See also Taylor, *Health Insurance and Canadian Public Policy*, 319.

67 Ibid., 297.

68 Tollefson, *Bitter Medicine*, 105.

69 Special half-hour public service telecast on doctors and medical care, CKCK-TV, 5 May 1962, mimeographed transcript.

70 *Regina Leader Post*, 4 May 1962.

71 Newsletter of the Saskatchewan medical profession, vol. 2, no. 13, (23 May 1962), quoted in Badgely and Wolfe, *Doctors' Strike*, 53–4.

72 *Regina Leader Post*, 28 May 1962.

73 These numbers are derived from Tollefson, *Bitter Medicine*, 111, note 20. See also Badgely and Wolfe, *Doctors' Strike*, 62; and Taylor, *Health Insurance and Canadian Public Policy*, 281. The numbers of physicians in the province are variously estimated at 700–25 practising and 900 in total.

74 *Regina Leader Post*, 27 June 1962.

75 Badgely and Wolfe, *Doctors' Strike*, 52.

76 Taylor, *Health Insurance and Canadian Public Policy*, 298.

77 Tollefson, 'The Medicare Dispute,' in Ward and Spafford, eds, *Politics in Saskatchewan*, 263.

78 Badgely and Wolfe, *Doctors' Strike*, 54, 57.

79 A.E. Blakeney, 'Press Coverage of the Medicare Dispute in Saskatchewan,' *Queen's Quarterly* 70, (Autumn 1963): 361.

80 Ibid.

81 Lloyd, *Woodrow*, 127.

82 Ibid.

83 Interview with Donald Tansley.

84 Taylor, *Health Insurance and Canadian Public Policy*, 315.

85 Ibid., 301.

86 Ibid., 300.

87 Frank B. Fiegert, *Canada Votes, 1935–1988* (Durham, NC: Duke University Press, 1989).

88 Sources for this sequence of events: chronology of discussions prepared by the secretary of the Medical Care Insurance Commission (1962), in the files of the MCIC; and Tollefson, *Bitter Medicine*, 105–7.

89 Premier W.S. Lloyd, 'Radio Address on Medical Care,' 26 June 1962, mimeo.

90 In its brief to the Royal Commission on Health Services (page 23), the college had said: 'We cannot agree to render service under the Plan. We would, however, continue to treat our patients in accordance with our capabilities. We would presume that patients presenting receipts of payment would be able to obtain reimbursement from the insurance program.'

91 *Regina Leader Post*, 27 June 1962.

92 Ibid., 6 July 1962.

93 Ibid., 27 June 1962.

94 Ibid., 30 June 1962.

95 Radio and television address by Premier W.S. Lloyd, 2 July 1962, mimeo.

96 *Regina Leader Post*, 30 June 1962.

97 See Badgely and Wolfe, *Doctors' Strike*, 61–2; and Lloyd, *Woodrow*, 129–31.

98 *Prince Albert Daily Herald*, 6 July 1962.

99 Tollefson, 'The Medicare Dispute,' in Ward and Spafford, eds, *Politics in Saskatchewan*, 263. This article provides a full and vivid recounting of these events.

100 CBC Radio broadcast by Premier W.S. Lloyd, 9 July 1962, mimeo.

101 Interviews with Woodrow Lloyd and Allan Blakeney, Oct. 1962.

102 All of these quotes are drawn from Taylor, *Health Insurance and Canadian Public Policy*, 307–11.

103 Saskatchewan Archives, Medical Care Insurance Commission documents.
104 Ibid.
105 Interview with Donald Tansley, July 2002.
106 Aside from fragmentary personal memories, the primary source for this part
of the story is Taylor, *Health Insurance and Canadian Public Policy*, 315–16.
107 This section relies generally on my Ph.D. thesis, and on Taylor's and Tollefson's accounts of these events. See Johnson, 'Biography of a Government';
Taylor, *Health Insurance and Canadian Public Policy*, 320–1; and Tollefson,
Bitter Medicine, 112–13.
108 *Regina Leader Post*, 17 July 1962.
109 A quite brilliant legal analysis of the changes involved in the medical care
settlement is found in Tollefson, *Bitter Medicine*, chapter 6. Taylor's recounting of the settlement in the context of the negotiations is admirably lucid.
See *Health Insurance and Canadian Public Policy*, 324–7.
110 Lloyd, *Woodrow*, 121.

Epilogue: The Legacy of the Douglas Government

1 Quoted in Taylor, *Health Insurance and Canadian Public Policy*, 342.
2 Ibid., 333.
3 This story – or elements of it – is recounted in Tom Kent, *A Public Purpose*
(Kingston and Montreal: McGill-Queen's University Press, 1988), 366–9; and
in Walter Stewart, *Dismantling the State* (Toronto: Stoddart, 1998), 53–5.
4 Taylor, *Health Insurance and Canadian Public Policy*, 374.
5 Ibid., 375.

Annex: Financing a CCF Program within the Canadian Federation

1 Three sources were relied upon in writing this section: A.W. Johnson, 'Social
Policy in Canada: The Past As It Conditions the Present,' in *The Future of
Social Welfare Systems in Canada and the United Kingdom*, ed. Shirley B. Seward
(Ottawa: Institute for Research on Public Policy, 1987), 29–70; David B.
Perry, *Financing the Canadian Federation, 1867 to 1995: Setting the Stage for
Change* (Toronto: Canadian Tax Foundation, 1997); and the author's own
recollections from his participation in many of these events.
2 Johnson, 'Social Policy in Canada: The Past As It Conditions the Present,' 32.
3 A. Milton Moore and J. Harvey Perry, *The Financing of the Canadian Federation:
The First Hundred Years* (Toronto: Canadian Tax Foundation, 1966), 26.
4 *Dominion-Provincial Conference* (Ottawa: Queen's Printer, 1960), 81. See also
the Conferences held in 1955 and 1957.

5 For a more complete story of these events, see Malcolm G. Taylor, *Insuring National Health Care: The Canadian Experience* (Chapel Hill: University of North Carolina Press, 1990); and Perry, *Financing the Canadian Federation, 1867 to 1995.*

6 Three sources were relied upon in writing this section: Moore and Perry, *The Financing of the Canadian Federation: The First Hundred Years*; Perry, *Financing the Canadian Federation, 1867 to 1995*; and the author's own recollections from his participation from 1955 to 1968 on the Continuing Committee on Fiscal and Economic Matters, and from his attendance at most of the federal-provincial conferences and finance ministers meetings for the same years.

7 Moore and Perry, *The Financing of the Canadian Federation: The First Hundred Years.*

8 Ibid.

9 Personal recollections of the author and Robert A. McLarty.

10 1961–2 Saskatchewan budget documents: 'Summary of Estimated Budgetary Revenues, 1961–62.'

11 The author's personal recollections, as deputy provincial treasurer from 1952 to 1964.

12 Right Honourable Pierre Elliott Trudeau, *Federal-Provincial Grants and the Spending Power of Parliament* (Ottawa: Queen's Printer, 1969).

13 'Budget Speech,' 15 March 1945, 15.

Index